THE CITY & GUILDS TEXTBOOK

LEVEL 3 DIPLOMA IN
HEALTH AND SOCIAL CARE

THE CITY & GUILDS TEXTBOOK

LEVEL 3 DIPLOMA IN
HEALTH AND SOCIAL CARE

SIOBHAN MACLEAN

ROB HARRISON

About City & Guilds

City & Guilds is the UK's leading provider of vocational qualifications, offering over 500 awards across a wide range of industries, and progressing from entry level to the highest levels of professional achievement. With over 8500 centres in 100 countries, City & Guilds is recognised by employers worldwide for providing qualifications that offer proof of the skills they need to get the job done.

Equal opportunities

City & Guilds fully supports the principle of equal opportunities and we are committed to satisfying this principle in all our activities and published material. A copy of our equal opportunities policy statement is available on the City & Guilds website.

First edition 2014
ISBN 978 0 85193 275 0

Publisher Charlie Evans
Development Editor Gaynor Roberts
Production Editor Natalie Griffith

Cover design by Select Typesetters Ltd
Typeset by Integra Software Services Pvt., Ltd
Printed in the UK by Cambrian Printers Ltd

British Library Cataloguing in Publication Data

A catalogue record for this book is available from the British Library.

Publications

For information about or to order City & Guilds support materials, contact 0844 534 0000 or centresupport@cityandguilds.com. You can find more information about the materials we have available at www.cityandguilds.com/publications.

Every effort has been made to ensure that the information contained in this publication is true and correct at the time of going to press. However, City & Guilds' products and services are subject to continuous development and improvement and the right is reserved to change products and services from time to time. City & Guilds cannot accept liability for loss or damage arising from the use of information in this publication.

City & Guilds
1 Giltspur Street
London EC1A 9DD

0844 543 0033
www.cityandguilds.com
publishingfeedback@cityandguilds.com

CONTENTS

ACKNOWLEDGEMENTS

City & Guilds would like to sincerely thank the following.

For invaluable subject knowledge and expertise
Gill Hall, Geraldine Donworth, Paul Robottom and Darryn Allcorn.

Picture credits
Every effort has been made to acknowledge all copyright holders as below and the publishers will, if notified, correct any errors in future editions.

Care Images.com: p119, © Julio Etchart, p201, p358 © Marc Morris p323 © John Edler, p348, p467 © Rick Matthews, p368 **City & Guilds**, p1, p4 **Fotalia**, p220-221 **Shutterstock** © Stocklite, p4, p123, p287, p443 © Michaeljung, p5 © Bevan Goldswain, p9 © Sergey Nivens, p10 © Monkey Business Images, p12, p15, p28, p83, p109, p135, p151, p158, p258, p296, p314, p351, p377, p427, p431, p446, p471, p487, p496 © ChmpagnDave p14 © Diego Cervo, p18, p169 © Ioannis Pantzi, p19 © wavebreakmedia, p21, p54, p139, p470 © Warren Goldswain, p26 © CREATISTA, p31, p333 © Fifian Iromi, p32 © MJTH, p37, p234, p263 © Blend images, p39, p66, p102 © baki, p41 © Lisa F. Young, p42, p47, p414 © Voronin76, p45 © CWA Studios, p53 © Timothy Large, p55, p203 © Christian Mueller, p56 © PaulPaladin, p57 © Susan Law Cain, p59 © Lighthunter, p61, p206 © Chepko Danil Vitalevich, p62 © mangostock, p64, p302, p529 © Robyn Mackenzie, p67 © RyFlip p73 © Andresr, p74 © chalabala, p77 © auremar, p78, p370 © wong sze yuen, p80 © stocker1970, p85 © Arvind Balaraman, p86 © Seregam, p91 © RTimages, p95 © Paul Fleet, p100 © bonchan, p105 © kazoka, p107 © Bobkeenan Photography, p108 © Dan Breckwoldt, p113, © Alexander Raths, p114, p121, p364, p411 © Kittisak, p118 © Sparkling Moments Photography, p125 © Champion Studio, p126, p523 © Brian A Jackson, p127 © MANDY GODBEHEAR, p129 © Jim Barber, p130 © 1000 Words, p133 © kurhan, p136 © Thorsten Rust, p141 © Gilles Lougassi, p143 © hans engbers, p147 © Goodluz, p153, p177, p405, p411 © Ensuper, p156 © iofoto, p157 © Iakov Filimonov, p163, p532 © bikeriderlondon, p172, p506 © Karuka, p174 © karamysh, p178 © Luis Santos, p180 © Carme Balcells, p183 © Ingrid Balabanova, p185 © Lane V. Erickson, p187 © Sim Creative Art, p188 © berna namoglu, p191, p295 © Shebeko, p194 © tungtopgun, p197 © Julio Etchart, p201, p358 © Tribalium, p209 © hxdbzxy, p210 © Vladislav Gadij, p214 © Ecelop, p215 © Phuriphat, p220 © Bartosz Ostrowski, p224 © scyther5, p228 © Africa Studio, p231 © Iancu Cristian, p237 © Jacek Chabraszewski, p240 © jcjgphotography, p242 © Karramba Production, p243 © Remik44992, p245 © Xavier Gallego Morell, p249 © ericlefrancais, p251 © Alan Bailey, p253 © Alexander Kirch, p261 © robert_s, p267 © AVAVA, p280 © Dimitar Sotirov, p281 © itsmejust, p281 © Chris Howey, p282 © Garsya, p283 © teguh_bosepro, p291 © mikie11, p299 © grafvision, p306 © mooinblack, p317 © Dmitry Kalinovsky, 9321 © Jack. Q, p326 © Aletia, p329 © Kzenon, p334 © John Kroetch, p335 © savageultralight, p339 © Brian Eichhorn, p339 © Nika Art, p340, p386 © Lisa S p341 © luxorphoto, p342, p437 © Pixsooz, p346 © Jorg Hackemann, p362 © Orange line media, p367 © Rasulov, p373 © Hannamariah, p375 © olmarmar, p376 © Sue McDonald, p378 © Rob Marmion, p382, p455 © Anetta, p384 © Aleksandr Bryliaev, p391 © Sklep Spozywczy, p395 © Stephen Finn, p396 © dutourdumonde, p396 © Robert Kneschke p400 © Peter Gudella, p401 © Jochen Schoenfeld, p403 © Ivonne Wierink, p419 © Tyler Olson, p420, p502 © Marc Dietrich, p422 © Dirk Ott, p432 © JustinRossWard, p435 © Ditty_about_summer, p445 © Andras_ Csontos, p448 © Vladimir Mucibabic, p449 © dotweb Steen B Nielsen, p450 © mykeyruna, p458 © Paul Maguire, p466 © Eugenio Marongiu, p474 © Featureflash, p475 © Ocskay Bence, p479 © amenic181, p481 © RomanSo, p483 © youlian, p489 © Glenn Price, p490 © Glovatskiy, p492 © Sue Robinson, p500 © design56, p503 © Denis Larkin, pg505 © Papik, p506 © Winai Tepsuttinun, p508 © Morphart Creation, p510 © jordache, p518 © Eurobanks, p519 © Marcel Jancovic, p531 © Vasiliy Koval, p539 © Anibal Trejo, p542 © holbox, p546 © zulufoto, p548 © Mike Flippo, p551 © Cheryl E. Davis, p554

Siobhan
My thanks have to go to the students and service users I have had the great privilege of working with and from whom I have learnt so much.

I would also like to thank my family for their support and encouragement. To my partner, Simon, and my daughters, Fliss and Rosie – thanks for putting up with me sitting at the laptop for hours on end and for doing so many of the things I should have been doing instead. To my parents – especially my mum – thank you for everything!

Rob
My thanks to everyone I have worked with over the years who have all taught me everything I know. I really do hope that readers of this book find it useful, whatever stage of your career you are at.

ABOUT THE AUTHORS

SIOBHAN MACLEAN

I started working in social care in a voluntary capacity when I was still at school, and since I was 18 I have worked in a variety of social care settings. I qualified as a social worker in 1990 and have since worked in a variety of service settings. I have a strong commitment to person-centred practice and to respecting the expertise of the people that social care seeks to support. I have written a number of publications for health and social care workers, many of them with Rob, and am committed to making the knowledge base accessible to busy practitioners.

ROB HARRISON

I began my work in this field as a volunteer, and have continued in a variety of voluntary roles to this day. I have worked in a range of services since 1996, primarily in the voluntary sector. Recently, I have managed advocacy services and services for carers. I am passionate about ensuring that the knowledge base is accessible across the profession, and about the ways in which the personalisation agenda can lead to better outcomes for service users and their carers.

FOREWORD

Working with people in any capacity is always interesting. Working with people who are in need of care or support is also a great privilege.

With nearly two million people now working in social care, and with the government expressing its commitment to making health and social care a priority in coming years, there has never been a more exciting time to work in the sector. Your professional knowledge, skills and expertise hopefully feel increasingly valued, and this qualification will enable you to define and communicate what it is that you do in your role, why you do it, and how you enable those you work with to live fulfilling and independent lives.

Whether you are new to health and social care or whether you have been working in the sector for some time, you will be working with people at times of need and often at crisis points in their lives, and what you do to support people can make a real difference to their lives. The *way* you carry out your work is what will make the real difference. People who receive health and social care services from professionals who work with compassion and who live out the values of professional practice really feel the difference. Working in this way is both a challenge and a joy – you will receive so much satisfaction from your work.

Be proud to be a health and social care worker – you can make a difference that makes the difference in society.

CASE STUDY CHARACTERS

The following seven characters are used in case studies throughout the book. Find out a bit more about them.

Jane is a senior support worker in a day service for people with learning disabilities. Many of the service users she works with have profound learning disabilities along with physical disabilities. Jane is responsible for organising day service activities and she supervises a small group of day service assistants.

Isabella is a senior care assistant in a respite care service that provides short-term stays for adults with learning and physical disabilities.

Chen is a senior care assistant in a residential service for older people. Many of the residents of the home have dementia.

Dee is a senior care assistant in a day service for older people. The people who attend the day service generally live at home with much of their support being provided by family members – a few service users also receive domiciliary care services.

Zakiyah is a senior domiciliary care worker. She provides care services to people in their own homes. The domiciliary care service provides support to all adults in need of support although most of the service users she works with are older people. Zakiyah is responsible for supervising a small team of other domiciliary care workers.

Jon is a senior support worker with a reablement team. He works with service users on a short-term basis to try to maximise their independence. His input is intensive but limited to a duration of six weeks. Many of the people he works with have recently been discharged from hospital. John works closely with the occupational therapists, physiotherapists and social workers on the team to develop individual reablement plans for service users.

Taju is a senior support worker with a mental health charity. He works some of his time in a drop-in centre for people with mental health problems and the remainder of his working week is spent in outreach services providing ongoing practical and emotional support for service users.

HOW TO USE THIS TEXTBOOK

Welcome to your City & Guilds Level 3 Diploma in Health and Social Care textbook. It is designed to guide you through your Level 3 qualification and be a useful reference for you throughout your career.

Each chapter covers a unit from the 4222 Level 3 qualification and also provides additional information.

Throughout this textbook you will see the following features:

KEY POINT

KEY POINT These are particularly useful hints that may assist in you in revision for your tests or to help you remember something important.

Key term ⚷

KEY TERM Words in colour in the text are explained in the margin to aid your understanding. They also appear in the glossary at the back of the book.

CASE STUDY

CASE STUDIES Useful, down-to-earth examples describing situations you may encounter in your work. There are usually questions at the end to help you shape your own thinking.

REFLECT

REFLECT Questions to encourage you to think more deeply about the topic you are studying.

RESEARCH

RESEARCH Useful pointers to finding out more about the subject you are studying.

APPLICATION OF SKILLS

APPLICATION OF SKILLS These are contexualised questions designed to develop your thinking and provoke further reflection on the skills you will need in your everyday work.

MESSAGES FROM RESEARCH

MESSAGES FROM RESEARCH These provide up-to-date extra background information.

CHAPTER 1
The role of the health and social care worker

As a professional in the field of health and social care, you need to be clear about your role, its boundaries, and the purpose of your work and working relationships. This chapter covers this in detail, as well as explaining some of the key issues around partnership working, which is an ever-increasing feature of all areas of health and social care work.

Links to other chapters

Your role extends into all of the units you will complete for your qualification. Specifically the content of chapters 2, 4, 6 and 7 link with this chapter.

UNDERSTANDING WORKING RELATIONSHIPS IN HEALTH AND SOCIAL CARE

To really understand working relationships in health and social care, you need to recognise the differences between working relationships and relationships in your personal life.

TYPES OF RELATIONSHIPS

Everyone who has a job of any kind has two distinct types of relationships:

Personal relationships

In our own personal lives, we all have a range of different relationships as shown here:

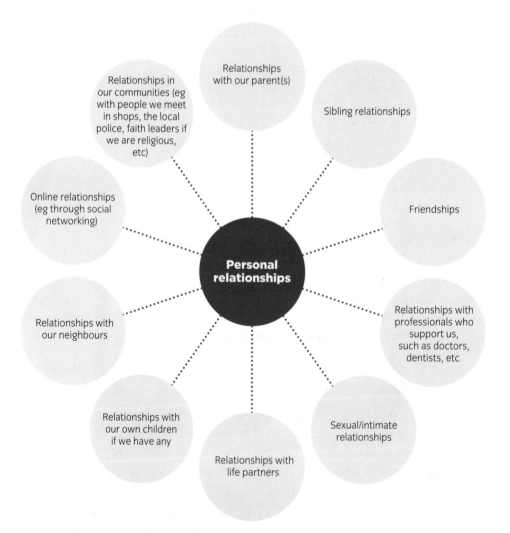

Working relationships

At work, we have a whole range of other relationships, which all differ in their nature from personal relationships. These include:

- relationships with supervisors/managers
- relationships with colleagues
- relationships with users of our services
- relationships with people's relatives, friends and informal carers
- relationships with colleagues and partners from other agencies.

THE DIFFERENCE IN WORKING AND PERSONAL RELATIONSHIPS

Personal relationships and working relationships are different in several key ways:

- You are paid to be at work, and you are not paid in terms of personal relationships.

- Being paid brings responsibilities with it (eg to follow your job description, to do your job according to the duty of care in this particular field of work, and to work according to national legislation and your employer's codes, policies and procedures). This could have some very specific results – eg if a friend tells you something you could choose to gossip about it (although you wouldn't be a very good friend!), but if a person tells you something as part of a working relationship you need to uphold professional confidentiality.

- When you are employed, you represent your employer/agency to everyone with whom you come into contact, so you need to be mindful of this and think about your employer's reputation as a responsible provider of services to people.

Relationships with service users are different from all of the other relationships discussed above, because these relationships involve power imbalance. This concept is explored more in Chapter 3 on equality, and is critical to consider because:

- service users rely on workers (ie you) in order to have their basic or other needs met

- people do not choose to have their needs met by others, so you have a duty of care to them. This involves doing your job to the best of your ability, safeguarding them, respecting their uniqueness and worth as a person, maintaining their dignity, and promoting their independence

- even if you do not feel powerful in relation to the service user, they are likely to perceive you as having power in the relationship because you are an employee

- you may hold societal power over them (as discussed in detail in Chapter 3) because of your age, gender, (lack of) disability, race, etc.

Therefore, in order to be an effective professional in this field of work you need to:

- understand power imbalances
- understand your role
- apply professional values to practice
- understand how your professional relationships differ from your personal ones, especially those relationships with service users.

THE IMPORTANCE OF PROFESSIONAL BOUNDARIES

In a professional relationship, you can be friendly with a service user but you are not a service user's friend. You should be clear on the limits of your role as a health and social care worker. Working within **professional boundaries** keeps you focused on the work you are doing with a service user. Without boundaries, you may overstep your duties and work outside of safe practice.

Key term 🔑

Professional boundaries: In work settings, refer to the limits of what we are allowed to do, and what is appropriate in our relationships with service users and other people.

WHAT COULD INDICATE POOR BOUNDARIES?

- A worker and service user call each other friends and interact outside of the working environment.
- Valuable gifts are exchanged between worker and service user.
- A worker shares personal information with the service user.
- A worker finds themselves discussing the service user and their circumstances with their family and friends.
- A worker has discussions with the service user about other workers or service users.

WHAT ARE THE CONSEQUENCES OF POOR BOUNDARIES?

Poor boundaries lead to poor practice, in a number of ways:

- Without professional boundaries the health and social care worker may not provide appropriate services to the service user. A worker without clear boundaries could over-identify with a service user that will make it difficult to provide the objectivity health and social care workers need.

- If you do not maintain professional boundaries, you may find yourself acting in an unethical manner.

- Professionals with poor boundaries often work outside of set policies and procedures which leaves them open to allegations and without the support of their employer.

CASE STUDY

Dee is a senior care assistant in a day service for older people. She becomes aware that Karen, one of the support workers in the day service where she works, is visiting one of the older residents at home at weekends – the worker is taking the service user some meals that she has prepared at home and is also doing some of his laundry. When Dee talks to Karen about this Karen says she feels sorry for the service user as he has no family members to support him and he has had some of his home-care services withdrawn. Karen feels that if she doesn't do this, the service user will be at risk.

- Should Dee be concerned? Why?

- What should Dee do?

- What should Karen do?

REFLECT

How do you define your own professional boundaries?

- How do your work relationships differ from your personal ones?

- Do colleagues have different boundaries from your own?

- Why are there differences?

- Can you identify common boundaries that all health and social care workers have?

- Where might these come from?

RESEARCH

Ask your supervisor what policies and procedures relate to working relationships and particularly professional boundaries. Ensure that you are fully aware of these boundaries so that you can work within them at all times.

APPLICATION OF SKILLS

Would you?

Think through the boundaries you have in your relationships with service users and the research you have carried out on policies and procedures, then look at the questions below.

You can talk some of these through with other workers and with your manager. It is interesting to see how different workers might have different boundaries – while it is important to be aware of the boundaries your employing organisation expects you to have.

Would you do the following? If so, why? If not, why not? If it depends, what does it depend on?

- If you saw a service user in town when you were out shopping would you stop to chat to them?

- When in a service user's home would you have a cup of tea?

- Would you tell a service user about your family? How much would you tell them? For example, if your partner had lost their job would you tell a service user?

- If a service user was struggling to get their clothes cleaned would you take their laundry home and do it when you do your own laundry?

- If a service user asked you to become a 'friend' on a social networking site would you accept the request?

- Would you accept a birthday card or gift from a service user?

- Would you send a birthday card to a service user?

WORKING RELATIONSHIPS IN HEALTH AND SOCIAL CARE SETTINGS

A health and social care worker's working relationships are with managers, supervisors, colleagues and other agencies as well as with users of services and their relatives.

Your role as a health and social care worker entails working to a shared set of values. The values of social care are also defined in detail in the equalities unit. These values involve a common understanding of what your role is and means, which will be shared by managers, colleagues and other professionals, as well as (hopefully) society more generally. Your role is to:

- communicate with people

- understand (assess) and meet people's needs

- respect differences and promote equality and inclusion for people who may otherwise be excluded from accessing resources

- empower people and enable the maximum possible independence for them

- keep accurate and up-to-date records

- work in partnership with other agencies

- keep people healthy and safe, and maintain a safe working environment for yourself and for others.

The health and social care worker's role is related to one of the mandatory units for this qualification. No matter what field of health or social care you work in, there is a common set of values, and a common agreement of what the role is and is not.

Your working relationships with other people should be based on this common understanding and shared set of values. Working with others is sometimes not as easy as it could be though, and issues surrounding partnership working across agencies are considered later in this chapter.

Unlike other fields of work, in health and social care, your conduct outside of work usually has to reflect a commitment to the values of your profession too, and a serious failure outside work to adhere to the standards expected can affect your employment. For example, workers in health and social care could lose their employment if convicted of certain offences, or if their conduct was seen to damage the reputation of their employer.

WORKING WITH OTHERS

Working in health and social care involves working with other people. Although many people work in an individual's home, they may still be part of a care team. Working with others can be a source of great support and of professional satisfaction. It can also be a source of stress and one of the harder things about the health and social care role as people's views and approaches may be very different.

Some key ways of working with others are linked to the principles of good care practice:

- Listen to other people's viewpoint – there is not always one way of doing things, and getting the best outcome can be far more important than how you get there. The exceptions to this are often in the area of health and safety (where the only way of doing something can be determined by legislation), safeguarding, and where procedures and policies prescribe a set way of doing a task and show the employer's expectations of consistency and best practice.

- Respect differences.

- Be open to trying out new ideas.

- Say if you have got something wrong.

- Praise people for doing a good job.

- Support others in the way you hope they would support you (eg at times of stress, if they need to swap a shift with you, etc).

- Find time to enjoy each other's company (where possible and appropriate).

- Find areas of common ground as well as difference.

- Understand how and when you may need to get support or advice from other people.

- Be clear in your role and on your own boundaries.

- Keep the focus on service users.

- Reflect on your practice and that of others.

TENSIONS IN WORKING RELATIONSHIPS

Even within one service, work setting or agency, working relationships can become strained for a range of reasons. The following is not an exhaustive list by any means, but indicates some of the possible causes of tension in working relationships:

- differences in values between two workers (despite the common values of the field of work, we are all still different)

- resource constraints

- stress

- differences in point of view towards an ethical dilemma

- differences in approach to work practices

- safeguarding issues

- whistle-blowing (ie where one colleague raises a concern about another person's work)

- our own health issues can make us unwell and/or tense

- different understandings of what an agreed procedure or practice is for the service

- different personalities can clash.

WORKING COLLABORATIVELY

The importance of effective collaborative working is recognised in the Code of Conduct for Healthcare Support Workers and Adult Social Care Workers, which states that you must:

- understand and value your contribution and the vital part you play in your team

- recognise and respect the roles and expertise of your colleagues both in the team and from other agencies and disciplines, and work in partnership with them

- work openly and cooperatively with colleagues including those from other disciplines and agencies, and treat them with respect

- work openly and cooperatively with people who use health and social care services and their families or carers and treat them with respect.

CASE STUDY

Zakiyah is a senior domiciliary care worker. Sophie has just started working for the same domiciliary care agency in which Zakiyah works. Sophie was supported by Zakiyah during her induction. Sophie has been providing support to Alf who has dementia and lives on his own in the community. Zakiyah used to support Alf and she introduced Sophie to Alf during the induction period.

Sophie sees Zakiyah when they are dropping off their timesheets at the office and asks Zakiyah if she can talk to her. Sophie tearfully tells Zakiyah that Alf has made some sexual comments to her and that he has tried to grab her breasts. Sophie feels really uncomfortable about going again but says she doesn't want to tell the manager as they might think Sophie isn't up to the job. Zakiyah is surprised that Sophie has chosen to confide this in her and is unsure what to do.

- Why might Sophie have confided in Zakiyah?

- What support might Sophie need in this situation from Zakiyah, and from others?

- How might Sophie feel if Zakiyah says that Alf is always like that because of his dementia, so she just needs to keep her distance from him?

- What should Zakiyah do?

- How might Zakiyah support Sophie in discussing boundaries with Alf?

WORKING IN WAYS THAT ARE AGREED BY THE EMPLOYER

It is vital that health and social care workers work in the ways that are required by their employer. Working outside of agreed ways of practice places the worker in danger of not being supported by their employer should something go wrong. Therefore, it is important that you understand the scope of your role and that you work within this agreed scope.

THE SCOPE OF YOUR JOB ROLE

Key terms

A **job description** describes the day-to-day tasks and responsibilities of the job.

A **person specification** is a list of criteria (skills, knowledge, experience, values and qualifications) which you need in order to do your job. These may either be 'essential' or 'desirable'.

When you apply for any job in health and social care, you are likely to have seen the job advertised somewhere, and submitted an application before being interviewed. When you were shortlisted for the interview, your application will have been tested against both the **job description** and in many cases a **person specification** for that role.

These two key documents provide the beginning of the scope of your job role.

Policies, procedures, legislation and codes of practice complete the scope of your role once you are employed.

Think of the scope of your job role as a building which you do not go outside of – the foundations are made up of the value base of health and social care, the walls are made up of your job description and the person specification, along with policies and procedures, and the roof is the law that you need to work within.

Policies are usually written and formal, and procedures can be:

Key terms

Policy: A policy in health and social care is a written statement explaining the service or agency's expected approach to an issue, area of practice, or key aspect of people's work. Policies can be local and/or national.

Procedure: A procedure is an agreed and understood way or order of doing something in work.

- presented in writing or in a flow chart or other formats

- formal

- informal (an informal procedure would be something that workers understand they follow in the work setting, but that is not necessarily written out in formal format – ie a way that people are expected to greet and sign visitors into the organisation or health and social care setting).

Policies and procedures will differ in every service setting, but they will always reflect the law and employer's responsibilities to both staff and service users. Health and social care workers need to have a working knowledge of their agency's policies and procedures in order to carry out their responsibilities.

ADHERING TO THE AGREED SCOPE OF YOUR ROLE

It is important to adhere to the scope of your job role because:

- the level of responsibility you have will be defined in the scope

- others will hold other duties and responsibilities which support and complement your role (ie those in higher and lower salary brackets than you, with different levels of responsibility, will have been measured against different criteria when they got their jobs, as will managers and supervisors)

- doing so keeps service users safe, and ensures that the right workers are in the right post, and that the right person does the right tasks to meet their individual needs.

Going beyond the scope of your job role can be dangerous and/or inappropriate because:

- there could be employer liabilities and insurance implications

- there could be safeguarding implications for the people you work with

- other people may be more skilled and more experienced, and therefore more effective in certain areas of work

- there may be a procedural, ethical or legal duty for certain workers to undertake certain tasks

- there could be consequences for you in terms of your own reputation for competence and potentially for your current (and future) employment.

Knowing your own boundaries, and understanding and adhering to those of your job role, are essential for good practice in this field of work.

RESEARCH

What do your job description and person specification say about your work role?

- When were they last reviewed?

- Do they reflect the actual job you do?

REFLECT

- When you applied for your current role (or for jobs in the past), how did you demonstrate in your application that you fully met the person specification?

- How could you improve future job applications based on your current experience and application of your skills?

CASE STUDY

Chen is a senior care assistant in a residential service for older people. Chen has worked in the same service for a number of years – working his way up to senior care assistant.

When Chen comes to reflect on the scope of his job role, he revisits his job description and realises that he has not recognised some of the aspects of his senior role. While he regularly offers support to other workers he did not see this as an essential part of his role – but recognises that the job description states that he is responsible for the staff on shift with him. Chen talks to his manager about what this actually means and asks if there is any training he can undertake to develop the skills he will need to support others. Chen and his manager agree that Chen will extend his work further and plan inductions for new staff, that he will also be involved in interviews for new care staff, and that next week he will get the opportunity to shadow some interviews so that he can develop his skills in this area.

- What might have been the consequences of Chen not being fully aware of the scope of his job role?

- How can Chen keep this under review?

ACCESSING FULL AND UP-TO-DATE DETAILS OF AGREED WAYS OF WORKING

It is important that you keep yourself up to date with the agreed ways of working in your organisation. Vital to this is ensuring that you are familiar with the policies and procedures of your employer.

Policies are statements that define the agency's stance on key issues, and provide some detail on how this stance should be implemented in practice. Most health and social care employers have set policies on the following:

- safeguarding
- health and safety
- equalities and diversity
- confidentiality and information sharing
- recruitment and selection of workers
- training and development
- bullying and harassment
- whistle-blowing
- an environmental policy
- grievance and disciplinary procedures.

As stated elsewhere, procedures are more about how things are expected to be done at work. Procedures can cover a wide range of tasks, including:

- anything to do with health and safety issues at work (see Chapter 6 for more details)
- fire
- recording
- opening up and locking buildings
- checking identity
- lone working
- hygiene (eg washing hands)
- administering medication
- complaints
- use of information technology systems.

It is your employer's duty to provide you with copies of all of the above when you start a job (or to give you the tools and time to research them for yourself). It is also your employer's duty to notify you of any changes to these key expectations. It is your duty to make sure you read up on any changes, stay up to date, and implement agreed ways of working in your work setting.

IMPLEMENTING AGREED WAYS OF WORKING

When there is a procedure in place in health and social care, this is because there either:

- has to be a set way of doing something (ie for legal reasons), or
- this is felt to be (or has been shown by evidence to be) the best way of achieving a task.

Your duty of care means that you have to follow procedures to keep people safe and ensure their needs are met.

Your contractual obligations mean that you have to abide by your employer's policies and procedures.

If you feel that a policy or procedure does not reflect actual practices in your work setting, part of your duty of care means that you either have to change your practices and follow procedure more closely, or that you need to alert your manager that the procedure may need to be changed or improved.

REFLECT

- How do you work in agreed ways in your work setting?
- Are there any procedures that you feel could be improved in your work setting in order to meet service users' needs better? What would you change and why?

CASE STUDY

Isabella is a senior care assistant in a respite care service that provides short-term stays for adults with learning and physical disabilities. She is concerned that since a recent change in the way that rotas are worked out, some shifts do not have sufficient staff to support service users to go out into the community – as the ratios cannot be maintained in the service. She feels that this goes against the service aspirations to support service users around their inclusion in the wider community.

Some staff have said that they feel it would be OK to take service users out even though there are not sufficient staff in line with the organisation's policy – they are confident that it would be safe and appropriate to go out with fewer staff. Isabella agrees that it is likely to be perfectly safe to go out with fewer staff than is laid down in the policy, but equally she feels that it is important that policy is followed.

- What should Isabella do?

MESSAGES FROM RESEARCH

The social care workforce

The State of the Adult Social Care Sector and Workforce in England 2012 provides the following information about the social care workforce in 2011:

- There were 1.63 million people working in adult social care in England.

- 85.8% of these were on permanent contracts.

- Almost half of the workforce were in full-time posts.

- 23% of the workforce work for recipients of direct payments.

- 36% of the workforce are employed in residential care.

- 45% of the workforce are employed in domiciliary care.

- 5% of the workforce are employed in day services.

- 14% of the workforce are employed in community services.

- 78% of the workforce are in direct care roles.

- The average age of a worker starting in social care is 35.

- 22,100 organisations provided adult social care.

- Services were delivered at an estimated 49,700 establishments.

(Skills for Care 2012)

WORKING IN PARTNERSHIP WITH OTHERS

Partnership working means working closely with others. Being able to work effectively in partnership with service users and their family members as well as a wide range of other agencies and professionals is an essential skill for everyone in health and social care.

Working in partnership with service users and their family members is a key theme throughout this book and involves:

- communicating effectively

- working in a person-centred way

- promoting the principles of active participation and self-directed support.

This chapter focuses on the issues of working in partnership with other professionals. Some of the skills you will use to work in partnership with service users and their family members are central to good

practice around working in partnership with other professionals too, although some of the challenges in working with people from other settings, services, professional backgrounds and agencies go beyond communication and interpersonal skills.

WORKING IN PARTNERSHIP WITH OTHER PROFESSIONALS

The agenda for skilling up all professionals to work together is at the heart of all governmental policy in health and social care work. The idea of a range of professionals forming a 'team around the person' is one which is key to providing person-centred services to vulnerable people which truly meet their individual needs. As Douglas (2008: 9) states:

Whilst many of us will receive the help we need from a single professional such as a GP, the persistent and enduring problems which form the average social care caseload will only be helped through a multi-agency or interdisciplinary approach.

The National Service Framework for Older People (Department of Health 2001a: 24–25) also outlines clear expectations around integrated working between health services and social care agencies, who are expected to work towards single assessment and joint commissioning:

Person-centred care needs to be supported by services that are organised to meet needs. The NHS and councils should deploy the 1999 Health Act flexibilities to:

- establish joint commissioning arrangements for older people's services, including consideration of a lead commissioner and the use of pooled budgets
- ensure an integrated approach to service provision, such that they are person centred, regardless of professional or organisational boundaries.

BENEFITS OF WORKING IN PARTNERSHIP WITH OTHER AGENCIES

There are a range of benefits to working in partnership with other professionals and other agencies, which might include:

Being able to 'tap into' resources which other agencies hold

Not only does this lead to better outcomes for service users, but it means that people can access specialist help from the right people at the right time. Being able to use a single assessment process means reducing the need for people to have to keep repeating their 'story' to different professionals.

Being able to be clear about service roles and responsibilities

Effective partnership working necessitates all workers being clear about the roles and responsibilities of other professionals. This means that workers need to be clear about the boundaries of their own role, so that this can be communicated to service users and other agencies. It also means that people working in health and social care need to be clear about the roles of others (eg occupational therapists, district nurses, community psychiatric nurses, social workers, etc), so that when a team is formed to provide support to a service user everyone knows:

- who is doing what
- when
- where
- why
- what each professional can and cannot offer.

Being clear in this way means that service users can also feel confident in understanding why so many people may be involved in their lives. It also means that service users can potentially be supported to understand what may be expected of them in terms of supporting themselves in line with the principles of active participation and self-directed support.

Being able to put into place effective and safe practices around confidentiality and information sharing

Where multiple agencies and workers are involved in someone's care, it is vital that good practice around confidentiality is organised and agreed. This is essential as working together usually means that certain information needs to be shared so that effective care and support can be offered. At the same time, it is a service user's legal and moral right to know which information is shared and what the purpose is for this sharing of knowledge about them.

Growing in confidence in professional knowledge and expertise

Working with others enables health and social care staff to learn, develop their skills and feel confident about their own role.

THE CHALLENGES OF PARTNERSHIP WORKING

Despite the various benefits to partnership working in health and social care, there are a number of challenges to effective partnership working. These can include:

Organisational culture

All organisations have their own values and culture. The concept of organisational culture applies to agencies, professional roles and to individual teams. This can mean that tensions arise where professional cultures are expected to work together as there may be several factors which create stress, such as:

- lack of a mutual understanding around the roles and boundaries of other professional roles

- stereotyping of other agencies and professionals (eg social workers just want to close cases, district nurses don't take enough time with people, etc)

- issues around leadership – managers need to be committed to the ideals of partnership working and communicate this consistently, as well as challenging stereotyping of other agencies

- factors within teams or services creating stress at certain times which lead professionals to 'shut down' and work in an insular way (eg when facing change, redundancy or high workloads).

Relative values of different professions and status issues

Tension can arise in decision making as certain professionals have more status granted them within society than others. This can be made apparent by differences around length of training, pay and by actions which accord some individuals more status. The obvious example of this is around general practitioners (GPs) – how many of us have found it hard to question decisions and actions taken by the GP because they are seen as so powerful? Similarly, this can apply for health and social care workers on a professional level as it can feel hard to challenge other agencies' views about a service user's needs.

Learning *how* to challenge others constructively

All relationships involve differences of opinion at some point. However, health and social care workers need particular sensitivity when challenging other agencies' views, decisions and actions. It is a difficult task to challenge other workers' decisions without it seeming like a reflection on their professional judgement. Being able to do this is a core skill in all professional practice in all fields. Sometimes, personalities may clash, or another worker may simply not be in the right frame of mind to hear a challenge which is made. Therefore, health and social care workers must be able to plan, weigh up and action the best way of making challenges in order to achieve the desired outcomes for an individual service user.

Protectiveness of jobs

Sometimes working in partnership can be difficult because other professionals might perceive unintended threats to their own jobs and status. One of the key skills in partnership working involves the ability to consider someone else's standpoint, their pressures and their anxieties, in the same way as with service users. Workers too can feel threatened by other people coming into the picture and offering support that they may feel is part of their job to deliver. The ability to share this openly can be a core skill for those working in health and social care, particularly when a relationship is new or already feels strained. Openness can achieve great change though, as other professionals may respond well to someone taking the time to find out what the barriers are to partnerships from their point of view. In this way shared solutions can be created so that closer partnership working can be achieved, although this can be an ongoing struggle in trying to form shared visions with some individuals.

Ethical issues

Sometimes there may be moral or ethical considerations which need to be looked at. This again might involve managers from two services taking a clear view together as to the way forward. An example of where this may be necessary could be around disagreements over information that can be shared. It is important for health and social care workers in this instance to ask managers for advice on the possible legal ramifications around partnership working and confidentiality (see Chapter 7 on handling information).

CASE STUDY

Jon is a senior support worker with a reablement team. He works in partnership with a number of other professionals – including hospital staff and a range of therapists. Jon sometimes finds this challenging. He is particularly challenged by his working relationship with hospital staff. He sometimes feels that they try to arrange discharges for people before they are ready to be discharged from hospital. He recognises the pressures that hospital staff are under, but feels that when people are discharged too early it affects how much he can do with them to support them in developing their independence.

- What could Jon do about his concerns?

WAYS OF WORKING THAT CAN HELP IMPROVE PARTNERSHIP WORKING

Partnership working can be improved in several ways, including:

- recognising the benefits of partnership working

- being committed to working in partnership – recognising the way that it can improve outcomes for service users

- managers and senior managers agreeing joint working protocols, which include detail on how disagreement will be resolved

- spending time with other professionals, and those working in partner agencies and disciplines

- understanding the challenges to partnership working

- developing skills in dealing with conflict

- attending joint training events

- shadowing colleagues from other agencies

- attending multi-agency meetings and listening to partners' views about an issue, someone's needs, or solutions to barriers

- co-locating teams in the same building; this is increasingly being used to aid partnership working, as people get to know each other informally and see how partners work on a day-to-day basis.

As with all good health and social care practice, listening to partners, respecting difference, and focusing on the service user are the key skills to ensure partnership working is improved.

WHEN AND HOW TO ACCESS SUPPORT AND ADVICE ABOUT PARTNERSHIP WORKING

Knowing when and how to access support around the challenges that partnership working can bring is important.

When:

- the above strategies have been tried but the tension remains in the relationship

- there are ethical dilemmas that may need someone else's input (see also Chapter 4 on duty of care)

- there may need to be an escalation of a specific issue or a use of joint working protocols.

How:

- usually workers would contact their immediate line manager for support, advice and information

- if they are not available, there may be a duty system for managerial support in some settings

- some issues may need escalating to more senior managers

- support may be available from employee assistance helplines, unions or from other agencies.

At all times, whenever there are issues in partnership working, and when additional support or advice is needed, keep the service user as the focus.

REFLECT

- Which agencies and other professionals do you work in partnership with in your role and work setting?

- What do you see as being the benefits of partnership working?

- What do you see as the tensions in partnership working?

- How would you resolve issues in your work setting?

- Have you had any experience of challenges within partnerships? If so, what worked in resolving these challenges, and what did not work so well?

RESEARCH

- Does your service or employer have any formal partnership agreements, or joint working protocols (either formally agreed in writing, or informal expectations around how partnership working will be conducted)?

- If not, are there any areas where you feel this could be helpful, and could improve outcomes for service users?

RESOLVING CONFLICT

Health and social care workers at all levels regularly find themselves in situations of conflict with others. This is particularly likely to occur in situations where they are working in partnership with others, which is why resolving conflicts is covered in this unit. However, it is important to remember that being able to work with and resolve conflict is an important skill in all aspects of health and social care work.

CONFLICT: POSITIVE OR NEGATIVE?

In our experience, health and social care workers often view conflict negatively. However, this can create difficulties in terms of conflict responses. In itself, conflict is neither positive or negative – it is the way that conflict is managed and the consequences of conflict which make it either positive or negative.

Many people who study organisational behaviour suggest that conflict is an essential aspect of life and should be viewed positively. In fact they believe that conflict-free, harmonious environments can be stagnant and non-responsive.

Conflict can be a positive force, in that it:

- enables a person to become aware of problems in a relationship
- serves as a catalyst for learning and positive change
- energises and motivates people to deal with immediate problems
- can stimulate interest and curiosity
- relieves minor tensions and can be liberating
- creates more creative approaches to decision making
- promotes self-awareness
- clears the air of unexpressed resentment.

WHAT MIGHT CREATE CONFLICT?

It is widely accepted that there are five main sources of conflict, as follows.

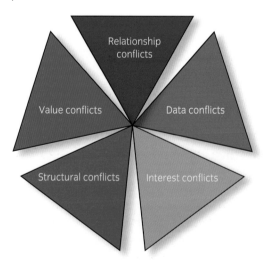

Relationship conflicts

When we think about conflict, conflicts between people or relationship-based conflicts are generally the first thing that comes to mind. Relationship conflicts can occur because of:

- poor communication
- strong negative emotions
- misperceptions or stereotypes
- repetitive negative behaviours.

Data conflicts

Data conflicts are sometimes referred to as informational conflicts. Essentially, they relate to conflicts where information is the source of the conflict. They might occur when:

- people lack the information necessary to make decisions
- people are misinformed
- there is a disagreement about which information is relevant
- there is conflicting information.

Interest conflicts

Interest conflicts are caused by competition between needs that may be seen as incompatible with each other. Conflicts of interest result when one or more of the parties believe that in order to satisfy his or her needs, the needs and interests of another person must be sacrificed.

Structural conflicts

Structural conflicts are caused by forces external to the people in dispute. Often they are related to the way in which society is constructed. Issues like limited physical resources, geographical constraints (distance or proximity), time (too little or too much) and organisational changes can make structural conflict seem like a crisis. It can be helpful to assist parties in conflict to appreciate the external forces and constraints that have an impact, as an understanding that a conflict has an external source can have the effect of bringing people together to jointly address the imposed difficulties.

Value conflicts

Value conflicts are caused by differences in value systems. Differing value systems do necessarily cause conflict. Value conflicts arise only when people attempt to force one set of values on others or lay claim to exclusive value systems that do not allow for different beliefs. Value conflicts can create internal conflicts for health and social care workers, for example where their personal values conflict with the professional values of social care or where organisational values conflict with professional values.

It can be useful when trying to resolve conflict to first of all analyse where the conflict is coming from. Understanding whether a conflict is a relationship conflict or a structural conflict, for instance, is a good starting point for resolving the conflict.

CONFLICT MANAGEMENT STYLES

Thomas and Kilmann (1974) studied the different ways in which people manage conflict. They identified five different styles and developed the Thomas–Kilmann Conflict Mode Instrument (TKI), a questionnaire that is used to assess an individual's conflict-handling style. The results from assessing a large sample using the TKI have demonstrated that although most people will use different styles depending on the situation, it is normal to have a preferred mode of handling conflict and this may well be related to personality type. The five styles can be categorised by the extent to which they demonstrate assertive and cooperative behaviour, as follows:

- competing
- collaborating
- avoiding
- accommodating
- compromising.

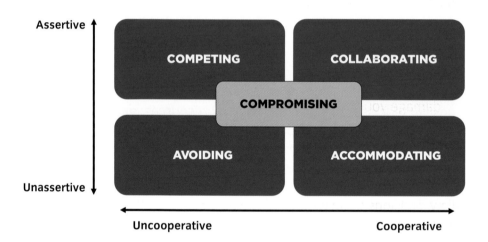

Competing: assertive and uncooperative

This individual is out to win, even if it is at someone else's expense. People who use this style are usually in a position of power. This may derive from their position in the hierarchy of an organisation or it may derive from a strong and dominating personality.

This style can be useful when:

- a decision has to be made quickly – for example, in an emergency situation
- an unpopular decision has to be made
- a defensive measure against people who will take advantage of more cooperative behaviour is required.

Collaborating: assertive and cooperative

This individual is looking for a solution that will suit all parties. Collaborators may be assertive, but unlike competitors, they are good at working with other people and recognise that other points of view may be as valid as their own. Effectively, this is the style that best suits partnership working.

This style can be useful when:

- the views of the different parties are too important for any compromise
- a project is more likely to succeed if all of the people involved feel they have been heard
- there has been conflict between people and this needs to be resolved before the project can move forward.

Accommodating: unassertive and cooperative

This individual is giving way to the interests of the other party and not looking after their own interests. The accommodator is too concerned about the opinions of other people and would prefer to 'lose' rather than hurt anyone's feelings.

This style can be useful when:

- you know that you are wrong
- the issue is much more important to the other person
- when there is no hope of winning and pursuing the issue would damage your cause.

Avoiding: unassertive and uncooperative

This individual is looking out neither for their own interests nor those of the other party. The avoider will delegate decisions to others or allow decisions to be made through default rather than tackle conflicts themselves.

This style can be useful when:

- there is no hope of winning
- the conflict is unimportant and not worth fighting for
- dealing with the conflict may potentially have a higher cost than resolving the conflict.

Compromising: midway in both assertiveness and cooperativeness

This individual is looking for a solution that will partially satisfy all sides. The compromiser expects that all parties involved in conflict will have to concede some ground, but they also accept that they will have to concede some ground themselves.

This style can be useful when:

- the cost of conflict is higher than the cost of giving up some ground
- the parties involved have equal power and have reached a stalemate because their aims are mutually exclusive
- a deadline is looming.

CASE STUDY

Taju is a senior support worker with a mental health charity. He is aware that Matthew and Dylan (two service users) do not get on. They have often argued with each other at the drop-in centre in the past. Recently, if Matthew is present when Dylan arrives at the service, Dylan simply turns around and leaves. Taju is concerned that Dylan isn't attending the drop-in centre very often and that he is becoming increasingly isolated. When he talks to Dylan about this Dylan says that he can't come if Matthew is going to be there as 'we hate each other'. Dylan agrees that he used to enjoy the drop-in and that he used to get on well with Matthew – but that this part of his life is now over.

- What could Taju do to address the conflict between Dylan and Matthew?

THE FIVE As APPROACH TO CONFLICT RESOLUTION

Borisoff and Victor (1998) identified five stages to conflict resolution, which we've summarised below.

Assessment

In this stage, the parties involved gather information to decide on the problem. They agree on the central nature of the problem and decide on which conflict management method would work best. Each party indicates what they want to achieve and where they might compromise.

Acknowledgement

Here, each party listens to the other. Active listening is really important and each person should indicate to the other that they have heard what is being said – even if they don't agree with it.

Attitude

This involves acknowledging diversity and the impact that culture and stereotyping might have on the situation. Any potential problems arising from difference should be explored.

Action

The parties implement the chosen action to resolve the conflict.

Analysis

Everyone involved agrees what they will do as the outcome of the discussions. A clear summary is needed and an agreement should be made about what will happen in the future. The short- and long-term results will be evaluated.

CONFLICT RESOLUTION: STAGES, SKILLS AND ATTITUDES

Conflict resolution is characterised by a number of stages and different writers have generated different numbers of stages. However, the general process can be summarised as follows.

1 Communication

When you are in a situation of potential conflict with another person, you need to avoid entering into an adversarial and defensive position. The initial task is to have an attitude where you want yourself and the person who is in dispute with you to benefit from any shared decision (ie win–win situation).

To do this, the starting point is to find out the needs of each party. Skills required include supportive questioning (to identify the other person's needs), effective listening and the ability to communicate your own needs. In communicating your own needs you should be assertive, use the 'I' word without expectations of what the other person should do. Conflict resolution recognises that the person could be very angry with you. Options include:

- Don't defend yourself at first; this will inflame the situation.

- Deal with their emotions; explicitly acknowledge that you recognise how angry they are.

- Acknowledge their perspective. You do not need to agree with them but you do need to understand them.

This process should enable the person to calm down. From then onwards the process should follow the same stage process.

One of the key elements to conflict resolution is attitude. There must be:

- an openness to recognise the benefit of differences

- a willingness to adapt or trade for mutual benefit

- a view that the difficulty is to be addressed and not the person

- a view that disagreements or potential conflicts are not a problem. They are an opportunity to engage with the other person.

2 Negotiation

Once the needs of each individual have been expressed, the next stage is negotiation. It is important that the focus remains on the issue. Where possible, explicitly acknowledge common ground. If it appears to be a big problem, can it be broken down?

If negotiations get heated:

- manage your own emotions
- let some barbed comments go without responding to them
- have a break but agree when to resume.

In seeking a solution:

- make a trial proposal
- suggest a trade, eg 'I will do this if you do that'
- make an agreement temporary or time limited so that agreements can be reviewed.

3 Mediation

If it is not possible to reach a win–win situation, it may be necessary to go for mediation.

A mediator requires various skills and must have a clear sense that both parties are willing to address the problem. She or he will:

- be explicit that mutual benefit is the aim
- enable each party to express themselves and check the other party has understood them
- encourage suggestions (the mediator should avoid making their own suggestions)
- discourage personal comments or behaviours that could be provocative (name calling, ignoring, threats, belittlement, etc).

4 Resolution

Be clear about the agreement that has been made. It is easy for two people to leave a conflict situation with each person having a different understanding of what has been agreed.

WHEN AND HOW TO ACCESS SUPPORT AND ADVICE ABOUT RESOLVING CONFLICTS

Knowing when and how to access support when you face situations of conflict is important.

When:

- you face a conflict that you feel cannot be easily resolved
- there is a range of conflicts that may need someone else's input
- there may need to be an escalation of a specific issue, or a use of joint working protocols

How:

- usually workers would contact their immediate line manager for support, advice and information

- if they were not available, there may be a duty system for managerial support in some settings

- some issues may need escalating to more senior managers.

At all times, whenever there are conflict issues, and when additional support or advice is needed, keep the service user as the focus.

REFLECT

Identify a situation where you have faced conflict, then consider the following:

- What was the conflict?

- How did you handle it?

- Could you have improved your response to this situation? How?

- If a similar situation were to occur again, how would you deal with it?

CODES OF PRACTICE FOR HEALTH AND SOCIAL CARE WORKERS

As professionals, health and social care workers need to follow the relevant codes of practice. The Care Standards Act 2000 placed a responsibility on the relevant care councils to produce a code of practice for social care workers. However, the Health and Social Care Act 2012 revised the arrangements for the regulation of social care such that the General Social Care Council was abolished. This has led to a change in the codes of practice for England. You need to be familiar with the relevant code for your area of work:

- In England the relevant code is the Code of Conduct for Healthcare Support Workers and Adult Social Care Workers (Skills for Care and Skills for Health).

- In Wales the relevant code is the Code of Practice for Social Care Workers (Care Council for Wales).

- In Scotland this is the Code of Practice for Social Care Workers (Scottish Social Services Council).

- In Northern Ireland this is the Code of Practice for Social Care Workers (Northern Ireland Social Care Council).

CODES OF PRACTICE FOR HEALTH AND SOCIAL CARE WORKERS (CONTINUED)

Since best practice in health and social care is built on firm foundations the codes of practice are very similar. Throughout this book reference is made to the Code of Conduct for Healthcare Support Workers and Adult Social Care in England. If you work in a different nation you will need to ensure that you refer to the code that is relevant for your area of work.

Code of Conduct for Healthcare Support Workers and Adult Social Care Workers

The Code of Conduct for Healthcare Support Workers and Adult Social Care Workers makes clear that you need to be accountable and that you must:

- be honest with yourself and others about what you can do, recognise your abilities and the limitations of your competence and carry out or delegate only those tasks agreed in your job description and for which you are competent

- always behave and present yourself in a way that does not call into question your suitability to work in a health and social care environment

- be able to justify and be accountable for your actions or omissions – what you fail to do

- always ask your supervisor or employer for guidance if you do not feel adequately prepared to carry out any aspect of your work, or if you are unsure how to effectively deliver a task

- tell your supervisor or employer about any issues that might affect your ability to do your job competently and safely (if you do not feel competent to carry out an activity you must report this)

- establish and maintain clear and appropriate professional boundaries in our relationships with people who use health and care services, carers and colleagues at all times

- never accept any offers of loans, gifts, benefits or hospitality from anyone you are supporting or anyone close to them which may be seen to compromise your position

- honour your work commitments, agreements and arrangements and be reliable, dependable and trustworthy

- comply with your employers agreed ways of working.

CHAPTER 2
Promoting communication in health and social care

The Social Care Institute for Excellence states that good communication skills are the starting point for all the other skills that health and social care workers need. The other skills that you will need in order to work in health and social care cannot be developed unless you have good skills in communication. Many people think that communication skills are 'natural' – that people are either good communicators or not. However, communication skills can be learnt. It is certainly the case that communicating where there are challenges can be learnt.

This chapter ensures that you understand and learn how to communicate effectively and overcome any barriers that you might face.

Links to other chapters

Communication is important for all aspects of effective work in health and social care. In particular, this chapter should be read with reference to chapters 1, 3, 5, 7 and 14.

UNDERSTANDING THE IMPORTANCE OF COMMUNICATION

In order to understand the importance of communication at work, you need to understand:

- what we mean by communication
- how people communicate
- why people communicate
- the way that communication impacts on your work.

WHAT IS COMMUNICATION?

On the face of it this might seem a very basic question, but there is a lot more to communication than you might first think.

Communication is a two-way process which is affected by the environment in which the communication takes place. It is never straightforward – it is never about one individual, but always about relationships, environments and understanding the specific needs of the individuals you work with.

Communication is about making sure that our needs are recognised or our wishes known by another being. It is about one living person interacting with another in any way, and about the other person listening, understanding and communicating back.

Every living organism communicates – communication is not something which only human beings can do. In the animal world, communication between creatures is essential for meeting basic needs for safety, food, company and warmth. Animals communicate via the sounds they make, their movements, the warning signals they give, and their posture. It is thought that even some plants communicate by releasing chemicals to warn their neighbours of risks in the area. Humans communicate on more complex levels partly because we have such a wide range of methods of communication to use.

Even newborn babies can communicate effectively because:

- their needs are unmet (hunger, warmth, comfort, affection, nappy needing changing)
- they want to be stimulated
- of fear or loneliness.

Many new parents will tell you that they quickly learn the difference in the way a baby cries – understanding the difference between a baby who is hungry or who wants attention.

COMMUNICATION AS A TWO-WAY PROCESS

Perhaps the most important aspect of communication is that it is a two-way process. It is about both giving and receiving a message. If you are alone, there is no one to see you, no one to hear you and your communication is not being picked up by anyone. Effectively there is no communication!

Communication, as we will see in other parts of this chapter, is as much about the listening and receiving of information from the other person, as it is about whatever we are trying to communicate to them. In order to relate to other people as individuals, we need to be considerate around their communication styles, preferences and needs, and to ensure that our own communication enables the other person to relate to us. *All* relationships are built on mutual, two-way communication.

Communication is:

- about understanding other people's needs and wishes

- about letting people know that you have heard and understood them

- about being honest and open about what you can and cannot do to meet those needs and wishes

- on its most basic level, about getting on with people – ie treating them with respect as individuals and as equals.

This is why good communication at work builds effective relationships with colleagues and service users, and why barriers to communication have to be overcome to aid effective mutual understanding.

> **KEY POINT**
>
> Communication is a two-way process. It is about giving a message and receiving a message.

WHY DO PEOPLE COMMUNICATE?

There are four main reasons people communicate:

Instrumental communication
We communicate in order to:

- ask for something
- refuse something
- choose something
- tell someone what we need or want.

Informative communication
We communicate in order to:

- obtain information
- give another person information
- to describe something.

Expressive communication
We communicate in order to:

- express our thoughts or feelings
- shares ideas.

Social communication
We communicate in order to:

- attract attention
- build relationships
- maintain relationships.

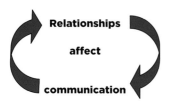

COMMUNICATION AND RELATIONSHIPS

Communication and relationships are very closely linked. The way in which we communicate with others will be affected by the relationship we have with them. In much the same way, the quality of communication has an effect on relationships. For example, when people don't communicate effectively their relationship suffers. The links between communication and relationships should never be underestimated by health and social care professionals.

In health and social care settings, communication occurs:

- between individual workers and individual users of services
- between individual workers and groups of service users
- within groups of service users
- between team members
- within staff groups
- between staff members and managers

- between staff members, managers and partner agencies
- between service users and their carers, family and friends
- between staff and service users' carers, family and friends.

REFLECT

Think about how the various ways in which you communicate at work affect your working relationships. You may have heard service users described as 'unable to communicate'. Given the complexity of communication, how is this so?

Communication is two way. If workers are failing to understand what a person is communicating, the problem is with the worker, not the service user. The view taken should be more along the lines of 'the person working with this service user can't understand their communication'.

MESSAGES FROM RESEARCH

Poor communication in health and social care

The Social Care Institute for Excellence highlights the extensive research demonstrating poor practice in communication in health and social care:

Care staff are regularly observed to use patronising styles of speech that feature exaggerated tones, inappropriate use of 'we' and 'our' instead of 'you' and 'your' and unsuitable endearments such as 'dear'. This way of talking is sometimes referred to as 'elderspeak'.

Other examples drawn from research observing health and social care staff in residential settings include making critical comments about residents within their hearing or carrying on conversations from which residents are excluded. This seems to stem from a mistaken belief that if residents' verbal communication skills have been affected, then they won't understand what is being said about them. The research indicates that even where residents' understanding is limited, they are likely to realise that something negative is being said by picking up on non-verbal signs such as facial expression.

A wide range of research indicates that where health and social care staff are reminded of the importance of respectful communication, this has an impact on their practice. Where the communication of care staff is improved through training and reflective practice this has a very significant impact on the outcomes for service users.

(Moriarty et al 2010)

UNDERSTANDING HOW PEOPLE COMMUNICATE

In order to meet the requirements of this chapter it is vital that you understand the different ways in which people communicate.

People communicate in a variety of ways, such as:

- touch
- gestures
- speech
- drawing
- facial expression
- sign language
- style of dress
- body movements and posture
- writing
- telephone
- electronically (eg text messaging and email).

All the different types of communication can be categorised into three main areas:

- verbal communication
- non-verbal communication
- written communication.

VERBAL COMMUNICATION

When thinking about verbal communication, people tend to focus on the words they use. However, research indicates that the words we use are less important than other aspects of communication in conveying or understanding our needs. Only a small proportion of communication is conveyed in the words we use with more being communicated by the tone, volume and pitch of the voice, and even more being communicated in the form of body language.

Therefore, in using verbal communication you not only need to think about using words that treat people with respect and using words that people can understand, but you also need to think about the following areas:

Speed

The speed at which someone talks is very significant. It might indicate someone's emotional state – for example, fast speech is associated with anger or excitement while slow speech can be associated with tiredness or a low mood. The speed at which someone speaks can be interpreted in a range of ways – for example, slow speech can be interpreted as showing a lack of interest.

Tone

People are often not aware of the tone of their own voice. However, it is important for health and social care staff to develop this awareness as tone of voice has such a significant impact on communication.

Volume

How loud or softly we speak has a very significant impact on communication. For example, loud speech can indicate anger or aggression and yet many health and social care staff raise the volume of their voice when talking to service users.

Register

The 'register' of speech refers to how formal or informal it is. You will be aware that people often change the formality of their speech depending on their situation.

NON-VERBAL COMMUNICATION

Non-verbal communication (also referred to as body language) refers to the messages given out by body actions and movements rather than words. Body language is an important part of the communication process. As the saying goes, 'actions speak louder than words'. Usually verbal and non-verbal communications are in agreement (eg someone saying 'I'm happy' and smiling) but at times they may contradict each other (eg someone saying 'I'm happy' while they look positively sad).

There are some key guidelines in terms of body language. When considering body language (and communication as a whole) try to remember the three Rs: Communication should always be:

- respectful
- receptive
- relaxed.

The table on the next page gives some guidelines on this.

Respectful, relaxed, receptive ✔	Disrespectful, tense, not receptive ✗
Resting and/or still hands	Fidgeting and/or clenched hands
Relaxed face	Creased brow, a drawn mouth
Relaxed shoulders	Raised and tense shoulders
Posture is upright, able to breathe easily	Strained or hunched
Slow and deep breathing	Rapid and/or shallow breathing
General position comfortable and easy to retain when either sitting or standing	Requires lots of fidgeting and movement to remain comfortable
Mouth visible	Mouth covered up or chewing finger nails
Feet and legs still and comfortable	Feet and legs fidgeting or tapping
Appear interested in what is being said	Doodle, sigh, look away, look at the watch, etc.

These descriptions can also act as indicators of how someone is feeling. Sensitive observation provides insight into how the exchange is progressing. This is an important point because communication depends upon responding to the verbal and non-verbal messages provided by others within the exchange. Therefore, if a person's body language becomes tense, the situation may be causing anxiety.

> **REFLECT**
>
> Spend some time observing people. You can do this anywhere – at work, at home, when you are out and about. Does a person's body language (non-verbal communication) always match what they are saying (their verbal communication)?

THE USE OF TOUCH IN COMMUNICATION

Touch is a very powerful form of non-verbal communication. Think about the way that you might experience touch yourself – when someone you know well touches you, you might feel comforted and safe, but when someone you don't know touches you, you might feel vulnerable and threatened.

When used appropriately, touch can be a very positive form of communication in that it can:

- provide comfort and reassurance when someone is distressed, making them feel safe and secure

- show respect

- calm someone who is agitated.

However, when used indiscriminately, touch can:

- invade privacy, making people feel vulnerable

- embarrass people

- undermine trust

- be seen as harassment.

So, this is a sensitive area. The best approach is to keep touch to a minimum, because it can easily be experienced as threatening, inappropriate or uncomfortable, especially for a service user who may already be feeling vulnerable. If a health and social care worker needs to touch someone as part of the care process, they should explain what they are doing and always ask permission. Failure to ask permission and obtain consent is an intrusion on that person and an abuse of power.

BEHAVIOUR AS A METHOD OF COMMUNICATION

Everything we do is communicating something. We even communicate in some way in our sleep – when you are asleep you are communicating that you are tired or that you are bored! Very often people behave in certain ways to communicate something to another person. It is important that when you see someone behaving in a certain way you ask yourself, 'What are they trying to communicate to me?' Recognising that all behaviour is a form of communication is a starting point for this chapter.

ALTERNATIVE METHODS OF COMMUNICATION

Where people experience barriers to the more common forms of communication they may use alternative methods of communication (sometimes referred to as **augmentative and alternative communication**). This might include communication methods as follows.

Key term

Augmentative and alternative communication (AAC) is a term which is used to describe a range of techniques which health and social care workers and other professionals use in order to aid communication and support people to understand. AAC can be pictorial (eg using photographs and symbols to mark out what will be happening and in what order), or it can be where sign and gesture are used in order to communicate certain words or ideas.

Objects of reference

Using an object or a picture to indicate what someone wants. They could pick up a cup to indicate that he or she would like a hot drink or could use a picture or symbol to indicate this. A particular object or picture may have a specific meaning for that individual which may not be immediately apparent, which is where observations, together with feedback from others, will be especially helpful.

Touch

Perhaps using a tap on the arm to obtain your attention or guiding you to indicate what the person requires. In this way, someone might guide you to a room where they want to be or show you something of interest.

Behaviour, gestures and movement

These can be used by many people as a communication method. Behaviour that may be labelled as challenging or difficult may in fact be much more about a person communicating some aspect of their needs.

Sounds

If people have relatively few or no words, they may use other sounds to indicate what they want. The meaning of some sounds may well be obvious, such as laughter or shouts of joy or pleasure. As with the use of objects of reference and touch, the association made with some sounds will be specific to that individual.

Smell

Where other senses are impaired, the sense of smell may take on added significance and some people may, for example, sniff different types of foods and toiletries to make their choice.

Drawing

Some people may prefer you to make a drawing to indicate what choices are available or what may be taking place. Symbols are often used in communicating with people to help understanding.

Writing

Some people may prefer to write rather than to speak. This may be the case if someone's speech is temporarily impaired due to illness or it may help them to clarify what they mean.

KEY POINT

The three Vs of communication
There are 3 Vs involved in the giving and receiving of a message:
Visual cues – body language such as eye contact.
Vocal cues – the tone and pitch of the voice.
Verbal cues – the choice of language.

REFLECT

Over the next few days think about the variety of different communication methods you use. If you were not able to speak, what other methods might you be able to use to communicate your wishes and needs?

MEETING PEOPLE'S COMMUNICATION AND LANGUAGE NEEDS, WISHES AND PREFERENCES

Every individual, whether they use or work in health and social care or not, has their own preferred methods, tools and means of communication. Within health and social care, it is our role to know about the needs and preferences of the people we are there to support. You therefore need to be competent at establishing *how* each individual communicates, and *what* they want to communicate about their needs and wishes.

Some of this is like a detective task, as you cannot assume that every individual communicates in the same way, as even when people have similar issues, they may communicate differently and want different things.

HOW DO YOU ESTABLISH A PERSON'S COMMUNICATION NEEDS, WISHES AND PREFERENCES?

Ask them. If they are not able to tell you then:

- Ask someone who knows them well, possibly a family member or another professional.

- Read their notes.

- Try different methods of communication and review what response you get.

When a health and social care worker meets a new service user, some documentation about this person should be shared – this might be assessment documentation or a care plan. This paperwork should provide information about how the person communicates. Occasionally, there may even be an assessment report by a communication therapist (sometimes referred to as a speech and language therapist).

Someone's communication needs are a key element of their care and support needs, and their preferred communication and any specific communication needs should be recorded in their care plan. As with any aspect of care planning, the process should begin with an initial or baseline assessment. Planning should then take place to find the best way to support the person's needs and help them to develop or maintain their skills if possible. The plan should be implemented and monitored to see what changes may be taking place. Periodically communication needs should be reviewed, as with any other aspect of someone's support needs, and they should be reassessed as necessary. A review may need to consider advice from relatives of the person or from a specialist, such as a communication therapist.

Even if all this information is carefully recorded, it is no use unless staff who are supporting individuals are aware of it and have had the necessary training to put it into practice. Information about someone's communication needs should be clearly and simply recorded and the record should be easily accessible by those workers who need to access it. It needs to be accessible in two respects:

- The information needs to be recorded in an uncomplicated format which is easy for the worker to grasp, perhaps on a profile card rather than having to wade through pages of care notes.

- A copy of the record itself should be with the worker rather than put away on a shelf in the manager's office. This is particularly important where staff are working alone, eg away from their practice or organisation, as is the case with domiciliary care services.

REFLECT

How do you establish the communication and language needs of the service users you work with?

PERSONAL COMMUNICATION PASSPORTS

Developed in the 1990s by Sally Millar, a specialist speech and language therapist at the Communication Aids for Language and Learning (CALL) Centre, personal communication passports are a person-centred and practical way of supporting people who cannot easily speak for themselves. Passports aim to:

- present someone positively as an individual, not as a set of 'problems' or disabilities

- provide a place for someone's own views and preferences to be recorded and drawn to the attention of others

- describe someone's most effective means of communication

- draw together information from past and present, and from different contexts, to help staff and conversation partners understand someone and have successful interactions

- reflect a 'flavour' of someone's unique character.

Some organisations have developed and adapted this approach and refer to the system as individual communication profiles or something similar.

PROMOTING EFFECTIVE COMMUNICATION

Since communication is about both the giving and receiving of messages, promoting effective communication requires you to consider both the way you give a message and the way that you receive a message.

Since the cycle of communication involves …

… there are various factors to consider when promoting communication.

All of these factors are covered in this chapter. You should reflect on how you consider these factors in promoting communication.

ENVIRONMENT

The environment can have a significant impact on communication. For example, if an environment is busy and noisy this can create barriers to effective communication.

Think about the way that you position the chairs in your own home so that people can face each other to facilitate communication between you – this demonstrates how much of an impact the environment has on communication.

PROXIMITY/PERSONAL SPACE

The physical distance you keep between yourself and others during social situations is your personal space. Everyone's personal space varies as it is based on gender, culture and personality differences.

In academic terms personal space and its impact on communication is referred to as 'proxemics'. The study of proxemics identifies that there are four levels of personal space:

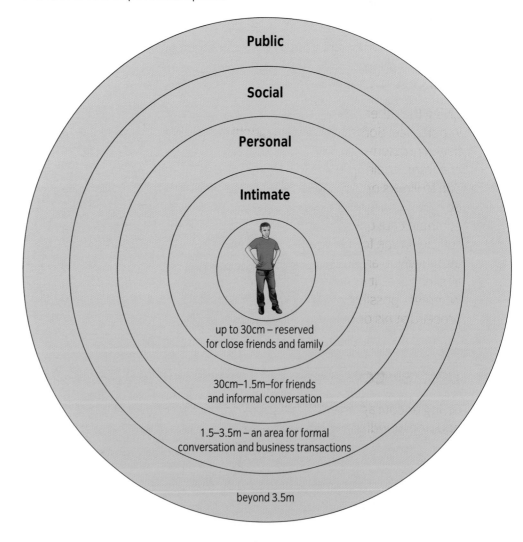

Public

Social

Personal

Intimate

up to 30cm – reserved for close friends and family

30cm–1.5m–for friends and informal conversation

1.5–3.5m – an area for formal conversation and business transactions

beyond 3.5m

Research demonstrates that people from different cultures have different personal space levels.

There are times when in health and social care these 'usual' areas of personal space are changed – for example, when you need to provide personal care for an individual. You need to think carefully about personal space issues and always check out a person's willingness for you to enter their personal space. You also need to respect the fact that people's preferences around this change over time, evolve (eg as they begin to trust you), and are likely to be specific to how someone is feeling and what they are experiencing that day.

> **KEY POINT**
>
> There is an Ancient Greek saying:
> 'We have two ears and one mouth so that we can listen twice as much as we speak.'

BEING A 'GOOD LISTENER'

Effective communication is not just about giving a message. A good communicator employs active listening skills. **Active listening** is of key importance in helping people feel valued and ensuring that their preferences and choices are recognised. Although some people are naturally good and attentive listeners, along with other aspects of communication, active listening is a skill that can always be further developed.

Key term

Active listening is about really listening to what a person is saying and showing them that you are listening to them.

There are several techniques that can help workers to be active listeners. While they might seem obvious, they are effective. In busy working environments they can easily be forgotten.

ALLOW SUFFICIENT TIME

Giving the other person the space and opportunity to talk is of great importance. Some people with learning disabilities, dementia or mental health problems may find it takes them a while to process information and frame their thoughts. People may have reduced energy levels due to illness or for other reasons. Giving an immediate response can be difficult and people may find it stressful to feel under pressure to communicate quickly. Health and social care workers need to allow sufficient time for people to communicate. Workers should listen attentively to anything someone says, but avoid feeling the need to fill silences as it may be sufficient just to be there with the person. Wherever possible, workers need to be led by the individual and to proceed at his or her pace.

USE 'ENCOURAGERS'

Giving encouragement to the person who is talking, perhaps by nodding or indicating in some other way that you are listening.

DON'T JUDGE AND DON'T ASSUME WHAT SOMEONE IS SAYING

Acknowledging what the other person has said without appearing to judge them is very important as is avoiding assumptions. If you are finding it difficult to understand what someone is saying, ask him or her to repeat themselves rather than pretend that you have understood.

USE SPECIFIC SKILLS SUCH AS REFLECTING AND PARAPHRASING

Reflecting is a skill drawn from counselling. It involves the listener repeating back what the person has said in their own words – this shows that you have listened and heard what they have said. This can also give someone the opportunity to check whether what the health and social care worker has heard is really what they meant, for them to take stock and then develop their line of thought further.

Paraphrasing is where the listener repeats back what they think they have heard using their own words – effectively summarising what they have heard.

THE SOLER MODEL OF COMMUNICATION

Developed by Gerard Egan and based on approaches used in counselling, the SOLER model of communication shows how active listening can be demonstrated to others:

Sit squarely in relation to the person – this demonstrates that you are ready to listen.

Open position – open body language indicates more attentive listening – this means not folding your arms, etc.

Lean slightly towards the person to whom you are listening – this indicates that you are interested in what the other person has to say.

Eye contact – maintain good eye contact.

Relax – it is important to sit still without fidgeting as this can distract the other person.

WHAT SHOULD I BE *LISTENING TO*?

On the face of it this seems a strange question: 'I should be listening to what the person is saying'. However, as we have covered, communication is about far more than words so we need to *listen to* far more than words. To listen effectively we need to listen to what a person is saying as well as:

■ *How the person is speaking.* You can tell a great deal from the way someone speaks. For example, if someone is speaking quickly they may be excited or anxious, and if someone is using a monotonous tone they may be feeling low. It is important of course not to make assumptions. Always check out your views, eg by saying 'it sounds as though you are happy/sad, etc about that?' By making the statement a question it is likely that the person will let you know how they feel.

■ *A person's body language.* Observe the whole person, but be aware that body language is culturally specific. In some cultures avoiding eye contact can be seen as ignorant while in others making eye contact can be seen as offensive. However, it is probably safe to assume that if someone is smiling they are happy, and so on.

■ *A person's behaviour.* Some behaviours such as crying and aggression can communicate a great deal. However you need to listen to the 'whole person' to be clear exactly what the behaviour is communicating. For example, people can cry tears of either joy or sadness.

The following poem written by an adult with learning disabilities demonstrates the way that listening is an active process:

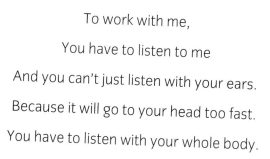

To work with me,

You have to listen to me

And you can't just listen with your ears.

Because it will go to your head too fast.

You have to listen with your whole body.

If you listen slow,

Some of what I say

Will enter your heart.

ENCOURAGING FURTHER COMMUNICATION

Active listening and employing skills such as using encouragers, reflecting and paraphrasing are likely to encourage people to communicate further and are therefore key skills in promoting effective communication.

Asking questions skilfully can also encourage further communication.

Questions are a vital part of the process of communication. While we all ask questions at different times, sometimes to be effective as a health and social care worker, people need to learn about different questioning techniques.

TYPES OF QUESTIONS

There are three main types of questions:

Question type	Example
Open	'What's your favourite drink?'
Closed	'Is tea your favourite drink?
Leading	'Tea is your favourite drink, isn't it?'

Open questions

Open questions generally start with the following:

- Why?
- Where?
- When?
- How?
- What?
- Which?
- Who?

Open questions:

- ask the speaker to think about their answer and give more information
- demonstrate an interest in a person because the questioner has effectively said 'Tell me more. I'm interested.'
- encourage people to think about the answer they are giving and the answer often gives a range of information to the questioner, allowing the conversation to develop further.

Closed questions

Closed questions are those that can only be answered by a 'yes' or 'no'. Closed questions:

- allow for limited responses
- are not helpful in gaining further information since the response is limited

- can be useful to gain very specific and basic information where the speaker regularly goes off the subject

- can be used to end a conversation.

Leading questions

This type of question gives the person being asked a clear indication about the expected answer. This can be done through the words that are used in the question or by the tone of voice in which the question is asked.

On the whole, leading questions should be avoided. However, it can occasionally be useful to ask some leading questions perhaps where a person lacks confidence in communication. A leading question can give the person a clue about how to respond – this can give the person initial confidence and if the leading question is followed up by an open question then this can lead to some useful communication.

CASE STUDY

Jon is a senior support worker with a reablement team. He is attending a review of Mr Wilder's needs. Jon has been working with Mr Wilder for over six weeks and his involvement is about to cease. The review is considering Mr Wilder's future needs. A social worker is chairing the review. The social worker asks Mr Wilder, 'Do you wash yourself in the morning by yourself?', to which Mr Wilder replies 'No'. She then goes on to ask other similarly closed questions to which Mr Wilder can only answer 'yes' or 'no'. Jon feels that the people at the review are not getting the full picture of Mr Wilder's needs. So he asks follow-up open questions such as 'How do you wash in the morning?' – these questions lead to much more useful information about Mr Wilder's needs.

- What might have been the result for Mr Wilder if Jon had not stepped in and asked more open questions?

USING A RANGE OF COMMUNICATION METHODS AND STYLES TO MEET INDIVIDUAL NEEDS

It is important for workers to be aware of the best way to communicate with individual users of health and social care services and to pay careful attention to such matters as the environment in which they are talking to the person. Even if someone normally communicates well using words, workers should bear in mind when and where they are speaking. Someone may be reserved by nature or, as is the case with many older people, may not want to 'be any trouble'. Some people, often those who have lived in institutional settings for some time, may be eager to please staff members and may communicate what they think staff want to hear rather than what they really think.

The type of questions to consider are:

- Is the person comfortable and relaxed enough to be able to respond well?

- Are there any distractions? Someone with a hearing loss may well find it difficult to distinguish what you are saying against background noise.

- If someone has a hearing loss, ensure that you are sitting opposite each other and that the light is good enough for you to be able to see each other's faces, particularly if the other person lip-reads. If the person has a hearing aid, ask them to ensure that it is switched on and operating correctly.

- Can you speak in a place where you are unlikely to be disturbed?

- Is the timing right for that person? If an individual has had a serious illness, or is on certain kinds of medication, he or she may be more alert at certain times of the day and may be more inclined to speak at those times.

- If someone has a hearing or speech disability, can he or she use or understand sign language and are you able to use this?

- Does the person respond well to pictures or symbols that you can use to communicate with them?

- Is the person happy to continue a discussion or do you need to consider changing the topic or ending a conversation? It is fine to do either and to return to discussing something on another occasion if this is appropriate to someone's needs.

Once you have established the answers to these questions you should be able to make use of a range of the communication methods covered in this chapter. Remember the wide range of communication methods you can use as shown on the next page:

Communication methods — Make good eye contact; Use augmentative and alternative communication where this will be useful; Listen actively; Observe the way a person is behaving; Think about your non-verbal communication; Use gestures; Put thought into the words you use and the way you communicate verbally

REFLECT

Consider an occasion in your work when you have adapted your communication style for an individual. What worked well, what worked less well, and why? How did you adapt your communication style and modify your communication according to the person's reactions?

IDENTIFYING APPROPRIATE AND EFFECTIVE COMMUNICATION

APPLICATION OF SKILLS

Mrs Akabogu has dementia. Communication can be problematic because she is experiencing intermittent memory loss.

- How would you identify the most appropriate methods of communication to use with Mrs Akabogu?

- What methods do you think you might be able to use to maximise communication with Mrs Akabogu?

Mr Thompson has a hearing impairment. He does have a hearing aid, but doesn't always use it.

- Why might Mr Thompson not always use his hearing aid?

- How might you get over this?

- How would you investigate the best way to communicate with Mr Thompson?

RECOGNISING THE BARRIERS TO EFFECTIVE COMMUNICATION

The barriers to effective communication come down to two areas – problems relating to the message being given and/or problems relating to the message being received.

Problems with the message being given

Problems with the message being given can include:

- It may be difficult to understand because of jargon.
- It might contain too much information.
- It might be distorted by perhaps being passed through too many people.
- Verbal and non-verbal messages may not agree.
- The message might be given inappropriately, eg aggressively.
- There might be cultural differences between the person giving the message and the person receiving the message.

Problems with the message being received

These can be varied, but basically all will fall into the following categories:

- environmental barriers
- 'clinical' barriers
- emotional barriers
- attitudinal barriers
- bureaucratic barriers.

Environmental barriers

The environment we are in can affect communication both in terms of being able to pass on a message or being able to receive a message. For example:

- In noisy surroundings, people may not be able to hear what is being said, or even be able to formulate a message to pass on ('It's so noisy I can't even think!').
- Poor lighting could be a barrier, particularly when individuals use lip-reading and also if facial expressions cannot be seen properly.
- In environments that are not private, people may not raise certain issues that they see as very personal.
- If people are not comfortable (eg if they are too hot or too cold) this will affect the quality of communication taking place.

■ The formality of the environment needs to be matched to the communication method. For example, a person may feel inhibited in communicating informally in a very formal environment. The furniture could be rearranged, where possible, to suit the situation.

There are a range of environmental barriers to communication and these will vary widely in terms of the environment in which health and social care workers operate.

Many health and social care staff have little, if any, influence over the environment in which they communicate, eg where a worker goes into a service user's own home. Others, however, can have control over environmental factors.

REFLECT

■ What environmental barriers do you face in terms of communication?

■ How much control over these barriers do you have in your work role?

'Clinical' barriers

According to the Royal College for Speech and Language Therapists, there are a range of clinical barriers to effective communication, such as:

■ genetic or medical conditions

■ trauma

■ mental health problems

■ learning difficulties or disabilities

■ speech (clarity, stammering, etc)

■ voice (lack of voice, low volume or hypernasality – this is where the speech sound is made primarily through someone's nose)

■ fluency (processing the delivery and receipt of language)

■ use of different languages, or of specific accents, dialects or jargons within a language

■ psychologically based communication disorders

■ social skills

■ problem-solving skills

■ literacy issues or dyslexia.

When considering specific clinical issues and the barriers that can be created, it is vital that staff do not 'blame' the individual for the communication barrier, but that they look at how the barriers can be overcome.

Working in a holistic way, recognising the individual needs of service users means that any specific 'barriers' should be addressed – but always remember that it is *not* the service user that is the barrier. Any difficulties faced in terms of communication can be as much about the staff member having a limited understanding and having a very rigid approach to communication.

Emotional barriers

A range of emotions can affect communication. Examples include:

- *Embarrassment*. If someone is embarrassed about an issue they may avoid discussing it.

- *Stress/distress*. It can be hard to communicate if you are feeling stressed or distressed.

- *Anxiety*. If people are particularly anxious they may find communication difficult. Having to communicate certain issues can create anxiety in itself.

- *Shock/anger*. People can be shocked or angry about what they are hearing. This may result in a person not listening effectively.

Other feelings that can have a signficant effect on communication are:

- fear

- powerlessness

- nervousness

- lack of confidence

- lack of self-esteem.

Attitudinal barriers

Where people have negative attitudes towards the person/people wih whom they are communicating, it is likely that the quality of communication will suffer. For example, prejudice, lack of respect and arrogance will create barriers to good communication. The barriers created by such attitudes are often referred to by staff in terms of service users (eg 'He's got a real attitude problem in terms of authority figures'). However, it is important to recognise that attitudinal barriers often lie with staff.

Addressing barriers created by attitudes can involve a range of approaches.

Health and social care workers need to take a whole system view of communication.

- What is the communication ethos, atmosphere or culture of the service?

- How do individual staff members reinforce that ethos or cut across it by their own style?

CASE STUDY

Muriel is a 92-year-old woman. She is admitted to a residential service. The home manager welcomes Muriel and introduces her to a care assistant to complete the admission process. The care assistant is friendly and welcoming. She sits Muriel in a vacant seat by the television in the main lounge and organises a cup of tea.

The care assistant notices that Muriel looks uncomfortable and keeps crossing and uncrossing her legs. She enquires whether Muriel needs the toilet. Muriel does not reply so the care assistant repeats the question, needing to raise her voice loudly because of the noise of the television. Muriel reacts badly to this, she shouts at the care assistant, accusing her of asking rude questions in public and treating her like a child.

At the end of the shift, the care notes are completed as follows:

Muriel was admitted today at 2.00pm. She is a highly sensitive woman, who is having difficulty in settling. Muriel likes to sit by the television. Muriel is deaf and can be aggressive. Please treat with caution.

- What difficulties in communication was Muriel experiencing?

- What could be done to address these difficulties?

- Within your own setting, what are the arrangements for supporting a person on their first visit?

- Are there any places that allow for privacy and exchange of confidential or sensitive information?

- If there are no places that allow for privacy, how could you discuss this matter in your team or with your manager?

Comments

- Muriel cannot hear what is being said to her. This could have been because of a hearing impairment or because she was placed by the television. The care assistant placed Muriel in that position because of the availability of the chair, rather than by first taking account of any need that Muriel may have. This is a typical example of an institutional bad habit.

- The care assistant was sensitive enough to recognise that Muriel may need the toilet, yet had become indifferent as to how personal a subject this is (a further example of an institutional bad habit).

- If at all possible, try to identify ways to make exchanges as private as possible. For example, by writing questions down.

- The case notes raise many questions about assumption and judgement, which could negatively influence workers on subsequent shifts.

MISUNDERSTANDINGS IN COMMUNICATION

People from different backgrounds will use and interpret communication methods in different ways. The term 'different backgrounds' does not just refer to people's race, ethnicity or culture. We all have a background of some form, which includes:

- where we grew up

- where we live now (consider the diversity of the UK in terms of culture, urban and rural areas, communities, financial wealth, etc)

- how our values were formed in childhood

- our current life circumstances and recent events in our own lives

- our language preferences, phrasing, understanding of some terms, use of jargon, etc

- our hearing or our interpretation of the tone of the person communicating with us

- our interpretation of another person's body language and non-verbal communication, which can also relate to our own background and prior experiences

- our age – think about the difference in the language that older people and younger people use.

Some of this is about 'culture' and some is more broadly about each person's background and prior experience and understanding of specific communication methods. Some examples of how communication methods may be interpreted differently include:

- differences between signs in British Sign Language, American Sign Language and Makaton

- different views on what non-verbal signals mean

- different interpretations of pictorial images (eg a symbol on a chart may mean different things to different individuals, and this can be influenced by the way in which different settings use certain symbols and systems)

- differences in terms of dialect/accent and what certain phrases mean to different people.

Where there are cultural differences between people, communication can be adversely affected. For example:

- Assumptions may be made, which can effectively prevent open communication.

- There may be differences in language, the use of words, accent, dialect etc.

- Non-verbal communication can be culturally specific (eg people from some cultures may like or dislike different uses of touch such as handshakes, and people have different tolerances around their personal space).

- Interpreters may need to be used which will clearly have an effect on communication (see below).

Don't forget that 'culture' covers a range of areas and could include generational differences as well as differences between people's backgrounds.

For more detail around what culture means and around the impact of stereotyping of cultures, see Chapter 3 on equality.

STRATEGIES TO CLARIFY MISUNDERSTANDINGS

Use of interpreters and translation services is considered below in more detail, but is the obvious strategy to use if language difference is the reason why a misunderstanding has occurred.

Other strategies to clarify misunderstandings should include:

- Check with someone that they have understood your communication before you finish discussing anything important with them. Getting someone to confirm their understanding is helpful for both them and for you as a worker.

- If someone's behaviour is displaying signals that they have not understood, eg signs of distress, fidgeting, expressions to show they feel annoyed, etc, then you can verbalise their non-verbal signs. For example, you could say, 'I see you are not looking happy about that. Can I check how you understood what I just said or how you feel about it?'.

- Consider using other tools in order to assist communication (see below). Email and text can be particularly challenging in terms of our common inability to interpret the tone. When this happens, it is often worth speaking to the other person (ideally face to face) to sort out any misunderstandings. It is also useful to consider reading an email or text through before you click send, especially if the content is potentially challenging to the reader. If there has been a genuine misunderstanding, acknowledge it, apologise and learn how to avoid this in future from the person and from others around them.

REFLECT

Consider occasions when other people have found you difficult to understand. What factors influenced this – was it your accent, words used, dialect, tone, non-verbal communication, or factors concerning the other person's needs being unmet? How could or did you adapt your own communication in order to clarify misunderstandings?

CASE STUDY

Taju is a senior support worker with a mental health charity. Taju is working with Ben, who has bipolar disorder. Taju and Ben have been working together around Ben's financial entitlements and access to work. Taju has tried to explain the recent changes in the benefits system and has offered to take Ben to the Citizens Advice Bureau (CAB) so that he can get more specialist advice on what he is entitled to. They have spent almost an hour looking at Ben's application forms and talking through the options. Previously, Ben has been anxious about this issue as he has been really struggling with his money and has been threatened with eviction by the housing association from which he rents his home.

Ben stands up during this meeting and starts to pace around the room. Taju asks Ben what is the matter and how he feels about them arranging a joint visit to CAB. Ben becomes angry with Taju quite quickly and shouts at him, saying 'What's the point? They don't listen and neither do you.'

- Why might Ben be feeling annoyed?
- How could Taju respond to Ben?
- How can Taju support Ben and move forwards?
- What strategies could Taju use to clarify any misunderstandings?

OVERCOMING BARRIERS TO EFFECTIVE COMMUNICATION

Communication is always individual. However, there are some basic guidelines in terms of overcoming the barriers to communicating with different groups of people which can be helpful for everyone to know. Although the following guidelines make reference to specific needs and certain conditions, good practice in communication is generic and the guidelines may provide pointers that are relevant to other service users, whatever their individual needs.

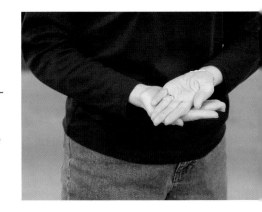

SIGNING SYSTEMS

The most well-known formal signing systems are British Sign Language (BSL), generally used by people who are deaf, and Makaton, generally used by people with learning disabilities. Many people develop their own signing systems built on gestures.

COMMUNICATION AIDS

Technology has enabled an increasing number of electronic and digital aids to communication that can help people who have difficulty speaking. Many of these devices enable messages to be recorded and stored and played at the touch of a button. The devices range in sophistication and price. Information, advice and guidance on choosing the most suitable devices is available from speech and language therapists to whom a referral can be made within the NHS.

SYMBOLS AND OBJECTS OF REFERENCE

Objects of reference can be used to help communication, eg showing someone a swimming costume when they are about to go swimming. For people with a visual impairment, objects of reference with a definite texture which can be held and felt can be useful. Objects that someone is familiar with should be used over a period of time so that the individual comes to associate the object with the message being conveyed.

Visual symbols and photographs can also be very helpful in promoting effective communication.

HEARING AIDS

Hearing aids make sounds louder and can make a big difference to the quality of life of people with hearing loss. They can be obtained free from NHS audiology departments or privately. Hearing aids can be in either analogue or digital formats. Digital aids are now increasingly available on the NHS and can be tailored to meet someone's own hearing needs and to suit different environments including those where there is more background noise.

OVERCOMING BARRIERS LINKED TO CHANGES IN PEOPLE'S NEEDS

It is important for workers not to become complacent once they have established effective communication with a service user – it is quite possible that their communication needs will change over time. For example, a health and social care worker could be supporting someone with dementia whose ability to communicate changes over time. The worker and the whole care team therefore need to be able to adjust and develop their approach.

OVERCOMING BARRIERS AROUND COMMUNICATING WITH PEOPLE FROM A DIFFERENT CULTURAL BACKGROUND

Communication techniques should be flexible in order to respect different cultural needs. The following guide provides key suggestions in communicating with people who are from a different cultural background from your own:

- There is no 'standard' form of address (eg 'Mr', 'Mrs' or use of first name). It is individual choice how different people would like to be referred to. The best way is to ask people what they would prefer to be called.

- The term 'Christian name' should not be used, as people may not be Christians. Use 'first name' or 'forename' instead.

- The use of tactile introductions, such as shaking hands, may be unacceptable in some cultures.

- Confirm with the individual that they are comfortable with your way of communication.

- Respect differences. You need to understand that diversity may affect a whole host of things including accent, dialect, slang and non-verbal communication. Find out as much as you can about the person's background and the effects this may have on communication.

OVERCOMING BARRIERS IN COMMUNICATING WITH PEOPLE WHOSE FIRST LANGUAGE IS NOT ENGLISH

Where a person is not fluent in English, health and social care workers will need to adapt their communication. The following pointers may be helpful:

- Speak clearly but not too loudly.

- Pace your communication well. If you speak too quickly people may not understand, but if you speak too slowly this can be patronising and it can be difficult to understand the whole sentence.

- Use clear language. When someone is from a different cultural background from your own they may not be familiar with idioms or culturally specific sayings (eg 'I've got a frog in my throat', 'it's raining cats and dogs', etc).

- Use pictures and symbols.

- Pronounce names correctly.

- Check and rephrase as you go along.

- Provide written information in the person's home language to back up other communication.

- Get a trained interpreter to help if possible (and do not use family, friends or especially children to enable this as this can be inappropriate).

OVERCOMING ATTITUDINAL BARRIERS

As professionals, we need to be very aware of our own attitudes when working with people whose first language is not English.

Always be aware of the dangers of:

- *Assuming.* People assume all sorts of things which clearly affect communication. For example, you may have assumed that in discussing people whose first language is not English we are talking about people whose first language is a foreign language. What about deaf people who use British Sign Language? English is not their first language.

- *'Dumping' responsibility.* In some health and social care services where one member of staff speaks the same language as a service user then it is sometimes thought to be best for that staff member to work with the service user which implies that other staff members don't need to think about their communication. The case study below gives an outline of such a situation.

KEY POINT

If you ASSUME you make an ASS out of U and ME.

CASE STUDY

Dee is a senior care assistant in a day service for older people. Eva Wengierska is Polish and speaks very little English. She attends the day service where Dee works. At the service a member of staff (Piotre) can speak fluent Polish. The manager and other staff think it best that Piotre communicates with Eva. Piotre and Eva have a good relationship so things work well, that is until Piotre finds another job. Eva is completely lost! No one else at the service has taken the time to develop their communication skills to be able to communicate effectively with Eva.

- What are the issues here?

- How might Dee have anticipated that there could be problems with this approach?

- What could Dee do now?

REFLECT

- What do you see as the main barriers to effective communication in your work practice?

- How can you overcome these in order to communicate with service users effectively?

- How do you support other staff and relevant people to understand and overcome the potential barriers?

ADDITIONAL SUPPORT AND SERVICES TO ENABLE INDIVIDUALS TO COMMUNICATE EFFECTIVELY

It may be important to access specific additional support or services in order to enable individual service users to communicate effectively. These could include:

- accessing additional support from others who know the person well already

- interpreting or translation services

- advocacy services

- speech and language therapy assessments, services and resources

- occupational therapy assessments and services.

USING INTERPRETERS

People who do not speak English as a first language may need the support of an interpreter. In certain circumstances, family or friends can act as interpreters. However, there are important disadvantages to this, such as:

- Individuals receiving care may not want members of their family or community to know personal details and information.

- Individuals may feel disempowered and they may feel that their control and choice may be adversely affected. This can be a particular issue if the family member or friend is seen to overpower the individual, or if there are concerns that they may not truly represent the individual's views and choices.

- Interpreting is a task that requires great skills in remaining objective and translating information in a completely neutral manner. Professional interpreters will be trained to do this.

- In rare circumstances, family or friends may be actually perpetrating abuse against the person receiving care.

When you work with interpreters, communication is clearly affected because instead of being a two-way communication process it becomes a three-way process. Therefore, perhaps the most important thing for a health and social care worker to consider when working with an interpreter is to ensure that they still create a relationship with the service user. Health and social care workers will also need to think about their relationship with the interpreter. They will need to be clear with the interpreter about each of their roles and to negotiate expectations of working together to facilitate effective communication with the service user.

Many people believe that their communication skills will not be used when working with an interpreter, because communication will be managed by the interpreter. However, professional skills will be more vital than ever. For example:

- Health and social care workers will need to maintain good eye contact with both the service user and the interpreter.

- Listening skills will be very important. The health and social care worker will need to listen to what the interpreter is saying, as well as attending to the non-verbal communication of the interpreter and the service user.

Using an interpreter adds another layer to listening.

COMMUNICATION TECHNOLOGY

Some issues around access to mobile phones and the internet are discussed in Chapter 5 on safeguarding. Communication aids and adaptations are considered in more detail in Chapter 14 on specific communication needs. However, it is also worth referencing here the fact that text, email, mobile phones and new technologies add a rapidly evolving layer into the means and methods by which we can communicate with users of services, and also how they engage with others in society.

ADVOCACY

In the context of health and social care, the word 'advocacy' means 'speaking for or on behalf of'. There are several different kinds of advocacy:

- *Self-advocacy* is about people speaking up for themselves. A commitment to self-advocacy entails enabling and empowering people to act on their own behalf.

- In *peer advocacy* the advocate shares a similar perspective to the individual. For example, when a person with learning disabilities supports another person with learning disabilities to get their views across.

- In *citizen advocacy* a volunteer is recruited to work with someone and build a strong relationship with them over time so that they can help them to put their views across.

- *Independent advocacy* is where either a citizen (volunteer) or a paid employee of an advocacy service takes on the role of the advocate for the individual.

The role of an advocate is one which takes skill to exercise and is different from that of a health and social care worker. Advocates can help in situations where:

- it is difficult for others to understand someone's means of communicating

- the individual is not happy with the service he or she is receiving and wishes to complain

- where supporters such as family, friends, paid carers or health and social care professionals disagree about how to support the person or with the individual's point of view

- when a significant change has taken place in relation to the individual – this may be in relation to someone's health or well-being or a major life change.

An advocate will initially work with someone to understand the way they communicate and to find out what is important to them so that they can represent them in a variety of situations. They will usually go to a meeting alongside the person they are supporting and must always be clear about representing their point of view even if the advocate believes that this may not be in the person's interests. The aim of the advocate is to empower the individual by making sure that their views and interests are heard. The advocate will try to obtain permission from the person to represent their views and to contact others who may be able to help.

Non-instructed advocacy

This is employed when someone is unable to put their views across, perhaps because of profound disability or very advanced dementia and where they lack the capacity or ability to make decisions. Just as with the various forms of instructed advocacy, the advocate will work hard to form a strong relationship with the person, to learn about their preferences and to do their best to represent their interests. See also Chapters 4 and 19 which cover your duty of care around the Mental Capacity Act which are relevant in relation to non-instructed advocacy.

REFLECT

What services do you use to promote effective communication?

RESEARCH

Look into some of the technological developments and adaptations that are now available to support people's communication.

- How would you enable people to access assessments in order to obtain such tools?

- Which agencies and professionals would you need to work with in order to enable people to get the right tools and support to communicate?

Jane is a senior support worker in a day service for people with learning disabilities. She has received a new referral about Jason. Jason has a severe learning disability and uses a wheelchair. He has previously accessed a very large service for young adults with learning difficulties. This service is about to close and so a referral has been made to the service where Jane works. In preparing to meet Jason, Jane reads the referral and Jason's case notes. She discovers that Jason has a communciation aid (a small keypad with about a dozen pictures loaded). When Jason presses one of the pictures, a computerised voice states which picture has been pressed. Extensive work by a speech and language therapist has concluded that this is the most effective way of Jason communicating. The pictures had been chosen to facilitate choices, so that when staff asked Jason a question he could indicate his choice using the pictures.

When Jason arrives to visit the service he is accompanied by a member of staff from the unit which is closing. Jane can't see the communication aid and so asks the staff member where it is. Jane is told that it is normally in Jason's rucksack, on the back of his wheelchair – and it is. When Jane gets it out and positions it so that Jason can use it, she finds that the aid isn't working.

The staff member tells her that it broke some time ago, adding 'It was so much trouble for just some minor communication that we left it. We muddle along pretty well without it.'

- What are the issues here?
- What should Jane do?

THE PRINCIPLES AND PRACTICE OF CONFIDENTIALITY

Health and social care workers must have an understanding of confidentiality and be able to implement this in their practice. This requires knowledge of what confidentiality entails and what dilemmas it might create.

WHAT IS CONFIDENTIALITY?

Confidentiality is a very important aspect of practice in health and social care. However, it is often misunderstood in that people think confidentiality is about keeping information secret. Confidentiality is about preserving information within a service and sharing it only on a need-to-know basis. When someone shares information with you it is confidential. But that doesn't mean it is secret – it means that the information should only be shared with your manager and others responsible for providing care to the service user.

The right to confidentiality is important to all of us, and especially important to individuals accessing health and social care services. This is because highly sensitive and personal information about individuals becomes known to people who hold a position of power over their lives.

Establishing clear boundaries around confidentiality within a service is vital. Confidentiality enables people who receive care services to have a sense of trust in professionals and a sense of control over their lives and the service they receive.

As a worker in health and social care, you will need to be able to:

- explain the idea of confidentiality to people who access the service, relatives, and other professionals
- understand and uphold your own boundaries around confidentiality
- understand, express and adhere to your service or agency's policies and procedures around confidentiality.

Aspects of confidentiality are covered in more detail in Chapter 7 on handling information. The key principles are that, as much as possible (in terms of consent, capacity and safeguarding), people should always know:

- what information you are sharing
- who with
- and why?

MAINTAINING CONFIDENTIALITY IN DAY-TO-DAY COMMUNICATION

Confidentiality needs to be maintained in:

- written communication about people
- storages of written records
- the way buildings and care environments are accessed and organised
- verbal communications within a care team

- communication with individual users of services about others who use a service (where services are accessed by groups of people)

- communication by members of that care team with other agencies and professionals, so that nothing is shared that is not pertinent to someone's care plan and that the other agency does not need to know

- communication by workers with family members and other carers

- communication by workers with their own friends and family outside of their work.

In the recent past, confidentiality has, arguably, not been treated seriously enough. At the same time, sometimes workers can lack clarity about what information needs to be passed on and to whom, and what information doesn't need to be shared.

It is important that workers only know information that is relevant to supporting the people with whom they work. Health and social care workers do not have a right to know everything about a person. It is also vital that health and social care workers realise that the information that they receive is given to them because they are professionals or members of a staff team, and that such information must remain confidential within the care team responsible for each individual person.

Where care teams support an individual, it is important that information is shared in order that everyone is working in a consistent way to meet a person's needs. However, when information is shared within one agency or even between agencies, this information remains confidential. The fact that it has been shared does not mean it can be shared further – the obligation to maintain confidentiality is shared just as much as the information itself.

The consequences of not maintaining confidentiality in these day-to-day communications are extremely significant for you as a professional, for your employer, agency or service, and, most importantly, for the dignity and rights of the people who use your service.

Support around these issues is available from a variety of sources, including:

- your manager(s), eg via supervision

- the local authority in the area where you work (and potentially their legal department if relevant and necessary)

- training courses

- regulators and inspection bodies.

Look at some records in your service (eg care plans, assessments or other documentation).

- How do these records show respect for people's confidentiality?

- Where are they stored?

- Who has access to them?

- If there are records or practices that do not uphold this right, what is your service or agency's policy around this?

INSTILLING CONFIDENTIALITY IN THE SERVICE CULTURE

It is vital for health and social care workers to demonstrate a commitment to confidentiality. This can be done in a range of ways:

- *Be transparent*. Users of services have the right to know that records are kept, that information about their needs is known (and who knows it), and when and why information may need to be shared with other people.

- *Act as role models*. If someone gossips about one member of staff to another, or makes jokes about a service user or their circumstances, then they are showing a lack of respect for the individual and for confidentiality. Health and social care workers should act as role models for effective practice in terms of confidentiality in all of their work.

- *Follow policy*. Services should have an effective confidentiality policy in place which makes the responsibilities of staff clear and which adheres to the Data Protection Act 1998.

- *Take action*. If people breach confidentiality, then you should take appropriate action. If a health and social care worker hears other people effectively 'gossiping' about a service user, eg during a break, then they should challenge this.

- *Ensure the security of information*. Make sure that lockable cabinets are available (and used) for the storage of personal information. For electronic records, services and agencies should have robust systems in place around access to and security of these records (see also Chapter 7 on handling information).

UNDERSTANDING AND WORKING WITH THE DILEMMAS AND TENSIONS CREATED BY CONFIDENTIALITY REQUIREMENTS

There is the potential for significant tension between maintaining confidentiality and disclosing concerns – particularly in relation to safeguarding. This is covered in more depth in Chapter 5. Remember, where there are concerns about a person's safety:

- *Check*. Check out your concerns and maintain your observations, as well as checking with the person (without investigating) how they are feeling.

- *Record*. As always, good practice in recording is part of good practice generally, but this is especially important when recording concerns about someone's well-being.

- *Report*. You cannot keep something to yourself if someone is being harmed by another person. You should always report concerns, first to your managers (according to service policies and procedures), and take action if required even where this may mean there is a tension with the person's wishes in relation to confidentiality.

- *Explain*. If you do need to pass information on to another agency or person, it is important that the person knows:

  - what you are doing

  - why you are doing it

  - what will happen next

  - who else might learn the information that was previously confidential

  - that you are there to support them

  - that they have done the right thing in telling you (in the event of a disclosure of abuse)

  - that they still have rights (eg to access records or to complain).

REFLECT

Recall an occasion where the tension between a person's right to confidentiality and the need to keep them safe or address certain concerns has occurred in your work.

- How did both you and the service user feel about this tension?

- What did you do?

CASE STUDY

Zakiyah is a senior domiciliary care worker. During a team meeting, Catherine, one of the domiciliary care workers in Zakiyah's team, talks about a person she is supporting.

Catherine says that she is worried that a person she works with, Bert, is being 'taken advantage' of by his son. Catherine says that Bert never seems to have any money but she thinks that Bert's son is taking about £100 a week off him. She suspects that Bert's son is a drug user (as she has heard rumours about this in the local community). She asked Bert about this one day and he told her to 'get her nose out of his business'. Jane is really worried she has offended Bert and since lots of her concerns are based on rumours, she is not sure what to do.

- What issues are there around confidentiality here?

- What are some of the dilemmas Catherine is facing?

- What should Zakiyah advise Catherine to do?

Code of Conduct for Healthcare Support Workers and Adult Social Care Workers

The vital importance of effective communication in health and social care is recognised in the Code of Conduct for Healthcare Support Workers and Adult Social Care Workers, which states that you must:

- communicate respectfully with people who use health and social care services and their carers in an open, accurate, effective, straightforward and confidential way

- communicate effectively and consult with your colleagues as appropriate

- recognise both the extent and the limits of your role, knowledge and competence when communicating with people who use health and social care services, carers and colleagues.

CHAPTER 3
Promoting equality and inclusion in health and social care

This chapter explores some key concepts in health and social care that are fundamental to the values of the profession. The information within this chapter is central to all acceptable and effective practice in working with users of health and social care services. Health and social care workers need to demonstrate their knowledge and commitment to the concepts within this chapter throughout their career and in each piece of work with every individual.

Your understanding and application of the knowledge and concepts in this chapter will be useful across all the units that you complete for the diploma. Inclusive practice and a commitment to equality of access and opportunity are central to health and social care in all its settings.

Links to other chapters

It is particularly relevant to consider this chapter in relation to its links with chapters 2 and 10.

Key terms

Diversity refers to difference. Everyone is unique and different in some way. There is a wide range of diversity in every population.

Equality is about treating people in a way which ensures that they are not placed at a disadvantage to others.

Inclusion is the word used to describe the opposite of social **exclusion**. It is where action is taken to address the effects of discrimination, and to strive towards preventing or ideally eliminating oppression.

Exclusion describes a situation where people face discrimination on many levels and are effectively 'excluded from society', ie where they have no voice and are not recognised in their society.

UNDERSTANDING DIVERSITY, EQUALITY AND INCLUSION

In order to understand the application of these three key concepts, you need to understand and work within the value base of health and social care work, as covered in Chapter 8 on personal development. **Diversity**, **equality** and **inclusion** are core aspects of the health and social care value base.

EQUALITY

Being committed to equality is often misunderstood as being about 'treating everyone the same'. Instead, equality recognises that we are not all 'the same'. Equality should be seen as offering the framework within which individuals and employers should show their commitment to promoting equality and treating people as they deserve to be treated, ie in accordance with their rights, choices and individuality, and with due respect.

DIVERSITY

Diversity is essentially about difference. Difference should be valued and celebrated. What a boring place the world would be if we were all the same.

Promoting diversity is about accepting the fact that we are all different and viewing this a good thing, and should be seen as so by everybody. Within all health and social care settings there will be a rich mixture of people from a variety of backgrounds and cultures. This diversity should be celebrated and reflected within the service.

Celebrating diversity is the next stage on from promoting equality, and it is the responsibility of both agencies and individuals to achieve this standpoint.

For one week, look at the images and messages all around us relating to one area of difference (eg disability, sexuality, age, ethnicity, etc). These could be images and messages within the media, on television, in advertising, newspapers and magazines, or in conversations with friends or colleagues.

Group the images and messages into those that are positive and inclusive and those that are negative and exclusive.

- What might be the impact of these messages on the people with whom you work?

- How are images and messages changing as society evolves? What impact of this can you see?

INCLUSION

If someone cannot access their entitlement to a service, education, employment or cultural resources because of:

- language barriers

- physical barriers (eg they cannot get into the building where the service is offered because it is not accessible)

- cultural barriers

then services need to find ways of ensuring that their provision *can* be accessed, rather than accepting the existence of such barriers and allowing someone to continue experiencing a lack of opportunity.

Inclusion focuses on the fact that people have the right to access resources and services without being discriminated against. Those in charge of providing resources have a responsibility to ensure their provision can be accessed.

Working in an inclusive way means celebrating diversity and promoting equality:

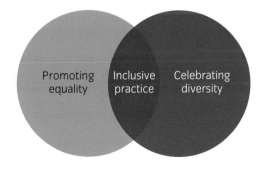

MESSAGES FROM RESEARCH

Equality, diversity and inclusion

There is a wealth of research available around equality and inclusion. Through the Equality Measurement Framework (EMF) the Equality and Human Rights Commission found clear discrepancies experienced by different minority groups in the UK around employment, earnings, participation, housing, health, education and access to care. For example:

- Black and black British people are less likely than any other group to feel that they are treated with respect.

- Younger people are more likely to feel that diversity is a good thing and one which is to be enjoyed and celebrated.

- There are specific barriers for older lesbian, gay, bisexual and transgender (LGBT) people in accessing social care services.

- Mixed-race Britons are the fastest growing minority group in the UK.

- Many people with disabilities experience violence and hostility on a daily basis in their communities.

- Gypsies and travelling communities face specific barriers and have a life expectancy which is 10 years lower than non-travelling people.

This framework also identifies a lack of data and the need for specific efforts to improve our understanding of the experience of people with learning disabilities, transgender people, homeless people, asylum seekers and refugees.

UNDERSTANDING DISCRIMINATION

Key term ⌐⊙━┅

Discrimination is where someone is treated less favourably than another person.

Promoting equality, diversity and inclusion is not easy. It requires health and social care workers to understand the way that **discrimination** operates and to develop skills in challenging discrimination.

WHO EXPERIENCES DISCRIMINATION?

Most people will have been discriminated against in some way at some stage of their life. However, it is widely accepted that some groups of people are more likely to experience discrimination than others, such as black people, women, older people, people with disabilities, and so on. Some of the main forms of discrimination that have been identified in British society are outlined here:

- *Adultism* describes the way in which children and young people can be oppressed by adults. It is based on the **prejudiced** belief that adults are superior to children and young people.

- *Ageism* describes the way that older people can be discriminated against. It is based on the prejudiced belief that older people are inferior to younger people.

- *Disabilism/ablism* is the term used when people with disabilities experience discrimination and oppression based on the prejudiced belief that those who do not have a disability are superior.

- *Heterosexism* describes the way that gay people are discriminated against. It is based on the prejudiced belief that only heterosexual relationships are 'normal' and therefore 'valid'.

- *Racism* describes the way that people are discriminated against because of their race. It is based on the prejudiced belief that people of some races are superior to others.

- *Sexism* describes the way in which people are oppressed based on their gender. It is based on the prejudiced belief that one sex is superior over the other. In British society the word sexism is usually used to describe the way that women are discriminated against.

These categories are by no means exhaustive. Other examples of groups who are particularly vulnerable to oppression include people who are homeless, people who use drugs, asylum seekers, people who have mental health problems, people with long-term health conditions – the list goes on.

Key term

Prejudice is where an individual makes a judgement based on either inadequate or inaccurate information that leads to the development of irrational preferences. One of the main features of prejudice is rigidity or inflexibility of ideas. This means that new information may not have an impact on prejudicial views.

DOUBLY DISADVANTAGED?

When looking at who is discriminated against, it is important to remember that discrimination is a complex process. Many people will be discriminated against because of more than one characteristic. For example, black people with a learning disabilities may be subject to racism as well as discrimination based on their learning disabilities. This complex process is often known as **double discrimination** or **triple jeopardy**.

Key terms

Double discrimination refers to oppression based on two characteristics.

Triple jeopardy refers to oppression based on three characteristics.

HOW DOES DISCRIMINATION WORK?

There are various ways in which people can be discriminated against. These are sometimes referred to as the 'mechanisms of oppression' and include:

- language
- the media

- stereotyping
- labelling
- jokes.

Health and social care workers should understand these mechanisms of oppression. It is too easy to subscribe to these mechanisms, often on an unconscious basis, and discriminate against people as a result. Enhanced understanding of the mechanisms of oppression can therefore help to avoid discriminatory practice and promote service users' equality, diversity and inclusion.

LANGUAGE

The subject of discriminatory or oppressive language is a complex one. Sometimes, issues around language that aims not to discriminate are described as 'political correctness' or a 'play on words', and dismissed. However, language is a living tool that grows and changes to reflect broader shifts in society. For example, the language that we use can affect the way we regard and interact with other people. Words and phrases project certain images. We must ensure that these images do not reinforce offensive or discriminatory attitudes.

The language that we use reflects our own value base, and therefore must receive careful attention in order to demonstrate an active commitment to inclusive practice.

Exclusion

Some of the language that we might use can make people feel like they are excluded. For example, it is now commonly accepted that referring to a position as 'chairman' may lead women to feel excluded. 'Chairperson' or simply 'chair' is therefore used instead. Using phrases that can exclude groups of people is potentially oppressive (eg 'every man for himself', 'young person's game', etc).

Depersonalisation

Language often depersonalises people, ie people can be viewed more as a label or as simply one of a group of people. For example, using language such as 'the disabled' or 'the elderly' means people's individuality is lost and they could be seen simply as a member of a group. The letters 'ic' are often added to a medical diagnosis and then used to describe someone, eg 'they are a diabetic', 'alcoholic', 'arthritic', or 'the schizophrenics', etc. These words are incredibly depersonalising. It is much better to refer to a person as having a diagnosis of diabetes rather than as a diabetic.

Dehumanisation

Dehumanisation is the process of people not being seen as a valued human being or the worth of a person being reduced so that they are seen as not quite human (sub-human). While it might sound extreme, dehumanisation through language is actually very common in social care. The language used around personal care is a good example. People generally 'eat' their meals but as soon as someone comes into contact with social care services they will be referred to as 'feeding' themselves or as 'needing feeding'. In other situations we only use the word feeding to refer to animals or babies. Some care services have a 'feeding rota' posted in the kitchen or dining area which we think makes it sound like a zoo. Another example is 'toileting'. People go to the toilet – they don't toilet themselves.

The combined effect of the use of this kind of language is that the language used to describe actions we all do changes when people are in need of care. The central message received by people is that they are now 'less than human'.

When we use dehumanising language, it becomes easier to abuse people and violate their rights. Therefore it is vital that health and social care staff do not use language that dehumanises people. We should think through the language that we use about ourselves and use this when referring to people who need care and support. For example:

- 'feeding' should be replaced with 'assisting to eat'

- 'toileting' should be replaced with 'assisting to use the toilet', etc.

CHECKLIST

It is important to continue to think about your use of language. Use the following points to prompt you as an ongoing checklist:

- Does the use of this word or phrase label people in a negative way?

- Does this use of language undermine people's strengths?

- Does this use of language depersonalise others, stereotype them, etc?

- Does this use of language devalue the individual/group?

- Does this use of language patronise?

- What can you do to facilitate positive images for all?

- Don't make assumptions that because one person/group has indicated a preference for certain words/phrases this will be shared by all.

- Treat the opportunity to learn about the use of language as an adventure in gaining new knowledge and understanding.

STEREOTYPING

Stereotyping is based on prejudiced ideas being applied towards all or most members of certain groups of people. Stereotyping becomes particularly dangerous when people begin to act towards individuals based on the stereotype of the group of people to which the individual belongs. For example, a common stereotypical comment about Asian people is that they 'look after their own'. This may lead to no services being provided for people from the Asian population, even though they may be needed. Stereotypes:

- lead to discrimination

- are resistant to change even in the face of evidence that conflicts with the stereotype

- are largely negative

- become so established that they are accepted as reality without serious question

- are often played out in the media and in comedy and jokes

- can lead to poor practice.

LABELLING

Labelling is closely linked with stereotyping, as people can be labelled based upon the stereotype. Once someone has been 'labelled', it can be very hard to move away from that label, and others see the 'label' before they see the individual!

Labelling is the process by which a negative blanket term is applied to somebody. The effect on other people, when they view that person, is to have a prejudiced and negative view that adversely influences their behaviour towards that person. The effect on the person, both of the label and of other people's actions towards them, results in their feeling judged and this undermines their confidence. Someone who is labelled may then act in ways that are a distortion of their true identity but, to the observer, result in confirming the validity of the label.

We all have labels given to us. A few people are fortunate enough to have the label of 'celebrity' or 'aristocrat'. Many of us have the label of worker or professional or student, partner, parent, etc. Most of these labels are seen positively.

Whether we like it or not, labelling is part of life; everyone is labelled in some way. The issue is really about whether the labels attached to people are positive or negative.

There are some labels that are negative and are not claimed by a person but are put on them by others. In health and social care, one of the problems is that most service users are given labels by professionals. In origin the intention by professionals is not to give someone a negative label, but to recognise that a person has identifiable specific needs. Unfortunately, many of the labels that professionals apply to service users are not neutral because they are used negatively within society.

Social care services and health services continue to use labels because it is the principal means they use to identify who should receive certain services. Therefore, there are benefits and disadvantages of having labels.

Benefits of labelling

- Having a recognised label can explain a characteristic of a person. If a child is struggling with reading and writing at school they may be at risk of being 'labelled' lazy or slow. If the child is then assessed and found to have dyslexia, this can be a relief (in part) for the child and parents in that it explains why the child is having difficulties.

- Having a specific label should enable someone to receive specialist services that are able to meet their needs.

- Some professionals find it beneficial to label an individual. For example, consider a professional who is working with a group of service users and one of them is presenting them with needs that demand more of their time and attention. Applying a label to the service user may result in the professional being given additional staff support or the service user may be moved to a more appropriate group of individuals who have similar needs.

- In a similar vein, organisations can benefit from labelling individuals if it results in being able to claim additional funds.

- Most statutory services for adults can only offer support to a person if they have a disability, mental health problem, are frail or infirm due to their age or have other support needs (eg an addiction to drugs or alcohol). Therefore, there is a requirement to give a person one of these labels if they are to 'reach threshold criteria' and receive services.

Some service users themselves also report that having a label enables them to receive support from peers with similar needs, and that this gives them a certain identity as part of a group of people.

Disadvantages of labelling

- The labels used by professionals are not neutral. They are nearly all viewed in society as negative. Some of the labels have a very significant stigma associated with them. The strength of this stigma should not be overlooked by those who are not given one of these labels.

- The label given by health and social care professionals to service users is often related to their perceived 'deficits'. Many service users see labels as operating solely for the benefit of services and not for them as individuals.

- The label may have originally had some meaning and purpose. However, it can quickly become misused and someone who has the label applied to them becomes covered by it as if covered by a blanket. The label becomes someone's identity and almost their name. For example, 'schizophrenic', 'alcoholic', 'epileptic', etc. When an 'ic' is attached to the end of a label, it is a sign that the person's individuality and identity have been lost under this label. Even without the 'ic', people can have their identity lost, eg 'she's a hair puller' or 'he has special needs'. Statements such as these place a judgement on a person.

- The label can become a 'self-fulfilling prophecy'. If somebody is given a negative label then health and social care staff are likely to be influenced by this and their behaviour could be different. If someone is given the label of 'aggressive' then staff may stand at more of a distance, be cooler in their whole approach and maybe have a colleague present. This could result in the service user recognising that a label has been applied to them and resenting the label. The service user is angry about the label, but this gets viewed by staff as confirming the claim that the service user is aggressive.

- Service users have *no* control over their label. It is passed to new staff by experienced staff. At one time or another, many of us have done something that could result in us being given a negative label. We manage to bury or lose the negative label. In Britain, by the age of 30, about 30% of men have a criminal record. Most men don't introduce themselves to someone new by saying, 'Hi, I'm Dominic, I've got a conviction for reckless driving. Do you want a lift home?' Most of us bury or lose our negative label by changing friends, moving home, etc and by not telling our new friends about our past. In care services, the label gets passed on and sometimes it is one of the first things a new staff member learns about a service user. Sometimes this label is inaccurate or exaggerated or it relates to an event that happened years ago. There are lots of ways to describe a person, but too often the negative labels are passed on to the new staff very early in their working life.

- Often service users can be given negative labels which have a profound effect on their lives and opportunities. For example, adults with dyslexia often relate how they were labelled as 'stupid' at school and were not given the support they needed. This has had a very profound effect on the self-esteem of many people with dyslexia.

- Adults may carry a mental health label such as 'schizophrenia' or a label like 'challenging behaviour'. Expectations of recovery or improvement may be low (or non existent) which can result in a care plan that is 'standard' and does not aid personal development.

Labels can be very damaging to service users. The Disability Rights Movement states that labels belong on jars and not people!

> **REFLECT**
>
> **Exploring labelling**
>
> Think of the ways in which you and other people are labelled. Think of both positive and negative labels. For example, a positive label might be 'friend' or 'home owner' and a negative label might be 'old' or 'unemployed'. Now consider the following questions:
>
> - What control do we have over the labels we are given?
>
> - How might people be able to get rid of the labels they don't want and acquire the labels they do want?
>
> - Now think about at least one of the service users with whom you work. Make a list of both the positive and negative labels they have been given, eg brother, service user, autistic, challenging, and so on.
>
> - Separate the list of labels into positive and negative labels. Look through the list of negative labels. Could more positive labels replace these?

SERVICE DECOR

Many services have realised the impact that service decor has on how services are viewed and how the users of services are labelled. Many services have also tried to maintain a good physical environment. But there will always be some exceptions. The way services look shows how the people who use them are valued, which links with the societal value put on certain labels and needs. Examples of how this can impact in a negative way include some day centres which have uncarpeted corridors and a communal wall with several coat hooks. By comparison, most offices are carpeted throughout and office workers keep their coats either in their own room or close to them.

NAMES OF SERVICES

As the saying goes, 'There's a lot in a name'. The names given to services very often have 'images' attached. For example, many older people's homes are called things like 'Greenfields', 'Green Meadows', etc. It sounds as though people are being put out to pasture! Swimming clubs for people with disabilities are often called names like 'Dolphins' or 'Penguins'. This gives a childlike impression as opposed to 'Burtonwood Swimming Club'. Many national organisations have changed their names or the names of individual service provision because of the importance of social imagery, eg the Spastics Society change its name to Scope.

The term 'social imagery' relates to how all of these issues, images and labels interact with each other, and shows how some qualities are valued in our society, and therefore how others are considered to have less value. The power of this can be belittled and minimised by reference to the term 'political correctness', but when people describe the negative impact social imagery can have on individuals, this should not be underestimated. However, generally people using this term are not devalued people who are affected by social imagery and oppression more generally.

APPLICATION OF SKILLS

Discrimination

Consider the following areas in which oppression and discrimination operate as described above. Complete the column on the right with ideas around how you and your service could work to challenge and be inclusive.

Discrimination and oppression operates via:	I/we can change this by:
Labelling people	
Stereotyping	
Service decor	
Service names	
Low expectations	
Loss	
Poverty	
Isolation	
Excluding friends, relatives and carers from being part of the life of the service user	

TYPES OF DISCRIMINATION

It is commonly accepted that there are three main types of discrimination.

Individual discrimination

This is where the actions and attitudes (often unconscious) of individuals towards people from excluded groups support and sustain a broader social pattern of discrimination.

For example, a man may believe that women should be responsible for all household chores and childcare. The way this man acts towards women will sustain the broader view of women in society.

Institutional discrimination

This is where institutions (such as schools, employers, churches, residential services and so on), in reflecting the structure of the society they serve, maintain a set of rules, procedures and practices that operate in such a way as to perpetuate discrimination against excluded groups.

For example, if in a secondary school English course all the main books chosen to read have central male characters but only minor female characters, this will reinforce society's view that men are more important or interesting than women.

Another example would be an organisation where 75% of the workforce are women but 75% of the managers are men. This also conveys that men are more important and the key decision makers. Both of these are clear examples of institutional sexism. These issues have recently been successfully challenged in terms of local authorities and equal pay for female employees. The Stephen Lawrence inquiry in 1993 also described the Metropolitan police as harbouring institutional racism as well as operating structural discrimination.

Structural discrimination

This is where organisations and institutions work together with the effect that a structural or societal system of discrimination is generated and sustained.

For example, residential care services generally have an accepted weekly costing that funding bodies (such as social services) are willing to pay. Above this cost, senior managers will need to agree the funding. The accepted weekly cost of older people's residential care is the lowest of all. The accepted weekly cost of residential care for adults with learning disabilities and adults with mental health problems is higher. The accepted weekly cost of children's residential care is higher still. This illustrates one structural inequality.

It is important to note that individual, institutional and structural discrimination are very closely linked. After all, institutions are made up of a number of individuals. Therefore, individual beliefs and actions will have a profound impact upon organisations, institutions and society as a whole. The key to the difference, however, is that where the discrimination is carried out by one or two people this is individual discrimination. Where the root of the discrimination is in an organisation this is institutional discrimination. When discrimination is endemic across a number of organisations this combination becomes structural discrimination.

Covert and overt discrimination

Discrimination can be described as either overt or covert. Overt is obvious discrimination and relatively easy to identify, eg some local youths shout racial abuse at an Asian woman. Covert is hidden (covered) discrimination and can be more difficult to identify, eg a company claims to have an equal opportunities policy but unofficially they won't offer jobs to young Muslim men.

WHAT EFFECT DOES DISCRIMINATION HAVE ON PEOPLE?

People who are discriminated against often have similar experiences. These can include:

Experiences	Examples
Rejection Kept at a distance from others; placed with people in similar situations.	Segregated services keep people away from the general population and in groups of people with similar needs.
Diminished experiences Less experience of different people, different places, different activities.	Excluded people may not be able to mix with the general population, activities may be limited etc. This is particularly so if people are in segregated services.
Low expectations People have limited expectations of what devalued people can achieve.	A classic example is when people ask a question to the person accompanying an individual in a wheelchair, rather than addressing the person in the wheelchair directly, eg 'Does he take sugar?'
Loss People who are discriminated against often experience significant loss in their lives.	As a result of the negative experiences people will experience a loss of power, control, choice, rights, dignity, etc.
Being seen as one of many Many people are not viewed as an individual, but as a label, or a condition or a problem.	Many people who are in receipt of services are viewed as a group. For example, in group outings, the needs of the group sometimes override the individual's needs. The general population may view people as a label, etc.
Artificial relationships A loss of real friends and contacts may lead to people's social networks being limited to paid staff and volunteers.	Many people living in residential services, or people who attend day services, are expected to rely upon other service users and staff to make up their social network.
Poverty People who are discriminated against are often reliant on benefits or trapped in poverty.	The weekly allowance of people living in residential care would not keep most people in the general population, even if all their daily living expenses (bills, food, etc) were paid for.
Labels People are often ascribed negative labels.	In the general population, people are referred to by negative labels or terms, such as 'mad', 'handicapped', etc. Within services people may be labelled as 'manipulative', 'attention seeking', etc.

Exclusion and discrimination creates a cycle where people have negative experiences which in turn can lead to:

- people having low **self-esteem** and a negative **self-image**
- feelings of anger and frustration
- a sense of powerlessness
- a sense of hopelessness
- a loss of motivation and engagement.

Key terms

Self-image is the way you see yourself. It is often influenced by the way others see you.

Self-esteem is the way you feel about yourself.

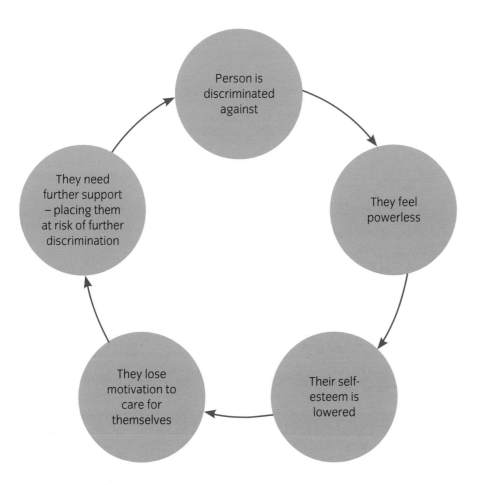

The cycle of discrimination (promoting inclusive practice is about breaking this negative cycle)

Isabella is a senior care assistant in a respite care service that provides short-term stays for adults with learning and physical disabilities. As a result of her upbringing and her religious beliefs, Isabella has strong personal values about gay relationships – she sees them as 'morally wrong and abnormal'.

Isabella is in the respite service lounge one evening with two young adults, Andrew and Tom. A soap opera has just finished which depicted two gay men kissing. Tom says, 'That was dirty and disgusting – it shouldn't be allowed on telly'.

Isabella feels torn to agree, but wonders what she should do.

- Is there a conflict between Isabella's personal values and the professional value base?

- What should Isabella do?

- Having thought about Isabella's dilemma, can you identify any value base conflicts that have arisen within your own practice?

- What did you do about them?

WORKING IN AN INCLUSIVE WAY

Workers in health and social care need to be able to demonstrate the actions that they take in their day-to-day working life to model inclusive practice. This is important because the role of the worker is about including people, tapping into people's strengths and talents, celebrating people's uniqueness and diversity, and enabling people who feel and often are disempowered in their lives.

To work in an inclusive way health and social care workers need to incorporate their understanding of equality and diversity into every aspect of their practice. Therefore, this section of the chapter links to many others in this book and to units across the diploma. See the following for examples.

COMMUNICATION

Chapter 2 on communication covers the need for health and social care professionals to consider their communication in a way that meets the needs and preferences of individuals more generally.

Workers need to ensure that communication is respectful of individuals at all times, and ensure that they communicate in ways that demonstrate respect and enhance people's dignity.

Perhaps most importantly in relation to communication, health and social care workers must take the time and energy to listen to people within the service – not assuming we know everything about people from reading an assessment, and not assuming that they are OK and satisfied with the service(s) on offer to them because they are not telling us otherwise.

PERSON-CENTRED PRACTICE

Person-centred approaches involve recognising and responding to each person as a unique individual and supporting people's rights to make choices. These are also key aspects of promoting equality, diversity and inclusion. See Chapters 9 and 10 for more details.

HANDLING INFORMATION

Health and social care workers should work towards handling information and access to records in an inclusive way. Chapter 7 on handling information goes through practical means of achieving this, eg sharing records with individuals and using good record-keeping practices to uphold people's rights.

PROMOTING ACTIVE SUPPORT AND SELF-DIRECTED SUPPORT

These aspects of practice are about understanding and applying the values of health and social care to practice through empowering individuals and ensuring that people can make active choices about their daily lives. Active support involves not doing things for people which they can and want to do for themselves. See Chapter 11 for more details.

PROMOTING INCLUSIVE PRACTICE

To understand which practices promote equality, diversity and inclusion it is important to recognise that the practices outlined in other chapters are vitally important.

Other aspects of inclusive practice include:

- Enabling accessibility. Ensuring people can access the right provision to meet their needs and preferences, whether this is within your own service setting or around you supporting someone to access another resource.

- Ensuring people can access advocates when necessary or when significant decisions are being taken.

- Working positively to include relatives, friends and carers of people within the service.

- Updating service decor to ensure the images are positive and inclusive, and that the messages displayed show that people within the service are important (ie no tatty or wordy papers on the boards).

- Developing means, methods and tools to enable choices about the provision that is available, and to ensure that the service continually develops and evolves in order to meet the changing needs and preferences of its users (not seeing people as static and not dynamic).

- Looking at events and promotional activity (where possible and appropriate) in order to celebrate achievement, and to enable services and local communities to interact with each other (as opposed to the service operating in isolation from its community setting).

- Putting on events or guest speakers to enable learning around faiths, cultures, languages and people's differences.

- Ensuring that complaints are actively responded to.

UNDERSTANDING THE LAW

In the UK we have a history of legislation designed to ensure that discrimination on certain grounds is unlawful. It is important to know about this legislation and to develop an understanding of the way in which this applies to your work setting. It is also important to have a clear understanding of the legislative framework in order to enhance your own practice in terms of challenging oppression. However, be warned that good practice is way ahead of the minimum legal requirements.

The two main Acts of Parliament that relate to promoting equality, diversity and inclusion are the Equality Act 2010 and the Human Rights Act 1998.

If you think of inclusive practice as a bag of tools then the legal framework is one tool to aid your practice. There are two other good reasons to be aware of what the law says in this area – first, you are required to work within the law. Second, you need to be aware of what action could be taken if any of the people you work with have been discriminated against and wish to take legal action.

THE EQUALITY ACT 2010

As the legal framework around equality and discrimination in the UK had developed since the 1970s, we were left with a complex and fragmented legal framework in this area. The idea of the Equality Act 2010 was to provide what is described by the government as a new 'cross-cutting' legislative framework to promote equality for all. It was designed to simplify and strengthen the legal framework.

The Act covers nine protected characteristics which cannot be used as a reason to discriminate against someone:

- age
- disability
- gender reassignment
- marriage and civil partnership
- pregnancy and maternity
- race
- religion or belief
- sex
- sexual orientation.

The Act outlines seven different types of discrimination:

- *Direct discrimination* occurs when someone is treated less favourably than another person because of a protected characteristic.

- *Associative discrimination* is direct discrimination against someone because they are associated with another person who possesses a protected characteristic.

- *Discrimination by perception* is direct discrimination against someone because others think that they possess a particular protected characteristic. They do not necessarily have to possess the characteristic, just be perceived to.

- *Indirect discrimination* can occur when you have a rule or policy that applies to everyone but disadvantages a person with a particular protected characteristic.

- *Harassment* refers to behaviour that is deemed offensive by the recipient. Employees can now complain of behaviour they find offensive even if it is not directed at them.

- *Harassment by a third party.* Employers are potentially liable for the harassment of their staff or customers by people they don't themselves employ, eg a contractor.

- *Victimisation* occurs when someone is treated badly because they have made or supported a complaint or grievance under this legislation.

The Act puts a new 'single equality duty' on all public bodies when they are making strategic decisions, such as new policies. The single equality duty means targeting services at people who are disadvantaged, so the real essence of this legislation is that it recognises that a person can experience several types of disadvantage at once. This makes sense. A single equality duty means that the focus is on the goal of equality, rather than a label or characteristic of a person or group of people. After all, if you are a black gay man with a disability who is discriminated against at work, why should you have to pinpoint the aspect of self that is being discriminated against?

This gives us the concept of 'intersectional multiple discrimination'. This is where there is discrimination against two or more such characteristics at the same time (see above as this links with the concept of people being 'doubly' or 'multiply disadvantaged'). This is all very new, and for employers and local authorities it is very complicated. It remains to be seen how it will work in practice and we can anticipate much of that practice being thrashed out in the courts to create case law.

How does this legislation apply in health and social care work?

The Equality Act 2010 is important to health and social care in that:

- service users are likely to experience (or have experienced) discrimination on the basis of their difference or the difficulty they may have in accessing the resources they need

- all services have duties to promote equality under this legislation

- as a professional, you have an individual duty to promote equality and inclusion

- you need to be able to understand what the law says about discrimination and equality in order to be able to challenge discrimination and exclusion effectively.

REFLECT

How do you meet the requirements of the Equality Act in your practice?

THE HUMAN RIGHTS ACT 1998

The Human Rights Act 1998 came into force in October 2000. It is, in effect, the European Convention on Human Rights. Listed in Schedule 1 of the Act are various rights, including:

- Article 2: Everyone's right to life shall be protected by law.

- Article 3: No one shall be subjected to ... degrading ... treatment.

- Article 5: Everyone has the right to liberty and security of person.

- Article 8: Everyone has the right to respect for his private and family life and his correspondence.

- Article 9: Everyone has the right to freedom of thought, conscience and religion.

- Article 12: Men and women of marriageable age have the right to marry and to found a family.

- Article 14: The enjoyment of these rights and freedoms set forth in this Convention shall be secured without discrimination on any ground.

EQUALITY AND HUMAN RIGHTS COMMISSION (EHRC)

The Equality and Human Rights Commission was established by the Equality Act 2006. It has a general duty to encourage and support the development of a society in which:

- people's ability to achieve their potential is not limited by prejudice or discrimination

- there is respect for and protection of each individual's human rights

- there is respect for the dignity and worth of each individual

- each individual has an equal opportunity to participate in society

- there is mutual respect between groups based on understanding and valuing of diversity and on shared respect for equality and human rights.

The EHRC is to pursue these objectives by:

- promoting equality of opportunity and diversity

- enforcing anti-discriminatory legislation

- promoting awareness, understanding and protection of human rights.

The EHRC has the power to:

- issue codes of practice to assist organisations to comply with legislation

- initiate enquiries and investigations

- issue notices requiring people to comply with anti-discriminatory legislation

- assist individuals to take legal proceedings where anti-discriminatory legislation appears to have been violated.

RESEARCH

Take a look at the EHRC website (www.equalityhumanrights.com). It has lots of useful information about equality and diversity. If you make some notes about your research this will provide you with evidence for a range of units.

INTERACTING WITH INDIVIDUALS IN A WAY THAT RESPECTS THEIR BELIEFS, CULTURE, VALUES AND PREFERENCES

CULTURE

Culture is an aspect of identity, where there can be significant diversity. Culture is based on a number of things shared with others such as language, shared history, beliefs, attitudes, celebrations, musical taste, dress, diet and many others. Culture is basically about a shared understanding with others of the same culture. Cultures are neither inferior nor superior – they are just *different*. It is important to recognise too that cultures are dynamic and constantly changing.

The term 'culture' incorporates concepts of differences between people's faiths, race/ethnicity and identity. However, it is a broader concept, as cultural diversity (difference) is not only created by these factors, but is also influenced by the following:

- *Generational difference.* Experience, identity and preference can be based on people's age. Consider how different your musical preferences, use of speech and language, sense of humour or identity might be from that of your own parents or grandparents.

- *Differences based on geographical location or between local communities.* Consider how towns in the UK which are 10 miles apart can feel very different culturally, and how areas within one town can have their own identity – this is all culture.

■ *Differences in beliefs (as opposed to faith).* People believe different things about what is right or wrong, about how life should be conducted and about what is important in life.

It is also important to recognise that culture is an aspect of a person's identity. It is not their 'whole' identity and it does not act as a prediction of how a person will behave and what they will believe. Everyone chooses which aspects of their cultural identity they wish to 'own' and which they do not. As such, each person has a unique approach to their culture – leading to a complexity of the way in which culture affects people's individual needs.

It is vital that health and social care workers do not make assumptions based on individuals' culture. Culture does not mean uniformity and we still need to treat people as unique individuals. For example, we could say that 'English culture' involves:

■ eating fish and chips or Sunday roast

■ attending Church of England services

■ monogamous relationships

■ wearing business suits, etc.

This would lead us to believe that all English people wear business suits, are in lifelong monogamous relationships, attend church every Sunday and eat fish and chips in the week and roast dinners on Sunday. Clearly this is not the case.

People working in health and social care settings should be well aware that making assumptions is dangerous. Assumptions about what people might eat or wear based on a basic understanding of cultural norms can be misleading. The best course of action is to simply avoid making assumptions about people.

The experience of service users from different backgrounds may differ radically from the cultural background of any member of staff. Cultural beliefs and practices may vary between generations and within a racial group. Certain cultural beliefs may be shared with others from the same background and certain things may not. The final collection therefore is completely unique to each and every individual.

DEVELOPING CULTURAL COMPETENCE

The concept of cultural competence is recognised as vital in social and health care. The fact that the word 'competence' is now being used suggests clearly that if workers are not good at working with difference, they will be seen as incompetent.

Culturally competent practice involves knowledge and understanding of:

- your own culture
- any culture bias you may have
- the concept of culture and how this can affect beliefs and behaviours
- specific cultural knowledge.

It requires a range of skills, including:

- culturally competent communication
- culturally competent assessment
- culturally sensitive care provision.

Plus, a range of values and attitudes, including a commitment to:

- valuing and celebrating difference
- respecting individuality and the role that culture plays in this.

Cultural competence is very often referred to as a journey. This is a useful image as it shows that everyone is on a journey towards cultural competence. We would encourage social and health care professionals to think about preparing for their 'journey' and to look towards the journey with excitement.

Communication and interaction in social care therefore needs to take account of and show respect for the fact that culture is something which:

- is part of every individual
- is important to every individual
- is essential for interaction with individuals to be effective and person centred
- cannot be assumed or generalised because it is individual in its nature.

RESEARCH

Talk to the individuals with whom you work about their culture with the aim of finding out more about the ways in which services could be improved in order to meet their cultural and individual needs.

If you need to, do some research into different faiths or cultural backgrounds of the people with whom you work. Remember that individuals interact with their faith and culture in unique ways, so it is important to avoid assumptions around how every person from one faith sees the world.

CASE STUDY

Dee is a senior care assistant in a day service for older people. She is working with an older Muslim man, Hasson, who has started to attend the day centre in which she works. Hasson is in his eighties and has had a stroke. Dee tries to engage Hasson in some of the regular activities at the centre, but he seems reluctant to participate. Some of the other people at the centre think he is aloof and rude. Dee, however, is concerned that Hasson's cultural needs are not being considered effectively in terms of the range of provision and the methods of communication that are being utilised with Hasson.

- What could Dee do to engage Hasson and find out more about his needs, wishes and culture?

- What assumptions should Dee avoid making about Hasson?

- Who else could Dee involve in considering these issues?

- What could Dee do to engage her colleagues in this dialogue with Hasson?

PROMOTING EQUALITY, DIVERSITY AND INCLUSION

Promoting equality, diversity and inclusion means modelling the components of inclusive practice, as covered on pages 88–89. It also requires health and social care workers to understand the barriers and enablers to equality, diversity and inclusion. When a worker understands these barriers and enablers, they can challenge the barriers and use the enablers. Promoting diversity, equality and inclusion might also call on workers to challenge people who are not employing inclusive practice.

UNDERSTANDING BARRIERS AND ENABLERS

There are potentially many barriers to promoting equality, diversity and inclusion in health and social care settings and these might hamper you in your work and your attempts to promote inclusive practice. It is also important to recognise that there are 'enablers' to inclusion and equality. Building on these enablers can help health and social care services find solutions to the barriers.

- What barriers to equality, diversity and inclusion do you face?
- How can you address and overcome these barriers?

PROMOTING A RIGHTS-BASED CULTURE

Health and social care workers need to work to cultivate a service culture where:

- all staff understand and have a commitment to service users' rights
- service user requests are responded to
- staff commitments and responsibilities are met
- tasks that are essential for service users' basic needs are carried out without service users having to make repeated requests
- staff ensure that service users are aware of their rights
- staff acknowledge and respond to comments and complaints without being defensive
- staff challenge one another positively
- positive values are promoted in the service at all times
- discrimination and prejudice are challenged
- service users are aware of their responsibilities towards others.

Many people who are in receipt of care services have, until recently, had many of their rights infringed or denied, or were never supported sufficiently to exercise their rights. Even now, many of the rights we take for granted may be only partially or half-heartedly upheld for people receiving a care service.

In health and social care it is vital that workers have a sense of the range of rights that we enjoy and that service users also have a right to enjoy. All care staff have a responsibility to assist people in exercising their rights in a real and meaningful way.

RIGHTS AND RESPONSIBILITIES

Closely tied to rights are responsibilities that somebody enjoying those rights has an obligation to observe. Various rights and responsibilities are listed in brief in the following table. The table is not comprehensive but gives an idea of some of the responsibilities that follow from exercising rights.

Right	Responsibility
To life	To respect the right of others to life
Freedom of movement	In exercising this right, not to violate or infringe anyone else's rights
Freedom of speech	To be prepared to hear what others say in response; not to say anything that incites racism or violence
Freedom of association	To seek to be with those who also want to be with you
To make decisions that affect own life	To acknowledge and face any reasonable and likely consequences of your decision
To practise religious beliefs	In exercising this right, not to violate or infringe anyone else's rights
To pursue cultural and other interests	In exercising this right, not to violate or infringe anyone else's rights
To vote (subject to age)	To make decisions based on knowledge of political options
To have sex (subject to age)	To ensure it is a mutual decision and to be aware of possible consequences, eg sexually transmitted diseases
To get married (subject to age)	To be aware of the nature of commitment and intent on upholding your promise
To own property	Stewardship of such property
To be treated with dignity and respect	To treat others in the same way
To be treated fairly and equally	To treat others fairly and equally
To due process of law and legal representation if arrested	To cooperate in police investigations; to comply with the law
To be protected from unnecessary risk of harm, neglect, abuse, etc.	Not to subject others to harm, abuse, etc and not to place oneself in situations where there is unnecessary risk of harm or abuse
To medical treatment based on clinical need	To provide relevant information to medical staff
To maximise personal development – spiritual, emotional, intellectual and physical	To pursue opportunities for personal development
To take risks	To accept the consequences that could reasonably be expected to follow
To privacy	In exercising this right, not to violate or infringe anyone else's rights

TENSIONS BETWEEN RIGHTS AND RESPONSIBILITIES

There can easily be potential conflicts when considering rights and responsibilities, which can take one of several forms.

Tension between a person's own rights and responsibilities

It may be that there are times when a person's rights conflict with their responsibilities. For example, an adult may have the right to smoke, but they also have the responsibility not to endanger others. In situations where a person smokes irresponsibly there is a danger of fire, eg a person smoking in bed and falling asleep as they smoke.

Tension between different people's rights and responsibilities

In any shared living or recreational environment tensions between people will arise. For example, one person's right to pursue their own interests can conflict with another person's right to do something different in the same place at the same time. A basic example of this is an argument between people about what television channel to watch.

So it can be seen that making a statement that someone has a right to something is not as straightforward as it seems. Each right needs to be taken individually and it needs to be 'unpicked' to see what it really means.

WHEN RIGHTS CANNOT BE UPHELD

At times in social care, the duty of care can be in conflict with upholding service users' rights. This may be because of some of the tensions between rights and responsibilities covered above.

Workers need to be very clear about the question, 'When should rights be overridden?' This is a difficult but vital question. Its answer relates to risk and to situations in which exercising a particular right may place someone in danger. Essentially, this applies in two main ways:

- *Danger to others*. No one has the right to violate or infringe the rights of someone else. If a person is acting in a way that intrudes on someone else's rights (eg hitting someone else), then action needs to be taken.

- *Danger to self*. Certain actions can place people at risk. Examples may include self-harm or even smoking in bed (which potentially may also pose a danger to others).

> **KEY POINT**
>
> Any situation that involves restricting someone's rights is very serious and decisions about this should not be taken by individual health and social care workers. Always speak to your line manager about any dilemmas in this area.
>
> It is vital if someone's rights are restricted (because of a danger to themselves or others) that the reasons for this should be explained to them clearly. Where people are unclear about boundaries and rights they may be left confused and frustrated.

APPLICATION OF SKILLS

Doing the rights thing?

- Miriam who is overweight is advised by her doctor to lose weight. The staff who support her at home draw up a diet with advice from a dietician. At mealtimes Miriam starts to complain that she doesn't get as much food as other people and staff become aware that when they are not close by, she is going into the kitchen to eat food. What are the concerns about rights here? How can Miriam's rights be upheld?

- Ted is in hospital recovering from a stroke. His partner, George, visits daily and is openly affectionate to Ted, holding his hand, kissing him and stroking his hair. The man in the next bed takes great exception to this and demands that staff speak to Ted and George about their behaviour. What are the concerns about equalities and rights here? How can Ted's rights be upheld?

- When staff try to involve Django in decisions in the residential home where he lives, he replies that it's not worth it since he didn't want to live there in the first place. The only decisions he feels he's asked about are minor ones. How should staff handle this?

- Shane has early-onset dementia and has recently moved to live in a residential home. One day, Shane says that he is going out and refuses to answer workers' questions about this, saying that where he is going and why is none of their business. How do staff manage and balance his rights and choices alongside their duty of care?

- Mrs Gable has smoked for over 40 years. Her doctor has said she must stop, so her daughter stops bringing her cigarettes when she visits her in the residential home where she lives. Mrs Gable pleads with staff to buy cigarettes for her and she has now started to take cigarettes from other people. What are the concerns about rights here? How can Mrs Gable's rights be upheld?

SUPPORTING OTHERS TO PROMOTE EQUALITY, DIVERSITY AND INCLUSION

There are a number of ways to support others to promote equality and work in an inclusive way. These include:

- challenging oppression (whether this comes from service users, relatives, colleagues or even managers)

- encouraging people to recognise, celebrate and positively respond to diversity (or 'differentness')

- implementing approaches such as advocacy and empowerment
- focusing on service users' strengths and encouraging others to do so
- avoiding using oppressive practices such as labelling and stereotyping, and ensuring that you challenge these processes
- understanding and challenging your own values
- challenging people who act in ways which deny equality, diversity and inclusion.

CHALLENGING DISCRIMINATION IN A WAY THAT PROMOTES CHANGE

Sometimes people aren't comfortable with the term 'challenging'. They might be unsure about what 'challenging' means and how workers can challenge effectively.

Whenever a worker comes across a situation which they feel they want (or indeed, need) to challenge, then they need to ask:

- Why?
- What?
- Who?
- How? and
- When?

Challenging may need to take place between workers, or workers may need to challenge service users or their family members.

Why challenge?

It is important to challenge poor practice and discriminatory behaviour because we all have a commitment to promote good practice. Through challenging we are able to ask questions about practice which otherwise remain unasked. We can make positive changes and we can ensure others adopt a challenging approach.

The purpose of challenging someone else, whether this is a service user, a colleague or another professional, should always be to promote change, and to enable more effective and inclusive practice to take place.

In a healthy, positive and inclusive working culture, challenging should be seen as:

- positive
- constructive
- enabling mutual learning

- respectful
- improving practice
- enabling inclusion and continuous improvement around this key issue.

Sadly, in many working environments, this can still be difficult to achieve as people may feel worried about challenging others, about how the other person may receive the challenge, or about not being supported sufficiently by their employer.

If people feel really concerned about someone else's working practice and they have tried to challenge this and it has not promoted change, their duty of care to individuals may mean they are required to take this challenge further. This is why agencies should have a whistle-blowing policy in place and this policy should detail what support is available to individuals who do escalate challenges in this way.

What is the challenge?

Someone making a challenge should be clear about exactly what is being challenged. Workers must listen, examine the issue, think about the context, and make the links with institutional oppression and structural forces. By working in this way, we avoid making challenging personally threatening.

Who is being challenged?

Workers must consider the person being challenged. Care workers should never avoid challenging because of the individual, but they should alter the focus and content of the challenge based on the understanding and experiences of the individual. Health and social care workers should think about communication in terms of the individual who is being challenged.

How should the challenge be made?

Workers should choose the right way of challenging and need to put thought into this. As a starting point, we suggest the following:

- *Understanding.* There could be a difference in understanding between a worker and a person being challenged.
- *Values.* There may be a difference between what is important to a worker and what is important to the person who is being challenged.
- *Styles.* There may well be a difference in the way in which a worker does things and the way the other person does things. That does not necessarily mean that the other person's way of doing something is bad practice.
- *Opinions.* There may be differences in opinion between a person making a challenge and a person being challenged.

If health and social care workers bear all of the above in mind, when deciding *how* to challenge, their approach is much more likely to be effective. In addition, we believe that it is important to choose the least oppressive way of challenging someone.

When should people challenge?

This is very closely linked to thinking around the area of *how* to challenge. It may be worthwhile considering the most appropriate time to challenge.

Consequences of challenging

In addition to considering the questions we have outlined, workers need to think about the consequences of any challenge both in terms of themselves and the person being challenged. They should also think about the needs of the 'victim' of the poor practice, the oppression, etc (ie the victim of whatever is being challenged). Support may need to be allocated for them too.

REFLECT

Consider a time when you have had to challenge somebody at work. This does not have to have been something that was a massive issue or which led to an escalation of the issue. It could have been quite an informal challenge to a person concerning their use of language, or perhaps it involved somebody making fun of somebody else without thinking that this could be upsetting for that person.

- How did you challenge?
- Why did you decide to challenge?
- How did it feel to challenge?
- What worked well and what would you do again in a similar situation?
- What would you do differently?
- What support did you need or might you need if this occurred again, or if the other person did not respond to the challenge you made?

EXPLORING YOUR TEAM COMMITMENT TO PROMOTING BEST PRACTICE IN EQUALITY, DIVERSITY AND INCLUSION

In order to ensure that service users experience services that promote equality, diversity and inclusion it is important that staff teams work together. If you feel that your team is not committed to equality, diversity and inclusion you have a responsibility to challenge your colleagues and to promote best practice. Read through the following case study which makes it clear that inclusive practice is a team responsibility.

CASE STUDY

The staff team of a service for people with disabilities is taking steps to meet the needs of black service users more appropriately. Only a few black people use the centre at the moment.

A year ago the whole staff team drew up an action plan. Since the training, only the two black members of staff and the manager have worked particularly hard to implement some of the items from the action plan, such as:

- cooking a wider variety of Asian, Afro-Caribbean and European foods for all service users as an alternative to the traditional daily menu

- taking small numbers of service users to the local shops to buy ingredients

- showing a wider variety of films during the video session

- playing music from different cultures.

About 30% of the white staff team members, including the deputy manager, have helped with and supported the work. The rest of the white staff members have taken little or no interest in the developments. At times they have shown hostility, eg they have supported service users who have made derogatory comments about the food, music or films.

- What are the issues here?

- What practical steps could you take as a staff member?

Code of Conduct for Healthcare Support Workers and Adult Social Care Workers

The Code of Conduct for Healthcare Support Workers and Adult Social Care Workers makes clear that you need to uphold and promote equality, diversity and inclusion. To do so, it states that you must:

- respect the individuality and diversity of the people who use health and care services, their carers and your colleagues

- not discriminate or condone discrimination against people who use health and social care services, their carers or your colleagues

- promote equal opportunities for the people who use health and social care services and their carers

- report any concerns regarding equality, diversity and inclusion to a senior member of staff as soon as possible.

CHAPTER 4
Principles for implementing duty of care

Health and social care work has a duty of care for others at its heart. This is a profession that cares for other people who need support or who require care in order to have their basic needs met. Providing this care or support ethically and professionally is one of the things that motivate competent workers in their job role.

This chapter considers what is meant by the term 'duty of care' and addresses some of the ethical dilemmas which can be involved in delivering a duty of care for and with individuals.

Links to other chapters

The duty of care applies to all aspects of your work, therefore this chapter links to every unit you will complete for the qualification. In this book, there are particular links with chapters 3, 5 and 6.

UNDERSTANDING THE DUTY OF CARE

The government defines the duty of care as:

An obligation placed on an individual requiring that they exercise a reasonable standard of care while doing something (or possibly omitting to do something) that could foreseeably harm others.

(Department of Health 2007)

This makes clear that your duty of care is an obligation – it is something you owe the people with whom you work, and it is their right to receive the best-possible care when they access services. The duty of care is a legal concept – when it is not exercised, there can be serious consequences.

This can apply outside of health and social care settings too. If someone trips in a shop or on a paving stone, they can argue that the company or local authority has not met its obligations to them. The ever-increasing frequency of legal action being taken around negligence is an example of how people exercise their rights when they feel that organisations have not met their duty of care.

The duty of care underpins all work in health and social care and is about:

- putting the needs of service users first
- ensuring that people's needs are met
- treating people with respect and respecting their rights
- working ethically and for people's best interests
- promoting people's independence and empowering them
- supporting people to keep themselves safe
- ensuring people are listened to
- carrying out your job competently
- doing your job to the best of your ability
- meeting legal requirements.

REFLECT

- What does the phrase 'duty of care' mean to you?
- What does it mean for your role at work?

HOW DOES THE DUTY OF CARE CONTRIBUTE TO THE SAFEGUARDING OR PROTECTION OF INDIVIDUALS?

At this point you should refer to Chapter 5 which covers safeguarding and protection and your role and responsibilities in this area in greater detail.

The duty of care that you have is vital in keeping people safe and ensuring that their rights are not contravened or ignored. This is because the duty of care involves:

- upholding people's right to feel safe from harm and abuse

- promoting people's right to be treated with dignity and respect

- ensuring that people are supported to take risks in a way that respects their individuality

- your duty to liaise with other professionals when you are concerned about someone's safety or welfare

- your duty to put people's 'best interests' at the heart of your work.

REFLECT

How does the duty of care apply when:

- providing personal or intimate care for individuals

- organising events and activities

- liaising with professionals from other agencies

- liaising with relatives and friends of individuals

- conducting your health and safety responsibilities at work

- recording your work?

DUTY OF CARE CONFLICTS AND DILEMMAS

The duty of care for individuals in health and social care settings can create a range of conflicts or dilemmas for workers. This is because:

- upholding people's rights is a complex business

- rights are balanced with responsibilities

- what one person wants might be in conflict with what another person wants

- what people want is not always what is best for them

- people have the right to do things which others may feel are not what is best for them.

ETHICAL DILEMMAS

The conflicts and dilemmas that can be raised by the duty of care are sometimes referred to as ethical or moral dilemmas. These conflicts and dilemmas generally occur when:

- there is a tension between rights and responsibilities (see Chapter 3 for more on this topic)

- there is conflict between different people holding different views about a situation.

- there is a conflict between values, eg between a worker's personal and professional values (see Chapter 3 for further information)

- a decision is not clear-cut or obvious

- every possible alternative in a situation would lead to an undesirable outcome for a service user

- there are concerns about the risks that a situation might pose.

Key terms O———

The terms '**ethics**' and '**morals**' are sometimes used interchangeably – there are some specific differences between them which are generally accepted.

Morals are about our belief in what is right and wrong, and are often associated with faith and our personal values.

Ethics are also about how we see right and wrong, but ethics are generally drawn from our understanding of responsibilities and so are closely linked with professional standards, codes of conduct and legislation. Ethics are closely related to the duty of care in health and social care.

WHEN EMPLOYERS' INSTRUCTIONS CONFLICT WITH THE DUTY OF CARE

UNISON (2012) points out that a health and social care worker may be placed in a difficult position where they are asked to do something by their employer that they feel conflicts with their duty of care. As examples, UNISON cites situations where:

- an instruction is unlawful

- an instruction is clearly unsafe

- an instruction is insufficiently direct, eg different managers giving conflicting instructions.

Where you consider there to be a conflict between what your employer is asking of you and your duty of care you must raise this with your manager. If the situation is not clarified or resolved then you should consider whether you need to follow whistle-blowing procedures. Remember the Public Interest Disclosure Act (see Chapter 5, page 174) will provide protection if you have followed your organisation's whistle-blowing policy.

REACHING DECISIONS WHERE THERE ARE CONFLICTS AND DILEMMAS

A FRAMEWORK FOR ETHICAL DECISION MAKING

Making a decision on situations where there are dilemmas and conflicts is often referred to as ethical decision making. It is useful to think about the process of making an ethical decision as a series of steps:

Make a decision.
Never make a decision in isolation – always discuss any dilemmas and the decisions with your manager and where the dilemma is significant make sure you consult with a range of different professionals.

Gather information.
Make sure that you have all the information you need in order to make a decision.

Identify the dilemma.
What exactly is the dilemma? What are the tensions and conflicts? Can any of these tensions and conflicts be eased?

Consider the risks and gains of each potential decision.
It is likely that you will have a variety of options. List the risks and the benefits of each option. Which option will do the most good or the least harm?

Think about different perspectives.
When working through each of the options think about different people's perspectives. Make sure that you consult with others in reaching a decision.

'DEFENSIBLE DECISIONS'

The lawyer David Carson introduced the concept of 'defensible decisions'. The idea of such decisions is that where there are major dilemmas and conflicts a decision can be defended if:

- all reasonable steps are taken
- reliable assessment methods have been used
- information is thoroughly collected and evaluated
- practitioners seek any information that they do not have
- decisions are clearly recorded
- practitioners work within agency policy and procedure
- practitioners communicate effectively with each other.

(Carson and Bain 2008)

WHAT ARE 'BEST INTERESTS'?

All decisions around dilemmas and conflicts must be made in line with the principles of best interests. The idea of people's 'best interests' is critical in health and social care work and it is a term that is used frequently in all fields. The following issues are key to considering best interests:

- It is important not to make assumptions about what is in someone's best interests. Decisions about best interests should be based on evidence, knowledge of the individual, and a deep understanding of risk and safeguarding practice.
- Decisions about best interests should not be made in isolation. Considering someone's best interests needs to involve discussion between a range of different professionals working in conjunction with the service user and their family.
- What is in someone's best interests is not always what they want.
- Your duty of care involves explaining best-interest decisions when this is an issue and evidencing the reasons for your decision making.

THE MENTAL CAPACITY ACT 2005

When formed, this Act represented a fundamental change for adult services and is particularly relevant to this chapter.

Where the Mental Capacity Act breaks new ground is that it departs from the idea that an assessment of capacity is made on a once-and-for-all basis and affects all other decisions that someone makes. It recognises that the ability to be able to make rational decisions may vary for a variety of reasons and according to the complexity of what is being asked of someone.

The Mental Capacity Act 2005 has five core principles:

1 A person must be assumed to have capacity unless it is established that they lack capacity.

2 A person must not be treated as unable to make a decision unless all practicable steps to help them to make the decision have been taken.

3 A person must not be treated as unable to make a decision just because they make an unwise decision.

4 Any decision made or act carried out on behalf of a person must be in their best interests.

5 Before a decision is made or an act is carried out, consideration must be given to how this can be achieved in a way which is least restrictive of the person's rights and freedoms.

THE IMPACT OF DECISION MAKING

When thinking about how to deal with conflicts and dilemmas several risks need to be considered. For example, there will be an effect on:

■ the individual concerned – they could be unhappy about decisions taken; they may feel unvalued and disrespected; they could feel that they have not been listened to

■ the individual's relationship with you and/or other workers

■ how the individual feels about continuing to access the service

■ the relatives and informal carers for an individual as decisions can often have far-reaching consequences

■ the service you provide or your employing agency (eg in terms of potential complaints).

Managing these risks and tensions is critical to maintaining working relationships and to working in line with your duty of care. Some ideas for achieving this include:

■ using good risk-assessment tools and practices which emphasise the dignity of risk and the protective factors around someone as well as the risks

■ involving people in risk assessments (see also Chapter 6 on health and safety)

- carefully considering how protective factors (eg support from family and friends) can be strengthened in order to reduce risk

- holding multi-agency or multidisciplinary meetings to look at either issues for individuals (involving the person in this as much as possible), or at themes within services in order to aid service development and continuous improvement of provision

- using advocacy services (see pp 64–65)

- providing clear and accessible information

- using your own active listening skills so that someone feels their views have been heard, even or especially when their wishes cannot be met

- being open, transparent and honest – feeding back to the person as soon as possible about any decisions (whether their wishes are being met or not), the reasons for those decisions, and their options and rights

- explaining the duty of care to the person, and that decisions are sometimes taken because people do care about them and their needs being met. People can usually accept when something they want cannot happen, as long as others are upfront and open about this. Others also need to be caring in their response to the annoyance or distress which this may cause. People usually become more unhappy when there are unnecessary delays in feeding back to them and when things are not explained clearly and respectfully.

MANAGING THE RISKS ASSOCIATED WITH CONFLICTS AND DILEMMAS

UNDERSTANDING RISK IN HEALTH AND SOCIAL CARE

Risk assessment is covered in detail on pp 192–194. However, here it is worth exploring how people understand risk in health and social care as this is closely related to the dilemmas and conflicts that people often face in relation to their duty of care.

APPROACHES TO RISK

In health and social care services, the main approaches to risk can be categorised as:

- risk elimination
- risk reduction
- risk minimisation
- risk management.

Risk elimination

Risk elimination is sometimes referred to as risk control. It refers to an approach that seeks to completely eliminate risks. This is a practically impossible aim in health and social care work. There are, however, a few examples where a risk is entirely influenced by one environmental factor and where this environmental factor can be changed (eg the risk of falls might be eliminated by changes to the environment such as removing rugs and trailing wires).

Risk reduction

This approach seeks to 'reduce' the risks or the likelihood of identified risks occurring.

Risk minimisation

This approach is often referred to as harm minimisation. Essentially, this approach is about minimising the impact of the risk.

Risk management

Risk management approaches seek to 'manage' risks rather than attempting to eliminate them. Risk management strategies are usually devised on a case-by-case basis using aspects of risk reduction and risk minimisation.

RISK-AVERSE APPROACHES

A number of social care services are seen as having a 'risk-averse' culture. That is, they seek to adopt a risk elimination approach rather than a risk management approach. It is widely recognised that services have often in the past been too protective of people. Services have always sought to minimise or eliminate any risk of harm, be it emotional, mental or physical. It is now accepted that the attempt to eliminate all risk undermines people's dignity and inhibits opportunities for personal development and growth. Often care environments that reduce risk as much as possible result in very poor care environments.

The key differences between risk elimination and risk management

	Risk elimination	Risk management
How risks are defined	Risk is viewed as wholly negative; seen only as a danger or a threat	Risk is viewed as potentially positive, ie risk is part of life, balancing risks and benefits is part of an individual's development, being self-determining and personally responsible
Priority principles	Professional responsibility and accountability	Self-determination, equality and inclusion
Practice priorities	Identification (assessment scales) and elimination (procedural, legalistic)	Partnership working, active support, empowerment

REFLECT

- What risk assessment and risk management procedures do you use?

- Having read through the models of risk assessment, can you identify how these affect the practice and policies in your organisation?

CASE STUDY

Jon is a senior support worker with a reablement team. Mr Lin is in hospital following a stroke. He wants to go home from hospital but his daughters want him to move into a residential service. They feel that it is 'too risky' for him to return home. They point out that Mrs Lin did most of the cooking when she was alive and that Mr Lin will struggle to look after himself now that he has some paralysis in his right side.

A hospital social worker assesses Mr Lin and decides that he has the capacity to make the decision about where he wants to live when he is discharged from hospital. She recognises that there are some risks to Mr Lin but the occupational therapists and physiotherapists on the ward feel that he has made good progress and that he has the potential to further develop his skills. She makes a referral to the reablement team and Jon is allocated to be Mr Lin's key worker when he returns home.

Jon works with Mr Lin on further developing his self-care skills. His daughters buy a microwave and Jon helps Mr Lin to learn to use this to cook his meals. After six weeks, Jon and Mr Lin meet with his daughters to review the situation. Mr Lin feels much more confident in caring for himself. His daughters are surprised by Mr Lin's level of motivation to learn new skills and are pleased that he is independent.

- What might have happened if Mr Lin had moved into a residential home as his daughters had wanted?

- How has Jon's work with Mr Lin helped to address the risks he faced?

- What approach to risk does this illustrate?

RECOGNISING THE DIGNITY OF RISK

It is now accepted that the attempt to eliminate all risk undermines people's dignity and rights and inhibits opportunities for personal development and growth. The answer to overprotection is not to ignore risks but to work in partnership to support people to take measured, reasonable risks.

Reasonable risk

The concept of 'reasonable risk' is important. Health and safety legislation often refers to what would be 'reasonable' and the expected actions of a 'reasonable person'. One of the difficulties in determining what constitutes a reasonable risk is that sometimes our view is coloured by our own anxieties about a person's safety and our attitude towards risk in our own lives. The Department of Health states that:

Because of perceptions of risk which may or may not be real, a person might be prevented from doing things which most people take for granted. So perceived risk must be tested and assessed against the likely benefits of taking an active part in the community, learning new skills and gaining confidence.

(Department of Health 2007)

Decisions about 'reasonable' risk must never be taken in isolation – what seems reasonable to one person may be unreasonable to another. People's personal values, for example, will significantly affect their view of risk, which demonstrates the importance of being clear about professional and organisational values.

A risk-enablement culture

If a health and social care worker works to the principles of active support, as covered in Chapter 11, they will be well on the way to promoting a positive culture in relation to risk. Taking some risks is a daily occurrence for everyone and must be necessary if people are to take a full and active part in their communities. Government guidance makes this clear:

The possibility of risk is an inevitable consequence of empowered people taking decisions about their own lives.

(Department of Health 2007)

Most people are able to balance risk against possible benefits and will take any necessary precautions to help minimise risk. It may not be quite so easy for the people that health and social care workers support to achieve this balance for themselves. This is where support will be required. It is where the key dilemmas will occur and where getting the balance right is perhaps the most difficult. Sometimes when providing support, social care staff can be anxious to eliminate

any identified risk of harm which can mean that a decision is made that a particular choice cannot be supported. As discussed in Chapter 11, this should only occur in extreme circumstances and where risk assessments clearly indicate the reasons why the person's choice cannot be supported.

Getting the balance right

Effective practice in working with risk within care environments is about balance.

It is vital that the duty of care is not used as a reason to deny the dignity of risk taking. The need to get the balance right has been made clear in various professional codes of conduct. For example, the code of practice for social care workers states that workers must 'promote the independence of individuals while protecting them as far as possible from danger or harm'.

The Nursing and Midwifery Code of Professional Conduct mirrors this by stating that nurses must 'respect the patient or client as an individual' and 'minimise risk to patients and clients'.

The emphasis must be on sensible risk appraisal, not striving to avoid all risk, whatever the price, but instead seeking a proper balance and being willing to tolerate manageable or acceptable risks as the price appropriately to be paid in order to achieve some other good – in particular to achieve the vital good of the elderly or vulnerable person's happiness. What good is it making someone safer if it merely makes them miserable?'

(Justice Munby quoted in the Department of Health 2010)

REFLECT

- What dilemmas have you faced in managing the balancing act between rights and risks?

- How did you promote the balance?

- Could you have dealt with this differently? How?

- If a similar situation were to occur again, what would you do? Why?

MESSAGES FROM RESEARCH

Balancing the duty of care

The Joseph Rowntree Foundation reports that a number of research studies have explored the dilemmas that health and social care staff face in balancing their duty of care with upholding service users rights – especially around the right to take risks. These studies have found that staff have a number of fears about service users taking risks, partly because they do not fully understand that the duty of care involves enabling service users to take informed and acceptable risks. The research identifies that many health and social care organisations take a risk-averse approach, denying service users the dignity of risk taking.

(Source: Mitchell, Baxter and Glendinning 2012)

GETTING SUPPORT AND ADVICE ABOUT CONFLICTS AND DILEMMAS

It is important that professionals in health and social care know when to ask for help and do not see needing support or advice as a sign of weakness. This is especially critical where there are complex dilemmas as sometimes there are no 'right' or 'wrong' ways to handle a situation, and a sound judgement can only be reached by sharing knowledge, information and dialogue with others.

Potential sources of support and information about conflicts include the following.

Colleagues

Resources such as books, leaflets, the internet

Managers

Potential sources of support and information

Advocacy services

Other agencies and specialist professionals

Your union if you belong to one

How would you access support, advice and information where you face a duty of care dilemma?

CASE STUDY

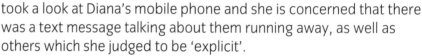

Jane is a senior support worker in a day service for people with learning disabilities. Diana and Lee attend the day service where Jane works. Diana has Down's syndrome and Lee has cerebral palsy. Diana's mother comes to see Jane one day to say she is concerned that Diana has been getting 'obsessed' with Lee. She says they are texting each other all of the time and Diana is talking about how she loves Lee. Her mother says she took a look at Diana's mobile phone and she is concerned that there was a text message talking about them running away, as well as others which she judged to be 'explicit'.

- How might Jane respond to this information?

- What other information might Jane need?

- What dilemmas does this situation present for Jane?

- Where could Jane go for support and advice?

- What support might Diana's mother need?

RESPONDING TO COMPLAINTS

All health and social care services are required to have a complaints procedure. To summarise the key issues around complaints procedures:

- It is vital that complaints procedures are clear and transparent so that service users (and their representatives or advocates) can access them and make effective use of them.

- If an agency or service has a complaints procedure, it must expect complaints. Workers should be able to pick up on situations where a service user or family member is unhappy about a matter, and, if possible, the worker should try to resolve the problem.

- If the concerns raised are outside of an individual worker's control, then they need to convey how it is important that a comments or complaints form is filled in. The worker can also help the service user and their family members complete the form.

WHY DO PEOPLE COMPLAIN?

People may complain for a variety of reasons including:

- They are not receiving a service to which they feel they are entitled.

- The service they are receiving is not what they expected it to be.

- The service they have the right to access is inaccessible to them.

- They feel they have been treated unfairly or without sufficient respect.

- They have not been informed about their rights.

- They are or feel unsafe.

- They feel that the duty of care of an individual or a service is not being met.

KEY PRINCIPLES IN RESPONDING EFFECTIVELY TO COMPLAINTS

- *Provide information.* People should be informed about what the service's procedure on complaints says, both when they begin to access a service and regularly after this. People need information around what is happening to their complaint when they have made one. They also need information about their rights (eg to an advocate or other support).

- *Provide support.* As a general rule, people do not want to complain and do not 'enjoy' complaining. People do so because they feel unhappy, aggrieved or unfairly treated. Your duty of care involves respecting people and supporting them through difficult situations.

- *Provide access to advocacy.* Ensure people know about advocacy services that are available to them and explain what an advocate does if they do not know this already. People often have the right to an advocate and this can be especially useful if they are making a complaint.

- *Follow the policy and procedures of your service setting.* Use good active listening skills – people have the right to be listened to and your skills in listening effectively when a person is unhappy about an issue are critical.

- *Record the complaint* (using the appropriate paperwork).

- *Do something with the complaint.* This sounds obvious, but this is essential, as is telling somebody what you are doing, what will happen next, and who will get back to them to inform them of the outcome of their complaint (where appropriate and possible).

- *If the complaint is about another worker,* consider how you will handle this with sensitivity and take any appropriate action to make sure that managers are aware as soon as you can.

- *If the complaint is about you,* maintain your respect for the person in how you handle this information and in your future work with them.

- *Respect the person's right to confidentiality.* If someone shares their complaint with you, you should not talk to colleagues or anyone else apart from your manager(s) about it.

PROCEDURES FOR HANDLING COMPLAINTS

Although the specific policy and procedure around complaints will be individual to each agency, service or employer, there are a few common elements to effective complaints procedures. Usually, a complaints procedure has three or four stages:

Stage 1: Informal or local resolution

The complaint is looked at by a manager who discusses with the complainant what they would like to see happen (eg an apology or a change of worker). The matter is resolved to the complainant's satisfaction and the complaint is recorded, but no formal investigation is completed.

Stage 2: A formal complaint which is handled within the service

This is where a formal investigation takes place, either by an immediate manager, or by a senior manager, or by someone who is independent from the service that is being complained about. Interviews may take place with the complainant (which is where an advocate can be extremely helpful), any witnesses and the person who is being complained about (if the complaint is about an individual). The outcome of the complaint may be shared with the complainant, as long as the confidentiality of anyone who has been complained about is respected.

Stage 3: The complaint remains unresolved

If the complainant is not satisfied with the outcome from stage 2, then the next stage may involve either:

- an independent person who is commissioned to come in and examine the complaint

- a panel of managers may look in more detail at the complaint.

Stage 4: The complaint goes to the ombudsman

Within local authority complaints procedures, the final stage is usually where the complainant asks the local authority ombudsman to look at how their complaint has been handled.

Some complaints may also be referred directly to the Care Quality Commission (CQC), in which case its procedures would be followed. Up-to-date versions of these are best found by contacting the CQC directly or researching them online.

RESEARCH

- Read your organisation's complaints procedure.

- How should you respond to a complaint?

CASE STUDY

Zakiyah is a senior domiciliary care worker. Margaret is an older woman who has a number of physical conditions which means that she requires support in daily living. Zakiyah supports her in the mornings. She helps Margaret to get out of bed and supports her with her personal care, helping her to get dressed and to get ready for the day.

Zakiyah is scheduled to visit Margaret at 9am. A different domiciliary care worker visits to help Margaret get into bed in the evening. Margaret tells Zakiyah that the times of her evening visit have been changed recently. She is now helped into bed at 6pm. Margaret feels unhappy that she is in bed for such a long time. She feels that it is unfair and she would like either her evening visit to be later or her morning visit to be earlier – in fact, she would prefer it if both were changed. She tells Zakiyah that she wants to complain about the recent change to her care, but she isn't sure what to do.

- How should Zakiyah respond?

Code of Conduct for Healthcare Support Workers and Adult Social Care Workers

The importance of responding effectively to complaints is recognised in the Code of Conduct for Healthcare Support Workers and Adult Social Care Workers, which states that you must:

- always take comments and complaints seriously
- respond to them in line with agreed ways of working and inform a senior member of staff.

CHAPTER 5
Safeguarding and protection

Safeguarding and protection are key aspects of every health and social care worker's role. Perhaps because they are so often used in the same sentence, the concepts of safeguarding and protection are often confused. Safeguarding refers to holistic practices which uphold rights and promote the safety of service users, predominantly through implementing good care practices. Protection refers to specific actions that may be taken where there are concerns about an individual being at risk of abuse.

Links to other chapters

Safeguarding the people that you provide care and support for is an integral aspect of your role. In particular this chapter links with the content of the chapters 1, 3, 4 and 7.

UNDERSTANDING ABUSE AND NEGLECT

Safeguarding is defined by the government as:

A range of activities aimed at upholding an adult's fundamental right to be safe. Being or feeling unsafe undermines our relationships and self-belief, our ability to participate freely in communities and contribute to society. Safeguarding is of particular importance to people who, because of their situation or circumstances, are unable to keep themselves safe.

(Department of Health 2010: 5)

WHAT IS ABUSE?

In 2000 the government issued 'No secrets'. This is a guidance document on the development of policies to protect adults at risk of abuse. This guidance recognised that abuse can be defined in many ways, but states that the starting point for any definition should be:

Abuse is a violation of an individual's human rights and civil rights by any other person or persons.

(Department of Health 2000: 9)

The guidance goes on to explain that abuse can:

■ be a single act or repeated acts

■ take a number of forms

■ occur when a vulnerable person is persuaded to do something that they do not (or cannot) consent to

■ occur in any relationship.

WHY DO YOU NEED TO UNDERSTAND ABUSE?

Understanding abuse and neglect is the first step in effective safeguarding practice. All health and social care workers need to develop their understanding in this area for the following main reasons:

■ Service users have a fundamental right to be free from abuse and the fear of abuse.

■ Care staff involved in intimate aspects of a person's life are in a position to identify suspicions of abuse.

■ Care staff may be part of a support package and care plan designed to monitor and reduce the risk of abuse.

- Disturbingly, much abuse actually stems from the care environment itself. Professional care workers need to be aware of, and be able to respond to, the complex reasons for this.

Media coverage of abuse tends to focus mainly on the abuse of children. Perhaps because of this and the distasteful nature of abuse, many people do not recognise the extent of abuse in the lives of vulnerable adults. The abuse of vulnerable adults tends to be a hidden and ignored problem in our society.

Key terms 🗝

Commission is where something is done by somebody who understands the implications of their act. For example, hitting someone would be an act of commission.

Omission is where something is not done (accidentally or on purpose). For example, not providing an adequate standard of care for a service user would be an act of omission.

> ### REFLECT
>
> Over the next few weeks do some research to find posters, magazine articles, news items, etc relating to abuse and neglect. Then consider how much of the news and publicity relates to the welfare/abuse or neglect of:
>
> - children
> - older people
> - other vulnerable adults
> - animals.
>
> Reflect on what you have learnt from this activity.

POWER AND ABUSE

Understanding abuse involves considering power, since power and abuse are linked in many ways:

- Abuse almost always involves a misuse of power (either deliberate or unintentional).
- Many victims of abuse are in some kind of relationship with their abuser which involves a power dynamic (eg the victim could be dependent on the abuser for basic care needs, etc).
- In their work, staff can feel powerless to deal with various issues, but they must understand that they have the power to respond effectively to abuse and suspicions of abuse.

Staff must understand that they are powerful in relation to service users. This is generally because service users are dependent on staff for the service.

Whenever a health and social care worker meets a service user, there is an immediate power relationship. In health and social care services, the power relationship is influenced by the following factors.

Power held by the service user:

- The service is meant to be for the benefit of the service user.

- The service user has the right to complain if not satisfied with the service provided.

- The service user may have other people to turn to for support (eg a family member).

- Personal qualities of the service user, eg articulate, confident, educated, etc.

The service user's perception of their own power may be undermined by:

- one or more negative experiences that have markedly reduced their confidence

- a profound sense of vulnerability due to the fact that they are dependent on the social care worker, which inhibits making complaints

- lack of knowledge of their rights

- isolation

- previous failed attempts at claiming power over their own life (learned helplessness)

- difficulties expressing themselves because of physical or mental health issues or a learning disability.

The health and social care worker may seem powerful by comparison with the service user. Possible reasons for this could include:

- The age, gender or race of the health and social care worker compared with the service user (eg a 30-year-old white woman supporting a black woman in her seventies).

- The worker has a role or a job to do. This sense is heightened if the worker presents as busy, with lots to do.

- The care tasks are one way – the service user needs care support, not the worker. The worker knows lots about the service user, etc.

- The worker is one of a team and has the power to influence the viewpoint of team colleagues through recording or team discussion.

It is vital to understand the links between power and abuse in order to work effectively to both recognise and prevent abuse. One very effective method of abuse prevention is to empower service users.

EMPOWERMENT

Empowerment is a developed concept. It requires an acknowledgement of how disempowered service users can be. To enable the service user to feel truly empowered, the service user needs to be supported on to a platform (or springboard) from which they can move. Empowering practice involves:

- recognising power differentials
- listening and hearing
- seeing people as experts on their own problems
- helping service users to develop resources
- developing positive attitudes and practices
- acknowledging the dignity of risk
- encouraging hopefulness
- facilitating user involvement
- implementing active support.

REFLECT

Consider the power that you have in your relationships with service users in your work setting.

- How do you acknowledge power differentials in these relationships with people?
- How would you put the features of empowering practice into effect with people in your own work?

TYPES OF ABUSE

Abuse is often divided into different forms or types. It is important to recognise that while understanding abuse in terms of the different forms it may take can be useful, people may experience more than one type of abuse at a time. For example, physical abuse is often accompanied by threats and abusive comments which means that the person is not only physically but also emotionally abused.

Abuse can be categorised into the following forms:

- physical abuse (which can include self-harm)
- sexual abuse
- emotional/psychological abuse

- financial abuse
- institutional abuse
- neglect (either by self or by others).

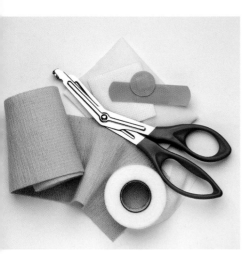

PHYSICAL ABUSE

Physical abuse includes any action that causes or is intended to cause physical harm to another, eg kicking, punching, pushing, slapping, scalding, burning, biting, etc. Most physical abuse would come within the remit of criminal law. However, particularly when dealing with vulnerable people, 'rough handling' and deliberately poor administration of care tasks (such as lack of physical sensitivity when handling dressings, catheters, etc, and lack of sensitivity and concern when helping someone to eat etc) would also constitute physical abuse.

EXAMPLE

Mary has been caring for her mother Elsie for some time and is finding this increasingly stressful. Elsie is becoming more confused and has a tendency to repeat the same questions again and again. Mary has become increasingly irritated by Elsie's repetition and when she was particularly stressed she hit Elsie.

Signs of physical abuse may include:

- various injuries which may not tally with the explanation given
- repeated injuries
- explanations for injuries that change over time, or are over-elaborate
- physical evidence of injuries, bruises, etc which have been acquired at different points in time
- injuries such as cigarette burns, finger tip bruising or bites
- inappropriate clothing intended to cover injuries
- unwillingness to undress or show parts of the body where there may be injury
- reaction to a particular person or people of a particular gender, etc.
- changes in appetite and weight
- anxiety
- agitation
- distress/tearfulness.

Isabella is a senior care assistant in a respite care service that provides short-term stays for adults with learning and physical disabilities. One day she is supporting Eldoran to have a bath. Isabella notices that Eldoran has a number of bruises but is unable to ask her what has happened because Eldoran has a severe learning disability and very limited verbal communication.

- Should Isabella be concerned? Why?

- What should Isabella do?

SEXUAL ABUSE

Sexual abuse includes any sexual act carried out against a person's wishes or when that person is unable to consent. This would include rape, touching sexual parts of the body, inserting objects into sexual organs, forcing the person to perform sexual acts, filming or photographing a person against their will for sexual purposes.

Sexual abuse can be categorised into two groups:

- *Non-contact sexual abuse*, which can include any sexual abuse where physical contact does not take place. Examples include sexual harassment, teasing, the taking of photos, the showing of pornography against a person's will.

- *Contact sexual abuse*, which is abuse where physical contact takes place. Examples include touching of the breast, genitals, mouth, etc; masturbation of one or both persons; and penetration of the mouth, vagina or anus by a penis or other object.

EXAMPLE

- Simon forces Joanne who has a learning disability to look at pornographic images on his phone.

- Mrs Wegierska was widowed several years ago. She moved into a residential service shortly after the first signs of confusion were noticed. In the service is another resident Mr Astbury. Mrs Wegierska has been calling Mr Astbury her husband. Recently, Mr Astbury has been taking Mrs Wegierska into his bedroom and having sex with her. Mrs Wegierska thinks Mr Astbury is her husband. She is not able to consent to this contact.

Signs of sexual abuse may include:

- injuries to genital areas or breasts that do not tally with explanations given
- repeated injury to the above
- repeated urinary or genital infections
- ripped or damaged clothing
- unexplained injury or bleeding from anus or genitals
- unexplained discomfort or unwillingness to urinate or defecate
- overly sexualised behaviour
- sexually explicit drawings/artwork
- sudden or unexpected changes in behaviour
- avoidance of a certain person/people
- low self-esteem
- difficulties in relationships
- changes in eating patterns
- hints/comments.

CASE STUDY

Chen is a senior care assistant in a residential service for older people. Chen has recently supported Mrs Clark as she has moved into the residential home where he works. Mrs Clark has dementia. She has been widowed for a number of years. Mr Dilkes has lived in the home for sometime. Mrs Clark has started to call Mr Dilkes 'Tom' (Chen is aware that this was Mrs Clark's husband's name). Mr Dilkes responds to Mrs Clark when she calls him this. Chen sees Mrs Clark going into Mr Dilkes's bedroom with Mr Dilkes.

- Should Chen be concerned? Why?
- What should Chen do?

EMOTIONAL/PSYCHOLOGICAL ABUSE

This includes the use of words and actions as weapons against a vulnerable adult that does not necessarily encompass physical harm. Examples of emotional abuse include racist or sexist taunts and discrimination, shouting, abusive language, belittling, mocking, threatening and bullying.

Emotional abuse can also include removing sources of comfort and reassurance, encouraging disruption and unhappiness in a person's life or preventing participation in activities that are important to social and emotional well-being.

When someone is subjected to physical or sexual abuse or to neglect, there are always elements of emotional abuse inherent within this treatment.

EXAMPLE

Ralph has a diagnosis of schizophrenia. He lives independently on a local housing estate. Other residents on the estate call him 'mad' and 'mental' and cross the road when they see him.

Signs of emotional abuse may include:

- anxiety
- sleeplessness
- reluctance to get up
- withdrawal and self-isolation
- anger
- distress/tearfulness
- fears and phobias
- low self-esteem
- comforting behaviour such as rocking
- weight loss or gain
- anti-social/destructive behaviour
- sudden changes in behaviour.

FINANCIAL ABUSE

This includes all issues around the misuse of finances, property or belongings of a person, including:

- robbery and fraud
- spending of allowances or savings of a person against their will or without their knowledge or informed consent
- misleading people about how money will be spent or the relevance of expenditure

- disposing of property against a person's will or without a person's knowledge

- displacing a person from their property.

EXAMPLE

Shortly before Christmas, Lena, a care assistant, agrees to go shopping for several residents to get their Christmas presents. She buys cheap presents for the residents and uses some of their money to do her own shopping.

Indications of financial abuse may include:

- sudden, unexplained withdrawals from savings accounts

- lack of finances to pay bills

- unexplained arrears or debts

- possessions going missing or being sold

- sudden and unexplained change in lifestyle

- unusual interest by another in the individual's finances.

CASE STUDY

Zakiyah is a senior domiciliary care worker. She has been working with Mrs Connor for some time. Recently, a young man has started to visit Mrs Connor. She tells Zakiyah that he is her nephew and says she is delighted that he has started visiting. Zakiyah notices that Mrs Connor seems short of money all the time, but she never had problems before her nephew started visiting.

- Should Zakiyah be concerned? Why?

- What should Zakiyah do?

INSTITUTIONAL ABUSE

Any of the types of abuse described can and do occur within institutions. However, institutional abuse itself refers to the abusive practices and behaviours that can occur on a widespread basis within an institution and that are considered 'acceptable'. Examples of institutional abuse include:

- uniform treatment of all service users

- possessions and clothes being used by anyone in the service

- service users being forced to follow routines that benefit the service and not the service user, eg setting bedtimes

- expectations that staff can impose punishments or 'withhold privileges'.

Monica (a care assistant) has already assisted Mr Patel to have a shave using his electric razor and he has gone to have his breakfast. Monica then goes to support first Mr Mathers and then Mr Gardner. Monica takes Mr Patel's electric razor and shaves both men before putting it back in Mr Patel's room. This is common practice in the service as it saves time.

Signs of institutional abuse can be considered in two different areas, as shown in the table below.

Signs of institutional abuse

Signs in the individual	Signs in the environment
Anxiety	Rigid routines and practices
Loss of confidence	People have a lack of choice
Submissiveness	Dignity is not upheld
Low self-esteem	Service is run to meet the needs of staff rather than service users
Weight loss, changes in appetite, etc	Poor standards of care
Difficulty in or anxiety about making independent decisions	Family members and friends have restricted visiting access
	Misuse of medication, eg medication used to sedate people so that staff have a 'quiet shift'

NEGLECT

Neglect can be divided into two types – direct and indirect.

Direct neglect is when a person knowingly and deliberately withholds something which should meet a person's essential needs.

Indirect neglect is where the perpetrator does not actively mean to cause harm, but is neglectful for other reasons. Indirect (or unintentional neglect) could be due to a person having a lack of information about the implications of their actions, or a lack of awareness about alternative means of addressing an issue.

Neglect can be carried out by the person themselves or by another person.

SELF-NEGLECT

Self-neglect describes a situation where a service user neglects themselves. They may do so on purpose or accidentally.

Self-neglect and active abuse are very closely linked. For example, research indicates that almost a half of all cases of active abuse also involve the service user self-neglecting and in cases where the service user is neglected by carers or staff teams almost two-thirds of the service users also self-neglect.

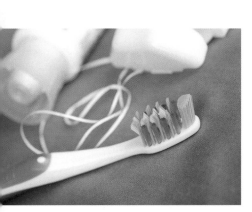

A whole range of behaviours constitute self-neglect, including:

- not eating adequately

- not attending to personal hygiene tasks (such as not using the toilet appropriately, not bathing or washing)

- not changing clothing

- not taking medication

- not engaging with health care provision or not cooperating with health treatment, etc.

Why does self-neglect occur?

There are many reasons that people neglect themselves, including:

- depression (people see no point in caring for themselves)

- low self-esteem (people can have a poor view of themselves and therefore see no reason to care for themselves)

- lack of motivation (people may have little to look forward to)

- abuse (self-neglect may be a sign that a person has been abused)

- control (if people have little control over their lives they may only be able to control their food intake, their personal hygiene, etc and may therefore choose to exert their control by not caring for themselves)

- mental health problems at that time

- confusion (possibly a temporary state) or dementia

- living alone and being isolated

- having alcohol or drug problems
- decreased physical abilities due to general or specific health issues resulting in a loss of motivation.

There are many dilemmas surrounding self-neglect. Since people have a right to make choices, care staff may allow a person to neglect themselves. However, staff have their 'duty of care' to consider and therefore need to address self-neglect. Where there are concerns of self-neglect, staff should discuss these as soon as possible with their line manager and strategies will need to be devised to deal with the neglect.

EXAMPLE

Daisy's husband died recently and she has only very infrequent contact with her grown-up children. Daisy has stopped taking care of herself and her home. She doesn't have any food in the house and hasn't eaten for several days. She does not get dressed most days and often does not even get out of bed.

NEGLECT BY OTHERS

Neglect by others involves situations where people fail to attend to the key needs of people who are dependent upon their support.

EXAMPLE

Fred is becoming doubly incontinent at night. His daughter feels that this is avoidable. To try to manage the situation, she refuses to give Fred anything to eat or drink from 4pm until the following morning.

Signs of neglect

The signs of neglect will be very similar whether the neglect is self-neglect or neglect by others. They could include:

- anxiety
- physical appearance of neglect and unkemptness
- weight loss
- increased susceptibility to illness due to lack of warmth or nutrition
- submissiveness/lack of confidence
- low self-esteem
- unsanitary living conditions.

> **REFLECT**
>
> How would you define the following forms of abuse:
>
> - physical abuse
> - sexual abuse
> - emotional/psychological abuse
> - financial abuse
> - institutional abuse
> - self-neglect
> - neglect by others?
>
> What are the key signs and symptoms of each of the forms of abuse?

THE SIGNS AND SYMPTOMS OF ABUSE

In detailing the different types of abuse, we have indicated what signs and symptoms there may be. However, it is important to remember the following when considering the potential signs of abuse.

- Particular signs are not necessarily indicative of a particular form of abuse (as discussed in this chapter, there is a great deal of crossover in terms of the signs and symptoms of abuse).

- There may be other explanations for the symptoms. It is important not to jump to the conclusion that just because someone is displaying some of the symptoms of abuse that they have been abused. However, it is also important not to miss issues that could be indicators of abuse.

WHO IS VULNERABLE TO ABUSE?

The short answer to this question is – everyone. But, of course, there is much more complexity to the answer than this. Media coverage of abuse tends to focus mainly on the abuse of children, although in recent years there have been some high-profile issues around the abuse of adults. It is vital to remember that adults are also open to abuse, with some people being more at risk than others.

The government's document 'No secrets' refers to a vulnerable adult as a person:

who is or may be in need of community care services by reason of mental or other disability, age or illness; and who is or may be unable to take care of him or herself, or unable to protect him or herself against significant harm or exploitation.

(Department of Health 2000: 8–9)

In 2009 the government carried out a review of 'No secrets' which involved 12,000 people. Ninety per cent of the respondents felt that the definition of a 'vulnerable adult' needed to be revised and there was a great deal of support for replacing the term 'vulnerable adult' with 'person at risk'. This same review made clear that some adults are more at risk of abuse than others.

'Safeguarding adults' published by the Association of Directors of Social Services in October 2005 identifies six aspects of people's lives that may indicate that they are more at risk of abuse:

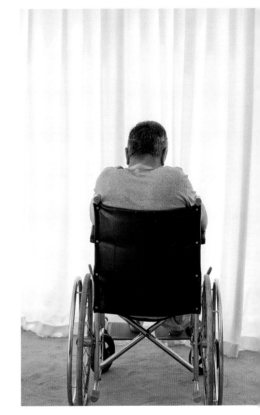

1 *Social isolation and lack of inclusion.* In general, the more social contacts that an individual has the more likely it is that others will notice if something is wrong. For example, if a person does not attend college, other students on the course may notice that he or she is missing, as might the friends of someone who usually joins in a lunch club or similar activity. Being a member of a social network whether at work, in leisure activities or as a member of a church congregation will make that person a little more noticeable and increase the possibility that someone will notice if the person is not their usual self.

2 *Dependency on others for essential needs.* This can include those who require support with shopping, personal care, finances and mobility and therefore includes the majority of those who make use of health and social care services. Paid support staff are sometimes the only people in the lives of service users and although most staff working in the health and social care field are well intentioned, there are others who may take the opportunity to abuse their privileged access.

3 *Poor-quality policies and information.* Inadequate policies and procedures can leave individuals unsure about what to do if they are the victims of abuse or suspect that it is occurring to others. This can result in a time delay before action is taken and, in the worst scenario, to nothing being done to protect the person. One of the most shocking aspects of dealing with abuse is that serial abusers will deliberately seek out organisations which they see as not having strong policies and procedures to protect adults at risk.

4 *Low standards becoming the norm.* This has happened historically in institutional services for people with learning disabilities, mental health problems and some services for older people, and occurs where people lose sight of what they should regard as acceptable and what they would not tolerate for themselves and their loved ones. Accepting low standards as the norm can happen where the setting is geographically or socially isolated as was the case with long-stay hospitals. However, it can also be the case where resources are under strain, where there are staff shortages or where training has not been adequate.

5 *Domestic abuse being seen as the norm.* Health and social care workers may provide services to individuals in homes which they share with their families and they may become aware of concerns around domestic abuse. As more services are provided to people in their own homes, health and social care workers may become more aware of behaviour within the home such as bullying. This behaviour may have become accepted within the family, but it would be unacceptable within any other setting. It remains unacceptable in the home too and should be confronted as it would elsewhere. Government documents on domestic violence make the point that violent, brutal or threatening behaviour within the home is as serious as a violent assault by a stranger.

6 *An unhealthy power balance.* Health and social care workers are in a position of significant power over people who use services. Where there is a lack of understanding of power or a deliberate misuse of this power, there is likely to be an abuse of power.

Some other factors that can also increase people's vulnerability are outlined below.

LOSS AND CHANGE

People may also be particularly at risk of abuse at certain stages of their lives because of the impact of loss or change, such as:

- the onset of mental health problems
- acquiring a disability
- increasing frailty due to the ageing process
- inability of family members to continue to provide care for the person.

LOW SELF-ESTEEM

Self-esteem is really the way in which we view ourselves. Where a person is described as having a low self-esteem or a poor self-image it basically means they 'feel bad' about themselves. Where someone has a 'healthy' self-esteem it means that they are confident and 'feel good' about themselves. Even though self-esteem is about our psychological well-being it can have a profound effect on our physical health.

It is important that care staff support service users to feel good about themselves. People in receipt of care and support are more likely to have a poor self-image and self-esteem, and they may feel dependent and even worthless. Negative feelings like these will then have a negative effect on a person's health and well-being. It will also leave people much more at risk of abuse and self-harm.

COMMUNICATION DIFFERENCES

Where there are significant challenges in terms of communication differences the risks of abuse increase. For example, a person with limited or no verbal communication may be especially vulnerable to abuse, not least because they may lack the means to disclose the abuse. This reinforces the need to listen to more than words and to develop effective methods of communication wherever there are differences in communication.

> ## REFLECT
>
> - In your work setting, what factors mean that individuals are more vulnerable to abuse?
>
> - How do you and your service attempt to support individuals through periods of particular stress (eg loss and change), and how do you meet individual communication needs in order to keep people safe?

RESPONDING TO SUSPECTED OR ALLEGED ABUSE

If care staff understand the nature of danger, harm and abuse, and why it can occur then the likelihood of it occurring is minimised. Likewise, if service users, carers and the general public are more informed about danger, harm and abuse, they will be more aware and risks will be reduced. However, abuse will still occur even with the best prevention strategies in place and health and social care staff need to know what to do where they suspect abuse is taking place.

HOW DO I KNOW THAT ABUSE IS OCCURRING?

Sometimes you will know that abuse is happening because someone will tell you that it is – or rarely because you actually see it happening. However, most of the time you will suspect that abuse is happening because you become aware that a person's behaviour is changing or you notice issues of concern occurring over a period of time. A service user may say things that appear out of place or their behaviour may change in a way that raises concern. The main skill lies in not jumping to a conclusion about whether abuse has occurred or not, but in 'listening' fully to what the person is communicating. However, it is equally important to recognise these signs as potential indicators of abuse.

KEY POINT

The worst thing you can do is to ignore the possibility that something could be the sign of abuse.

DISCLOSURES OF ABUSE

A significant amount of abuse is discovered because the victim declares that it is happening – often to someone they trust. A disclosure can take any of the following forms:

- *Full disclosure.* This is where the victim tells a person directly that they are being abused. A full disclosure may be totally unexpected and so may come as a real surprise.

- *Partial disclosure.* This is where the victim hints to a person that they are being abused. However, they may change the subject quickly and may seem reluctant to give details.

- *Indirect disclosure.* This is where the victim talks about abuse in a general sense or with regard to someone else. They may be looking for the person's response, and trying to find out how they would respond if the victim declared the abuse that they were experiencing.

RESPONDING TO DISCLOSURES OF ABUSE

When a person discloses abuse, it is important that a health and social care worker passes this information to their line manager or the senior member of staff on duty immediately. It is also important to record accurately what the person said.

Any disclosure should be followed up with an investigation – these are almost always multi-agency. Investigations should never be undertaken by individual care staff. The way that the disclosure is handled and the recording and reporting of the disclosure will be vital in terms of the progress of any investigation.

Sensitive interpersonal skills are required in order to support a person who discloses abuse (ie says that they are being abused). These skills include:

- believing the person
- showing concern
- listening effectively.

Dos and don'ts of disclosures

If abuse is disclosed to you ...

You must:	You must not:
Listen	Ask any 'leading' questions
Believe	Appear shocked, horrified, disgusted, etc
Stay calm	Pressurise the person
Allow the person to talk	Ignore what you have been told
Reassure the person that they are doing the right thing by telling someone	Promise to keep what you have been told a secret
Tell the person that you believe them	Put opinions in your recording
Tell the person that you need to pass this information on	Pass judgement on either the victim or the abuser
Record accurately the date, time and place of the disclosure and what was said (using the person's own words as far as possible)	Confront the alleged abuser
Report the disclosure to your manager immediately	

RECORDING DISCLOSURES

If someone has disclosed abuse or the possibility of abuse, it is very important that a clear and accurate record is made of the disclosure. Making a note at the time will probably distract from the work of supporting the person and he or she may find this off-putting, but this must be done at the first possible opportunity.

If anyone who is involved with a disclosure is making notes for their own records, they must bear in mind that these may be needed for any subsequent investigation or for a court case. Any rough notes made at the time must therefore be placed in the service user's file.

Records should contain:

- the date, time and where the person disclosed the information
- the date, time and place of the alleged incident disclosed by the person or witness
- the name of anyone else who was there when the alleged incident took place or anyone else who was present when the person disclosed the information
- what the person said in his or her own words
- any other information that is relevant to record without going into unnecessary detail.

CASE STUDY

Jane is a senior support worker in a day service for people with learning disabilities. Morten attends the day service where Jane works. Morten has a learning disability and lives at home with his mother. Jane knows that Morten enjoys swimming so she arranges for him to go swimming with a small group from the day service. Morten isn't able to go on the organised sessions to the pool as he never has any money with him. Morten tells Jane that his mum told him he can't have any money because she needs it all. He says that they have lots of rows about this and sometimes his mum hits him.

- Is this a disclosure of abuse?
- What kind of disclosure is this?
- Why might Morten have decided to disclose now?
- What should Jane do? Why?

SUSPICIONS OF ABUSE

Often people do not disclose abuse for a variety of reasons, including:

- fear of the abuser

- fear of not being believed

- communication barriers

- feelings of guilt

- confusion.

This means that health and social care workers need to be alert to the possibilities of abuse and need to be aware of the signs and symptoms of abuse.

Where there are suspicions of abuse, it may feel like there are various pieces of a jigsaw that need to be put together to get a clear picture. Sometimes different people hold different pieces of the jigsaw, which can make it more difficult to put the pieces together.

Often workers in health and social care will have a significant amount of contact and time with the people who use a service. This gives workers the opportunity to:

- observe any changes (eg in a person's appearance, behaviour or responses to situations)

- spend time talking with people and building up trust (which is what enables people to disclose when abuse has occurred to them)

- observe changes in the presentation and behaviour of others (eg a person's relatives, friends or your own colleagues)

- reflect in supervision and discussions with managers (and other agencies) on these sorts of changes in order to put together any pieces of a 'safeguarding jigsaw'. Sometimes workers may have suspicions and no direct disclosure of abuse occurs, but by putting all of the pieces of information and observation together, a real need for action can be identified.

POTENTIAL INDICATORS OF ABUSE

Physical signs may include:

- injuries
- pain
- unexplained accidents
- infections.

Emotional signs may include:

- distress
- tearfulness
- anxiety
- fear
- agitation
- lack of self-worth
- low self-esteem
- compliance
- anger.

Health-related signs may include:

- changes in appetite and weight
- deterioration in health
- sleep disturbance.

Behavioural signs may include:

- any sudden changes in behaviour
- comfort behaviours such as rocking
- unusual responses to individuals or people of a particular gender, etc
- wetting/soiling.

Environmental signs may include:

- rigid routines
- lack of choice
- staff demonstrating little concern for service user's dignity.

Other signs can include aspects such as:

- sudden lack of funds
- loss of possessions
- changes in communication
- hints or full disclosure.

Always remember that just because a person is displaying one or more of the signs of abuse it does not automatically mean that they are being abused.

SUSPECTED ABUSE

Where you suspect that someone is being abused, there are a number of things you should do. Your priorities should be to:

1 ensure that the person is safe

2 preserve any evidence

3 record and report it as soon as possible

4 follow up by ensuring that a referral has been made.

Ensuring the person is safe

A person's immediate safety is the first concern when there are actions to be taken around keeping them safe. The key questions to ask are:

- If the person is due to be leaving the service today, when is this taking place, where are they going and will they be safe?

- If the answer is 'no', and the concern is around a risk in the place they are going to, discuss this with your managers, and stay with the person until an agreement can be made around where it is safe for them to go.

- If the person is not due to be leaving today (and potentially, the concern or risk to them is within your service setting), ensure someone is with them and agree with your manager how their immediate need for safety will be met.

- In any scenario, your duty of care means you cannot leave issues of immediate safety without full consideration and you cannot leave the person until you know that:

    - they will be safe when you do leave them

    - the issue that has been raised is being dealt with

    - there is support for the person after you have left them.

Health care emergencies where abuse is suspected

Should the individual be injured or unwell as a result of the incident you should:

- give the person first aid treatment but remember to inform the emergency services what you have done

- call an ambulance

- notify the police who will arrange for a police surgeon to examine the person

- follow organisational procedure and the policy for the local authority area.

Preserving evidence

Preserving evidence in the case of immediate reporting to the police

If a criminal offence such as assault or a sexual offence has been committed, the police will need to be notified. Who should do this will be indicated in local procedure.

The person concerned is likely to be very distressed and may well want to have a bath or shower for reasons of cleanliness and because they feel 'dirty'. The worker will need to reassure the person and comfort them until the police arrive. The worker will need to explain to the person what will be happening as far as they are able to, which may not be easy, particularly if the person is distressed by the fact that the police are involved. Similarly, the person may wish to change their clothes, but this must not take place until the police have arrived. Some people may be unhappy and distressed about police involvement as it may heighten any fears they may have about events spiralling out of their control and it may also prompt fears of retribution by the abuser.

It is also important to ensure that the person is not given anything to drink until the police arrive as they may wish to take a swab from the person's mouth.

The scene of the incident should also not be disturbed. Do not strip the bed, wash bedclothes or disturb any items in the room. Do not allow anyone else to go into the room until the police arrive.

If there are any tissues, condoms or other material contaminated by blood, semen or other body fluids, either leave these in situ, or if this is not practical, put them in a clean envelope or glass.

Ensure that the person who has disclosed the possible abuse and the alleged abuser are apart and under no circumstances have one worker supporting both people.

CASE STUDY

Taju is a senior support worker with a mental health charity. Taju is due to visit Sophie at home as part of his outreach work. When he arrives at Sophie's home, she is in a dressing gown and has clearly just had a shower. Taju notices that the room is a mess, with clothes on the floor and a lamp tipped over – Sophie is normally very tidy. Sophie starts crying and tells Taju that she invited a man back to her flat last night. He wanted to have sex but Sophie asked him to leave. Sophie says that then 'something terrible' happened.

- What should Taju do?
- Why?

Preventing 'contamination' of an investigation and any potential evidence

Where an individual discloses abuse health and social care workers need to think about not 'contaminating' evidence or hindering the investigation process. A worker should not stop someone recalling events but they also need to keep in mind that it will be someone else's role – possibly the police – to investigate and find out more information. To pursue too much detail at this stage risks compromising any subsequent investigation and could mean that the person could be needlessly distressed by being asked the same questions again.

The health and social care worker will need to ensure that emotional and practical support is provided to the individual who may have been the victim of the alleged abuse. They need to ensure that the organisation's procedures on dealing with abuse and their local authority's guidelines on protecting vulnerable adults are followed, and that the appropriate personnel are notified according to your procedures.

Preventing contamination of evidence is a key issue for health and social care workers. For example, if a health and social care worker suspects that abuse has been taking place and they ask a **leading question** the potential evidence will be contaminated. So, if a health and social care worker asked something such as, 'He kicked you, didn't he?' or later say something like, 'You're acting like this because of the abuse, aren't you?', this would make anything the service user said inadmissible in court. For this reason, careful recording and reporting is critical.

Key term

Leading question is a question that gives the person being asked a clear indication about the expected answer, eg 'He hit you, didn't he?

Recording suspicions

Recording potential signs and symptoms is important as these can help build a picture to aid in the detection of abuse. Any investigation of abuse will involve a consideration of any relevant recording. Indeed, records can be used as evidence in legal proceedings, investigations and inspections.

It is important that all records follow principles of good recording (see Chapter 7 on handling information), but it is even more important where there may be concerns about abuse.

Principles of recording

- Recording should be in black ink.

- Recording should be legible. It doesn't matter what the quality of the information is if it cannot be easily read by others. If your handwriting is poor, slow down when you write; it may well help.

- If you make a mistake, do not use correction fluid. Cross out your mistake with a single line ensuring that what you wrote can still be read. Initial the error. This is important because if the records are required, for whatever purpose in the future, it is clear that they have not be falsified.

- Always attribute the source of the information being recorded. For example, if a service user's relative told you something make this clear in the records, eg 'Soriya's mother said that Soriya fell down and had a nosebleed yesterday', rather than 'Soriya fell and had a nosebleed yesterday'.

- Recording should be contemporaneous – ie completed at the time and not several days later.

- Records should be dated, timed and signed by the person completing the record.

- All documentation should be objective. It should not contain information about your feelings, thoughts, instincts or assumptions.

- Documentation should be fact based.

- Judgemental language must be avoided.

If you have concerns about abuse or someone has made a disclosure to you about abuse, it is vital that the recording you complete follows these guidelines. If you are unsure, ask a senior worker or your manager to support you as you complete the record. Remember though that good recording should be usual practice.

EXAMPLE

Rose is a support worker in a residential service providing day care places for older people. Rose is a key worker to an older Asian woman named Mrs Asma Kahtun. Asma attends the service with her arm in plaster. Rose asks how she has obtained this injury. Asma tells her, hesitantly, that she fainted at home and fell over. Rose is suspicious and observes that Asma appears particularly anxious and unhappy.

When Asma's husband arrives to collect her, Rose enquires again about how Asma obtained the injury. Asma's husband informs Rose that his wife fell when she was out. When Rose challenges him about this, he becomes annoyed and refuses to answer any more questions. He informs his wife that they will leave immediately.

Rose provides a written report on this incident to her manager. It reads as follows:

11 February 2013

Asma Kahtun attended the service today with a broken arm. Her husband may have inflicted this injury, as he acted in an extremely suspicious manner. It is to be noted that the family are strict Muslims, Asma is very docile and her husband does not like to answer too many questions!

EXAMPLE (CONTINUED)

The report by Rose is making assumptions; it is not reporting the facts in an objective manner. The report also demonstrates some underlying racist and sexist beliefs. This report could also be considered libellous – it is not up to Rose to decide upon the guilt of anyone. A more accurate report about this incident would read:

11 February 2013

Asma Kahtun attended today with a broken arm. I asked her how she had obtained this injury. Asma said that she had fainted and fallen over in the house.

I asked Asma's husband how his wife had acquired the injury. He said that his wife had fallen when she was out.

I also observed that Asma seemed anxious today. She did not wish to participate in activities and kept pacing up and down. This behaviour is uncharacteristic.

Asking about injuries is a sensitive subject and tact is always required. Direct confrontation antagonised Asma's husband and did not encourage a constructive working relationship. The investigation of suspected abuse is beyond the role of individual workers.

Reporting to your line manager

Responding to suspicions of abuse quickly is very important. As soon as you suspect that abuse is occurring you must report this to your line manager and get guidance on what to do next.

You should report any suspicions or concerns to your line manager immediately. If your manager is on leave or 'off shift', you must pass the information to whomever is responsible in their absence. DO NOT wait for your manager's return.

In reporting to your manager you need to:

- keep the information factual

- tell your manager whether you have recorded any relevant information yet and where this is to be found

- ask your manager for guidance and ask them what will happen next.

THE NATIONAL AND LOCAL CONTEXT OF SAFEGUARDING AND PROTECTION FROM ABUSE

UNDERSTANDING THE LEGAL CONTEXT

There is a clear and extensive legal framework surrounding child protection. However, the legal basis for safeguarding adults from abuse is much less developed.

The picture is very different across the United Kingdom. Scotland is furthest ahead since it passed the Adult Support and Protection Act in 2007. This placed adult protection on a statutory basis. In England and Wales, the picture is much more patchy, where there is statutory guidance on the development and implementation of policies and procedures for the protection of adults at risk of abuse. In England this is called 'No secrets' and was published by the Department of Health and the Home Office in 2000. The Welsh guidance was published by the Welsh Assembly and the Home Office in the same year and is called 'In safe hands'.

'NO SECRETS: GUIDANCE ON DEVELOPING AND IMPLEMENTING MULTI-AGENCY POLICIES AND PROCEDURES TO PROTECT VULNERABLE ADULTS FROM ABUSE' (2000)

This is guidance issued by the Department of Health and as such it does not have the full force of statute law. It is important for all health and social care staff to be aware that the government wants all agencies to take it seriously and to respond as fully as possible to situations where vulnerable adults are being abused.

In 'No secrets', the Department of Health makes clear its expectations for individual providers of care to minimise the risk of abuse by:

- rigorous recruitment practices
- requiring written references
- ensuring that all volunteers are subject to the same checks as paid staff.

Provider services are also to have in place guidelines detailing staff responsibilities and how they should respond to concerns about any abuse of a vulnerable adult. These guidelines are to link into, and be consistent with, the local multi-agency policy (bringing together social services, police, health services and provider services).

Provider services are also expected to ensure that service users, carers and the general public have accessible information detailing what abuse is, how they can raise concerns and/or make a complaint.

'STATEMENT OF GOVERNMENT POLICY ON ADULT SAFEGUARDING' (2011)

This document sets out the government's policy on safeguarding vulnerable adults. It includes a statement of principles for use by local authority social services and housing, health care, the police and other agencies for both developing and assessing the effectiveness of their local safeguarding arrangements.

This is a very useful document setting out the key principles for organisations to benchmark their existing arrangements to see how they support this aim and to measure future improvements. A series of outcomes are set out as a starting point for assessing progress and the basis for locally agreed outcomes.

SAFEGUARDING ADULTS BOARDS

As a result of the 'No secrets' guidance, local areas have developed safeguarding adults boards. At the time of writing, the government announced plans to make these boards statutory.

Safeguarding adults boards generally include membership from local agencies engaged in health and social care, community groups and people who use services and carers. The Social Care Institute for Excellence (2011: 20) states that safeguarding adults boards have a strategic role to:

- determine safeguarding policy

- oversee development and implementation of procedures

- raise public awareness

- ensure staff are trained

- monitor performance

- improve the quality of safeguarding practice.

THE 'NO SECRETS' REVIEW

In 2009 the government reviewed 'No secrets'. The review involved 12,000 people and more than 68% of these supported bringing in safeguarding legislation. However, there were also arguments against legislation for safeguarding adults, including:

- Much has been achieved in adult safeguarding without legislation and improvements are felt to be likely to continue.

- Legislation will not necessarily lead to adult safeguarding becoming a priority.

- The experience in Scotland should be studied over some years before conclusions are drawn.

- Some of the possible new legislative powers would extend the government's power over people's lives in a dangerous way.

- The most effective safeguarding was when it became part of mainstream activity and was effectively part of the choice agenda.

(Department of Health 2009a: 7)

The four key messages from the review of 'No secrets':

1 Safeguarding must be built on empowerment – or listening to the victim's voice. Without this, safeguarding is experienced as safety at the expense of other qualities of life, such as self-determination and the right to family life.

2 Everyone must help to empower individuals but safeguarding decisions should be taken by the individual concerned. People wanted help with options, information and support. However, they wanted to retain control and make their own choices.

3 Safeguarding adults is not like child protection. Adults do not want to be treated like children and do not want a system that was designed for children.

4 The participation/representation of people who lack capacity is also important.

(Department of Health 2009a: 6)

The Law Commission's review of adult social care law found that the existing framework for adult protection 'is neither systematic nor coordinated, reflecting the sporadic development of safeguarding policy over the last 25 years' (Commission for Social Care Inspection 2008: 3).

What this means is that in England and Wales a kind of patchwork quilt of legislation exists – in that there is a great deal of legislation that relates to safeguarding adults from abuse. Some of the key legislation is outlined in the following table.

Legislation	What it covers
Family Law Act 1996	Makes arrangements for non-molestation orders to protect people from domestic abuse.
Youth Justice and Criminal Evidence Act 1999	Provides for special measures to be taken to support vulnerable people who are victims or witnesses to an offence.
Health and Social Care (Community Health and Standards) Act 2003	Although many of the provisions of this Act have been changed by the Health and Social Care Act 2008, Section 114 of the Act remains in place. This gave the government powers to issue and enforce regulations about the provision of complaints procedures in health and social care services.
Sexual Offences Act 2003	Defines 'consent' to a sexual act and outlines sexual offences clearly. Protects service users with a mental health problem or a learning disability from sexual exploitation by staff.
Domestic Violence, Crime and Victims Act 2004	Makes it an offence to cause or allow the death of a vulnerable adult.
Mental Capacity Act 2005	This introduced a new offence of ill treatment or wilful neglect by any person who has the care of another person who lacks capacity or who the offender believes to lack capacity. A number of health and social care staff have been charged and imprisoned for this offence. Includes deprivation of liberty safeguards.
Fraud Act 2006	Created an offence to abuse a position of trust; can be used in situations of financial abuse.
Safeguarding Vulnerable Groups Act 2006	This Act set up a new system of vetting people who work with children, young people and vulnerable adults.
Forced Marriage (Civil Protection) Act 2007	Provides a range of civil remedies for the victims of forced marriage.
Health and Social Care Act 2008	Introduced wide-ranging changes to the regulation of health and social care services. Established the Care Quality Commission.

This demonstrates that the legislation that surrounds safeguarding adults from abuse is very complex. Legal advice should always be sought where there are any concerns.

SERVICE-SPECIFIC POLICIES AND PROCEDURES

All organisations providing health and social care services should have a policy relating specifically to safeguarding vulnerable adults – these may be referred to as POVA (protection of vulnerable adults) policies or safeguarding procedures. Health and social care staff must ensure that they are familiar with the policies that relate to their working environment.

LOCAL AUTHORITY POLICIES AND PROCEDURES

Every local authority in England and Wales will have locally specific policies, procedures and expectations around safeguarding adults. Training will be available on these within localities, and it is vital that you know about these in order to be able to work to local protocols and best practice, and to make the local links that you may need to access in the event of a safeguarding concern.

RESEARCH

Find the specific policy about safeguarding adults in your agency.

1   What does it say about your role in safeguarding the people you work with?

2   Does it provide any information on the roles and responsibilities of other agencies and other professionals?

3   Ensure that you are clear on what the policy says about:

- what actions you should take if there are suspicions that a person is being abused
- what actions you should take if a disclosure of abuse is made
- how you should preserve evidence.

This activity will help you with your assessment task.

UNDERSTANDING ROLES AND RESPONSIBILITIES

Whenever a disclosure of abuse is made or there are suspicions that abuse is taking place, an investigation must take place. However, the responsibility for investigating situations does not lie with any one individual (even a senior manager). Alleged abuse must always be investigated in line with an agreed protocol.

Investigations will usually be multi-agency since different agencies and individuals can offer a range of skills, knowledge about a specialist area (such as the law or medicine), different knowledge about the individual concerned, and different resources and means of support. It is this combined multi-agency approach that can offer a holistic approach in both detecting abuse and in formulating a way to best support and protect the vulnerable person.

The role of individual health and social care staff is limited in the investigation of abuse. The role will be in contributing to the overall process of multi-agency investigation. Objective verbal and written communication, with vigilant regard for facts such as dates and times, will be the principal ways in which health and social care staff contribute to the investigation of alleged abuse.

YOUR RESPONSIBILITIES

Care staff responsibilities in this area can be summarised by three points (ROC):

- *Report.* Always report any disclosure or concerns to your line manager immediately.

- *Observe.* Make careful observations and record these accurately.

- *Care plan.* Be aware of a person's care plan and work to it carefully. The care plan may contain specific information about reducing the risk of abuse (eg increased observation, restriction on certain visitors, etc).

YOUR MANAGER'S RESPONSIBILITIES

A social care manager's responsibilities in relation to this area can be summarised by four points (CAMS):

- *Collate.* Managers need to collate all the information they receive from staff members and pass this on where necessary. It may be that individual staff don't have enough of the 'jigsaw', but that when the manager reviews what all staff are saying, they can recognise patterns of behaviour which may indicate abuse.

- *Advise.* Managers should keep the individual and the staff team advised about the investigation process and progress (as far as confidentiality allows), and advise staff about their roles and the limits to these.

- *Monitor.* Managers should monitor the work of staff (eg that staff are recording effectively) and observe the service user themselves, if possible, to monitor the situation fully.

- *Support.* Managers should support the individual, as well as the staff working with the individual who may also find the situation distressing.

WIDER RESPONSIBILITIES

Local authority social care services

Local authorities have a key role in safeguarding adults where there are concerns about abuse. For example they will:

- receive and manage safeguarding alerts

- coordinate adult protection investigations

- provide information and advice on safeguarding issues

- arrange and chair investigation meetings and case conferences.

Police

The police will usually be involved in investigations of abuse and will always be involved (possibly taking the lead) where a crime is suspected. Their involvement will include:

- investigations

- gathering evidence

- pursuing criminal prosecution with the Crown Prosecution Service where relevant.

Health services

Health services, particularly doctors, will have a role in providing:

- medical treatment to people where necessary

- medical evidence.

SAFEGUARDING IS EVERYONE'S CONCERN

Despite the fact that some professionals and agencies have specific tasks in relation to safeguarding people from abuse, it is vital to recognise that safeguarding is a shared concern. Everyone has a responsibility to:

- work within their organisation's safeguarding policy and procedures

- liaise with other professionals where there are safeguarding concerns

- recognise and report the signs of abuse

- provide information and advice on safeguarding issues and support services

- work safely and report any unsafe working practices.

SERIOUS FAILURES TO PROTECT INDIVIDUALS FROM ABUSE

There have been a variety of serious failures to protect people from abuse in care and support in both health and social care settings. Following such failures, inquiries are often set up to investigate the failings and to support people to 'learn the lessons' so that similar failings do not happen again.

It is a sad fact that in reviewing the reports into serious failures in health and social care over the past 20 years, many of the same issues arise again and again. This begs the question, 'When are we going to learn the lessons?'

'LESSONS FROM CHI INVESTIGATIONS 2000–2003' (2004)

Between 2000 and 2003 the Commission for Health Improvement (CHI) carried out 11 investigations into serious failures in the NHS. The report found that the following issues contributed significantly to the service failures:

- lack of effective leadership

- staff shortages

- poor induction, training and supervision

- poor team relationships

- poor incident reporting and poor recording

- poor information for service users.

ROWAN WARD INQUIRY (2003)

Following allegations of abuse on Rowan ward, a hospital ward for older people with mental health problems, the CHI's investigations concluded that:

The Rowan ward service had many of the known risk factors for abuse: a poor and institutionalised environment, low staffing levels, high use of bank and agency staff, little staff development, poor supervision, lack of knowledge of incident reporting, closed inward looking culture and weak management ...

(Commission for Health Improvement Investigations 2003: 2)

A range of recommendations were made, including:

- strengthening management and leadership
- that all staff receive training on vulnerable adult procedures
- a requirement for robust information systems
- improving multi-disciplinary working
- prioritising the continuing professional development of staff
- raising expectations in terms of basic care standards.

'SIX LIVES: THE PROVISION OF PUBLIC SERVICES TO PEOPLE WITH LEARNING DISABILITIES' (2009)

Following a request from Mencap, the Local Government Ombudsman looked into complaints from family members of six adults with learning disabilities who died while in health and social care services between 2003 and 2005. The investigation 'illustrated some significant and distressing failures in service across both health and social care'. A range of recommendations were made, including:

- People must be treated as individuals.
- Basic care must be well provided.
- Leadership needs to be improved.
- Policy, standards and guidance must be followed.
- Workers should demonstrate empathy for service users.
- Communication at all levels needs improvement.
- There needs to be improvement in partnership working and multi-agency cooperation.
- Services need to find constructive and positive ways to work with families and informal carers.
- Advocacy may provide additional support for service users and families and opportunities to work with advocates should be available.

INVESTIGATION INTO WEST LONDON MENTAL HEALTH NHS TRUST (2009)

This investigation by the Care Quality Commission was triggered by concerns about the Trust's responses to suicides within the Trust. The investigation found that:

- the Trust failed to properly investigate or report serious incidents

- the Trust did not learn from previous incidents or implement all previous recommendations

- some of the hospitals and wards were not a safe environment for care

- some wards were overcrowded

- people had limited access to primary care services

- there was a shortage of staff with high rates of sickness absence

- staff attendance at mandatory training was extremely low.

WINTERBOURNE VIEW

In late 2012, six workers from Winterbourne View, a private care home near Bristol, were jailed for abusing residents, following exposure in a BBC documentary. The Panorama programme, aired in 2011, showed people being slapped, pinned under chairs and subjected to cold showers as punishment.

The people living in the home were subjected to appalling treatment and the exposure of this led to high-profile public debate around the placement and treatment of adults with learning disabilities.

Key learning from the Serious Case Review into what happened at Winterbourne View highlights that:

- there is a very negative perception of people with learning disabilities

- the inspection of institutional care and the monitoring of safeguarding notifications by local authorities is inadequate

- there is a clear need for better planning and commissioning of services

- whistle-blowing policies must be applied properly

- other forms of alert must exist

- there needs to be an improvement in access to advocacy services.

MID STAFFORDSHIRE NHS TRUST

The most in-depth inquiry in recent times into NHS failings was around the Mid Staffordshire NHS Foundation Trust hospital in Stafford. A local pressure group of patients and relatives formed together and called themselves 'Cure the NHS' after identifying common concerns around the standard of care and treatment at the hospital. A lengthy and detailed public inquiry was held involving ministers, the Department of Health, the Care Quality Commission, the local Primary Care Trust and the West Midlands Strategic Health Authority.

The conclusions included:

- The culture and systems at the hospital led to failures to diagnose people's conditions and neglectful treatment, which may have resulted in or hastened the deaths of up to 1,200 people between 2005 and 2009.

- There were confusions around the number of agencies and bodies involved in monitoring the hospital, as listed above, and this is part of a bigger picture of systemic change in health care that the current government is progressing.

- Whistle-blowers were not listened to – one nurse submitted 50 reports and concerns which senior managers were seen not to take account of.

- There were serious concerns about 'the quality, competence and humanity' of the nursing care and practices in the hospital, especially in relation to care for older patients.

REFLECT

Locate one of the reports highlighted above or research other serious failures in health and social care services.

- What 'lessons' can be learned from what went wrong?

- How might you use what you have learnt to improve your own practice?

KEY ISSUES IN FAILURES IN HEALTH AND SOCIAL CARE

Reports into serious failures often highlight similar themes, which may include issues around values, power, isolation, staff culture, failures to follow policies and procedures, and failures to apply person-centred approaches.

VALUES

The attitudes that staff have (both direct care staff and managers) towards service users appears to be the key as to whether a service effectively safeguards service users from abuse and neglect.

The inquiries into serious failures in health and social care highlight that attitudes held by staff towards some or all service users have included a sense of contempt and disrespectfulness. Staff perceive the person or people in various negative ways, including:

- seeing the person as not understanding what they are experiencing

- saying the person has a poor quality of life 'anyway'

- saying that a harsh and punitive punishment was 'good for them' or 'they deserved it'

- dehumanising the person by seeing them as lesser than others, as a problem, or as an object.

Negative attitudes like these are always behind situations where services have left people more vulnerable to abuse.

POWER

Related to values is the issue of power. Where there have been failures of practice there appears to have been an abuse or misuse of power – sometimes relating to a lack of understanding of power and where it lies. Many direct care staff feel relatively powerless – it is important that all staff recognise that they are in a position of significant power in relation to service users.

Inquiry reports show that some staff who have felt powerless in their own work situation or life have used the power they have over service users in a manner that is destructive towards the service user.

ISOLATION

Inquiry reports also show that abusive situations are more likely to arise in services that are isolated. There is increased risk of negligence, neglect or more active abuse where service users:

- receive all their support from within one service

- are placed a long way from family members

- have few or no visits from family

- have little contact with other professionals.

STAFF TEAM CULTURE

Where abuse or service failures have occurred it is not unusual to find that there are features of the staff team that raised concerns. Aspects include:

- Staff teams consisting of some family members.

- There is no or little interest in training and development.

- There is resistance to advice or information from visiting professionals.

- Some staff cultures can act as barriers to reporting poor or dangerous practices.

- Loyalty to colleagues is considered far more important than upholding the well-being of service users.

FAILURES TO FOLLOW POLICIES AND PROCEDURES

Many inquiry reports have identified that appropriate policies and procedures were in place within the organisation but these were not effectively followed. Clearly this reinforces the need for health and social care workers to follow policies and procedures.

FAILURES TO APPLY PERSON-CENTRED APPROACHES

Inquiry reports generally identify that services that fail to protect service users do not apply the basic principles of person-centred practices, and fail to uphold the dignity of service users and employ good care practices such as active support.

REFLECT

The Department of Health and the NHS Commissioning Board's (2012) 'Compassion in practice' document outlines the need for all services to apply person-centred approaches more effectively in practice. This document contains a vision and strategy around the six Cs which are care, compassion, competence, communication, courage and commitment. The strategy 'sets out our shared purpose as nurses, midwives and care staff to deliver high quality, compassionate care, and to achieve excellent health and wellbeing outcomes'. It comes from the government's response to the concerns around dignity in care and reported poor practice, as outlined above in this chapter.

- Have you or any of your colleagues worked in settings where some of the issues highlighted in these reports were present?

- If so, what did or could you do in order to flag up these issues and address them?

CASE STUDY

Jon is a senior support worker with a reablement team. Jon often visits people at hospital just before they are discharged to discuss their care plans with them. He is concerned that one of the wards he goes to provides poor care to patients. He has noticed, for example, that food and drink is often left out of reach of patients at mealtimes and he has seen staff taking it away untouched. He has talked to other members of his team about this and they say it is well known as a poor ward. On a recent visit, he heard a patient ask a staff member if they could go to the toilet. The staff member shouted at the patient and said, 'For goodness sake, I've already taken you three times. I have a lot to do. You'll just have to wait.' The patient that Jon is visiting says, 'Oh she's a real nasty one that one.'

What should Jon do:

- immediately

- when he leaves the ward?

REDUCING THE LIKELIHOOD OF ABUSE

Sometimes it feels like this. There I am standing by the shore of a swiftly flowing river and I hear the cry of a drowning man. So I jump into the river, put my arms around him, pull him to shore and apply artificial respiration. Just when he begins to breathe, there is another cry for help. So back in the river again, reaching, pulling, applying, breathing and then another yell. Again and again, without end, goes the sequence. You know, I am so busy jumping in, pulling them to shore, applying artificial respiration, that I have no time to see who the hell is upstream pushing them all in.

(McKinlay 1994: 509–510)

Prevention depends on accurately identifying why abuse occurs in the first place and then establishing work-based practices that aim to counter (and if possible eliminate) those factors.

As with all work in health and social care, best practice involves working proactively. In terms of abuse, this means working assertively to reduce the likelihood that abuse can occur.

If care staff understand the nature of abuse and why it can occur then the likelihood of abuse occurring is minimised. Likewise if service users, carers and the general public are more informed about abuse they will be more aware and risks will be reduced.

Reducing the likelihood of abuse occurring is an important aspect of a care worker's role. As the saying goes, 'prevention is better than cure'. Ensuring good care practice can be very effective in minimising the risks to service users.

Safeguarding must be built on empowerment – or listening to the victim's voice. Without this, safeguarding is experienced as safety at the expense of other qualities of life, such as self-determination and the right to family life.

(Department of Health 2009a: 6)

PERSON-CENTRED PRACTICE AND REDUCING THE LIKELIHOOD OF ABUSE

Below are ways to help reduce the likelihood of abuse occurring in health and social care settings.

- Work in a person-centred way and with person-centred values at the heart of all practice (see Chapters 9 and 10.) Treating people with respect and dignity and working within the value base of health and social care increases people's self-esteem. This in turn increases people's abilities to protect themselves and recognise abuse.

- As part of this, involving service users in risk assessment is important. Services should also complete risk assessments around specific issues of concern for individuals, in a way that enables people to enjoy the dignity of taking risks, but which also ensures that risks have been fully considered in partnership with the individual (see Chapter 11 on active support).

- Ensure good care practices that promote people's choices and rights. Informing people about their rights can again empower people and reduce vulnerability (see Chapter 4 on duty of care).

- Ensure that robust and agreed policies and procedures are in place and that they are followed by staff (see Chapter 4).

- Ensure that all staff members have a shared understanding of abuse and that continuing professional development and ongoing learning are expected and valued by all (see Chapter 8).

- Have good links with other agencies and opportunities for multi-agency working. Effective multi-agency working and information sharing are also key aspects of preventing abuse and reducing the risks for service users.

- Services will also be responsible for checking and vetting that their own employees are suitable to work there (according to the Disclosure and Barring Service requirements), and that contractors and visitors are safe and supervised appropriately while they are on service premises (see Chapter 6 on health and safety).

It is therefore clear that the areas covered in the other sections of this book all contribute to effective safeguarding and reducing the likelihood of abuse. Safeguarding is not something that workers do in isolation from the rest of their practice or only in response to an incident or disclosure. It is something that cuts across all practice in health and social care, and that is an essential component of being person-centred in your work because:

- a person with a voice (and who feel their voice is listened to) is more likely to say if they are being hurt or abused

- people with positive and supportive relationships around them are less vulnerable to abuse and feel more confident that they will be listened to and believed if they are abused

- if people direct their own support they are more likely to feel in control of their own lives (and therefore to experience fewer feelings of powerlessness, vulnerability and isolation which increase the risk of abuse occurring)

- people who feel respected and important are more likely to complain if the high standards of care that they deserve are not met.

SAFEGUARDING AND TECHNOLOGY

In recent times, the emergence of new technologies has been rapidly changing our lives, often in positive ways for those with whom we work, but also in ways that can present new concerns in terms of keeping people safe. Access to mobile phones, the internet, and social networks can reduce isolation for many people and keep them connected with those who care about them. However, concerns around predatory grooming, e-safety and cyber bullying are regularly discussed in the media, and are issues that service organisations need to consider in order to protect those who access services. It may be that some services want to develop policies, access training, or run group sessions on issues like e-safety. It may be for other services that specific issues have presented, and led to targeted work being commissioned by a service, or referrals to social care being required. In any case, it is part of your duty of care to the people with whom you work to keep up to date with these issues, and to monitor any effect the use of new technologies has on people's safety (without being risk averse and without denying people access to resources that may benefit them).

HOW POLICIES AND COMPLAINTS PROCEDURES REDUCE THE LIKELIHOOD OF ABUSE

One of the ways in which health and social care services seek to reduce the risk of abuse occurring is through the development and implementation of policies and procedures that, if followed, markedly reduce the likelihood of abuse occurring in the first place. An example of this is policies around the handling of service users' money. If these are followed by staff then service users' money and valuables should be protected, and if any allegations against staff were made then staff can produce evidence that they have acted professionally and responsibly.

This also explains why other policies have been developed, eg policies relating to providing intimate personal care, risk assessment procedures, etc. A vital aspect of reducing the risk of abuse is therefore following all policies and guidelines carefully.

Ensuring the service has a complaints procedure and that service users have the opportunity to complain can help to empower people, and therefore make them less vulnerable to abuse. Knowing that service users have access to an effective complaints procedure may also prevent potential perpetrators from abusing.

In health and social care one of the best ways to prevent abuse and safeguard service users is to follow good care practices.

- What might these include? (Try to list three or four).

- How might each of these be effective in preventing abuse and safeguarding people?

THE PROVISION OF INFORMATION

The provision of information is a key aspect of safeguarding people. Clear and accessible information should be provided for service users about the expectations they can rightly have over how they are addressed, their right to make choices, take risks and the freedom to meet with others. Service users also need to know about their rights to complain to service managers, social workers, inspectors, etc. Additionally, family members and friends should be informed about their rights to advocate for the service user as well as what support they could enquire about, for example, an advocacy organisation.

One of the most effective ways of safeguarding people builds on the provision of information, by ensuring that service users are meaningfully involved in the life of the service and its development. Service users should be involved in the different levels of service provision such as:

- their own care and care plan

- the provision of the service generally

- service developments

- future service provision

- wider discussions about community care.

Many services and service providers are beginning to recognise the need to encourage service user participation and have responded to this in various ways through actions such as:

- involving service users in management groups and service planning groups

- involving service users in staff interviews, induction and training

- setting up service user consultation groups, etc.

Whether or not these processes are in place, service users should be encouraged to make comments and complaints about service provision.

COMPLAINTS PROCEDURES

An effective complaints procedure is essential for service users, but it can also be helpful for health and social care workers in that it can:

- bring attention to lack of resources
- emphasise the need for a high-quality service provision
- identify areas of poor practice
- support staff to develop their practice
- clarify misunderstandings.

It is therefore important that health and social care professionals do not view complaints procedures negatively or as a threat. A good-quality complaints procedure is a positive attribute to a service. It will encourage recipients of the service to participate more in the service and have more control over the care they receive.

However, service users often experience problems in making use of complaints procedures.

Happless Care, Complaints Procedure

As part of our commitment to improving all our Care Services, any person wishing to make a complaint may do so, following the procedure outlined below:

1. Please make your complaint using form C7.0000.bd.XIX.

2. If your complaint is made on behalf of a relative, then please use form C7,0090.SS.XXXX (part A) only. Parts C and D should only be completed if your relative incurred any financial loss in relation to the complaint, but no personal injury.

3. If personal injury was incurred, please complete parts D, supplemented by form C3.0010…S. (ignoring part B).

4. Forms are available from floor 40, Bleak Tower, Middle of Nowhere. Please collect by hand.

5. Please collect the appropriate form prior to the incident in question.

6. Please return the form promptly, making sure all 50 questions are answered in full, with supporting evidence from your GP and other referee.

7. Please complete your full name and address, and include a photograph of yourself and/or your loved one. This is to ensure that members of staff can be absolutely clear about who is making a nuisance of themselves.

8. Please obtain a receipt of postage, though a Microchip trace may be the only means of ensuring the complaint will not get completely and entirely lost.

9. If you do not have any response within 12 months of making your complaint, please complete form ZZ.23,000,SSI.

10. Forms are available in a variety of languages, though it is doubtful if these can be found anywhere at all.

"HAPPY TO HELP"

(Basnett and Maclean 2000)

Some of the difficulties experienced in putting a complaints policy into effect can be caused by the following.

LACK OF ACCESSIBILITY

A complaints system may exist in the form of a paper document in the policy manual, for example, but it can only be a living document if those who may need to use it are aware of it and understand how they can use it. So health and social care services should:

- refer to the complaints policy in any brochures or explanatory information which they give to people when they begin receiving the service

- ensure that relatives and other people who are important in the lives of the service user are aware of the policy, together with who they might need to raise a complaint with and how to do so

- ensure that the policy is available in different formats depending upon the needs of the people who use the service, eg on an audio tape or in larger font for people with impaired vision.

NEGATIVE POWER BALANCE

- Although individual members of staff may not feel as if they are especially powerful individuals in their own right, they will be perceived by the people to whom they provide a service as being more powerful than they are. For this reason, service users may find it more difficult to raise concerns if they have them.

- Individuals may feel that they do not have much control over their own lives. This could be because they may require assistance in many aspects of their lives and they are dependent upon members of the staff team to enable them to access the community.

- Service users and their family members may be afraid to raise a complaint in case they lose the service. They may feel no one will listen or they may find it difficult to act assertively.

Therefore health and social care professionals need to:

- recognise power differentials and work with them effectively

- ensure that service users are empowered by the service

- promote a positive culture of support which welcomes comments and complaints about the service provided.

INDIVIDUALS' PAST NEGATIVE EXPERIENCES

- Past experiences of 'care' (perhaps in long-stay institutions where people may have had even less control and where many elements of daily life were directed by nurses, doctors and others) may mean that individuals have low expectations of service provision.

- Memories of institutional care and behaviour patterns learned in this environment are often very difficult to shift, even many decades later, and we may see this in behaviours such as a reluctance to raise complaints.

THE NEED TO COMBAT DEFENSIVENESS ON THE PART OF STAFF

One of the most difficult elements of a healthy complaints policy to establish is a positive culture towards complaints. Staff often fear that a complaint will inevitably lead to disciplinary action being taken and could lead to a person losing their job. In some organisations where the culture is quite punitive, people may have grounds for thinking in this way.

This feeling can also come about because employees habitually regard a complaint as reflecting solely upon their own work. It is preferable that everyone in a service shares the understanding that complaints need to be dealt with as a reflection on the service as a whole, rather than any specific worker's failing.

MESSAGES FROM RESEARCH

Experiences of complaints procedures

Research by Finnegan and Clarke in 2005 identified that:

- 76% of staff agreed or strongly agreed with the statement that 'very few service users use the formal complaints procedure'

- 82% agreed with the statement that service users 'do not understand the process'

- 76% agreed with the statement 'they do not understand their rights'.

Comments from the staff about the lack of use of complaints procedures included the following:

Service users just don't like complaining. I can see why they wouldn't because I don't think I would feel at ease doing that if I was them. I'd be worried about being seen as a troublemaker I suppose, and you might be worried about how you might get treated afterwards.

My worry is that they complain less and less because nothing is ever done ...

The service users really do not feel that they can complain against someone who has power over their lives. It stays within the house and is not properly recorded or followed up.

I know that every time there is an incident or complaint, everything should be written down but that is never the case.

(Finnegan and Clarke 2005)

REFLECT

- Are you aware of the complaints procedure in your workplace?

- How do you ensure that service users are aware of the procedure and that they receive any support they might need to complain where they are not satisfied with their care?

RECOGNISING AND REPORTING UNSAFE PRACTICES

WHAT ARE UNSAFE PRACTICES?

Unsafe practices can include:

- poor working practices (either accepted practices within a service or individual practices by workers that do not meet the expected standards of good care practice)

- resource difficulties (where the resources are not available within a service to provide adequate or safe care practice)

- operational difficulties (eg where staff absence means that a service is not staffed to a safe ratio).

HOW DO UNSAFE PRACTICES AFFECT THE WELL-BEING OF INDIVIDUALS?

If practices such as those outlined above take place within a service, people are not going to receive a standard of care and support that:

- is individual to their needs

- is sufficient for their needs to be met

- respects their dignity and uniqueness

- is safe.

WHAT IS THE LEGAL FRAMEWORK AROUND REPORTING UNSAFE PRACTICES?

Workers who identify and report unsafe practices are protected by the law. Stating this does not make it easier to take action, but it is important that workers know about the legislative duty and protection in order for anyone to feel able to escalate issues appropriately.

PUBLIC INTEREST DISCLOSURE ACT 1998

This is often referred to as the 'whistle-blowers' legislation. It was implemented in July 1999. This Act gives significant statutory protection to employees who disclose malpractice reasonably and responsibly in the public interest and are victimised as a result. If an employee is victimised or dismissed for this disclosure they can make a claim for compensation to an industrial tribunal. There is no cap to the amount that can be awarded.

While it is not a statutory requirement, there is an expectation that organisations will establish their own whistle-blowing policies and guidelines. These guidelines should:

- clearly indicate how staff can raise concerns about malpractice
- make a clear organisational commitment to take concerns seriously and to protect people from victimisation
- designate a senior manager with specific responsibility for addressing in confidence concerns that need to be handled outside the usual management chain.

Staff receive the full protection of the Act if they seek to disclose malpractice responsibly, eg by following the organisation's whistle-blowing policy or guidelines.

WHAT ACTIONS SHOULD BE TAKEN IF UNSAFE PRACTICES ARE IDENTIFIED?

Where unsafe practices are identified, you have a duty to report these. This forms part of your duty of care to those you support (see Chapter 4 for more details on this). Part of your duty as a professional in the field of health and social care means that you:

- cannot ignore practices that are unsafe and that impact upon individuals' rights and well-being
- have to report concerns
- should expect to justify your concerns with evidence, knowledge and understanding of the impact of unsafe practices.

WHAT ACTIONS SHOULD BE TAKEN IF NOTHING IS DONE?

If you report a concern, identify a practice as unsafe in your service, or inform your employer that a colleague's practice is unsafe or abusive, you should expect the person you inform to take action. It is reasonable that where a colleague's practice has to be investigated, that you may not get to know all of the detail of this investigation or its outcome (eg if a person were to be disciplined for a conduct issue at work). However, you should expect that the person:

- records what you are concerned about and why

- takes your concerns seriously

- agrees with you what will happen in terms of feedback to you following this

- identifies sources of support (either internally or externally) and recognises that coming forwards and sharing concerns is not easy to do.

If you have reported concerns and the above does not happen or if you do not see change as a result of the action, then there are other actions you may need to consider taking, such as:

- escalating the issue to the next level of management

- talking to your union

- notifying the local authority and/or police (in cases where someone is being abused, you would follow safeguarding procedures immediately anyway as described elsewhere in this chapter)

- notifying the regulator (ie the Care Quality Commission).

REFLECT

- How and when should you report any resource or operational difficulties that might affect the delivery of safe care?

- How and when should you report the practice of colleagues which is or may be unsafe?

- Why should you report any such concerns?

- If you report unsafe practices and no action is taken, what should you do?

- Does your organisation have a whistle-blowing policy?
- Where can you find it?
- What does it say?

Code of Conduct for Healthcare Support Workers and Adult Social Care Workers

The Code of Conduct for Healthcare Support Workers and Adult Social Care Workers makes clear that you must:

- always make sure that your actions or omissions do not harm an individual's health or well-being. You must never abuse, neglect, harm or exploit those who use health and social care services, their carers or your colleagues

- challenge and report dangerous, abusive, discriminatory or exploitative behaviour or practice

- always take comments and complaints seriously, respond to them in line with agreed ways of working and inform a senior member of staff

- always treat people with respect and compassion

- always maintain the privacy and dignity of people who use health and care services, their carers and others

- always discuss issues of disclosure with a senior member of staff.

Report any actions or omissions by yourself or colleagues that you feel may compromise the safety or care of people who use health and care services and, if necessary, use whistle-blowing procedures to report any suspected wrongdoing.

CHAPTER 6
Promoting and implementing health and safety in health and social care

Health and safety issues are important in all work settings and sectors. However, in health and social care settings you are working with people who have particular vulnerabilities and specific care needs, so this means that you need to be especially vigilant in relation to health and safety at work.

Links to other chapters

Health and safety issues should be considered in all aspects of health and social care work. The contents of this chapter will therefore be useful to you in completing any qualification units. There are particular links with material in the chapters 4 and 15.

HEALTH AND SAFETY: THE LEGAL FRAMEWORK

It is important that health and social care workers understand their own responsibilities and the responsibilities of others in relation to health and safety. Responsibilities in terms of health and safety are drawn from legislation and associated policies and procedures.

The main piece of legislation in terms of health and safety is the Health and Safety at Work Act 1974.

HEALTH AND SAFETY AT WORK ACT 1974

This Act outlines a number of responsibilities for employers, managers and employees.

Employers have a duty to:

- ensure the health and safety at work for all employees

- provide and maintain equipment and systems which are safe and not a risk to employees' health in terms of use, handling, storage and transport of articles and substances

- provide information, training and supervision relating to health and safety at work.

Managers have a duty to:

- maintain a safe working environment for all staff

- ensure that all staff adhere to policies, procedures and instructions

- provide training for staff practices and work methods

- explain hazards and safe working practices to new employees before they start work

- report/record all accidents.

Employees have a duty to:

- adhere to instructions relating to the operation of a site and equipment

- ensure that they use materials in line with recommended procedures

- utilise protective clothing and equipment as directed

- not to misuse anything provided for health, safety and welfare.

THE UMBRELLA EFFECT

The Health and Safety at Work Act 1974 is known as an umbrella piece of legislation in that it covers a wide range of areas and a number of associated regulations are issued underneath the 'umbrella' of the original Act. Regulations are used in health and safety as they are more easily changed than an Act of Parliament, and health and safety issues need to be kept under constant review.

ASSOCIATED REGULATIONS

There are a range of regulations in the health and safety area, including:

- Reporting of Injuries, Diseases and Dangerous Occurrences Regulations (RIDDOR) 1995

- Safety Representatives and Safety Committees Regulations 1997

- Health and Safety (First Aid) Regulations 1981

- Workplace (Health, Safety and Welfare) Regulations 1992

- Manual Handling Operations Regulations 1992

- Health and Safety (Consultation with Employees) Regulations 1996

- Management of Health and Safety at Work Regulations 1996

- Control of Substances Hazardous to Health Regulations (COSHH) 2002

- Provision and Use of Equipment Regulations (PUWER) 1998

- Lifting Operations and Lifting Equipment Regulations (LOLER) 1998

- Food Hygiene Regulations 2006

- Fire Safety Regulations

- Display Screen Equipment Regulations

These are covered throughout this chapter. To aid compliance, the Health and Safety Executive (HSE) implements new regulations on only two dates per year. These are:

- 6 April

- 1 October.

It is hoped that the implementation of new regulations being kept to twice a year will enable organisations to foresee change and plan for it. The HSE publishes an excellent (and brief) overview of current legislation – 'Health and safety regulation: a short guide'. This can be downloaded from the HSE website at www.hse.gov.uk.

Another Act that relates to health and safety at work and provides information on responsibilities is the Corporate Manslaughter and Corporate Homicide Act 2007.

This Act covers fatal accidents and redefines the offence of corporate manslaughter.

- For a case of corporate manslaughter to be brought, a death must have occurred. This sounds obvious, but if someone is 'only' severely injured, standard health and safety legislation still applies.

- The death does not have to be an employee of the company concerned but it does have to result from the way that company's activities were managed or organised.

- The death must have arisen from a gross breach of the company's duty of care to the victim.

- The organisational failings that led to the death must have been somehow authorised by senior management; that is to say, practices that were authored, or agreed to, or known about by senior management. Senior management does not just include the company directors.

This Act demonstrates the vital importance of all health and social care staff being clear about policy and procedure and following this consistently. It also lays out responsibilities for managers to:

- ensure that policy and practice are fit for purpose

- keep policy and practice under review

- monitor that staff follow policy and procedure.

HEALTH AND SAFETY REGULATION IN HEALTH AND SOCIAL CARE

The Health and Safety Executive (HSE) is the national independent regulator for health and safety in the workplace. As such it covers all workplaces. The HSE works in partnership with sector-specific regulators, so in relation to health and social care it works closely with the Care Quality Commission and local authorities to inspect, investigate and, where necessary, take enforcement action.

The Health and Safety Executive recognises that health and social care is a sector where health and safety issues are vitally important. It therefore provides a range of information specifically for health and social care services on its website. This is worth reviewing as you work towards completing this unit for your diploma.

RESEARCH

You should have read your organisation's health and safety policies during your induction. It is worth revisiting these now to ensure that you are fully informed about the relevant policies and procedures. Make a list of all the policies and procedures that relate to health and safety in some way and ensure that you have read these. If you struggle to follow any of the policies for any reason, make a note of this and ensure that you discuss this with your manager.

SAFETY REPRESENTATIVES AND SAFETY COMMITTEES REGULATIONS

If an employer recognises a trade union and that union has either appointed or is about to appoint safety representatives, then the employer must consult those representatives on matters that will affect the employees they represent.

The roles of trade union safety representatives appointed under these regulations are:

- to investigate possible dangers at work, the causes of accidents and general complaints by employees on health and safety and welfare issues, and to take these matters up with the employer

- to carry out inspections of the workplace particularly following accidents, diseases or other events

- to represent employees in discussions with health and safety inspectors, and to receive information from those inspectors

- to attend meetings of safety committees.

An employer must set up a safety committee if two or more trade union representatives ask for one.

WORKPLACE (HEALTH, SAFETY AND WELFARE) REGULATIONS

These regulations complement the Management of Health and Safety at Work Regulations, and cover the management of workplaces. Duties are placed on both employers and employees (in the sense that both have control over a workplace).

The main requirements created by these regulations are:

- The workplace, equipment, systems, etc must be maintained in an efficient state.

- Enclosed workplaces must be ventilated by a sufficient quantity of fresh and purified air.

- A reasonable temperature must be maintained inside buildings and a sufficient number of thermometers must be provided.

- Lighting must be suitable and efficient.

- Workplaces must be kept sufficiently clean.

A **policy** in health and social care is a written statement explaining the service or agency's expected approach to an issue, area of practice or key aspect of people's work. Policies can be local and/or national.

A **procedure** is an agreed and understood way or order of doing something in work.

HEALTH AND SAFETY POLICIES AND PROCEDURES

WHAT ARE POLICY AND PROCEDURES?

A **policy** is usually written and formal, and a **procedure** can be:

- presented in writing or in a flow chart or other formats

- formal

- informal (an informal procedure would be something that workers understand they follow in the work setting, but that is not necessarily written out in formal format, eg the manner in which people are expected to greet and sign in visitors).

Policies and procedures differ in every service setting. Health and social care workers need to have a working knowledge of their agency's policies and procedures in order to carry out their responsibilities in terms of health and safety. As a minimum, workers need to be familiar with the policies and procedures covering the following:

- communicable diseases/infection control policy

- confidentiality and information disclosure

- control of exposure to hazardous waste (based on COSHH regulations)

- fire safety

- hygiene and food safety

- record keeping and access to files

- moving and handling

- dealing with accidents and emergencies

- responding to abuse.

It is important that all services have policies and procedures that reflect national legislation and good practice guidelines in this area. Individual workers may not have very much control over the nature of an organisation's policies, particularly in large organisations. However, all workers should:

- be aware of the legislative context in which they operate

- know about relevant policies and procedures, and know how to access them if they need to

- understand policies and procedures

- keep up to date with the necessary training to enable them to put policy safely into practice.

WHY HAVE POLICIES AND PROCEDURES?

Policies and procedures are necessary in all sectors, but perhaps more so in health and social care, for various reasons, including:

- *Legal compliance.* Legislation (eg the National Minimum Standards) requires services to have policies and procedures in specific areas.

- *Good 'business' sense.* Having policies and procedures (particularly those relating to human resources issues) makes good business sense.

- *Consistent practice.* Clear policies and procedures ensure consistent practice in a staff team and staff will be aware of minimum standards for their practice.

- *Managerial accountability.* Good-quality policies and procedures protect managers in terms of their accountability for the actions of staff.

USING POLICIES AND PROCEDURES

In terms of health and safety, candidates may be unsure about the evidence they need to provide in this area. It is important to remember that competent health and social care workers will generate the necessary evidence for health and safety as a matter of course as it is central to all good practice in health and social care.

Workers who provide personal care will need to use gloves, aprons, etc in their work, and are therefore likely to have evidence of their competence in terms of health and safety. However, health and social care workers can still be fulfilling their health and safety requirements even in mundane and everyday activities. Think about:

- using the kettle safely in making a cup of tea

- using the shredder

- moving a box to a different area in a store cupboard in an appropriate way

- supporting a service user to use a kettle, a cooker, a vacuum cleaner, etc

- supporting a service user to cross a road

- using a computer safely or organising desk space.

The list goes on and on. These may seem like obvious examples but often health and social care workers miss them. Providing evidence of health and safety doesn't mean workers need to do anything new or different, as it's about the detail of everyday health and social care practice.

BEING CLEAR ABOUT ROLES AND RESPONSIBILITIES: INCREASING CONFIDENCE

Having policies, responsibilities and procedures that are clearly stated can increase confidence in the service from the perspective of the service users, their families and carers. Health and safety in any workplace is a shared responsibility.

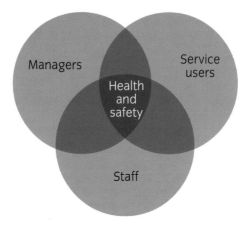

Under health and safety legislation, managers have specific responsibilities. These include:

- to ensure all equipment is properly maintained and safe to use

- to explain health and safety procedures to new staff

- to provide training to enable staff to follow all necessary procedures and to use equipment safely

- to assess any risks of harm that could arise in work and to take steps to reduce risks of harm to a minimum

- to provide protective clothing, such as gloves and aprons.

Arguably the three key health and safety responsibilities that fall on management relate to:

- ensuring that all staff are familiar with health and safety practices

- monitoring their staff's compliance with procedures

- assessing new risks as they arise and either addressing these within the service or involving others to address and manage the risks.

Equally, under health and safety legislation all staff have a responsibility to:

- follow all instructions and procedures to ensure risks of harm are minimised

- use any protective clothing as expected (eg gloves, aprons)

- act responsibly

- to report any dangerous occurrences, accidents, etc to the senior member of staff on duty

- to report any avoidable health and safety risks in the environment.

Service users also have a responsibility in terms of health and safety, but the extent of this will depend on their circumstances.

MAXIMISING SERVICE USER INVOLVEMENT

Values should always inform our practice. Involving service users in discussions about health and safety conveys respect and the fact that service users have a responsibility to maintain certain standards around health and safety if they are able to do so.

Discussions with service users could relate to what to do following an accident or supporting the service user to maintain their own personal hygiene or assisting them to follow accepted guidance on handling food safely.

Discussing matters with service users conveys to both the service user and colleagues that such involvement is a key aspect of good practice.

RESPONSIBILITIES TOWARDS NEW WORKERS

Health and social care workers are often involved in supporting new colleagues within a team. New workers need to have an induction plan, which could include:

- a tour of the service, highlighting health and safety and security matters

- shadowing a colleague as they carry out their ordinary responsibilities and asking the colleague to talk through health, safety and security matters

- reading through policies, procedures and summaries of key regulations and legislation, or being given a ralk on there subjects

- watching health and safety training DVDs or videos

- completing or meeting the Common Induction Standards for adult social care to training events about health and safety matters

- reading through some care plans and discussing the risk assessments and management plans with them.

ONGOING RESPONSIBILITIES

Health and social care workers are likely to communicate regularly about health and safety issues within services. This communication is part of everyone taking an active responsibility around their own well-being and that of their service users. Examples might include:

- At the beginning of a working day, discussing issues relevant to that day.

- At team meetings, having a health and safety 'slot' on the agenda.

- Discussing 'buddying' arrangements each day in a service that involves lone working.

- Use of written communication such as communication books or memos.

- Discussions around changes to policies in supervision sessions.

The list could go on. The idea is that health and safety should not be seen as something extra to good practice or a pain imposed from external forces, but as something integral to all good health and social care work.

HEALTH AND SAFETY (CONSULTATION WITH EMPLOYEES) REGULATIONS

Any employees not in groups covered by trade union safety representatives must be consulted by their employers under these regulations. An employer can choose to consult them directly or through elected representatives.

Elected representatives of employees must:

- take up with employers concerns about possible risks and dangerous events in the workplace that may affect the employees they represent

- take up with employers general matters affecting the health and safety of the employees they represent

- represent the employees who elected them in consultations with health and safety inspectors.

Employers may choose to give elected representatives extra roles.

UNDERSTANDING THE WORK ENVIRONMENT

Health and social care staff work in a wide variety of environments, such as residential services, day services, service users' own homes, and so on. While some staff have a regular place of work, eg a nursing home, others work in a range of environments in any given day.

For example, a community care worker who visits seven service users in their own homes and drives two of these people to a drop-in service and accompanies one person shopping will have worked in more than ten environments in one day. In this scenario, there are seven houses, a car, a drop-in service, a supermarket and the car park as a minimum.

Candidates should consider their work environment and view it in the way that someone new to the environment would view it. This is because assessors will be seeing the candidate's health and safety practice for the first time, and therefore will need to know that the basic daily duties are followed. We all often take these practices for granted for the very reason that we do follow them each day.

SPECIFIC TASKS THAT NEED SPECIAL TRAINING

Some tasks cannot be carried out without specific training because:

- of your liability and duty of care to the people you support

- of your employer's duties and responsibilities to you and to the users of the service

- it is not safe or appropriate for people with care needs to receive certain interventions if people have not had the right training.

These tasks include:

- moving and handling
- use of equipment
- first aid
- administering some types of medication
- clinical interventions
- preparing food.

CARRYING OUT YOUR RESPONSIBILITIES FOR HEALTH AND SAFETY

Now that you understand the responsibilities that you and others have, you need to think about how you carry out these responsibilities and how you support others to carry out their role safely.

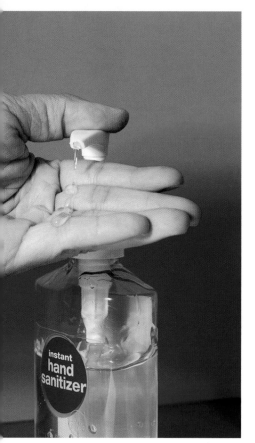

USING POLICIES AND PROCEDURES

We have explored policies and procedures in relation to health and safety and you have revisited these in your work role. It is important now to think about the impact that these have on your work. Try developing the following table: the first example has been filled in for you, but you should add further policies.

Policy/ procedure	What effect these have on my work	What difficulties I encounter	What I can do to address these difficulties
Infection control	I wear gloves and an apron. I use cleansing gel on my hands between visits.	I do not always have a full supply of gloves. I feel uncomfortable putting on gloves – it feels very clinical.	Talk to my manager to ensure that I have a sufficient supply.

The policies, procedures and agreed ways of working you cover in this table should be those that are most relevant to your role, and might include:

- fire safety procedures (drills, exit points, expectations in the event of a fire). These are likely to be formal because of employers' legal duties regarding building and fire safety, but for social care workers who support people in their homes, these may not be quite so formal

- procedures for cleaning and storage of cleaning products (linked to COSHH)

- food preparation responsibilities and procedures

- procedures relating to access to buildings and information

- procedures for storage and administering medication to people

- procedures and expectations for storage of your own belongings and your own medication

- risk-assessment policies, paperwork and procedures

- procedures to monitor safety warnings and equipment (eg ladders, hoists or annual electrical PAT checks)

- lone working systems and policies

- agreed ways of opening up and locking up a building safely

- expectations for training in the use of equipment (eg for moving and handling).

SUPPORTING OTHERS TO UNDERSTAND AND FOLLOW SAFE PRACTICES

Part of your responsibilities in terms of health and safety can be cross-referenced with your duty of care for the people you support. Service users may need support in order to keep themselves safe because of:

- a specific health need or disability

- their communication needs

- their understanding of risk

- their sensory needs.

Supporting service users to understand and follow safe practices is important in:

- promoting person-centred working (people should understand safe practices and be encouraged and enabled to keep themselves safe with the minimum level of support from workers)

- promoting active support (people should feel in control of their care plan, able to make decisions and enabled to understand risk)

- enabling independence

- empowering people (see also below in terms of risk assessment and promoting a positive culture that acknowledges the dignity of risk).

Below are some ways to support service users to understand and follow safe practices:

- Talk to people about risk and discuss their level of need for support.

- Involve them in risk assessments (see below).

- Model the procedures and practices for them and with them.

- Use leaflets, visual images, colleagues, relatives and managers to help demonstrate practices, and involve people as a whole care team in modelling safe practices and managing risk.

You may also be involved in supporting colleagues (particularly new workers as part of their induction) in understanding your service's health and safety practices and procedures.

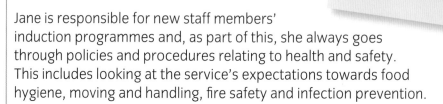

CASE STUDY

Jane is a senior support worker in a day service for people with learning disabilities. Many of the service users she works with have a profound learning disability along with physical disabilities. Jane is responsible for organising day service activities and she supervises a small group of day service assistants.

Jane is responsible for new staff members' induction programmes and, as part of this, she always goes through policies and procedures relating to health and safety. This includes looking at the service's expectations towards food hygiene, moving and handling, fire safety and infection prevention.

Jess is a new worker who starts at Jane's service. Jess is experienced and has worked in other similar services for many years. Jane goes through the service's expectations as she would with any other worker. She asks Jess to sign a document to show that she has had her induction, and that she understands the service's policies and procedures, and her own duties and responsibilities.

In the second week Jess is employed there, Jane is told by another colleague that Jess is not following correct food preparation procedures, and says things like 'we always used tea towels to dry up odd bits and bobs where I used to work'. Jane then observes Jess letting a visitor into the service without checking their ID properly.

- What does Jane need to do next?

- How can she approach Jess to make sure she is on board fully with the service's expectations?

- What might Jane need to consider if Jess does not address these concerns?

MONITORING AND REPORTING POTENTIAL HEALTH AND SAFETY RISKS

As a professional, you have a duty to monitor and report risks to people's health and safety. This is about keeping yourself safe, considering your colleagues, and being respectful and vigilant for the additional needs of your service users.

In considering health and safety risks, it is vital to understand the concept of hazard and risk.

Hazard and risk

REPORTING OF INJURIES, DISEASES AND DANGEROUS OCCURRENCES REGULATIONS (RIDDOR)

These regulations are often referred to as RIDDOR. The regulations require the reporting of work-related accidents, diseases and dangerous occurrences. Under the regulations, employers, self-employed people and people in control of work premises have duties to report:

- deaths or major injuries at work
- work-related injuries which result in people being away from work for over three days
- work-related diseases
- dangerous occurrences at work.

Hazards can present quite rapidly and the **risks** presented by the hazard are constantly changing. One of your duties is to keep considering hazards and risk. Often the hazards that present risk are not the ones where a risk assessment has been completed (eg a frayed wire or a person turning round and banging into someone else with a hot cup of tea in their hand). This is why you need to operate as a 'walking risk assessment' in your job role, so that risk is something that is always at the forefront of your mind, not in a way that restricts normal activity, but in a way that considers all aspects of the environment.

You also need to follow your service's agreed policies and procedures for reporting risk.

ACCIDENT AND INCIDENT FORMS

Every service has to have either an **accident** form or an accident book as part of the RIDDOR regulations. Accident forms are often preferred these days as they can be filed in a way where confidentiality and data protection concerns are addressed (as an accident book may contain lots of different people's names and details).

Likewise, your service will have required paperwork for recording any incidents that occur.

You need to familiarise yourself with your agency's paperwork, and ensure you know who is responsible for collating these forms and where they are stored. Both accident and incident forms need to contain:

- names of those involved
- names of any witnesses
- date and time of the of the accident/**incident**

Key terms

A **hazard** is a possible source of harm.

A **risk** is the likelihood that a hazard will actually cause harm.

Although these words are sometimes used interchangeably it is important to recognise that there is a clear difference between a hazard and a risk. For example, if there was a spill of water in a room then that water would present a slipping hazard to persons passing through it. If access to that area was prevented by a physical barrier, then the hazard would remain though the risk would be minimised.

Key terms

Accidents are events that take place which were not predicted and where someone is hurt.

Incidents are events where something unpredictable or unsafe has taken place – it might be that no one is hurt in an incident, but recording and reporting are necessary in order for monitoring and learning to take place.

- a (brief) description of what happened
- a description of any injuries (possibly pictorial)
- what action was taken and why
- how the issue was escalated.

USING RISK ASSESSMENT IN RELATION TO HEALTH AND SAFETY

MANAGEMENT OF HEALTH AND SAFETY AT WORK REGULATIONS

These regulations place on employers a duty to assess all health and safety risks associated with their work, and to introduce procedures and practices that minimise the likelihood of any identified risks occurring.

Additionally, employers have to provide training for staff:

- when they start work
- when their work or responsibilities change and there are new or greater risks
- periodically if needed (ie if the skills do not get used regularly)
- during working hours and not at the expense of employees.

All workers should be familiar with the importance of risk assessments as everyone has duties to be aware of their own safety and that of other people. Often a risk assessment is required in various aspects of promoting health and safety.

Risk assessments assess hazards and what can go wrong (from minor to worst possible) and what the likelihood (probability) is of each possibility occurring.

The Management of Health and Safety at Work Regulations place a legal responsibility on employers to carry out risk assessment as the first step in ensuring a healthy and safe workplace. Risk assessments should identify possible hazards, assess the likelihood of harm resulting and identify what measures could be taken to manage the risks.

For health and social care services, the employee's workplace, in practice, can be a variety of different locations which may include the homes of those to whom they are providing a service. By extension then, risk assessments must take into account the different locations in which you may be working.

In assessing the extent and nature of the risk, workers will need to take into account the severity of the hazard and the likelihood or probability that it will occur. This is often represented as a calculation where both severity and probability are given a numerical value and multiplied to form the risk factor.

In this way the worst-possible outcome is balanced against the probability that this outcome will occur. For example, someone who is prone to prolonged epileptic seizures may have their condition well controlled by medication. The worst-possible outcome from a prolonged seizure may conceivably be death, but this may be balanced by the fact that the medication controls the epilepsy so well that it has been several years since the person last experienced a seizure. Therefore, although the severity of the hazard is high, we can justifiably assess that the probability of a seizure occurring is very low.

The Health and Safety Executive (2006) identifies five steps in undertaking a risk assessment.

Five steps to risk assessment

Step 1

Identify and document possible hazards.
These are usually environmental hazards which might be in the home of the individual being supported, such as very hot water coming from a bath tap, or in the external environment, such as a busy road nearby.

Step 2

Identify who might be at risk of harm and what form the harm might take.
The hazards do not present a danger in themselves but individuals may be put at risk by the actions they take. An individual may be at risk of scalding if he or she decides to take bath in water that is extremely hot. Someone crossing a busy road who has relatively poor pedestrian skills may be at risk of being struck by a car and being injured if they take insufficient care.

In Steps 1 and 2 it is not just the person who is being supported who may be at risk. Any visitor lacking the necessary skills may be at risk of scalding while other road users may also be at risk of injury if involved in an accident.

Step 3

Evaluate risks arising from hazards and determine whether any existing precautionary measures are sufficient.
Someone who lacks the ability to run a bath unaided and judge the safety of the water temperature may be at significant risk of injury or even death from scalding unless steps are taken to protect them.

One option might be to have a mixer system installed which gives a controlled, lower water temperature. This can be quite costly to install but removes the possibility of scalding, although the problem would still remain should the individual need to access a bath in a different location which does not have this system. Alternatively, a member of staff could help the person to run the bath supporting them to do as much as possible for themselves and ensuring that the water temperature is safe.

A person with poor pedestrian skills may benefit from a programme being devised to help them to improve their skills, perhaps incorporating progressively reduced degrees of supervision with the aim of becoming fully independent.

In both Step 3 instances the degree of risk can be reduced by providing supervision and additional support where necessary. The amount of supervision over time might be reduced as the person's competence grows.

Step 4

Complete a risk assessment.
Under the regulations there is a requirement that risk-assessment documentation is completed if an organisation employs more than five people. In fact, under the Care Standards Act 2000 there is an expectation that risk assessments will be completed in all cases and it is regarded as good practice within health and social care organisations.

You must record significant hazards, assessment of risk and reasonable precautions that can be taken. This documentation must be recorded carefully and must be accessible to all workers who might have to use it. It must be dated and available for future inspection if required.

Step 5

Review the assessment periodically and update it if necessary.
Risk assessments will require review at regular intervals (at least annually) and as circumstances change. Examples of changes that may signal the need for an earlier review include:

- an improvement or deterioration in the skills or ability level of the person being supported
- a change in the service user's environment
- a change in health or in the level of impairment requiring more or less support
- a change in service level not influenced by the above.

Ensure that the review date is accurately recorded on the risk assessment.

Aside from the legal requirement to produce and use risk assessments, there are further reasons to do so. Risk assessments:

- provide a measure of protection to the individual and to others who may be either directly or indirectly at risk

- provide protection to yourself which may be quite literally by safeguarding you from a possible consequence of taking the risk and by ensuring that you can justify any actions you take in respect of the risk

- can also help to protect other people, including the general public who may be exposed to risk.

IDENTIFYING HAZARDS AND RISKS IN SERVICES AND IN THE COMMUNITY

Identifying risks is a responsibility of all workers. However, just because a hazard or risk is identified, it does not necessarily mean it can be eliminated.

The types of risk that a worker needs to be conscious of will be determined by their work role and type of service.

In a community-based team, the hazards and risk areas could include:

- lone working and risk of violence (either from a stranger, service user or carer)
- stress
- risks to service users (eg mental health issues, risks of falls)
- vulnerability to abuse.

In a domiciliary service, the hazards and risks could include:

- lone working and risk of violence
- manual handling
- trips and falls
- stress
- risk of abuse (in respect of vulnerable service users)
- other risks to service users (eg fire).

In a care home or day centre, the hazards and risks could include:

- manual handling and risk of injury
- risk of violence to staff and service users
- risk of abuse (of vulnerable service users)
- trips and falls

- fire

- stress

- handling of medication

- handling and preparation of food

- risk of infections

- risks to service users (eg leaving the building alone)

- other work-related risks (eg use of disinfectants).

Field workers in the community may need an added awareness of the risks during a home visit. These lists are by no means exhaustive.

Responding to risk is not just the responsibility of managers or any worker on their own. As already touched upon, health and safety is a joint responsibility. All services and teams should maintain an open dialogue around health and safety, including risk assessment and reviews of everyday practices. Service users should also be involved in discussions as appropriate.

Some risks will need the involvement of the whole team, while other risks will need discussions with line managers and other agencies.

Reviews of risk assessments are crucial because sometimes situations change and the risk assessments are not amended. This can result in the importance of risk assessments being belittled.

OVERPROTECTION

It is widely recognised that in the past services have often been too protective of people. Services have always sought to minimise or eliminate any risk of harm, be it emotional, mental or physical. It is now accepted that the attempt to eliminate all risk undermines people's dignity and inhibits opportunities for personal development and growth. Often care environments that reduce risk as much as possible result in impoverished environments. Effective practice in risk assessment within care environments is about balance.

The answer to overprotection is not to throw any sense of service responsibility to the wind and claim that whatever happens to people upholds their dignity. The aim should be for services to support people to take measured risks. The first time tasks are initiated they should be at the top end of someone's present capability. If the task is successfully completed the person's sense of confidence and self-esteem should be notably enhanced. If the person is not successful, while there is a risk that their confidence and self-esteem is knocked, there should be support to assist people through this. The person still has the sense that at least they tried it even if it wasn't successful.

Examples of risk taking could apply in all aspects of a service. For example, instead of a staff member actively assisting someone to bathe, the service could seek to support someone to bathe independently. If this resulted in there being no need for a staff member to be in the bathroom, then this is a significant enhancement of the person's dignity.

Another example would be supporting someone to develop pedestrian skills. If a person who formerly always needed a staff escort to go out could be given the opportunity to learn to cross roads safely on their own, then this is a positive move towards increased independence. At one level, learning pedestrian skills represents a big risk and staff may be tempted to say, 'What if she or he gets hit by a car?' We could always point to the worst-possible outcome, even in our own lives. Any of us could be involved in a car crash, but that doesn't mean we sell our cars or don't cross the road.

In any programme that is intended to maintain or extend a person's level of independence and involves risk, there must be planned stops that enhance the person's skills and control the level of risk. In essence, services should actively use risk assessments in a constructive manner. As people are supported to develop and extend their skills, the risks associated should be evaluated to see if the person can extend their level of independence.

Risk taking is an integral part of daily life and is a significant route to supporting service users to maintain a sense of achievement and fulfilment. When risk is handled in a planned and conscious way it can be a great springboard for all.

MINIMISING POTENTIAL RISKS AND HAZARDS

While risk can never be fully eliminated, as it is a part of everyone's everyday life (and promoting positive and informed understanding of risk in health and social care can be a good thing), you have a duty to minimise potential risks.

To minimise risks you need to work through three steps:

1 Identify the hazard.

2 Identify the possible risks from the hazard.

3 Identify 'control measures' (ie what controls can be used to minimise the risk).

Some risks are easier to minimise than others, as the table on the next page demonstrates.

Examples of risks and control measures

Hazard	Possible risks arising from the hazard	Control measures (ideas to minimise risk)
Trailing wires	A person could trip and fall	Use a cable tidy or move items around so they do not trail in people's way
Wet floor	A person could slip and fall	Put a barrier around the wet area of the floor to prevent people slipping Dry the floor
Smoking	Short term: risk of fire	Education on the risks, eg not smoking indoors
	Long term: health risks	Education on the risks and smoking cessation support
Medication	Possible overdose or a person using medication which isn't theirs	Secure storage of medication Training for people who administer medication Supporting people to self-medicate where appropriate
Bleach bottle on the table	A person could drink the bleach	Ensure correct labelling Store safely
When out in the community cars pose a hazard	A person could be involved in a road traffic accident	Provide education and support in road safety and training in pedestrian skills
In carrying out a personal care task you may come into contact with bodily fluids	Risk of infection	Wear personal protective clothing

RISK COMPENSATION

It is widely accepted that people adapt their behaviour based on their perceptions of risk. For example, where people feel that they face significant risk, they tend to ensure that they employ safety-conscious behaviours. Where people feel 'safe' in the knowledge that risks are minimised, their behaviour often adapts to their perception of risk so that they place themselves at heightened risk. People are in essence lulled into a false sense of security. This is widely demonstrated in research relating to road safety, eg cyclists wearing helmets take more risks because they feel 'safe' wearing helmets.

In devising control measures or risk-management strategies, it is important to address potential behaviour changes created by risk compensation. Understanding the concept of risk compensation is important in terms of discussing risk management strategies with service users. How will they ensure they contribute to the strategy?

It is also important in understanding how staff could place themselves at additional risk where they feel 'safer' because of a particular strategy put in place.

ACCESSING ADDITIONAL SUPPORT OR INFORMATION RELATING TO HEALTH AND SAFETY

Additional support and information about health and safety will be available from:

- your colleagues

- your managers

- the internet

- training providers (eg the Health and Safety Executive's website)

- books and leaflets

- local authority and service health and safety advisors, trainers and experts.

It is part of your responsibility as a professional in the field of health and social care to know your duties, know your limitations, know your learning needs, and to access help, advice, training, information and support when you need this.

APPLICATION OF SKILLS

'Thinking' health, safety and security

Over the next few days keep health and safety at the front of your mind, as you carry out your everyday practice.

- Have you worked with others to assess, minimise and manage a risk or address a hazard?

- In what way have you acted as a role model in observing health, safety or security practices and procedures?

- Have you monitored practices or procedures to identify if changes or improvements are needed in a service user's risk assessment?

RESEARCH

Look into the risk assessments that exist in your service.

- Which issues and needs have been subject to a risk assessment?

- How often are these reviewed?

- Who is responsible for reviewing them?

- How could you input these into future reviews?

APPLICATION OF SKILLS

Changing needs and circumstances

Example 1

A woman with severe learning disabilities, Rhiann, requires a significant level of support that includes personal care. When Rhiann transfers from her bed to her commode she is able to do so with just some guidance from the member of staff with her.

Over the past few weeks the situation has started to change. Rhiann is now noticeably leaning on staff when she transfers.

- What are the health and safety issues in this scenario?
- What action should be taken?

Example 2

Mrs Scoles is an older woman living in a care home. Over time her degree of confusion has increased. Mrs Scoles regularly tries to leave the care home but she is unable to open the door without assistance. Staff are concerned about Mrs Scoles leaving the home as there is a very busy road outside.

The service convenes a meeting to discuss their options. This includes a community nurse and a social worker. It is agreed that the next time Mrs Scoles tries to open the door a staff member will unlock the door and go out with Mrs Scoles.

The plan is applied. Mrs Scoles walks for a short distance but then just walks up and down the road. She is smiling. Mrs Scoles makes no attempt to cross the road and she is happy to return with the worker after 15 minutes or so.

- What should happen now? You may want to think in terms of both short-term and medium-/long-term issues.
- What would you have done in a similar situation?

PROCEDURES FOR RESPONDING TO ACCIDENTS AND SUDDEN ILLNESS

In any work setting, a range of accidents or sudden illnesses could occur and create an emergency situation. In health and social care work, we are working with individuals who often need services because there are increased risks to their health and well-being.

The following accidents could occur:

- fire
- falls

- trips

- spills

- road accidents (eg where a service user is accessing a resource in the community or being transported as one of a group)

- scalds or burns

- fractures or broken bones

- cuts causing sudden or severe bleeding.

Sudden illnesses could occur (either to yourself, colleagues or service users, although service users may be more vulnerable to certain conditions), such as:

- heart attacks/cardiac arrest

- asthma and respiratory difficulties

- epileptic seizure

- losing consciousness

- choking.

PROCEDURES TO BE FOLLOWED IF AN ACCIDENT OR SUDDEN ILLNESS SHOULD OCCUR

Every service or setting will have its own procedures for responding in the event of accidents or sudden illness. It is important that you are aware of these before an event occurs, as it is no use in an emergency if you have to spend time finding out what to do when you should be doing it.

One of the key skills of competent workers is to remain calm and not to add to the sense of drama or crisis by panicking, or by getting angry or irritated.

If a worker is the first person at an emergency scene (or the first person who appears able to act), then their response should include the following:

- assessing the emergency

- maintaining their own and others' safety

- summoning help

- supporting the casualty

- understanding their own limitations

- handing over the casualty to the emergency services and giving them relevant information

- seeking appropriate support for yourself and others, if required

- completing the appropriate paperwork.

Assessing the emergency

It is important that the worker remains calm and tries to think rationally. Trying to gauge the casualty's condition is helpful.

There may be environmental clues as to why the accident has occurred (eg a wire cord from, say, a vacuum cleaner lying across the floor).

Maintaining one's own and others' safety

If there is anything the worker can do to make the area safe, then they should do so. It is often more important for you to make sure that you are safe, so that you can respond better to the needs of others who require support in a crisis situation when there are others who are more experienced or more able to deal with the person who needs immediate help.

Summoning help

If the emergency situation occurs in a care home or a day centre, the worker will usually need to call for the manager on duty. It is usually up to the senior staff member to either call the emergency services or delegate that task to a staff member.

If the incident occurs in a service user's own home, then a worker may well be working alone. The worker may be able to contact the emergency services while with the casualty.

Supporting the casualty

If the person is conscious, the worker should inform them what has been done, ask them what happened and how they feel at the time.

Handing over the casualty to the emergency services

If trained and authorised to do so, then workers should administer first aid if required. When the emergency services arrive, the worker should inform them about:

- what they know about the cause of the emergency and when it happened

- the casualty's name and relevant personal information

- what actions the worker has undertaken

- any changes in the casualty's condition that they have observed, eg when did they become unconscious?

HEALTH AND SAFETY (FIRST AID) REGULATIONS

These regulations require employers to provide adequate equipment, facilities and personnel to enable first aid to be given to employees if they become ill or are injured at work. The regulations do not oblige employers to provide first aid for members of the public, though the Health and Safety Executive strongly recommends that employers make provision to do so.

BEING CLEAR ABOUT YOUR ROLE

In all aspects of health and social care, workers should be clear about their role and responsibilities, to work within this framework and not to exceed their role (or competence). It is never more important than in terms of dealing with emergencies at work. If a worker exceeds their role in an emergency, they may well put their own safety and perhaps even their life (and those of others) at serious risk.

It is difficult to explore the whole range of potential emergencies in any detail. Candidates should know what sort of emergencies could occur in their own work role and should also be familiar with which policies and protocols are in place to give guidance on the management of these emergencies.

REFLECT

- Have you ever been in a crisis situation in your work?

- What were the policies and procedures that you followed?

- How did you feel, and what support were you offered at the time and afterwards?

RESEARCH

Find out who the trained first aiders are in your service.

- What training is available to you and how would you access this?

- What procedures does your current employer have in place for dealing with accidents or sudden illness?

- Does your employer have regular test runs of these procedures to make sure that everyone is confident in what they should do in an emergency?

CASE STUDY

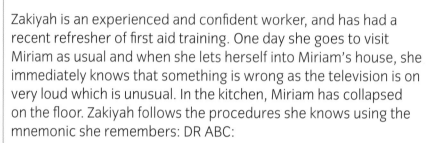

Zakiyah is a senior domiciliary care worker. She provides care services to people in their own homes. The domiciliary care service provides support to all adults in need of support although most of the service users she works with are older people.

Zakiyah has worked with Miriam for many months. Miriam is an older person who has physical health difficulties and restricted mobility.

Zakiyah is an experienced and confident worker, and has had a recent refresher of first aid training. One day she goes to visit Miriam as usual and when she lets herself into Miriam's house, she immediately knows that something is wrong as the television is on very loud which is unusual. In the kitchen, Miriam has collapsed on the floor. Zakiyah follows the procedures she knows using the mnemonic she remembers: DR ABC:

- **D**anger: checking there is no immediate danger to herself
- **R**esponse: calling Miriam's name (she does not respond)
- **A**irways: checking Miriam's airways are not obstructed
- **B**reathing: checking Miriam is still breathing
- **C**irculation: checking Miriam's pulse which is faint and irregular.

- How might Zakiyah feel at this point?
- What does Zakiyah need to do next?

REDUCING THE SPREAD OF INFECTION

Since care work regularly involves personal care there are immediately risks of cross-infection. The risk of cross-infection is increased given that one staff member often supports various service users. Additionally, service users and staff are often in close proximity and are likely to use some shared facilities, eg bathroom/toilet.

Individuals do sometimes become ill. Some illnesses cannot be transmitted to other people, eg cancer, heart disease, etc, but there are a variety of illnesses that can be passed on to others (that are communicable). Within care services, staff should be able to work in ways that reduce the likelihood of communicable illnesses or diseases being passed on to other people.

If two people in a service develop the same communicable disease at the same time (or one soon after the other) this could be considered an outbreak. For some communicable diseases one person with the infection can be a cause for concern in its own right (depending on what the infection is) and so be considered an outbreak.

Management are responsible for notifying local health and environmental health staff of outbreaks of certain communicable diseases and to take action to prevent **cross-infection**.

Key term

A **cross-infection** is when an infection spreads from one person to another.

HOW PEOPLE CAN BECOME INFECTED

Within any setting there are four potential ways that infection can be passed on:

- inhalation (eg breathing in minute droplets/particles of infection)
- ingestion (eg eating foodstuffs that carry the infection)
- direct contact with the skin or mucous membranes
- through the skin (eg being pricked by an infected needle, contact with open wounds).

Inhalation
Communicable diseases that can be contracted through breathing in bacteria include:

- tuberculosis
- shingles, mumps, rubella
- methicillin-resistant *Staphylococcus aureus* (MRSA)
- influenza.

Ingestion
Communicable diseases that can be contracted through a person eating or drinking the infectious agent include:

- food poisoning bacteria, eg salmonella, *E. coli* 0157, listeria, etc.
- dysentery
- typhoid.

Contact with the skin
Communicable infections that can be acquired by contact with the skin (eg where the skin is broken or inflamed) include scabies.

Contact through the skin
Infections that can be transmitted either by the skin being pierced or through already open wounds include:

- hepatitis A

- hepatitis B

- illnesses that cause diarrhoea, eg dysentery

- human immunodeficiency virus (HIV).

HIV transmission only occurs where body fluids (eg blood, semen or breast milk) infected with HIV are transferred from one person's body into another person's body. Urine, faeces and vomit are not considered to pose a risk of HIV infection, unless they are contaminated with blood. However, urine, faeces and vomit could be the means by which other diseases are transmitted and so staff must always wear gloves and aprons if there is a risk of coming into contact with them.

> **KEY POINT**
>
> **Washing your hands**
> Evidence consistently indicates that the single most important work practice that should be observed by staff is effective hand-washing.

PREVENTING THE SPREAD OF INFECTION

There are a variety of work practices that should be applied ordinarily by staff to prevent infection. Additionally, if a person develops a communicable disease in a service, the managers of the service may need to introduce other measures (hopefully only until the risk of further infection has passed).

WHEN SHOULD STAFF WASH THEIR HANDS?

- Before and after any personal care task.

- After handling clinical waste (eg body fluids, incontinence wear), linen or emptying bins or handling any bags intended for disposal.

- Before handling food, eating or drinking.

- After using the toilet.

- After removal of protective gloves and aprons.

- After blowing your own nose.

- After contact with animals.

GLOVES AND APRON

It is important to note that hands should be washed after providing intimate personal care or after dealing with body fluids even when gloves have been worn since gloves do not provide 100 per cent protection.

Even considering this gloves and aprons should always be worn whenever it is necessary. They do reduce the risk of infections being spread. Always remove and dispose of the apron and gloves after you have provided personal care (or dealt with a body fluid spillage or whatever the task was).

Gloves should always be removed by pulling down the hand from the wrist and left inside out. Used gloves can be disposed of in the normal household rubbish.

HEAVY-DUTY GLOVES

Rubber gloves should be used when you are dealing with practical household duties. They must always be worn when emptying and cleaning commodes and toilets.

Care should be taken when handling household chemicals and cleaning agents. These gloves do not need to be disposed of after use. They should be rinsed in cold water after use, dried and kept for future use.

SINGLE-USE ITEMS

Various items are single-use only and this must be observed. Simple examples of this are gloves and aprons.

INDIVIDUALS WITH SPECIAL NEEDS

Some service users have specific needs, such as having a urinary catheter. Only staff who have been trained in catheter management should be actively involved in assisting a service user with their catheter.

BLOOD-BORNE TRANSMISSIBLE DISEASES

Blood-borne transmissible diseases such as hepatitis B and HIV are very significant diseases. Good working practices can markedly reduce the risk of acquiring such a disease.

SPILLAGES OF BODY FLUIDS

- Whenever there are spillages of body fluids they must be cleaned up quickly and safely.

- Any body fluid is a potential source of infection and so staff must respond in a way that protects themselves and other people.

- Staff need to have clear information about how body fluid spillages are to be responded to.

- Staff must wear disposable gloves and an apron before attempting to clean up a body fluid spillage.

- Body fluid spillages must be disposed of following agreed workplace procedures.

- Any items or surface area in contact with body fluids should be thoroughly cleaned or disposed of (if the item is disposable) as necessary.

GENERAL CLEANLINESS

As a general rule, it is best if rooms are kept clean and free from clutter. Areas where personal care has been provided should be as clean as practicable.

DEALING WITH BODY WASTE

The contents of commodes, bedpans and urine bottles must always be emptied into the lavatory. They should be washed thoroughly and dried, before replacing ready for reuse.

METHICILLIN-RESISTANT *STAPHYLOCOCCUS AUREUS* (MRSA)

MRSA is a type of bacterium that may be harmlessly carried by many people on their skin and in their noses without causing an infection. It is carried more easily on skin that is broken, eg where there is a rash, a cut or a sore. It can, however, cause abscesses, boils and wound infection, particularly in people who are unwell.

MRSA is resistant to treatment with some antibiotics and may be more difficult to treat if it does cause an infection.

The bacteria spread easily from person to person by sticking to the hands or clothing of staff or service users and then passing on to the next person they touch. Careful hand-washing with an antibacterial wash is important and helps to prevent the spread of bacteria.

Clothing and bed linen of infected people should, where possible, be washed separately and you should try to reduce the amount of times the laundry is handled. Protective clothing, disposable gloves and aprons must be worn, and disposed of immediately by tying into plastic bags and placing into a dustbin.

MRSA may have come on to service users' skin when they went into hospital or it could have been picked up since being in hospital. It can be treated very successfully by prescribed ointments, washes or antibiotics.

People with MRSA do not look or feel different from any other people. The germ can only be found by growing it from swabs taken from the skin and wounds. Swabs will be taken from different parts of the body to see whether the germ is just in one or two places or if it is widespread. After a week, the swabs will be taken again to check that the germ has gone. Sometimes it may take several weeks to completely clear from the skin. Good hand-care precautions are essential. You must wash your hands prior to commencing any tasks and putting on gloves, and then you must wash your hands on completion of the task.

On leaving a property, further protection can be gained by blowing your nose.

DISPOSAL OF WASTE (PERSONAL)

When disposing of service users' body waste, make sure infection-control guidelines are kept to, which includes the use of protective clothing.

Waste from commodes and urine bottles must be emptied into the lavatory.

Commode pots and urine bottles must be washed thoroughly on each occasion of emptying, then rinsed using a bleach solution diluted to 1:10. The pot should be thoroughly dried and replaced. Over-the-counter purchased disinfectants may also be used.

Commode chairs also require wiping down daily with solution and disposable cloths or a cloth kept specially for this activity. This will prevent cross-infection.

GENERAL PRINCIPLES IN INFECTION CONTROL

Some practices that can help reduce the risk of infection spreading include:

- following the recommended methods for washing hands

- using personal protective clothing, eg gloves and aprons

- ensuring that cleaning methods and practices are safe, rigorous and regular

- ensuring people who undertake cleaning are trained and that their work is monitored and checked as necessary

- following food hygiene practices

- ensuring that service users are supported with their hygiene needs as pertinent to their care plan

- ensuring that you and your colleagues' own hygiene is good.

CODE OF PRACTICE ON THE PREVENTION AND CONTROL OF INFECTIONS

A code of practice on the prevention and control of infections and related guidance was introduced by Regulation 12 of the Health and Social Care Act 2008. This code of practice sets out 10 criteria against which the Care Quality Commission judges a registered provider on how it complies with the cleanliness and infection control requirement which is set out in guidance. The document also helps registered providers interpret the criteria and develop their own risk assessments. The guidance is proportionate in that the requirements for social care services are less rigorous than for clinical medical facilities and examples of this are shown in the text.

THE RECOMMENDED METHOD FOR WASHING YOUR HANDS

In health and social care practice, the Department of Health's (2007a) 'Wet, soap, wash, rinse, dry' model is the accepted best practice in hand-washing technique.

ENSURING THAT YOUR OWN HEALTH AND HYGIENE DO NOT POSE A RISK TO AN INDIVIDUAL OR TO OTHERS

There are a number of ways to ensure that your own health and hygiene are appropriate to meet the needs of those with whom you work. These ways include:

- wearing uniforms in some settings, and personal protective clothing (PPE) as required in other environments

- ensuring your own clothing is clean and appropriate to the work you do

- wearing gloves for certain tasks

- not wearing jewellery

- tying your hair up in certain settings or for specific tasks

- considering your footwear and its appropriateness to your work

- taking time off work if you are not well enough and if there is a risk that you could spread an infection to the service users whom you support. Remember that many service users are more vulnerable to many conditions (coughs, colds, stomach bugs, etc), and that for some people, a relatively minor infection could become something which is potentially life threatening.

REFLECT

- How do you ensure your own hygiene and health do not increase the risk of infection for colleagues or service users?

- What practical measures do you use in your work setting to reduce the risk of infection?

RESEARCH

- What is your service or agency's agreed procedures for washing hands?

- How are these expectations adhered to by everyone in the service?

- How do you support service users to follow best practices too?

CASE STUDY

Chen is a senior care assistant in a residential service for older people. He has worked there for many years, and usually enjoys good health. However, this winter he has had three periods of absence because of a persistent cold, a sickness bug and diarrhoea.

After the third absence, Chen has a return-to-work meeting with his manager. At this meeting, he is warned that he has reached the threshold for concern because of his sickness absence record. Chen is annoyed as he has not had any previous absence for a long time, and he has taken time off this winter in order to avoid spreading infections to the residents in the home, many of whom are extremely frail and vulnerable.

- What could or should Chen do in this situation?

MOVING AND HANDLING EQUIPMENT AND OTHER OBJECTS SAFELY

MANUAL HANDLING OPERATIONS REGULATIONS

These regulations contain the following main requirements:

- Suitable and efficient assessment of all moving and handling should be made, if the handling cannot be avoided.

- Risk-reduction strategies must be considered by employers to reduce the risk of injury to the lowest level reasonably practicable.

- Employers must provide reasonable information about moving and handling.

- Employers must review assessments where there is reason to suspect that circumstances have changed, and then make any necessary changes.

- Employees must make full and proper use of any system of work provided by the employer.

PROVISION AND USE OF EQUIPMENT REGULATIONS (PUWER)

These regulations impose a range of duties on employers (and to a limited extent to the employees who use the equipment). Aspects include:

- the initial state of the equipment
- use of equipment for the proper purpose
- suitability of equipment
- maintenance
- inspection
- training staff in its use.

The scope of these regulations has been interpreted very broadly so that it includes cupboards and curtain rails as well as equipment that is subject to heavy usage. The employer's liability is strictly applied. Even if the equipment were regularly inspected and then it unexpectedly fell and injured a staff member, the employer would still be liable. The employer would not be liable for negligence if the equipment was satisfactorily maintained and inspected, but they would still be liable for any injury under these regulations.

LIFTING OPERATIONS AND LIFTING EQUIPMENT REGULATIONS (LOLER)

These regulations apply to lifting equipment used at work. Lifting equipment would include hoists, stairlifts and through-floor lifts. The regulations impose a range of duties on employers and to a limited extent on staff who use or supervise the use of the equipment. Duties include:

- ensuring adequate strength and stability
- positioning and installation
- marking of safe working loads
- organisation of lifting operations
- examination and inspection
- reporting defects and acting on these reports.

There is no set guidance as to how frequently lifting equipment should be inspected. This is partly dependent on whether the equipment is exposed to conditions that could cause it to deteriorate so that dangerous situations could arise.

Some hoist manufacturers recommend a thorough examination of their hoists every six months. Against this, the Health and Safety Executive has published a document recommending that hoists are inspected at least every 12 months. The implication is that some manufacturers could have a conflict of interests. That is, they can charge a care organisation every time their trained inspectors go out on a visit. What is clear is that the timescales for thorough inspections should be drawn up by a competent person who is aware of all relevant facts.

PRINCIPLES FOR SAFE MOVING AND HANDLING

Moving and handling includes:

- moving objects in the work setting (eg boxes, water cylinders, filing cabinets, bags of rubbish)

- supporting people to move.

The key principles are as follows:

- *Avoid.* Do not undertake any moving or handling without having had the necessary training (eg to use specific equipment). Do not undertake moving and handling if you do not feel it is safe to do so.

- *Assess.* Ensure that moving and handling activities have been properly risk assessed. In risk assessing moving and handling, consider the following TILE model:

  - *Task.* What is the precise task that is required? What factors make the task more or less difficult to achieve? What obstacles might there be?

  - *Individual.* What specific needs, capabilities or difficulties does the individual doing the moving or handling need to consider for themselves to be able to perform the task safely?

  - *Load.* Consider the actual load that the task presents, and how this load can be moved most safely.

  - *Equipment* and *environment.* Consider the impact of temperature, space, flooring, hazards, posture, handles on equipment, wheels, training, and maintenance of equipment.

- *Reduce risk.* Do not undertake any moving or handling without the right equipment. Do not undertake moving and handling by yourself if the task actually requires more than one or two people to do it safely.

- *Review.* Following any moving or handling, review how this went and update risk assessments as required for future activities.

- *If in doubt, don't do it.*

More information on the TILE model is available on the Health and Safety Executive's website: www.hse.gov.uk.

SUPPORTING A PERSON TO MOVE

The first and most important key principle links to the value base of social care – in order for practice to be person centred, people should be involved in planning any moving of themselves. People are not objects to be moved about without their full involvement and their active participation in this personal form of support. People should be supported with the minimum of input from others – ie people should be supported where they need support, and enabled and empowered to do everything for themselves that they can do. This is an area where the principles of active support are at their most apparent and powerful.

Use of hoists should be undertaken by people who have been trained to use this equipment, and the safety of hoists, stairlifts and other equipment involved in moving people should be regularly reviewed.

In terms of legislation (and the duty of care in your role), it is your employer's responsibility to provide the necessary tools, equipment and training for moving and handling to be done safely, and it is your duty to use them safely and appropriately.

REFLECT

- Have you been involved in any moving and handling activity (either at work or in your personal life, eg lifting items at home when moving house) that has concerned you?

- What could you and others have done to make this activity safer?

- If your role involves moving people, how do you achieve the principles of active support?

RESEARCH

If your job role involves moving and handling, review the risk assessments on the equipment in your work setting. When were these last reviewed, and how do reviews take account of the need for any changes?

CASE STUDY

Dee is a senior care assistant in a day service for older people. The people who attend the day service generally live at home with much of their support being provided by family members – a few service users also receive domiciliary care services.

Dee is organising for the main seating areas to be redecorated as the decor has been looking a little tired and shabby for some time, and everyone feels that a refresh would be timely. While this is being done, the conservatory is going to be used as the seating area.

Dee and her team have a staff meeting where they look at the timescales for the redecoration and roles and responsibilities around this. Dee advises the team that professional decorators have been booked, and it is the team's role to support service users on the day the decorators come in as there will be nowhere to sit while the chairs are moved from the lounge to the conservatory. Dee thinks this should take approximately an hour, and asks staff to consider spending planned time with certain service users on activities outside or in other areas of the building.

When Dee comes into work on the Monday morning when the decorating is to commence, she sees that eight large comfortable chairs and the full-sized television have already been moved into the conservatory. She asks her team who moved them as the decorators have not arrived yet, and the workers tell her that the people who worked over the weekend moved them as they were concerned that some service users would have nowhere to sit if they arrived before the decorators. Dee is concerned that these chairs are extremely heavy and that the risk assessment around moving them has not been followed.

- What could Dee do in this scenario?

- How can she ensure that proper moving and handling procedures are followed in the future?

HANDLING HAZARDOUS SUBSTANCES AND MATERIALS

Substances can be hazardous in a range of ways:

Explosive (E)
Flammable (F)
Toxic (T)
Irritant (I)
Corrosive (C)
Harmful to the environment (H)

Hazard symbols

TYPES OF HAZARDOUS SUBSTANCES THAT MAY BE FOUND AT WORK

In health and social care settings, the types of hazardous substances can include:

- human waste
- cleaning products and bleach
- office equipment (eg correction fluid and photocopier/printer cartridges)
- needles and sharps
- medical equipment (eg used dressings and linen).

All such items will need:

- clear labelling
- risk assessing
- controlled access
- safe storage of the items
- a file to be kept with information on these items so that everyone in the team can access this.

CONTROL OF SUBSTANCES HAZARDOUS TO HEALTH REGULATIONS

These regulations are often referred to as COSHH and cover substances that can cause ill health. Any substances such as cleaning materials, waste products, fumes, etc are covered. In order to comply with the regulations employers must:

- assess the risks to health arising from work
- decide what precautions are needed
- prevent or control exposure to substances hazardous to health
- ensure that control measures are used and maintained
- monitor exposure of workers to hazardous substances and where assessment shows that health surveillance may be needed to carry out such surveillance
- ensure that employees are properly informed, trained and supervised.

SAFE PRACTICES FOR STORING, USING AND DISPOSING OF HAZARDOUS SUBSTANCES AND MATERIALS

As has been described, both you and your employer have specific responsibilities for ensuring safe practices in terms of COSHH. The table below details some of these responsibilities.

Responsibility of the employer	Responsibility of the employee
Ensure there is an assessment from COSHH of the risks to health arising from work	Assess the risks to health arising from work
Decide what specific precautions are needed	Know about these precautions that have been identified, and follow them
Prevent or control exposure to substances hazardous to health	Prevent or control exposure to substances hazardous to health (for you, your colleagues and your service users)
Ensure that control measures are used and maintained	Ensure that control measures are used and maintained
Monitor exposure of workers to hazardous substances and where assessment shows that health surveillance may be needed to carry out such surveillance	You may be involved in monitoring the exposure of others to hazardous substances, or in carrying out surveillance (recording/reporting) of the effects of COSHH on yourself or other people
Ensure that employees are properly informed, trained and supervised	Access the training that is made available and put the learning from this training into practice

STORING HAZARDOUS SUBSTANCES

You should follow agreed procedures for storing substances that are potentially harmful. These could involve:

- use of a lockable cabinet (eg for cleaning products)
- safe storage of sharps
- procedures for ensuring cabinets and storage facilities have limited access and that they are locked at all times when they are not in use.

USING HAZARDOUS SUBSTANCES

This sounds self-explanatory, but again your service is likely to have procedures and/or informal expectations in place in order to ensure that substances are used safely and appropriately. For example:

- ensuring that there is no cross-contamination where two substances are mixed when they should not be

- making sure substances are used in the right/safe quantities

- using the right containers to put products in.

DISPOSING OF HAZARDOUS SUBSTANCES

Disposal of hazardous substances is critical in order to ensure that there is no harm caused to people and the environment.

Some items are required to be disposed of in certain ways (eg sharps and dressings). Sometimes there will be best practices for disposal (eg of bodily fluids or human waste) that will include agreed expectations of how a work area should be cleared and made safe after the substance has been disposed of.

REFLECT

- In your work setting, how do you apply the principles above relating to COSHH?

- What training have you had on this, and how are you involved in reviewing and updating or amending risk assessments for COSHH?

RESEARCH

Look at the Health and Safety Executive's website and the information on COSHH. How does your agency or service meet its duties relating to hazardous substances?

PROMOTING FIRE SAFETY AT WORK

REGULATORY REFORM (FIRE SAFETY) ORDER 2005

This statutory instrument reforms the fire safety regulations that apply to England and Wales. In any workplace the employer has a responsibility to:

- take fire precautions to ensure, as far as possible, the safety of all employees

- ensure there are general fire precautions to keep the property safe (and so protect the general public) (article 8).

The employer's duties are to:

- carry out a risk assessment to identify the general fire precautions that are needed (article 9), and then to

- apply any fire prevention measure and have in place an evacuation procedure (articles 10 to 18)

- inform employees of the risks and the fire prevention measures (articles 19 to 21).

Employees have duties which include (article 23):

- following all fire safety requirements as directed by their employer

- informing the employer of any risks not adequately addressed.

UNDERSTANDING FIRE PREVENTION

Prevention is more important than cure, especially when it comes to fire. Employers and services will have specific measures in place to ensure fire safety is considered, such as:

- electrical checks

- risk assessments

- regular fire drills

- fire exits with clear standard labelling

- signing in and out procedures (in a portable form which can be taken out of a premises for a register check in the event of a fire)

- fire alarms (regularly tested)

- fire wardens with specific responsibilities

- fire extinguishers in key places in the premises

- fire blankets

- training on fire safety (updated regularly)
- posters to show where the designated fire assembly point is (all service users, staff, visitors and contractors should always be made aware of this when they access the premises or service).

All fires involve:

- oxygen
- heat
- a fuel (something that burns).

KEY POINT

Without any one of these factors in place, a fire cannot start. In order for any fire to be put out safely, one or more of these factors need to be tackled.

FIRE EXTINGUISHERS

You need to have some awareness of which colour fire extinguisher is used for which type of fire. Extinguishers should always be labelled, but it still is helpful for you to have basic knowledge about this. You should always read instructions before you activate any extinguisher too and, if you are uncertain, it is better to evacuate everyone safely instead of tackling a fire and possibly causing greater harm.

For solid-fuelled fires, you usually need to point the extinguisher at the bottom of the flames and move it across the area of the fire. For all fires, make sure that all of the flames are out before you finish using the extinguisher.

Colour on extinguisher	Contents	Used on	Do not use on
Red	Water	Solids, eg paper, cloth, wood	Electrics or burning liquids
Black	Carbon dioxide (CO_2)	Some liquids, eg paint, petrol, fats Electrical	Chip-pan or fat fires Do not use in areas without sufficient ventilation as fumes can be harmful

Colour on extinguisher	Contents	Used on	Do not use on
Blue	Multi-purpose dry powder	Solids, eg paper, cloth, wood / Some liquids, eg paint, petrol, fats / Electrical	Chip-pan or fat fires
Blue	Standard dry powder	Some liquids, eg paint, petrol, fats	Chip-pan or fat fires
Cream	AFFF (Aqueous Film Forming Foam)	Solids, eg paper, cloth, wood / Some liquids, eg paint, petrol, fats	Chip-pan or fat fires / Electrical
Fire blanket		Can be used on both solids and liquids / Make sure the whole fire is completely covered in order to cut off the oxygen supply to the fire	

EMERGENCY PROCEDURES TO BE FOLLOWED IN THE EVENT OF A FIRE IN THE WORK SETTING

The emergency procedures will be slightly different in every work setting you access and it is important that you familiarise yourself with procedures including:

- how to raise the alarm
- fire exits
- who is the person responsible for fire safety
- telephone points
- risk assessments for fire
- fire assembly point.

Doing so when you provide care in people's own homes, or where a service user employs you using their direct payments, is really different (but no less important) from where you work as part of a day centre or residential provision.

STANDARD PROCEDURES AND EXPECTATIONS IN THE EVENT OF A FIRE

1 Sound the alarm.

2 Call the fire brigade.

3 Evacuate the premises safely and without causing increased risk. In health and social care settings, the needs, mobility and vulnerability of service users should be considered and addressed at all times. Planning and identifying specific actions and necessary support is a critical element of good fire risk assessment in social care. You need to know about people's individual needs as part of your job role, and you need to enable people to move if they can do so themselves, or to be moved quickly and safely in the event of any emergency. As part of this, you also need to know what your service setting's expectations are about people who cannot be safely moved to a safe area in an emergency.

4 Do not stop for belongings.

5 Do not use lifts. Do not try to be a hero – the fire service are the experts. If you feel it is safe to, attempt to use the correct extinguisher to attack the fire, but if it is not safe, it is better to evacuate the building and let the fire service do their job.

6 Consider your own safety – eg do not take hold of a door handle which may be very hot and present a risk to you (test it with the back of your hand instead).

7 Go to the identified fire assembly point.

8 Take the register with you so you know who is in the building and can check that everyone is out.

9 Do not go back to the service premises until it is safe to do so.

ENSURING THAT CLEAR EVACUATION ROUTES ARE MAINTAINED

Trailing wires, office equipment, clutter in people's homes or frayed carpets could all cause a hazard in the event of an emergency evacuation because of a fire, bomb threat, chemical spill, or any other reason. Maintaining vigilance, updating risk assessments, monitoring and reporting any concerns, and completing regular tests or practices of service procedures are critical in order to ensure that if an emergency does occur, evacuation is swift and safe.

KEY POINT

It is essential that you ensure that clear routes to evacuate are always maintained.

REFLECT

- What are the procedures for fire safety in your work setting?

- Have you signed something to say that you have read and understood these?

- On a scale of 1 to 10, how confident do you feel in applying these procedures in an emergency?

- If you need further training, this is a good opportunity to request this.

- If you feel there are other training needs or issues in your work environment that you have identified, this is a good opportunity flag these up too.

RESEARCH

What are the expectations in your service regarding the following:

- fire training

- risk assessment

- emergency evacuation (especially of vulnerable people)

- fire extinguishers

- fire notices

- assembly points, etc.

If you provide services in people's own homes, how do all of the above look in practice?

IMPLEMENTING SECURITY MEASURES AT WORK

ENSURING THE SECURITY OF PREMISES AND INFORMATION

Ensuring the security of information is also covered in more detail in Chapter 7 on handling information.

Ensuring the security of premises is important in order to keep service users, colleagues, yourself and information safe and secure. Each work setting is likely to have different procedures, and for health and social care workers who support people in their homes, these procedures are likely to be very informal in their nature (but no less important for that).

Agreed procedures and systems may include:

- use of doors and locks where people's identity is checked before the door is released

- asking people for their identity badge (many have a number on the back of the person's employer which you can ring to verify the person's identity)

- ensuring people sign in and out of buildings (for fire purposes and for verifying who was in the building on any day)

- use of logbooks or daybooks

- verifying people's identity with their employer (especially where there may be concerns and double checking is felt to be needed)

- calling people back on the telephone when they have rung in for information, so that you can check their identity

- using agreed policies relating to access to records and formal requests for information from other agencies

- ensuring that contractors sign a document to show that they understand local/ Service safety procedures – this also provides a record that their identity has been checked.

For your assessment, you are likely to need to demonstrate your understanding of your service's procedures and your application of these procedures in a consistent way to your practice.

MAINTAINING YOUR OWN SECURITY AND THE SECURITY OF OTHERS AT WORK

Measures to maintain your own security and those of colleagues and service users include:

- training in risk identification, assessment and minimisation
- confidence in using procedures (eg emergency procedures and procedures for locking up a building at the end of a day)
- tools and measures to secure people's personal belongings away
- skills in de-escalating situations
- safe keeping of tools that are within a work environment (eg limiting access to a building or areas of a facility).

In health and social care, workers need to be skilled in protecting themselves and those with whom they work. Organisations should provide workers with the information to enable them to work through the following steps:

1   Identify potential risks.

2   Avoid potentially dangerous situations.

3   De-escalate.

4   Disengage.

5   Call for help.

6   Use appropriate physical interventions.

Since staff work in a wide range of areas it is difficult to give examples that apply to all staff. Therefore what follows is bound to be limited. Staff do need to develop their own sense of risk awareness and to plan what to do should a situation become dangerous.

Identify potential risks

In terms of identifying the behaviour an individual may engage in, the biggest single indicating factor is previous behaviour. If a person has been violent in the recent past, there is a risk that they could be violent at some point in the future.

If an individual is on the whole reasonable but once they drink alcohol they become aggressive then the consumption of alcohol is a risk factor. If a person is in group care (at a day centre or residential care home) and the presence of a certain service user triggers an aggressive cycle then that would be a risk factor.

Avoid potentially dangerous situations

Having a sense of the potential risks should lead a worker on to seeking to minimise the likelihood of an aggressive incident occurring. Once a potential risk is identified, how to manage this should be included in a care plan. The service user should also have been consulted about what response staff will be required to take.

If two particular service users in the same room results in a difficult situation, can the two service users be supported to engage in activities in different rooms?

If a home care worker arrives at the home of a service user and it soon becomes clear that the person has consumed alcohol, and this is a known risk factor, then it could well be written into the care plan that at this point the care worker leaves.

Within care plans there could be comments about what staff should or should not do to reduce the risk of dangerous situations arising.

De-escalate

In some situations it may be possible to calm a situation that has started to become of concern. Aspects of de-escalation include remaining calm, listening to the person and, wherever possible, acknowledging that the service user has a point and recognising that the person's concern can be pursued through normal routes, eg a complaints procedure.

Disengage

Staff need to be aware that leaving a potentially dangerous situation is a legitimate and responsible reaction to a threatening situation.

A staff member may enter a situation that they quickly perceive is potentially dangerous. To keep open the option of leaving the staff member needs to consider practical aspects such as remaining near the door.

Call for help

Staff should be aware of how to summon assistance. This is usually easiest when an incident occurs in a service or office. Home care staff working alone are the most vulnerable and must know how to call for help.

Use appropriate physical intervention

Any staff who are expected to use physical intervention will receive training as to what is expected, what physical interventions are acceptable and they will rehearse applying these in training.

One common feature of such training is to convey that using physical interventions should be the option of last resort.

If any staff member is in a situation that is so threatening that they are actively concerned for their own well-being, then there is a common law right to use reasonable and proportionate force for the purpose of self-defence.

VIOLENCE AGAINST WORKERS

In 2001 the Department of Health published a document called 'A safer place'. This was developed by a task force set up to look into violence against social care staff.

The document is essentially an audit tool for managers to consider whether their organisation minimises the potential for workers to be subject to violence or abuse.

The document defines violence and abuse as:

Incidents where persons are abused, threatened or assaulted in circumstances relating to their work, involving an explicit or implicit challenge to their safety, well-being or health. This definition is taken to include verbal abuse or threat, threatening behaviour, any assault (and any apprehension of unlawful violence), and serious or persistent harassment, including racial or sexual harassment, and extends from what may seem to be minor incidents to serious assault and murder, and threats against the worker's family.

(Department of Health 2001b)

It goes on to cover the following principles:

- Violence, threats and abuse to workers are unacceptable.

- Good policies need to be developed, in consultation with service users, workers and other relevant people.

- Managers and environments should maximise workers' safety.

- Good-quality risk assessments should be developed and these should be kept under regular review.

The document outlines various responsibilities that managers have towards staff and the type of actions they can engage in to uphold these responsibilities.

One of the management responsibilities is to ensure that all staff are aware of what they should do to reduce the risk of violence occurring in the first place and what to do once a situation starts to develop.

ENSURING THAT OTHERS ARE AWARE OF YOUR WHEREABOUTS

In health and social care, workers are frequently doing their jobs in situations where there may be risks to:

- people who are being supported

- the worker themselves – these could be risks presented either from the person being supported, from relatives or others known to the person, or from others in the community.

Workers can often be working in very isolated settings and it is important that someone knows of your whereabouts at all times. This should be done via the service or employer, as it is not appropriate in terms of confidentiality for your own family or friends to know the addresses of service users with whom you work.

Most services have or should have agreed and understood procedures in place to ensure the safety of workers who provide services in people's homes and in the community. These procedures might involve:

- *Signing in and out of the office.* Usually the administrator or manager should monitor the 'in and out' board and flag up any concerns if people do not return at the time they have specified they are due back.

- *A named buddy for work out of office hours,* so that someone knows where you are, what time you are due out, and what to do (ie to call a manager or police) if you do not buddy in at an agreed time or respond to their efforts to contact you.

- *Lone working.* Most services that are delivered primarily by lone workers will consider this in detail in the risk assessment. For example, if you are working in the community, you will need to consider issues relating to finding people's homes, where you park for a visit (eg ensuring that if you need to leave somewhere suddenly for your own safety, you can do so safely), what to do in extreme weather conditions, etc.

- *Using a system that the service purchases from an independent agency (or call centre).* In these systems, the worker texts or calls into a central point of contact that coordinates the information on workers' visits, and knows when the person has said they are due to be out of a visit. The coordinator also has the number of a named person to contact if the worker does not make contact at the designated time.

Of course, all of these systems are only effective in keeping workers safe if they are used regularly by everyone in the team, and if their effectiveness is tested and reviewed.

Even where all your work is within one building, it is still important that others know your whereabouts within that building, and know what to do if you are not where you should be.

RECORDING AND REPORTING

Accurate recording and reporting of health, safety and security matters is another key responsibility of workers. Whatever the service's setting, professional honesty is crucial.

For a variety of reasons there can be wide variations in the number of actual or potential incidents that are reported by services. One care service may report that there were 12 violent incidents in a six-month period while another care service reports that there were two violent incidents in the same period. Assuming that the two services were similar (in size and the needs of service users) why is there such a difference? Possible reasons include:

- more accurate recording in one service compared with the other

- one staff team manages risk better than the other (so the number of incidents reported is accurate in both services).

Without wanting to sound cynical, it is likely that both care services are under-recording and under-reporting the number of incidents. However, one service under-records more than the other. Workers need to have the professional strength to recognise that reporting incidents is not a bad reflection on themselves or their team. It is also a key component of evaluating the effectiveness of risk management procedures that have been put in place.

REFLECT

- Have there ever been occasions when you have felt unsafe at work?

- What did you do or what could you have done?

- If you work out of hours and in the community, how are buddying/lone working policies and procedures applied and implemented?

- Are there any gaps that you can identify in your local procedures?

MESSAGES FROM RESEARCH

Violence against care staff

- Violence and abuse are more common in the care sector than for comparable professions.

- Violence and abuse in health and social care are significantly under-reported, because:

  - staff believe managers will not support them

  - staff feel they will be seen as incompetent

  - there is a belief that verbal abuse and threats are part of the job

  - complex and inconveniently situated forms deter reporting.

- Violence and abuse against staff need to be taken more seriously by managers and the organisation as a whole.

- Immediate support for staff after an incident is essential and valued by staff.

- Research indicates that effective support involves:

  - effective communication within the team

  - the offer of counselling

  - recognition that everyone present might need support

  - provision of practical advice

  - calling specific debriefing meetings (if possible using an external facilitator).

(Source: Osser 2000)

APPLICATION OF SKILLS

Implementing security measures

Example 1

Ella is a woman with severe and enduring mental health problems. Support workers who visit her have noted that her back door (which they are expected to enter by) is often actually ajar. Ella usually leaves most of her money on the kitchen surface near the back door.

- What are the safety and security issues in this scenario?
- What action should be taken?

Example 2

In a care home for older people, Mr Bates has been a resident for some time. He has managed to establish a routine which includes watching a certain TV programme most days of the week on the communal television in the residents' lounge.

A new resident, Mr Charnock' moves into the service. After a few weeks he starts arguing with Mr Bates about what to watch. Mr Charnock does not have his own television and argues that the communal one should not be Mr Bates's 'own'.

One day the disagreement between Mr Charnock and Mr Bates becomes particularly heated during which Mr Bates wields his walking stick as if to hit Mr Charnock.

- What are the safety and security issues in this scenario?
- What should be done?

MANAGING STRESS

Stress can have positive as well as negative effects, but in the context of this chapter the word is used to refer to negative stress. For most of us, especially at work, a little pressure can be helpful as it enables us to feel motivated and to be able to respond. Stress is the effect when the pressure becomes too much and therefore overwhelming.

Stress is a feature of everyday life, but is particularly relevant in health and social care where the work is about working with people who need support, are often vulnerable and who can display challenging behaviours.

WHAT ARE THE SIGNS AND INDICATORS OF STRESS?

As individuals, everyone will react to stress in different ways. However, people generally react to stress in three dimensions – physical (sometimes referred to as physiological), emotional (psychological) and behavioural.

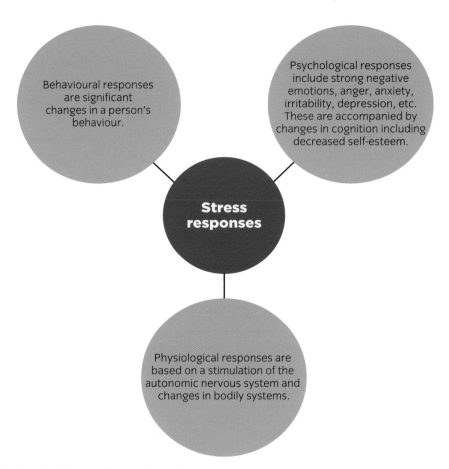

Physical reactions to stress

Someone experiencing stress might experience the following symptoms:

- muscle tension
- aches and pains
- sweating
- twitches
- pins and needles
- nausea
- dry mouth
- tiredness
- headaches
- frequency in urinating

- dilated pupils
- rapid or uneven heartbeat
- sleep disturbance
- restlessness and fidgeting
- indigestion
- hair loss
- chest pain or tightening
- butterflies in the stomach
- high blood pressure
- rapid breathing

- constipation or diarrhoea
- palpitations
- changes in appetite
- lack of concentration.

Emotional reactions to stress

Sometimes, stress can be caused by emergency situations or incidents, and the symptoms of stress can relate to the human instinct of 'fight or flight'. Feelings of panic, surges of adrenaline, and gut reactions in extreme situations can be part of our make-up as human beings, and therefore may not necessarily be fully within our conscious control. It is important to be able to recognise this, and access support from managers, colleagues or other workplace support mechanisms in order to manage the serious impact which these sorts of events can have upon all of us.

Someone who is experiencing stress may have exaggerated emotional reactions. They may feel some of the following emotions:

- tense
- under pressure
- mentally drained
- fearful
- frustrated
- angry
- irritable
- tearful
- unable to relax

- conflicted
- gloomy
- embarrassed
- agitated
- suspicious
- restless
- indecisive
- negative.

Behavioural reactions to stress

Someone experiencing stress might:

- sleep much less than usual or much more than usual
- become irritable and snap at people
- smoke more
- become dependent on drink or drugs
- change their sexual behaviours (loss of interest, increase in casual sex)
- become withdrawn where they were once very sociable
- engage in behaviours to constantly seek reassurance
- make more mistakes
- engage in self-harming behaviours
- engage in obsessive type behaviours (eg excessively checking that things are switched off).

MESSAGES FROM RESEARCH

Stress in health and social care

A wide range of research indicates that the occupation of health and social care has one of the highest raters of work-related stress. This is because health and social care work has many of the characteristics that are related to workplace stress, such as:

- long hours
- poor work–life balance
- the speed of work expected
- lack of clarity about requirements
- overloaded work schedule
- lack of support
- significant consequences when things go wrong
- high emotional demands at work
- lack of recognition and value
- regular changes in the work environment
- conflicts of values
- risk of violence and harassment.

(Milczarek, Schneider and Gonzalez 2009)

UNDERSTANDING YOUR OWN STRESS

As everyone is different, what makes us feel stressed and the way in which we show our stress will be unique for us.

HOW DO I RECOGNISE THE SIGNS OF STRESS?

It is important to be fully aware of the signs and symptoms of stress. However, when people are experiencing chronic stress they are often unable to recognise the signs of stress in themselves.

It is much more likely that those around you will recognise the signs of stress and the changes in your behaviour.

There are a range of warning signs that someone is experiencing 'dangerous levels' of stress:

- thinking you are indispensable
- negative thinking

- extreme, exaggerated or misplaced emotional reactions

- getting away from the workplace physically, but not being able to properly 'switch off' mentally

- fatigue and lack of energy

- frequent illness

- poor relationships.

KEEPING A STRESS DIARY

It is useful to keep a record of stress as you experience it – although this need not necessarily be kept in a diary form. The record can help give an insight into your own reactions and can provide a clear benchmark against which you can measure any significant changes. The record must be kept under regular review if it is to be of any use.

Various methods can be used to keep the 'stress diary'. It could be as simple as, for example, taking the list of stress signs and symptoms on pages 232–233 or the list of warning signs above and adding a tick or cross each month. How many crosses do you get? At what point do you decide you are experiencing a dangerous level of stress?

Or you could try writing a 'free narrative' or reflective account once a week or fortnight or month about your feelings, focusing on any issues relating to stress levels. Keep any significant changes under review.

AM I IN CONTROL OF STRESS OR IS STRESS CONTROLLING ME?

Remember, the aim is not to eradicate all stress – the aim is to use stress positively and to ensure that you are controlling stress rather than the other way around. So as part of keeping your stress diary regularly ask yourself:

- When I feel agitated, do I know how to quickly calm and soothe myself?

- Can I easily let go of my anger?

- Can I turn to others to help me calm down and feel better?

- When my energy is low can I boost it easily?

- Do I often feel tense or tight somewhere in my body?

- Does conflict absorb my time and attention?

FACTORS THAT TEND TO TRIGGER STRESS

Everyone is different and we all have different triggers for stress. The following is a non-exhaustive list of possible factors that cause stress in health and social care practice:

- *A busy workload.* Most workers in this field understand this stressor all too well. There are often not enough hours in the day to do all the things that need doing, and it is stressful for well-motivated and caring professionals to sometimes feel that they are not giving the best-possible service to people because of their hectic workload.

- *Long hours.* Health and social care work frequently involves long hours and shift work, and people can feel tired and stressed at the end of a long and busy day or week.

- *Issues in our personal lives.* We may work to the best of our ability, but sometimes when there are issues outside of work, this affects work itself. Modern life is busy and stressful, and when something does happen in our personal lives, it can be hard to be as focused and calm at work as we may be in happier times.

- *Working with individuals who challenge us.* Professionals in health and social care should be experienced in remaining calm, professional and respectful in work. We all know though that some people respond better to different workers and sometimes the work itself can be challenging. People who display challenging behaviours can challenge our sense of our own skills in our job role, and we all need support at times to consider and address the impact which this can have at work.

- *Feeling unsupported by colleagues and/or managers.* This one is obvious, but maybe this is a greater cause of pressure in times of tight budgets and anxiety over the future of some services.

- *Job security.* As mentioned above, people often feel extremely stressed when their own job role may be at risk, and uncertainty about the future causes stress for most people.

- *Working with other agencies and professionals.* Sometimes other people will have a different view of an issue and this can be challenging and stressful.

- *Inadequate resources.* Not having the resources you may need or wish for to do your job is challenging and likely to create stress.

- *Safeguarding.* Dealing with safeguarding issues or concerns is stressful and workers need to acknowledge the effect this has upon us personally.

- *Personal health.* Workers may have their own health issues to deal with.

- *Isolation.* Many workers feel increasingly isolated in the role – perhaps more so when support is provided with individuals in their own homes, so workers feel less of a team and therefore less supported by colleagues.

- *Administrative duties.* Keeping up with paperwork can be difficult for some people or particularly difficult in some work settings. The paperwork never reduces, and certainly never goes away, and for some workers, this is harder than for others to deal with.

REFLECT

- Do any of the above factors cause you stress in your work?

DEVELOPING A PERSONAL STRESS MANAGEMENT PLAN

Stress is a very personal experience and what helps one person deal with stress won't necessarily work for another, so stress management plans need to be unique to every individual. In developing your own personal stress management plan you need to think about:

- *Reduce.* How can you reduce the stress in your life?

- *Recognise.* How do you know when you are stressed?

- *Reverse.* What helps you to de-stress?

- *Resilience.* How can you develop your resilience to stress?

STRATEGIES FOR MANAGING PERSONAL STRESS

Again, everybody's strategies for managing stress are different, and some ideas that work well for some people will not work for others. There are some strategies that people use that are also often not good for us (eg a drink or a big bar of chocolate after a stressful day).

It is important for you to know what works best for you, and to apply the principle of 'self-care' to your work and life. Caring for ourselves enables us to care effectively for others and not doing so makes us ineffective.

Ideas for self-care:

- exercise (letting off steam through exercise is proven to help and improve mental well-being)

- keeping a diary (bearing confidentiality in mind)

- keeping up with friends
- taking time to relax (music, TV, walks, or whatever works for you)
- laughter (often the best tonic in the world)
- hobbies
- taking care of animals (again proven to help reduce stress)
- trying relaxation techniques
- herbal teas and health foods.

Do something to make a clear distinction or break between work time and your own time, such as going for a walk, reading for half an hour, going to the gym.

Other ideas that could help reduce stress at work:

- Talk to your manager. If you have not had supervision for a while, make sure you ask for this. There is nothing 'weak' or wrong in acknowledging that the work we do is stressful, and asking for the help that we need to do the job to the best of our ability. Doing this is actually part of the duty of care for those we work with.

- If paperwork is an issue, as discussed above, are there adaptations that can be made to help you get back on track and stay up to date with recording? Can time be set aside to help you get up to date? Can others help you with this? Often spending time worrying about this is not productive and sitting down and doing some helps relieve the stress.

- Many employers provide confidential and free counselling or telephone support for staff.

- If an individual is causing you concern or causing you to feel stressed because of their behaviour or needs, it can be helpful to take advice from your manager, access training or talk to colleagues about what works for them in dealing with this person. Also, accessing specialist input from other agencies can help.

If the stress continues despite trying these strategies or other techniques that usually work for you, it may be important to talk to your GP about stress that is enduring and limiting you at or outside of work.

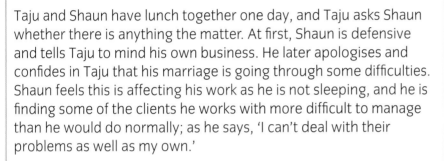

CASE STUDY

Taju is a senior support worker with a mental health charity. He works some of his time in a drop-in centre for people with mental health problems and the remainder of his working week is spent in outreach services providing ongoing practical and emotional support for service users.

Taju works in a team with three other staff members who have similar roles. One of his colleagues, Shaun, has been looking increasingly frustrated at work, and has snapped at the service administrator on a couple of occasions.

Taju and Shaun have lunch together one day, and Taju asks Shaun whether there is anything the matter. At first, Shaun is defensive and tells Taju to mind his own business. He later apologises and confides in Taju that his marriage is going through some difficulties. Shaun feels this is affecting his work as he is not sleeping, and he is finding some of the clients he works with more difficult to manage than he would do normally; as he says, 'I can't deal with their problems as well as my own.'

- What could Taju suggest to Shaun?

- What support may be available for Shaun in and outside of work?

DEVELOPING A 'STRESS AID KIT'

First aid kits are an essential requirement in every workplace and we all know how important they are in terms of health and safety. A 'stress aid kit' builds on the idea of first aid kits. A personal stress aid kit should be made up of things that someone finds helpful in combating or addressing stress. A stress aid kit might include:

- a favourite music CD

- a favourite DVD

- something that encourages someone to take time out to do something they enjoy (it might be something as simple as some bubble bath)

- a favourite book or magazine

- some special treats

- positive images and photographs that bring back happy memories.

REFLECT

What would you include in your personal stress aid kit?

TOP TIPS FOR STRESS MANAGEMENT

The International Stress Management Association (2009) recommend the following 10 tips for avoiding stress:

1 Learn to manage your time more effectively.

2 Adopt a healthy lifestyle.

3 Know your limitations and don't take on too much.

4 Find out what causes you stress.

5 Avoid unnecessary conflict.

6 Accept the things you cannot change.

7 Take time out to relax and recharge your batteries.

8 Find time to meet friends.

9 Try to see things differently; develop a positive thinking style.

10 Avoid alcohol, nicotine and caffeine as coping mechanisms.

REFLECT

- What works for you in managing stress?

- Which strategies work less well for you?

- Is there a strategy you have not tried before which you could make a deliberate effort to implement, and then reflect on whether this works for you?

CHAPTER 7
Promoting good practice in handling information in health and social care settings

Handling information in an appropriate manner is particularly important in health and social care settings because care workers get to know a range of personal information about service users. Often this information includes very sensitive details about people's individual needs, choices, wishes and care.

Links to other chapters

Whatever aspect of work you are carrying out you will need to handle information about that task appropriately, therefore the content of this chapter will be useful in relation to all the units you complete. The content of this chapter has specific links with chapters 1 and 5.

YOUR ROLE AND RESPONSIBILITY FOR HANDLING INFORMATION

The way that information is recorded and handled is vitally important in health and social care settings, not just because there are legal requirements about this, but because you are dealing with both personal and sensitive information about people and their needs.

Personal information includes:

- someone's name
- their address
- their date of birth
- their ethnicity
- the nature of any disability
- their phone number(s)
- their email address
- their family details.

Sensitive information includes:

- information about someone's needs
- assessment information, which contains judgements about a person's care or needs
- information relating to a **diagnosis** or someone's **prognosis**
- information about a person's rights
- financial information.

> **Key terms**
>
> **Diagnosis** is the identification of an illness or other problem by examination of the symptoms.
>
> **Prognosis:** the likely course or outcome of a medical condition.

YOUR RESPONSIBILITIES

Your duties and responsibilities in relation to handling information include:

- knowing the legal framework for handling both personal and sensitive information
- knowing about when, how and why to share (and not share) such information
- storing information securely and appropriately
- following good recording practices
- being transparent with people about what information is recorded and shared with others, and why
- ensuring that others handle information appropriately.

THE LEGAL FRAMEWORK FOR HANDLING INFORMATION

Reflecting the fact that this is such an important area of practice, there is a clear legal framework around the handling of information in health and social care. The following pieces of legislation are relevant to all workers in health and social care:

■ Data Protection Act 1998

■ Human Rights Act 1998

■ Access to Medical Reports Act 1988

■ Freedom of Information Act 2000.

DATA PROTECTION ACT 1998

The Data Protection Act 1998 concerns the recording of personal and sensitive information. It also covers requirements for confidentiality and access to records. The Act sets out eight principles for the recording and use of information. Personal data must:

1 be processed fairly and lawfully

2 be used only for a particular and lawful reason

3 be adequate, relevant and not excessive

4 be accurate and up to date

5 not be kept for longer than is necessary

6 be used in line with the right of individuals

7 be kept securely

8 not be transferred between countries which do not have adequate protection for individuals' personal information.

The Data Protection Act is enforceable by law. In addition to the eight principles being followed, it requires that organisations have appropriate measures in place to ensure personal information is not unlawfully processed, lost or destroyed.

HUMAN RIGHTS ACT 1998

The Human Rights Act 1998 states in article 8 that 'Everyone has the right to respect for his private and family life and his correspondence'.

ACCESS TO MEDICAL REPORTS ACT 1988

This Act gives individuals the right to see a medical report that is written by a doctor for employment or insurance purposes. The individual can comment on the report or ask for changes if they feel it is inaccurate.

FREEDOM OF INFORMATION ACT 2000

Direct care staff, support workers and professionals in regular contact with service users and family members should not get confused by this Act which relates more to general rather than specific information.

The Freedom of Information Act 2000 gives ordinary people the right to request information from public authorities (eg local authorities, the police, NHS organisations) about statistics, about decision making and policy making.

Information about specific individuals remains confidential and can only be accessed by the service user themselves in line with the Data Protection Act 1998.

REFLECT

In what ways does your practice meet these legal requirements? Try to think of four or five specific examples.

RESEARCH

What are your service's policies and procedures for:

- handling of information
- confidentiality
- access to recording systems
- service users accessing files?

CODES OF PRACTICE

All of the codes of practice that could be relevant to health and social care practitioners (such as the Code of Practice for Social Care Workers and the Health and Care Professionals Council code of practice) make clear reference to the importance of all health and social care staff upholding confidentiality.

CODES OF PRACTICE (CONTINUED)

For example, the Code of Practice for Social Care Workers includes an expectation that social care staff should:

- respect and maintain the dignity and privacy of service users, and

- respect confidential information and clearly explain agency policies about confidentiality to service users and carers.

OTHER LEGAL GUIDANCE

INFORMATION SHARING: GOVERNMENT GUIDELINES

Guidance from the Department for Education

As part of the Every Child Matters: Change for Children initiative, the government published a practitioner's guide to information sharing in 2004. With a number of inquiries and investigations identifying social care staff's uncertainty about the sharing of information, the government revised their guidance in 2008 and extended it to cover professionals working with adult service users. The focus of 'Information sharing: guidance for practitioners and managers' is on sharing information legally and appropriately. The guidance comes with a range of associated materials designed to support good practice in information sharing between professionals.

The guidance contains the following seven 'golden rules' for information sharing:

1. *Remember that the Data Protection Act is not a barrier to sharing information* but provides a framework to ensure that personal information about living persons is shared appropriately.

2. *Be open and honest* with the person (and/or their family where appropriate) from the outset about why, what, how and with whom information will, or could, be shared, and seek their agreement, unless it is unsafe or inappropriate to do so.

3. *Seek advice* if you are in any doubt, without disclosing the identity of the person where possible.

4. *Share with consent where appropriate* and, where possible, respect the wishes of those who do not consent to share confidential information. You may still share information without consent if, in your judgement, that lack of consent can be overridden in the public interest. You will need to base your judgement on the facts of the case.

5   *Consider safety and well-being.* Base your information-sharing decisions on considerations of the safety and well-being of the person and others who may be affected by their actions.

6   *Necessary, proportionate, relevant, accurate, timely and secure.* Ensure that the information you share is:

   ■   necessary for the purpose for which you are sharing it

   ■   shared only with those people who need to have it

   ■   accurate and up to date

   ■   shared in a timely fashion

   ■   shared securely.

7   *Keep a record of your decision and the reasons for it* – whether it is to share information or not. If you decide to share, then record what you have shared, with whom and for what purpose.

The guidance also contains a framework for decision making in relation to information sharing. It clearly identifies that a practitioner should make decisions in conjunction with their manager about the sharing of information working through the following seven key questions:

1   Is there a clear and legitimate purpose for you or your agency to share the information?

2   Does the information enable a living person to be identified?

3   Is the information confidential?

4   If the information is confidential, do you have consent to share?

5   If consent is refused, or there are good reasons not to seek consent to share confidential information, is there a sufficient public interest to share the information?

6   If the decision is to share, are you sharing information appropriately and securely?

7   Have you properly recorded your information-sharing decision?

RESEARCH

Try to read some information-sharing guides for practitioners. 'Information sharing: guidance for practitioners and managers' is a very useful guide and contains a range of case studies and guidance. Don't worry, it is accessible and not written in highly legal language!

It can be downloaded from the Department for Education's website at www.education.gov.uk/publications/standard/publicationdetail/page1/DCSF-00807-2008.

CALDICOTT GUIDANCE

Caldicott guidelines govern the management of patient information in the health service and it is essential for professionals working with health agencies to understand the key principles involved.

The Caldicott guidelines were originally developed for the health service as the result of a report by a committee chaired by Dame Fiona Caldicott in 1997 on the flow of patient-identifiable information in the National Health Service and subsequently extended as guidance to social care services in 2002.

Caldicott guardians

All organisations in the NHS and councils with social services responsibilities must have a senior manager with responsibility to ensure that personal and sensitive information is safeguarded. The key principle of the Caldicott report is that every use or flow of **patient-identifiable information** should be regularly justified and routinely tested against the principles below which were developed in the Caldicott report.

Key term

Patient-identifiable information is any personal or sensitive information that can identify a patient.

Principles

1 Justify the purpose(s) for using confidential information.

2 Use it only when absolutely necessary.

3 Use the minimum required.

4 Access should be on a strictly need-to-know basis.

5 Everyone must understand their responsibilities.

6 Understand and comply with the law.

These principles are in accordance with those in the Data Protection Act, but have been developed in much more detailed procedures for the security of information in health organisations, eg the security of faxes.

GOOD PRACTICE IN HANDLING INFORMATION

To meet the legal requirements in this area and to carry out your role effectively, you need to consider two main areas in relation to handling information:

1 How you record information.

2 How you store and access information safely.

EFFECTIVE RECORDING

We are all 'service users'. If you are registered with a general practitioner, a credit card company or even if you have been to school, you have used a service and people have written information about you. There are files about you out there. If you were left alone in a room with these files how long would you wait before taking a peek? What might your concerns be about the things that have been written about you?

Here are a few key issues in recording:

- *Accuracy.* Is it all correct?

- *Veracity.* Is the record true?

- *Timeliness.* Is the record up to date?

- *Completion.* Are there gaps in the record? If so, why?

- *Judgement.* Are facts and opinions clearly differentiated, and are opinions backed up by evidence?

- *Power imbalance.* The record is about you. How do you feel?

As you think about these things you get some idea of the power of information, or, more specifically, the power of actually holding it. The point is we all have a duty to record and handle information in a way that respects the truth and makes clear the difference between fact, opinion and hearsay. You should record information in a way that you would like information about you to be recorded. It's that simple – in theory. In practice though, it may not be so simple.

RECORDING AS A FORM OF COMMUNICATION

It is not unusual for people working in care to complain that too much time is spent on paperwork as though 'paperwork' is a pointless task, whereas it is a vitally important aspect of good-quality care. An essential aspect of a health and social care worker's role is recording information (eg in a person's care plan, in risk assessments, etc).

Recording information is a form of written communication. Written communication is of vital importance in care work – particularly in terms of completing care plans and contact sheets.

Perhaps the key difference between written communication and other methods of communication is that written communication is more permanent than any other form. While what someone has said may be forgotten or confused, what is written is permanent – it can be read time and time again. Written work remains 'on file' for years and can therefore influence future actions. For this reason it is vital that you recognise the importance of developing your skills in recording.

WHAT TO RECORD

One of the difficulties in keeping records is that different people may choose to record different information, eg what one person sees as important another may not. Some people may record too much information and others too little. Since the recording of information is so vital to effective health and social care practice, it is important that there is consistency in *what* is recorded. We will therefore consider the process of deciding *what* to record before looking at *how* to record the information.

Getting the balance

Too much? As stated, some people may record too much information. In fact, this is pointless. No one will have the time to read through reams of information just to pull out one or two key points.

Too little? On the other hand, it is important that sufficient information is recorded so that all relevant information is shared with the team responsible for providing the individual's care and support.

To get the balance of what to record try using the following pointers:

- *Match what is recorded to the purpose of the record.* Different records require different information. For example, a medication chart and an incident report form will require very different information to be recorded.

- *Record what is important for other staff to know.* In a contact sheet or a message book, health and social care workers will need to record what other staff will need to know to provide the care and support an individual requires. Workers should be aware in doing so that they should record positive as well as negative messages; for example, always recording when a service user displays aggressive behaviour, but rarely recording when they are respectful and thoughtful. This can result in a person being labelled as aggressive because of behaviour that actually only occurs very infrequently.

- *Record information that is not held elsewhere.* A great deal of information is recorded in care plans and review notes. In your day-to-day recording you do not need to repeat this information, record new information rather than repeating what is already known.

- *Check with your line manager if you are unsure.*

POOR RECORD KEEPING

- undermines good care practice
- leaves health and social care workers vulnerable to legal and professional problems
- increases workloads.

HOW TO RECORD

Having considered what to record it is important to explore how information should be recorded. You should make sure that your recording follows LACES. It should be:

Legible

Accurate

Concise

Equality based

Shareable

Legible

Some people's handwriting is very difficult to read. It doesn't matter what the quality of the information is if it cannot be easily read by others in the care team. If your handwriting is poor, slow down when you write as this may well help.

Accurate

Accuracy includes aspects such as making sure you have recorded the information correctly and keeping it factual.

Recording should always be based solely on facts, without opinion. Where a particular record asks for opinion (which is rare), workers should make clear that it is their opinion by adding *'in my opinion ...'*.

Where a worker has observed something, the record they make should include only what they have observed and not their interpretation of the information.

Keeping records factual is vitally important, not least because one person's opinion might be wrong!

EXAMPLE

Opinion based	Factual
Mrs Holden was very depressed today.	Mrs Holden was tearful today; she didn't eat her meal and didn't join in with the afternoon group session.

These two examples show clearly the difference between factual and opinion-based recording. There could be many reasons for Mrs Holden's behaviour – she may be feeling ill or may have had an argument, etc. The opinion-based record tells us nothing about Mrs Holden's behaviour but in fact gives her a clinical diagnosis, which the care worker completing the record is not qualified to do.

Concise

While workers do need to record everything that is important, recording should be as concise as possible. This means that less time will be taken in recording, and it makes it more likely that the information will be read and understood by others. Remember KISS:

Keep

It

Short and

Straightforward

Equality

It is important that health and social care values underpin all record keeping. Workers need to use positive language to reflect, respect and value diversity and equality, and should avoid recording in a manner which, for example:

- labels people (eg 'Santok has challenging behaviour'; or 'Helen is aggressive')

- refers to people in a childlike way (eg 'Moira had a big tantrum'; or 'Mr Antoir was really naughty').

If recording keeps to factual information, then it is more likely to promote equality and less likely to be disrespectful.

Shareable

It is important to remember that service users have the right to access their records and therefore the recording must be fit for sharing with service users. Recording may also be shared with colleagues and possibly other agencies – so it must be understandable and fit for purpose.

PRINCIPLES OF GOOD PRACTICE IN RECORDING INFORMATION

All agencies have different requirements in terms of the recording of information. Even within agencies there may be different requirements in terms of different forms of recording, but the following general rules for good practice in recording will always apply:

- Records should be made in black ink as photocopies may need to be made at a later stage and black ink is more legible once photocopied.

- Records should centre on the facts rather than opinion and speculation.

- Make it clear where your information has come from. For example, if a service user's relative told you something, make this clear in the records, eg 'Soriya's mother said that Soriya had a nosebleed yesterday', rather than 'Soriya had a nosebleed yesterday'.

- Records should be signed, dated and timed.

- If any mistakes are made, a single line should be put through the error. Correction fluid must never be used. Whatever was originally written – even if it is a mistake – must still be visible.

- Any crossing out or changes made (eg to spellings) must be initialled and dated to show who made the changes and when.

USING RECORDING TO UPHOLD RIGHTS

Records can be used to uphold people's rights in that records can:

- assist in looking at a person's progress and can help to develop a picture over time of a person's needs

- inform decision making at reviews. This can be particularly important if a person is unable to express their views verbally – the records can inform professionals about a person's behaviour and therefore what they are trying to express

- be used to support an application for additional support/services

- be reviewed to ensure that a person's rights have been upheld.

APPLICATION OF SKILLS

The write stuff?

Read through the following extracts from some records and consider the questions that follow.

- 'Yasmin is attention seeking and manipulative.'

- 'Sushna has BO. She needs a bath urgently.'

- 'Patrick was a real problem today.'

- 'Mohammad is very easily offended by other service users.'

- What do you think of these extracts?

- Do they meet the principles for good record keeping? (Think about LACES too.)

- What would you do if you read anything like this in your work practice?

KEY PRINCIPLES TO COMPLETING DOCUMENTATION IN CARE SETTINGS

- The rules of confidentiality always apply to all records.

- All records could be read by the service user in question. All workers should bear this in mind when recording.

- All documentation should be objective. It should not contain information about the feelings, thoughts, instincts or assumptions of the carer.

- Documentation should be fact based.

- Judgemental language must be avoided.

- If there are particular concerns about a person, then committing those concerns to paper will ensure that other people are aware.

- Paperwork should be clear, concise and to the point.

- In completing paperwork, workers must consider what it is important for someone else to know if they are absent.

BE AWARE OF USING JARGON IN RECORDING

Professional jargon can interfere with communication on many levels.

Abbreviations are perhaps what most of us think of when we hear the word 'jargon'. Abbreviations tend to be put together as a form of shorthand but they can be one of the most dangerous forms of jargon. What one person believes an abbreviation to stand for may not be the same as another person's understanding and confusion can occur with the different use of abbreviations in different professions. For example, 'NFA' can either mean 'no fixed abode' or 'no further action', which could lead to a real problem in terms of communication about someone's needs.

Abbreviations often exclude and confuse people, so the best advice is to try not to use them – but this is easier said than done. Most of us will use some form of abbreviation in our work. However, it is vital that abbreviations are never used in communicating with service users. This can lead to real confusion and potentially dangerous problems.

We were once told a story about a man who, when his care plan was reviewed, asked why no one had come to cut his grass when it clearly said this on the care plan. In fact, what was written on the care plan was 'MOW' – the service user was receiving meals on wheels. Although this is perhaps a funny story, imagine how the service user felt and what other more serious forms of misunderstanding can occur.

- Abbreviations should never be used in case files.

- Abbreviations should never be used in communicating with service users.

- Never make an assumption about what an abbreviation means – the person using the abbreviation should always be asked to clarify what they are saying.

As a general guide, health and social care workers should try to avoid professional jargon as much as possible since it is one of the most widely acknowledged barriers to effective communication at all levels.

For guidance on how to avoid jargon and make use of clearer, straightforward language, it is worth visiting the Plain English Campaign website at www.plainenglish.co.uk.

STORING AND ACCESSING INFORMATION

INFORMATION STORAGE SYSTEMS

All agencies have their own systems for handling information securely, whether this is using paper records, electronic recording, or a combination of both. It is important that any records relating to service users, any documentation containing names, and any other personal and/or sensitive information are kept securely in order to maintain confidentiality.

Key features of different systems that help ensure security

Manual systems	Electronic systems
Always use lockable filing cabinets	Passwords are required to access the system
Install systems to monitor when files are requested, eg booking a file out	The agency monitors who has access and vets people before they are provided with access
Keep cabinets in an office area that's out of the public part of a building and in a room that is also locked at the end of each day	Keep computers in a room that's separate from publicly accessible areas and in a room that is locked at the end of the day
Managers should have oversight of files and conduct spot checks	Managers should have oversight of files and conduct spot checks
Service users are allowed access to files and/or key documents	Service users are allowed access to files and/or key documents
People should be trained not to leave files, letters or other paperwork lying around the office or in public view	People must lock their computers if they leave their desk for a period of time (and the system also auto-locks after five or ten minutes of inactivity)
Policies and procedures should be in place (and understood by all workers) about access to records for service users, and when, how and why information can and should be shared with other agencies	Policies and procedures should be in place (and understood by all workers) about access to records for service users, and when, how and why information can and should be shared with other agencies

RESEARCH

Find out more about the information systems used in your organisation. Using the table above, which key features are in place in the systems? What other features of the systems uphold the security of information?

REFLECT

How do you use the information systems in your organisation to ensure the security of information?

CASE STUDY

Zakiyah is a senior domiciliary care worker. Her domiciliary care agency has a system where care plan folders are kept in people's own homes. When Zakiyah visits a service user to provide care she makes a note in the folder about what she has done and any issues. One of the other care workers on her team always leaves the folder open – as she thinks it speeds things up if she doesn't have to look for the place to write. However, Zakiyah is concerned that this means very personal information about service users is open for everyone to see. On one occasion Zakiyah notices that a neighbour has popped by to see one of the people she supports and she sees that the neighbour has been looking at the file which is open on a coffee table in front of her.

Zakiyah feels that the system in place is not ensuring that personal information is handled securely. She can see the other worker's perspective about it taking time to find the right page to record but she feels that the system could be improved in some way and decides to take this to the next team meeting for discussion.

- What are the problems with the current system?

- What options might there be for improving the system?

- Having read about Zakiyah's experiences, can you identify any factors about the information systems used in your agency that might be improved?

PRACTICES THAT ENSURE SECURITY WHEN STORING AND ACCESSING INFORMATION

As part of the requirements for the diploma you will need to show that you use practices that ensure security when storing and accessing information. Using the systems in your workplace and being clear about how these improve the security of information are obviously vital for this.

In terms of your own assessment, you will probably need to show evidence to your assessor that contains personal and sensitive information about service users. This information should be located in confidential records. The way you share this information with your assessor will demonstrate whether you are employing practices to uphold the security of information. The only 'safe' method to use the recording you make as part of your work as evidence for the diploma is for assessors to view the evidence in the place where you undertook the recording and then to make a note about this evidence (and where it can be found should there be any queries later). This verification by the assessor that they have seen the original recording is what needs to go into your portfolio.

ACCESS TO RECORDS AND ACCOUNTABILITY

Service users have a right to see their own files. Within a service or organisation there may be a procedure that the service user has to follow to see their file. In some provider services access can be quickly arranged. Every health and social care worker needs to ensure that they are familiar with the access to files procedure in their service.

People who work in a large organisation will probably have a system for service users to request access to their files. In some settings, service users can see their files almost immediately. In some situations, a health and social care worker might sit in private with a service user and provide an opportunity for them to look through their file, offering them support to understand the records.

In other services it might take time to provide access for a person to see their records. How records can be accessed and the length of time it will take must be clear in agency policy.

RESEARCH

What is your organisation's policy for service users accessing their files?

CASE STUDY

Chen is a senior care assistant in a residential service for older people. Dan lives in the residential care home where Chen works and Chen is his key worker. Dan has dementia and is not able to communicate his wishes and needs verbally.

Dan's daughter visits her father one day and asks Chen if she can see Dan's record. Chen is unsure what to do with this request as he thinks it is Dan's own record and is unsure whether his daughter should be able to read it.

- What should Chen do in this situation?

- What legislation and guidance would inform his decision making?

- What might the consequences be if Chen does share the record with Dan's daughter?

- What might the consequences be if Chen does not share the record?

SUPPORTING OTHERS TO HANDLE INFORMATION

One of your duties as a health and social care professional is to ensure that the people you support understand their rights and your responsibilities under the Data Protection Act 1998 and other relevant legislation. Service users should be informed:

■ that information about them is recorded

■ where information about them is kept and how it's security is ensured

■ how they can access these records.

Supporting colleagues around the handling of information is equally important. This could take place in several contexts, including:

■ with you supporting a new worker through their induction and enabling them to shadow you at work, including observing you recording, sharing and storing information about service users

■ when you work with one or more other people directly as part of a care team and share responsibility for handling information

■ when you cover for a colleague in the event of someone's sickness or annual leave

■ when you work in partnership with other agencies

■ when you refer to or take referrals for people from other agencies.

You may also need to challenge colleagues occasionally or report any concerns about the inappropriate handling of information to your manager. Remember, one of your key duties as a professional in health and social care is to uphold the dignity and safety of the people you are paid to support. If a colleague does not do the same, if they record in a way that is oppressive or inappropriate, or if they handle or share information in a way that does not follow the guidance and law detailed here, you have a duty to report this.

REFLECT

In your organisation what practices take place when a new member of staff joins and has their induction to make sure they comply with legislative requirements and service-specific policies?

APPLICATION OF SKILLS

Who needs to know?

Think through the following situations.

- You are referring someone you work with to a college of further education. The admission tutor asks you if the person has any personal care needs and whether they are a hepatitis B carrier. What do you do? Why?

- You receive a phone call from a woman who introduces herself as a new social worker for a service user for whom you are their key worker. She asks for some information about the service user. What do you do? Why?

- You are with a group of service users. A colleague comes and asks you about the financial situation of one of the service users. They need to know this so they can arrange a service that the service user needs. What do you do? Why?

- One of your colleagues tells you that she has just heard that a service user you work with was married four times and had several children by different men. She tells you that she is surprised at what she describes as the service user's 'colourful background' as the service user seems so quiet. She goes on to say that the other staff will never believe it when she tells them. What do you do? Why?

RECORDING WITH CARE

In 1999 the Social Services Inspectorate and the Department of Health published *Recording with Care: Inspection of Case Recording in Social Services Departments* (Goldsmith, 1999). This followed inspections of recording systems in social services and highlighted some interesting views and opinions of managers, such as:

> I couldn't believe the information wasn't there! I kept thumbing through the file trying to find it. I know we've talked about lots of other things in supervision. I thought it was being written down – but I don't have the time to check.

The report included a range of recommendations about the role of people in management positions in relation to recording:

- Recording is an organisational responsibility: managers need to emphasise case recording as an essential part of the service and ensure policies and procedures are established.

- Recording policies should set out how equality of opportunity will be addressed in recording practice.

- Information technology systems need to be explicitly linked with case-recording policies and procedures: cross-referencing between paper-based records and those held on IT systems is essential.

- Managers should aim to streamline the process so that what is recorded is clearer, more succinct and avoids duplication.

- Staff recording should be used in supervision, read and endorsed by managers and periodically, audited.

(Goldsmith, 1999)

SUPPORTING RELATIVES, COLLEAGUES AND OTHER AGENCIES TO UNDERSTAND AND CONTRIBUTE TO RECORDS

One of your roles in health and social care may be around enabling others to contribute to assessments, plans and records. This could be in order to ensure that these documents and the resulting interventions with service users are appropriate to their needs and inclusive of everyone working with the person.

You can support others to contribute by:

- enabling face-to-face communication with key people (ensure this is planned ahead and does take place so that it does not feel rushed or like an 'add-on' or afterthought)

- organising and/or attending multi-agency care planning meetings

- working with other agencies and advocates to ensure the service user's voice and wishes are kept central to these documents

- taking the time to consider the communication needs and preferences of the service user, the person's relatives, and also of other professionals (we are all different and approach our work in different ways, even if we wear the same badge of being a 'professional')

- sharing records and enabling contributions according to the relevant legal guidance.

SUPPORTING SERVICE USERS TO UNDERSTAND AND CONTRIBUTE TO RECORDS

The most effective way to support service users to understand and contribute to their records is to ensure the accessibility of records and other written communication.

For some time the Department of Health has advocated an open-file approach. In other words, professionals should not need to wait for a service user to request to see their own file. It is best practice for health and social care workers to sit with the service user and agree what is recorded, or at least ensure the service user knows what is being recorded. It is important that service users are aware that any viewpoint they have can also be written down.

When service users access the information in their files they should be able to understand it. The simplest way to do this is to use a member of staff to go through the information with them. They can read or even translate the written information if necessary but can also interpret it and explain it.

The right of individuals to see their own records could be developed much further if systems are designed with this in mind from the outset and by ensuring that both the presentation style and language are fully accessible.

Person-centred planning techniques (see Chapters 9 and 10) often allow more scope for creativity than would be possible using conventional assessment and planning methods. Graphic symbols and pictures are sometimes used to record ideas and thoughts which are often more memorable and personal for those involved, and are usually more immediate in nature than waiting for minutes or formal notes. Digital photographs can also be taken and used in this way, eg by building up a profile of people and places that are important in the life of an individual. Presented pictorially rather than as a list on a more usual form this information can usually be understood quickly and is more meaningful than the more usual methods.

REFLECT

How could you work with service users so that they contribute more fully to their own records?

CASE STUDY

Dee is a senior care assistant in a day service for older people. Sayeeda starts work at the day centre where Dee has worked for some time. Sayeeda comments during her induction that in her last job there were some practices around record keeping which she thinks would be useful to implement here.

For example, Sayeeda thinks that the storage of information could be more secure as she has noticed that some colleagues leave letters unfiled at the end of the day in their in-trays. She also talks with Dee about the ways in which she has involved service users in assessments and plans via reminiscence work. Sayeeda is used to scanning old photographs and collating personal photo albums which she thinks would be useful and inexpensive to do here in order to engage individuals who would enjoy this.

- What could Sayeeda and Dee do to change practices in the centre?

- How could they demonstrate that this would improve people's experience and the security of information?

Code of Conduct for Healthcare Support Workers and Adult Social Care Workers

The importance of handling information effectively is recognised in the Code of Conduct for Healthcare Support Workers and Adult Social Care Workers, which states that you must:

- maintain clear and accurate records of the health care, care and support you provide. Immediately report to a senior member of staff any changes or concerns you have about a person's condition

- treat all information about people who use health and social care services and their carers as confidential

- only discuss or disclose information about people who use health and social care services and their carers in accordance with legislation and agreed ways of working

- always seek guidance from a senior member of staff regarding any information or issues that you are concerned about

- always discuss issues of disclosure with a senior member of staff.

CHAPTER 8
Continuing personal and professional development

The concept of continuing personal and professional development is vital in health and social care. Whatever qualifications and experiences a health and social care worker has, they should never feel they have nothing further to learn. Health and social care and the evidence base for it are constantly changing and we therefore all have much to learn in order to provide the best-quality service to the people with whom we work.

Links to other chapters

You will want to consider your development in relation to all of the units you complete for your qualification and will therefore find this chapter useful across your whole qualification. In particular this chapter links to chapters 1, 4, 9 and 16.

UNDERSTANDING COMPETENCE IN YOUR OWN WORK ROLE

In order to understand what is required for you to demonstrate competence in your work role it is important to understand what is meant by competence. Competence is made up of three aspects:

Knowledge + skills + values = competence

To be competent in your role you must therefore understand what knowledge you need, what skills are important for you to have and what values should influence your practice.

Competence isn't simply about having the right knowledge, skills and values – it is about:

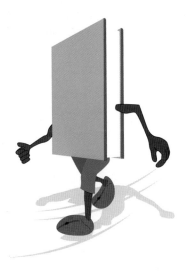

- the way in which you use your knowledge in practice
- the way that you use your skills at work
- understanding the way that your values affect your work, your skills and your knowledge.

A walking encyclopedia does not make a good health and social care worker.

The knowledge, skills and values required for effective practice in health and social care work are expressed in various standards, such as the National Occupational Standards. This is why working towards this qualification will significantly enhance your understanding of your role and help to improve your practice.

You will have a **job description** and this might have some associated documents such as a **person specification**. This will detail your role and responsibilities and may also provide some specific information on what knowledge and skills are the most important for your role. Quite often people don't look at their job description once they are employed in a particular role. It is worth looking at your job description again as you work on this chapter.

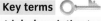
Key terms

A **job description** is a written outline of the role and responsibilities of a specific job.

A **person specification** a list of criteria (skills, knowledge, experience, values and qualifications) that you need in order to do your job. These may either be 'essential' or 'desirable'.

> **REFLECT**
>
> How would you describe your role and responsibilities at work?

WHAT STANDARDS SET OUT EXPECTATIONS FOR THE HEALTH AND SOCIAL CARE WORKER'S ROLE?

Standards	Status of the standards	Impact on your work role
National Occupational Standards	There are National Occupational Standards in many occupational areas. They are used to describe the standards that everyone working in that occupational area need to meet. They are intended to be used in a variety of ways including design of job roles, appraisal systems, procedures and in the development of qualifications in the area.	You need to meet the National Occupational Standards for health and social care in all of your work. They will be used to assess you when you are working towards a qualification. Your job role or job description could be based on them or they could be used in practical appraisals by your line manager.
National Minimum Standards	These are published by the government and cover a wide range of areas – eg there are national minimum standards for domiciliary care. They cover expected standards of care.	These will cover what standards you and your service should meet. They describe the standards of care that people can expect to receive.
Care Quality Commission: Essential Standards of Quality and Safety	These describe what health and social care workers and services should do in order to meet the requirements of Section 20 Regulations of the Health and Social Care Act 2008. The standards are written in the form of outcomes for service users, providing detail on what health and social care professionals need to do in order to achieve these outcomes.	The Care Quality Commission is the current regulator of health and social care services. The CQC uses these standards in order to inspect the quality of health and social care services.
Codes of Practice	The Social Care Council relevant to the specific country develops these codes of practice which refer to the way in which health and social care workers should operate.	These mostly describe the specific values that health and social care workers need to employ.
Legislation and government guidance	Various legislation and governmental directives set out standards for practice for both employers and practitioners in health and social care.	As a health and social care worker you need to understand the requirements of law and meet these in your practice.
Organisational requirements	Every organisation will have policies and procedures that need to be followed. They may also have specific standards of practice and mission statements.	As an employee you have a specific contractual responsibility to meet the standards of practice outlined in your job description.

Locate at least three of the standards detailed on the table and make some notes about the key implications these have for your practice. It will be particularly helpful for your work for this chapter if you can detail what skills, knowledge and values these standards say you should have to carry out your role effectively.

CASE STUDY

Jon is a senior support worker with a reablement team. Although Jon has worked in health and social care for some time he has only recently taken up his post in the reablement team. The team is a fairly new initiative in the local area where he works. As a result of a pilot period, the team has developed a mission statement that details what the team wants to achieve and the way it expects workers to develop reablement practice in the area. Jon looks at this and makes some notes about what skills and knowledge he will need to put the mission statement into action.

He also draws up some notes about the values he will need to put into his practice. Jon then revisits his job description and the associated person specification and makes some similar notes. Jon also looks at his employer's code of conduct and the code of practice for social care workers.

Jon spends some time reflecting on the list of knowledge, skills and values, and then scores each of the items on the list using a scale of 1 to 5. He gives a score of 5 where he feels very confident that his skills or knowledge are high in this area. Where he feels he is less confident he gives a lower score. This enables Jon to work out where he might need to improve his practice in order to be the most effective reablement worker he can be.

- How might Jon be able to use this in his work towards the diploma?

- What other standards could Jon look at?

- Jon has scaled the items he has listed in terms of his confidence in that area – how else might he score the items?

REFLECTIVE PRACTICE

The basic idea of reflective practice is that people learn based on experiences and then reflecting on the experience. Reflecting on the experience means looking back on it, considering how well it went and how your practice could be improved. If someone fails to reflect on their experiences then they will learn little from them.

So you need to reflect to learn and to develop your practice, but sometimes people need to learn *how* to reflect. In busy working environments you may feel the need to move quickly from one thing to another and sometimes you may feel that you have no time to reflect. However, it is vital that everyone makes the time to reflect on their own practice. Thinking about what you are doing shouldn't mean that a task takes any longer but it is likely that the task will be carried out more effectively than if you were thinking about something else. Sometimes people can be doing one task and thinking about the next task and then neither task is carried out effectively.

People use a mirror to look at themselves and perhaps to try to look the best they can. Reflection in professional practice is about looking back at your practice and getting a clear idea about how you can improve what you see.

Reflective practice is about:

- keeping an open mind about what, why and how we do things
- questioning what, why and how we do things
- asking what, why and how other people do things
- generating choices, options and possibilities
- comparing and contrasting results
- viewing our activities and results from various perspectives
- asking 'what if …?'
- seeking feedback and other people's ideas and viewpoints.

WHY IS REFLECTIVE PRACTICE IMPORTANT?

Reflective practice improves health and social care practice in a range of ways. Perhaps most importantly reflective practice opens up options; when we reflect on a situation it enables us both to see more and to see things differently. Effectively, it 'illuminates' our practice so that we can see things more clearly. This can lead to improved, more effective practice.

Reflective practice improves practice in a range of ways as it:

- helps people to identify gaps in their skills and knowledge (this helps them to identify their learning needs and improve their practice)
- encourages people to analyse communication and relationships (this means that working relationships can be improved)

- supports people to examine the decision-making process, so that they are able to justify practice more readily

- encourages a healthy questioning approach which can help people to 'find their way'.

REFLECT

Why is reflective practice important in continuously improving the quality of service you provide?

WHAT IS REFLECTIVE PRACTICE?

To fully understand reflective practice it is important to recognise that there are three forms of reflection:

REFLECTION IN ACTION

Reflection in action is the process of reflection when you are working. Essentially, it is working and being aware of what you are doing at the same time. Reflection in action involves:

- thinking ahead ('Right if that's happened, then I need to …')

- being critical ('That didn't work very well …')

- storing up experiences for the future ('I could have dealt with that better, next time I will try …')

- analysing what is happening ('She's saying that to test me – I think I should …').

Reflection in action is happening all the time – if your mind is on the job! While reflection in action is good practice and can help people to develop their practice, it does have drawbacks. The main problems with reflection in action are:

- you can only see things from your own perspective ('I think', 'I feel', 'I'm not sure', etc).

- you will only have short-term reflection. If your mind is on the job, when the job changes so will your thoughts.

REFLECTION ON ACTION

This is separate from, but linked with, reflection in action. It is the reflection done later, after the event – talking things through informally or formally with colleagues and maybe talking things through in supervision. Reflection on action is free from urgency and any pressures of the actual event. As such it allows for longer-term reflection and addresses the drawbacks of reflection in action. For example, reflection on action allows for the opportunity to explore other people's views on the event. Feedback from others therefore adds an extra dimension to the reflection – allowing for more depth.

Reflection on action requires space and time and this is perhaps one of the most significant challenges for busy health and social care workers. One of the main drawbacks of reflection on action is that because of time constraints practitioners tend only to think in this way about more complex or critical work issues. In terms of more routine events and work practice, there is a tendency for practitioners to only reflect in action. This can mean that people do not make many changes to routine work practice. It is therefore important to plan reflection on action to ensure that it covers every aspect of practice.

REFLECTION FOR ACTION

Reflection for action describes the stage of reflection where future actions are considered. As such, reflection for action serves to guide future action. It is essentially reflection before an event.

If we apply the stages of reflection to a health and social care worker's role then it could look something like the following.

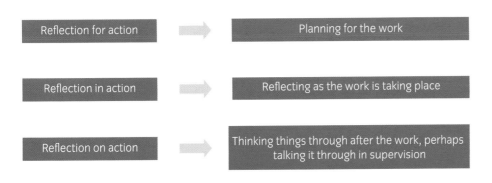

Reflection for action	→	Planning for the work
Reflection in action	→	Reflecting as the work is taking place
Reflection on action	→	Thinking things through after the work, perhaps talking it through in supervision

So the basic framework for reflection consists of three stages. This is often depicted as a cycle in the following way.

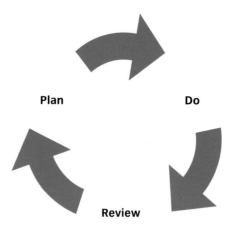

Plan   Do

Review

Reflection on action should lead to further reflection for action in terms of planning what to do next. Essentially, a reflective cycle is produced, in which a truly reflective practitioner will be reflecting all the time, at different stages:

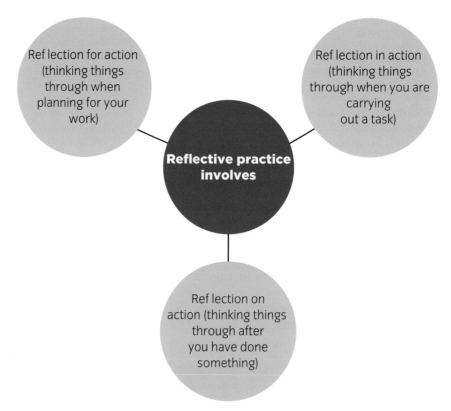

Ref lection for action (thinking things through when planning for your work)

Ref lection in action (thinking things through when you are carrying out a task)

Reflective practice involves

Ref lection on action (thinking things through after you have done something)

A number of frameworks have been developed to support reflective practice. The framework that is arguably used most extensively in health and social care is that of Gibbs (1998).

FRAMEWORK FOR REFLECTION

Gibbs (1998) suggests a six-stage process as follows:

Stage 1

Description of the event
Think about what happened? Who did what? What were the results? And so on.

Stage 2

Feelings and thoughts
This stage is essentially about self-awareness. You need to think about questions like:

- How were you feeling when the event began?
- How did your feelings change as the event unfolded?
- How did you feel about outcomes?
- How do you feel about it now?

Stage 3

Evaluation
In this stage the person needs to think through what was good and bad about the experience. What went well? What didn't go so well?

Stage 4

Analysis
This develops on from Stage 3 but involves breaking down the event into component parts so that they can be explored separately. It may involve considering more detailed questions than those covered in Stage 3. For example:

- What went well?

could be followed up with:

- What did I do well?
- What did others do well?

and:

- What didn't go so well?

could be followed up with:

- What didn't turn out as it should have?
- In what way did I contribute to this?
- In what way did others contribute to this?

Stage 5

Conclusion
Now that the event has been explored from a range of perspectives, you should be able to draw some conclusions. This will involve you asking yourself what you could have done differently and what impact this would have had on the outcome. If the previous stages have not been fully and honestly explored, then the conclusions reached in this stage will be fundamentally flawed.

Stage 6

Action planning
During this stage, you should think about what you would do if you encountered the event again. Would you do anything differently or take similar action?

Gibbs sees this process as a cycle, such that when the action plan is put into place the event should become the focus of further reflection, as follows.

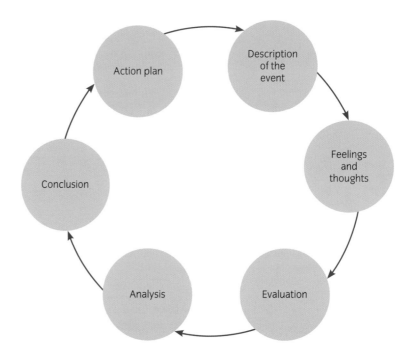

CASE STUDY

Jane is a senior support worker in a day service for people with learning disabilities. She has responsibility for planning day service activities and for organising a small staff team. Jane notes that a number of service users seem to be interested in musicals – they choose to have the soundtracks of musicals on when they have music in the day service room. One of the team members comments on this interest in a short morning meeting saying that she has brought in a few CDs of other musicals to try to vary the background music. Over the next few days Jane reflects on this interest and decides that it might be useful to set up a group activity based on musicals. She makes this suggestion to the service manager who agrees that this would be a good idea, but says that there are no additional resources.

Jane and the staff team arrange a group session that is based on listening to some music from different musicals and ask service users to point to some pictures to show what emotions they think the singer is feeling. During the session Jane notices that service users seem very engaged with the activity. She notes that two service users who are generally quite withdrawn respond to staff much more.

After the session Jane and the staff team arrange a discussion about how they think the session went. Jane asks the staff to think about what went well and what could have been improved. She also asks for ideas about how the service users' interest in musicals could be further developed. A couple of staff members say they really don't like musicals and offer other suggestions for activities.

- Can you identify where Jane was employing:
  - reflection in action
  - reflection on action
  - reflection for action.
- Should Jane take notice that some of the staff team members don't like musicals?
- How might Jane encourage the staff team to be more reflective in their approach to their work?

SUMMARISING REFLECTIVE PRACTICE

The key aspects of reflective practice in health and social care are:

- developing self-awareness
- being aware of values and the impact that these have on practice
- exploring emotions (how you feel about things)
- using your knowledge and developing new knowledge.

VALUES IN HEALTH AND SOCIAL CARE PRACTICE

It is generally accepted that **personal values** are influenced by a number of factors, which might include:

- our background and upbringing
- personal experiences
- education
- religious beliefs
- cultural background.

Because we are all individuals and the above factors will be different for us all, then everyone will have a different set of personal values.

Key terms

Values: what is seen as important.

Personal values: what is important to an individual.

Professional values

Choosing to work in health and social care means that you need to adopt a set of **professional values** – the values of health and social care. While the professional value base does not replace each individual's personal value base, professional values do override personal values in terms of the way in which we work.

Individual organisations and services have also often developed their own internal codes of practice, codes of conduct or value statements. The field of work that you have chosen to enter is one which is about:

- people providing some form of support to other people (medical, social, personal, etc)

- getting the best for people who for some reason need to rely on others to meet some of their needs, whether these are basic needs for care, or needs around being part of society and accessing services

- empowering people so that their own voices are heard and respected, and so that they do those things for themselves that they are capable of doing.

Key to this then are the following values of health and social care:

- *Dignity*. The need for people to be treated with respect and as unique individuals with rights and choices.

- *Rights*. Upholding the rights of vulnerable people.

- *Fairness*. Society can be unfair in its treatment of individuals, and health and social care needs to model fairness in treating people in the best possible way. This is not just because fairness is the right thing to do, but also because the users of health and social care rely on services in order to have their needs met in some way.

- *Empowerment*. Enabling others to do everything they can for themselves and supporting them in areas where they feel they need this support.

- *Equality*. The belief that every individual is equal and worthy of being treated in ways that respect this and their uniqueness.

- *Diversity*. The idea that our differences and uniqueness are things to be enjoyed and celebrated, as opposed to treating people differently based on these differences.

- *Inclusion*. The idea that services and society should include everybody and that exclusion and inability to access resources are unfair.

KEY POINT

Many of these issues are covered in separate chapters and within specific units of the diploma and you should recognise the importance of these as the key values of health and social care practice.

CASE STUDY

Chen is a senior care assistant in a residential service for older people. He has a large extended family who all live very close to each other. Chen and his sisters provide a lot of support to their mother so that she can remain living at home. Chen and all his family believe that older relatives should be supported by their family – they are determined that no one in their family will ever go into a care home.

In a team meeting one day at the service where Chen works, a number of members of staff talk about a particular resident (Mrs Lathbury) who has a number of adult children. Mrs Lathbury hardly gets any visitors although her adult children often phone to speak to their mother. The staff comment that as Mrs Lathbury is becoming more confused she doesn't have any idea about who is talking on the phone and the phone calls are distressing her. They feel that Mrs Lathbury's family should visit rather than 'just taking a couple of minutes to phone – when it only upsets their mum'.

- How might Chen's personal values affect his response to this situation?
- How might Chen reflect on what to do in this situation?

REFLECT

- How might your own values, belief systems and experiences affect your working practice?
- Try to identify three or four specific issues that might affect your practice.

EVALUATING YOUR OWN PERFORMANCE

In health and social care evaluation is seen as reviewing three things:

- *Efficiency*. Did we do the right thing, at the right time, and in the agreed timescale?
- *Effectiveness*. Did we do it in the best possible way?
- *Economy*. Did we get the best value?

You need to be able to evaluate your own performance against required standards. Effectively, you should know how well you do your job. In order to do this you need to understand the requirements of your role and you need to reflect on how well you meet these requirements. To reflect effectively you should draw on feedback from others and use systems such as supervision and appraisal.

RECEIVING FEEDBACK

Receiving feedback is a fantastic learning opportunity. The learning is maximised by the feedback being constructive. The feedback process will only be constructive if the person seeking the feedback has developed the necessary skills in receiving feedback. When receiving feedback at any stage, health and social care professionals should work towards the following:

- *Maintain an open attitude*. Don't be defensive or 'defend' yourself. This may sound easy, but it isn't easy to do. If you find yourself feeling defensive about a piece of feedback, you need to remind yourself that the reality is that a defensive reaction to feedback generally results from it being accurate.

- *Employ your active listening skills*. Listen actively, look at the person providing feedback and maintain an open body language.

- *Clarify the feedback*. Ask any questions you need to in order to make sure you understand the feedback.

- *Recognise the person giving the feedback*. Providing feedback is not an easy task. The person providing feedback is likely to have put a great deal of thought into the feedback – it takes a great deal of time and effort to provide thoughtful feedback. It is advisable to thank the person giving you feedback – just something like 'You've really given me something to think about there. Thanks', not only demonstrates your commitment to learning but also helps you to maintain that vital positive and open attitude.

- *Write down the feedback*. Try to write down what you can remember of what was said as soon as possible. You will find this assists with your reflection later.

- *Don't take criticism personally*. Feedback is a professional process. Recognise that part of being a professional is learning from how others view your practice.

- *Recognise learning*. Remember that simply because someone has picked up on an area of your practice that can be improved, this does not mean you are not a good health and social care practitioner. Even the very best worker can improve on some aspect of their practice.

- *Reflect*. If some aspect of the feedback puzzles you, take some time to reflect. How might the person's perception have been formed?

- *Focus.* Make sure that you are not distracted so that you can focus fully on the feedback. Stay 'in the moment' and try to truly understand the meaning behind the feedback. Try to avoid framing a response in your mind until you have heard all of the feedback.

- *Recognise your reactions.* Notice your own reactions and how the feedback is making you feel. Sometimes it helps to partially disassociate yourself and imagine you are a 'fly on the wall' witnessing feedback being given to someone else. This can help you to view feedback objectively, rather than emotionally.

In receiving feedback, people take either a negative (closed) style or a positive (open) style. The following table summarises this.

Negative/closed	Positive/open
Defensive: defends actions, objects to feedback	Open: listens without frequent interruption or objection
Attacking: turns the table on the person providing feedback	Responsive: willing to truly 'hear' what is being said
Denies: refutes the accuracy or fairness of the feedback	Accepting: accepts the feedback without denial
Disrespectful: devalues the person giving the feedback	Respectful: recognises the value of the feedback
Closed: ignores the feedback	Engaged: interacts appropriately seeking clarification where needed
Inactive listening: makes no attempt to understand the meaning of the feedback	Active listening: listens attentively and tries to understand the meaning of the feedback
Rationalising: finds explanations for the feedback that dissolve personal responsibility	Thoughtful: tries to understand the personal behaviour that has led to the feedback
Superficial: listens and agrees but does not act on the feedback	Sincere: genuinely wants to make changes and learn

REFLECT

Think about a time when you received feedback on your practice. How did you use this feedback?

CASE STUDY

Isabella is a senior care assistant in a respite care service which provides short-term stays for adults with learning and physical disabilities. She is asked to act as key worker to a new service user – Louise Hamlin. Louise has a condition called Rett syndrome. Isabella knows nothing about Rett syndrome and decides to do some research into the condition so that she can provide the best possible care to Louise. Isabella does an internet search and finds out that there is a UK support group – she prints off some fact sheets from its website and provides these to the whole staff team.

Isabella reflects on what specific skills she will need to work with Louise. She recognises that as Louise has seizures she can draw on some recent training she attended on epilepsy management. Louise does not communicate verbally so Isabella reflects on how she can draw on her skills in communication. Isabella writes some notes on how she can work with someone with Rett syndrome and takes these to her next supervision session.

Isabella's supervisor says she is pleased that Isabella has done some research and prepared effectively, but she advises Isabella that she has a concern that Isabella may have focused too much on Louise's diagnosis. She has not met Louise or her parents yet, but has still started to prepare a care plan. Isabella's supervisor reminds her of the need to remain person centred and not to make assumptions based on a diagnosis.

Initially Isabella is upset by this feedback – as she has put a lot of work into this preparation. After the supervision session Isabella reflects on her manager's feedback and recognises that in her enthusiasm to understand Louise's needs she has focused on her diagnosis rather than on Louise as a unique individual.

- Why might Isabella have been initially upset by her manager's response?
- How has her manager's feedback helped Isabella?
- What should Isabella do now?

RESEARCH

Go back to the list of knowledge, skills and values you listed at the start of your work on this chapter (p 264).

- How can you evaluate your own practice against this list?
- What might you use to inform your evaluation?

UNDERSTANDING LEARNING

To support you in developing your own practice, you should have an understanding of adult learning theory and approaches.

EXPERIENTIAL LEARNING

Experiential learning theory is probably the most influential adult learning theory in health and social care. The idea of experiential learning can be traced back to thousands of years ago and the famous quotation said to be made by the Chinese philosopher Confucius:

Tell me, and I will forget.

Show me and I might remember.

Involve me and I will understand

Perhaps because of this quote, experiential learning is sometimes misinterpreted as simply saying that people learn through experience. To some extent this is true but it's not enough for people to have an experience – they won't learn from this unless they spend some time reflecting on the experience. Experiential learning basically states that there is a four-stage process to learning:

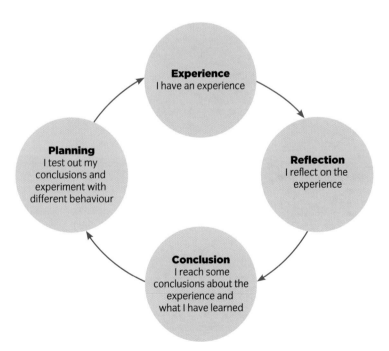

This theory of adult learning is particularly helpful in understanding continuing personal and professional development, as it clearly demonstrates that it's not enough for someone to simply have lots of experiences. They won't necessarily learn from the experience unless they are supported to follow through the whole learning cycle.

In order to learn effectively, health and social care workers need to reflect on their experiences, make wider links, draw conclusions and plan any necessary changes to their practice.

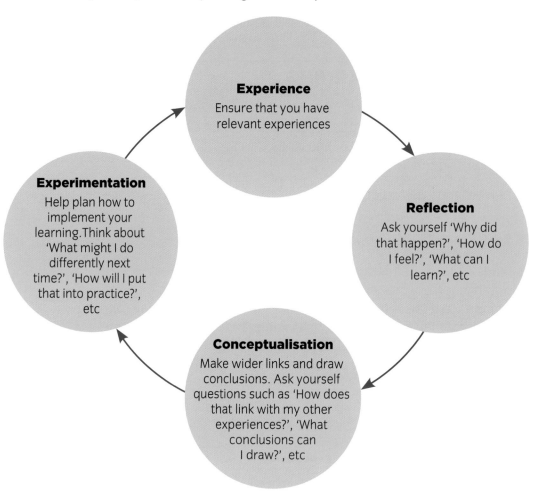

Experience
Ensure that you have relevant experiences

Reflection
Ask yourself 'Why did that happen?', 'How do I feel?', 'What can I learn?', etc

Conceptualisation
Make wider links and draw conclusions. Ask yourself questions such as 'How does that link with my other experiences?', 'What conclusions can I draw?', etc

Experimentation
Help plan how to implement your learning. Think about 'What might I do differently next time?', 'How will I put that into practice?', etc

LEARNING STYLES

Honey and Mumford (1982) identified four different learning styles:

- *Activists* are often open-minded and enthusiastic – they like new experiences and want to get involved in the here and now. They enjoy getting involved and they learn by 'doing'. Activists can become bored when an activity stops and will want to quickly move on to the next challenge or activity, rather than dwell on reflection of the last activity.

- *Reflectors* do just what it says on the tin! They stand back, reflect, ponder and consider many perspectives before acting. Reflectors mull over things before reaching a conclusion. They observe, gather information and use plenty of time to think things over.

- *Theorists* are logical thinkers. They analyse, question and learn step by step in a logical way. Theorists question any new learning and want to ensure it fits and makes sense with their logical approach. Theorists are often perfectionists and don't appreciate a flippant approach to a subject.

- *Pragmatists* like to try out something new to see if it works in practice. They like experimenting with new ideas. They will often take a problem-solving approach to learning and will seek to apply something that they have learnt straight away. However, if it doesn't work they are likely not to try the approach again. Instead, they will look for something new to try.

We all have a little of each style in us (and some of us are evenly matched across all four styles), but most of us favour one style over another. It is vital to remember that no one style is 'better' than another – they are simply different.

REFLECT

- Which learning style from those suggested by Honey and Mumford above do you think you have?

- How does this have an impact on the way you learn and how you improve your practice?

PERSONAL DEVELOPMENT PLANS

To develop an effective development plan you need to understand the process of personal and professional development. This is often referred to as the continuing professional development (CPD) process.

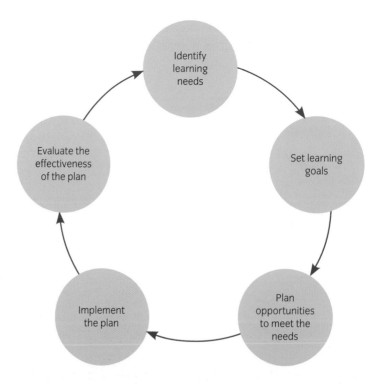

IDENTIFYING LEARNING NEEDS

In order to take a positive approach to your continuing professional development you need to begin by identifying your learning needs so that you can plan learning and development opportunities that will address these needs.

To identify your learning needs, you need to take into account:

- the standards you are expected to meet in your practice (these might include regulations, codes of practice, National Occupational Standards, etc)

- any specific issues as a result of changes in your role and responsibilities

- any forthcoming changes in your employing organisation

- the needs of the service users with whom you work

- your aspirations for the future (perhaps in terms of career goals, improvements in practice, etc).

Identifying gaps in knowledge and weaknesses in practice can be particularly challenging and so it is important that you evaluate your practice effectively, drawing on feedback and reflection.

SETTING LEARNING GOALS

A goal can be defined as the point to which operations are directed or the point to be reached. If you think about setting a goal as planning a journey then this can be helpful. The learning need is the starting point while the goal is what you want to achieve/the destination you want to reach.

PLANNING OPPORTUNITIES TO MEET THE NEEDS

This will become the worker's professional development plan (sometimes referred to as a PDP). When planning development opportunities, it is important to think more widely than simply training opportunities. You need to think about the whole range of development opportunities available to you. These opportunities then need to be accurately matched to your learning needs. For example, if a person wants to develop a particular skill they may feel it would be useful to ask a colleague who is skilled in this area to assist them by talking them through the skill, observing them and providing feedback, etc.

In devising learning plans, you will need to consider:

- any requirements for mandatory training (such as health and safety)

- any individual needs you have

- your learning style
- the views of service users
- any specific needs of service users and how you can learn about these.

Whenever you devise a development plan, you need to ensure that you keep the plan and goals set:

Specific. Your goals need to be clearly defined.

Measurable. You need to be able to measure your progress towards the identified goals.

Achievable. Make sure that you can meet the goals.

Relevant. The goal needs to relate to the standards for your practice.

Time-bound. There should be a deadline for you to meet the goals.

IMPLEMENTING THE PLAN

You need to engage in the opportunities you have planned. In doing so you will find it helpful to consider the following questions:

- What do I want to learn?
- What are my expectations?
- How will I know when I have learned it?
- How will I use what I learn?

Thinking through questions such as these will help you to take a proactive and reflective approach to your learning. It might be useful to make some notes on your responses to the questions and on your experiences as you implement the professional development plan. This will assist with the next stage of the process.

EVALUATING THE EFFECTIVENESS OF THE PLAN

Once the plan has been actioned and you have effectively engaged with all the planned opportunities, it is vital that you evaluate what you have learnt. A key aspect of the evaluation will be in revisiting the originally identified learning needs and associated goals, then considering to what extent they have been met by the plan.

If the needs haven't been met, are there different opportunities that could be used? Would a different approach help? Where the learning needs have been met, this won't be the end of the process as it is likely that the learning will have highlighted some further needs and so the cycle continues – hence the phrase continuing professional development.

KEEPING A RECORD

Keeping a record of professional development is a requirement for those staff who are registered with a regulatory body. Even though not all health and social care staff are currently required to be registered, it is good practice for all professionals to keep track of their professional development in a systematic way. There are a range of benefits to this, including:

- The record can be used as evidence for a range of professional qualifications.

- The record can be used in appraisal systems.

- Continuing professional development records can be used to update CVs or provide useful information in job interviews.

- Reflection will be easier with a record on which to base your thoughts.

Some organisations provide a system for recording professional development, which makes it much easier for staff who simply need to complete the documentation. Other staff can choose how to record their professional development. Whatever system is used it should be easy to identify:

- your learning needs and the associated goals

- the activities you have undertaken to address these

- your progress towards the goals.

SOURCES OF SUPPORT

It is important that you make use of a wide range of support in order to plan your own development and keep this under review. For example:

- *Informal feedback*. You might get feedback informally in a range of ways, eg through a person's body language, through individuals and their family members making comments about your practice, etc. Draw on this feedback to help you evaluate your practice and plan your future development.

- *Formal feedback*. You should receive feedback formally through supervision and appraisal. You can make use of this to evaluate the effectiveness of your practice and to plan how you need to develop your practice.

- *Learning activities*. See pages 287–288 which provide information on the range of learning activities you can use to develop your practice. You can make use of these and reflect on your learning in order to evaluate your practice and to plan other learning activities.

- *Within the organisation*. Your colleagues will be able to provide you with support to identify your development needs and with support to improve your practice. For example, if you have a colleague who has a particular skill you could ask them for support if you want to develop your skills in that area.

- *Outside the organisation*. A range of support might exist outside of your own organisation, eg there may be careers advisors that could assist you with planning your career goals. There are also a number of national organisations that can support health and social care workers, which you can find online.

RESEARCH

Put some thought into the formal and informal support networks you can use to plan and review your own development. Separate these into support within your own organisation and outside of your organisation.

- Are there any systems that you don't make use of?

- How could you draw on these support systems to plan and review your development more effectively?

WORKING WITH OTHERS

You will need to involve a range of other people in planning your learning and keeping this under review, eg:

- *Service users, carers and advocates* will have a fuller understanding of the needs of the people you support and they will therefore have ideas about how you should prioritise your learning needs. They will also be able to provide you with useful feedback about how effective your practice is which will help you to reflect on your practice.

- *Supervisors, line managers and employers* will be clear about the standards you need to meet and can therefore provide valuable advice on what you need to develop by providing you with feedback and guidance.

- *Other professionals* will be able to identify what you need to do to provide a good service and will be able to provide you with feedback on your practice, helping you to identify your own needs.

All of these people may also be able to support you in accessing learning activities that can meet your development needs.

DEVELOPING YOUR PRACTICE THROUGH LEARNING OPPORTUNITIES AND REFLECTIVE PRACTICE

Not too long ago learning and development opportunities were viewed almost purely in terms of training courses. The learning and development plans which health and social care staff developed appeared to be little more than a 'shopping list' of training courses. However, there is now an increasing level of understanding about the range of learning opportunities that exist, and it is clearly recognised that reflective practice enables people to learn and develop their practice on a range of levels.

Some of the most widely utilised learning opportunities in health and social care include:

- supervision

- performance review or appraisal

- mentoring and coaching

- training

- e-learning

- assessment and feedback

- independent research

- supporting others' learning (eg working with students)

- team meetings

- reading.

Health and social care professionals can utilise all of these opportunities to improve their practice if they are using a reflective approach.

SUPERVISION

It is generally accepted that there are four functions (or purposes) of supervision.

Accountability

This refers to the fact that the supervisor is responsible in various ways for the supervisee's work. The supervisor and supervisee will need to discuss the work that the supervisee is undertaking. Where this function is carried out well, it provides a safety net for the supervisee who will recognise and value the opportunities to share their work and the challenges they face with their supervisor. The supervisor can use this discussion to ensure that legal requirements are being met and that organisational policies and procedures are being followed.

Professional development

This involves the supervisor and supervisee discussing the supervisee's development needs and how these can be addressed. Skilled supervision discussion in itself should provide extensive opportunities for reflection and learning.

Personal supports

Supervision should always involve discussion about what support the supervisee needs. Supervision should allow time for health and social care workers to explore their feelings about the work they are undertaking.

Mediation

This function involves the supervisor making clear what the policy, procedure and expectations of the agency are and why the supervisee needs to apply these to their practice. It might involve negotiation about dilemmas faced by the supervisee in relation to organisational requirements and how these can be managed.

Very often agency supervision policies refer to the various functions of supervision, but managers may focus on one function at the expense of the others.

Good-quality supervision balances all four functions such that health and social care workers have opportunities to explore their work, organisational requirements, their learning and the support they need.

Good practice in supervision is a joint responsibility and involves the following aspects being in place:

- Supervision should be planned and thorough.

- The process of supervision needs to be explicit and there should be a clearly agreed working definition of supervision.

- Past experiences of supervision should be acknowledged, in order to clarify current expectations.

- Supervision should be accurately recorded and this should be shared, with both parties' signatures included.

- Power imbalances should be acknowledged and discussed. By virtue of the fact that one worker is accountable to the other in an arrangement formalised within the agency, the supervisor is in a more powerful position. However, it is important to remember that other general power imbalances may exist.

- A written agreement (supervision contract) should be in place and this should be regularly reviewed.

- A safe environment should be fostered. This basically involves all of the above points being covered.

Supervision is a vital activity for all health and social care professionals. Unfortunately, some staff value supervision more than others – this includes supervisors and supervisees. Both parties need to value the process and be committed to it in order for it to be effective.

Supervision has a range of benefits for health and social care. It:

- allows workers to share any concerns, dilemmas, etc

- provides opportunities for growth and professional development

- can provide a safe forum for the provision of feedback

- provides a useful forum for reviewing actions and monitoring progress against plans – providing a safety net for workers and organisations

- leads to improved outcomes for service users.

PERFORMANCE REVIEW AND APPRAISAL

Performance review or appraisal takes a much broader view than supervision and should draw together the themes, feedback and learning that has emerged from regular supervision sessions over a longer period (generally six months to a year). As with supervision, the process varies between organisations but will usually cover a worker and their manager meeting together and:

- reviewing previously set objectives

- considering performance over the last year

- giving and receiving constructive feedback
- looking at the wider organisational context
- agreeing a personal development plan
- agreeing performance objectives for the year ahead.

MENTORING

Mentoring has a long history. The term itself is drawn from ancient Greek mythology – when Odysseus went to Troy he left Mentor to be the trusted friend and adviser to his son. Since then, the term mentoring has been used to describe a relationship where one person who is more experienced than another takes on a role to assist, support and advise. Traditionally, people have sought informal mentors. For example, when a person has joined a new team, they may approach a worker they trust, and whose practice they respect, to ask questions, etc. Many organisations have begun to recognise the value of mentoring and have set up formalised mentoring schemes, where workers new to a role or task are linked with a more experienced worker who will act as a mentor.

COACHING

A coach could be formally matched or introduced to a worker or a coach could be informally approached by a worker who feels they would benefit from a supportive relationship. The main difference between coaching and mentoring is that generally a coach supports a person to develop a specifically identified area. A coach might use a range of tactics to support an individual to learn, such as:

- *Modelling*. This involves carrying out a behaviour/skill in what is considered to be the 'correct' way while the learner is able to observe and ask questions.

- *Rehearsal*. This involves the coach supporting the learner to practise the skill or activity with the coach observing/supporting and then providing feedback. This is sometimes referred to as role play.

- *Coaching conversation*. This involves the coach talking to the learner using a questioning approach to enable the learner to work through the process and learn for themselves.

TRAINING

Not too long ago training in health and social care meant the worker going away from the workplace for a day or more to take part in a course. However, nowadays training opportunities are much more varied and might include:

- a traditional 'course'

- a presentation given to the team (maybe in a team meeting)

- a distance learning course

- online or computer-based training (often referred to as e-learning)

- in-service training (eg a supervisor showing a worker a new task).

Learning from training isn't automatic whatever the content and quality of the training. It is important that anyone going on training takes responsibility for their own learning. This will involve preparing for the training by thinking through questions like:

- What do I want to learn?

- Why do I need to learn this?

- How will I use what I learn after the training is over?

It will also involve reflecting on learning after the training:

- What did I learn?

- How can I use this learning in my practice?

ASSESSMENT AND FEEDBACK

Health and social care workers regularly undertake competence-based qualifications. People can learn a great deal from being assessed and receiving feedback, not least because of the fact that being assessed encourages people to reflect on their practice.

RESEARCH AND EVIDENCE-BASED PRACTICE

There is an increasing emphasis in health and social care on evidence-based and research-based practice. This basically means practice that draws on what is known, eg from research in the service area. Many health and social care workers learn a great deal and develop both their own practice and service delivery based on their own reading and research. Within this book, the research sections will draw your attention to some up-to-date knowledge and research evidence. This research is used to inform local and governmental policy direction and to improve services, eg following a safeguarding investigation.

JOB ENLARGEMENT OR ENRICHMENT

Concepts of job enlargement and enrichment are drawn from theories about job satisfaction and the way that different work roles motivate people in different ways. When people have been in a particular role for some time, their satisfaction with the role may reduce and their performance may be affected. This can be addressed by changing jobs either through *enlargement* or *enrichment*.

Enlargement means extending the scope of the job by combining two or more jobs into one, giving greater variety and a more 'holistic' feel. Job enrichment means giving people more responsibility for setting their own pace, deciding their own methods and correcting their own mistakes – resulting in greater autonomy.

PROVIDING SUPPORT TO STUDENTS/ NEW STAFF

Staff teams can learn a great deal from supporting learners in the workplace. Many health and social care settings offer practice placements to students and supporting their learning can assist staff to learn a great deal themselves. When new members of staff begin in a team, other team members may act as mentors or supporters (eg during induction). This can also assist the existing worker to develop their own practice.

As a Level 3 candidate you may well be assisting other staff members to develop their practice in some way – use this opportunity to further develop your own practice. Adult learning is a two-way process and everyone can learn from the experience.

EVERYTHING IS A LEARNING OPPORTUNITY

It is important that professionals recognise the whole range of opportunities that can be accessed in terms of learning and development. Some opportunities are formal and have formal access procedures, such as training. Other opportunities are informal, where everyday activities are undertaken in a reflective way in order to aid learning. Absolutely anything can be viewed as a learning opportunity and recognising this is, in many ways, what makes a worker a professional, what makes a job a career.

CASE STUDY

Taju is a senior support worker with a mental health charity. He keeps a CPD portfolio, a folder where he keeps a range of material:

- certificates of training (he jots some notes down to go with these outlining the key learning he gained and how he has used these in practice)

- his supervision notes

- reflective notes about his practice experiences

- feedback he has received about his practice

- a copy of his job description.

Every six months Taju refers to his portfolio and makes some brief notes about his progress and his aims for the next six months.

- What else could Taju include in the portfolio?

- How might Taju make use of this portfolio in his work towards the diploma?

- What else could Taju use the portfolio for?

SURFACE AND DEEP APPROACHES TO LEARNING

Surface learning approach

This approach focuses on acquiring and memorising information. An uncritical, unquestioning approach is taken to acquiring new knowledge and there is little reflection. Learning is motivated by external factors such as demands from employers or meeting the requirements of an assessment.

Deep learning approach

This approach involves critically analysing new ideas and linking them with existing knowledge. This approach means that a learner will understand and be able to apply the learning in new and different contexts. Deep learning assists with problem solving and making wider connections.

KEY POINT

You should always try to take to take a deeper approach to your learning.

Code of Conduct for Healthcare Support Workers and Adult Social Care Workers

The Code of Conduct for Healthcare Support Workers and Adult Social Care Workers expects you to 'strive to improve quality through continuing professional development' and states that you must:

- ensure up-to-date compliance with all statutory and mandatory training, in agreement with your supervisor
- participate in continuing professional development to achieve the competence required for your role
- carry out competence-based training and education in line with your agreed ways of working
- improve the quality and safety of the care you provide with the help of your supervisor (and a mentor if available) and in line with your agreed ways of working
- maintain an up-to-date record of your training and development
- contribute to the learning and development of others as appropriate.

CHAPTER 9

Facilitating person-centred assessment, planning, implementation and review

Health and social care work is generally seen as having an underpinning process beginning with an assessment which is then followed by a cycle of planning, implementation and review. Reviews can then lead to a reassessment of need, which begins the process again. This chapter is focused on how this process works in order to continue to meet individuals' needs as they change over time.

Links to other chapters

The underpinning process covered in this chapter is reflected in almost all of the units of the qualification. Each time you do some work with an individual you should assess the need, plan what to do, carry out the work and then review its effectiveness. There are specific links between this chapter and the content of chapters 2, 5, 10, and 12.

THE HEALTH AND SOCIAL CARE PROCESS

Health and social care is generally seen as having an underpinning process, as depicted in the following cycle.

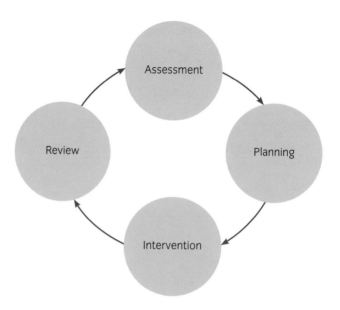

Depending on their role different health and social care workers are involved in different ways at the different stages of this cycle.

KEY PRINCIPLES OF PERSON-CENTRED ASSESSMENT AND CARE PLANNING

Person-centred assessment builds on the principles of person-centred practice, as follows:

- *Individuality*. Recognising each person as an individual and ensuring that their assessment and care plan reflects this individuality.

- *Choice*. Ensuring that people are given choices throughout the assessment and planning process.

- *Privacy*. Promoting an individual's privacy by only sharing assessment information on a need-to-know basis.

- *Independence*. Promoting a person's independence and ensuring that any assessment reflects the individual's strengths and that care plans promote the person's independence.

- *Dignity*. Promoting a person's dignity in the assessment and planning process.

- *Respect*. Respecting the individual at all times.

- *Partnership*. Working to complete the assessment, plan and review in partnership with the individual.

Person-centred assessment is also about ensuring that the person is at the centre of the assessment process and that the assessment is holistic in nature.

HOLISTIC ASSESSMENT AND CONCEPTS OF NEED

In order to understand **holistic approaches to assessment**, it is first essential to consider the concept of 'need', as assessments aim first and foremost to identify people's needs, so that these needs can then be met.

In recent years an emphasis has been put on needs-led assessment. Yet as the people carrying out assessment are often employed by agencies with limited resources, many would argue that assessment can never be truly needs led. There are further arguments that the concept of need in itself is not clear, so it is worth developing an overview of theories of need.

There are a number of theories of need. Perhaps the most well known of these is Maslow's hierarchy of needs.

Key term

Holistic approaches to assessment take account of all of the needs that people have and look at the person 'in the whole'. This means looking at people's culture, environment, resources, social networks, and all of the levels of need described in this section.

MASLOW'S HIERARCHY OF NEEDS

Maslow (1970) argues that all humans have a hierarchy of needs. We first need to satisfy basic biological needs (eg food, warmth, etc) and then we are successively drawn to meet higher needs.

Originally, Maslow created a pyramid of needs with five levels. He later extended this to seven levels.

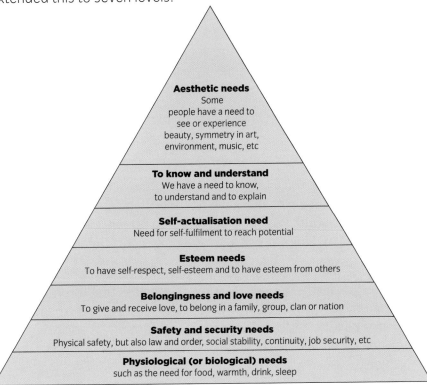

Aesthetic needs
Some people have a need to see or experience beauty, symmetry in art, environment, music, etc

To know and understand
We have a need to know, to understand and to explain

Self-actualisation need
Need for self-fulfilment to reach potential

Esteem needs
To have self-respect, self-esteem and to have esteem from others

Belongingness and love needs
To give and receive love, to belong in a family, group, clan or nation

Safety and security needs
Physical safety, but also law and order, social stability, continuity, job security, etc

Physiological (or biological) needs
such as the need for food, warmth, drink, sleep

(Source: Adapted from Maslow 1970)

Maslow argues that each level of need is a very powerful motivating force for each person.

At first, we are preoccupied with meeting our physiological (or biological) needs. If our need for food, water, warmth, etc is not being met, then all the other 'higher' needs are unimportant. We *must* satisfy our biological needs. Once we are in a situation where our biological needs are largely or fully met, we start to experience a craving for safety and security. The more fully our biological needs are met, the stronger is our desire to establish safety and security. The safety and security needs are not just about being free of the fear of being physically attacked. It also refers to our need for stability, order and routine. This includes social and economic stability.

Once the safety and security needs are largely or fully met, then our need for belonging and love becomes as intense as the two preceding needs once were. We crave the opportunity to love and to be loved, to belong to someone else, to be part of a wider group or community.

When we satisfy or largely meet our need to love and be loved, the importance of our need for self-esteem starts to rise. This need includes being able to achieve tasks, being competent, independent and having personal strength. Additionally, we need respect from others in the form of prestige, status, even fame. Maslow notes that basing self-esteem solely on the opinion of others is inviting insecurity. We need a sense that self-esteem is based on deserved respect from others rather than celebrity or unwarranted adulation.

The need for what Maslow describes as self-actualisation increases as our need for esteem is satisfied. Maslow assumes that all people will experience this need. How this need is satisfied will be an expression of our individuality. For one person, it will be through being an ideal mother; for another person, achieving a physical, athletic goal; for yet a different person, developing a new invention, etc.

In his later writings, Maslow then adds on two higher stages. In some respects they are extensions of the self-actualisation stage rather than entirely new stages.

In the first of the two new stages (the sixth stage of the whole pyramid) Maslow argues that we have a need to know, to be curious to seek to understand our world. People who enter into boring, unstimulating lifestyles are sometimes at risk of developing mental health problems.

The second of the two new stages (the seventh stage of the whole pyramid) is the aesthetic need. Maslow recognises that this need may only be felt by some people. However, for these people the need to experience beauty, symmetry and idealised harmony is so strong that Maslow feels it should be considered a need.

Maslow makes clear that people do not need to work through the stages in a methodical, rigid manner. A person could be seeking to meet their needs from two or three stages at the same time. But a person is able to increasingly devote their personal resources to a higher stage only once a lower stage is largely satisfied.

Maslow's hierarchy of needs in services

There are too many services that support service users only as far as level two (safety and security). Some services don't even get as high as level two. Very few service users are actively supported to have their needs for love and belonging met. Additionally, the use of labels in services undermines the idea of upholding a person's self-esteem and their sense that others respect them as competent people.

BRADSHAW'S TAXONOMY OF NEED

First developed by Jonathan Bradshaw in relation to the needs of older people, this was entitled a taxonomy of social need (1972). However, it is now probably more widely used in terms of health care than social care.

Bradshaw refers to real need. He believes this to be a combination of four types of need:

- *Normative need*. This refers to needs that the expert or professional defines – these needs tend to be based on the professional's view of societal 'norms'.

- *Perceived/felt needs*. This refers to needs felt by the individual – in a way a kind of self-assessment. This type of need is sometimes referred to as a 'want' rather than a need.

- *Expressed need (demand)*. This refers to the needs expressed by people – this can be seen as a felt need converted into expressed need when the person seeks assistance.

- *Comparative need*. This refers to the comparison that people make in defining needs – do we need what others have? etc. This is often referred to in understanding poverty. The concept of comparative poverty recognises that people may perceive themselves to be poor in comparison with others but this would not necessarily be viewed as 'real' poverty.

Bradshaw claims that each of these areas of need overlaps and that it is perhaps somewhere in the overlap that 'real need' can be found.

Do you really need it, or do you just want it?

CASE STUDY

Taju is a senior support worker with a mental health charity. He spends some of his time in a drop-in centre for people with mental health problems and the remainder of his working week is spent in outreach services providing ongoing practical and emotional support for service users.

Taju is working with Pam, who has recently begun to access the mental health charity's services. As part of his assessment with Pam, Taju has been working with her to help her identify her needs, hopes, goals, wishes, worries and the things she wants.

Pam began to experience depression and anxiety after her divorce, and she talks about needing company, as she finds herself feeling lonely and isolated, which she feels contributes to her depression. Pam also feels strongly that she needs to develop new friendship groups and social opportunities as the friends she used to have were all part of couples. She feels many of these 'fair-weather' friends took her partner's side after their divorce.

Taju understands that Pam is very concerned about these issues, and is keen to explore this further in his assessment and the support plan which he and Pam can agree. As Taju continues to talk to Pam, she begins to open up more about some of the other issues that are preventing her from moving on in her life. She says that her partner left her with some debts, and that as her benefits have recently been reviewed she is worried that she may lose her home if she falls into rent arrears. She also talks about how trapped she feels as she has not had a weekend away from the area or a holiday in several years.

- Which of Pam's issues are needs and which are wants?

- Using Maslow's hierarchy of needs how would you categorise Pam's needs?

- Using Bradshaw's model how would you categorise Pam's needs?

USING THE ASSESSMENT 'TRIANGLE'

When you are assessing any particular needs it is important to use the triangle approach. This means getting information from:

1 what you see (your own observations)

2 other people (this includes what the service user themselves tell you and what others say)

3 reports and records about the person.

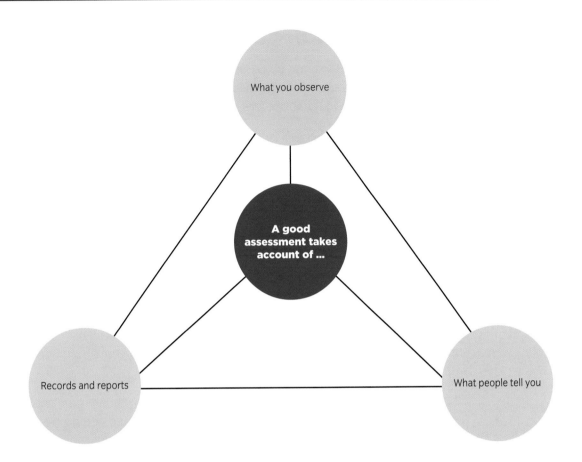

REFLECT

- What is your understanding of the concepts of need as explored above?

- How do your assessments and plans focus on people's needs, and which levels of need in Maslow's hierarchy are most often the ones you are working to meet in your work role?

HOLISTIC APPROACHES TO ASSESSMENT

Holistic approaches look at:

- the person's needs (according to every layer of the hierarchy)

- their systems, networks and support

- their emotional and mental well-being

- the home, area and situation in which they live

- their access to financial, community and other resources.

These ideas link strongly with the concept of social models as opposed to medical models of disability (see Chapter 18). Social models see people in the full context of their lives, and try to assess needs and plan cares holistically as opposed to 'treating' conditions in isolation from the context in which people live.

FOCUS OF PERSON-CENTRED ASSESSMENT

Person-centred assessments focus on the individual needs that a person has rather than on what services can do. Health and social care workers can get confused about this at times, eg:

- Mrs Jones needs to go to a day centre.

  or

- Mr Gardner needs home care.

These statements demonstrate a service-led approach to the assessment. The assessor has listed services that are available as the need.

Perhaps Mrs Jones is socially isolated and needs opportunities to meet and engage with others to prevent loneliness – this need could be addressed at a day service but it could be addressed by a wide range of other services. For example, maybe Mrs Jones could be supported to go to local community activities, perhaps she would find a befriending service useful, etc.

Possibly Mr Gardener needs support with his personal care. Again this need could be met by home care, but Mr Gardener's needs could be met in a range of other ways – perhaps he could employ a personal assistant, perhaps his family could provide support with personal care, etc.

An assessment is not about prescribing a service – it is about beginning with identifying a person's individual needs in detail, then looking at what they want to achieve. Only then are the different options for meeting those needs considered.

THE SINGLE-ASSESSMENT PROCESS (SAP)

The single-assessment process (often referred to as SAP) was introduced in the National Service Framework for Older People (Department of Health 2001a). SAP aims to make sure older people's needs are assessed thoroughly and accurately, but without procedures being needlessly duplicated by different agencies, and that information is shared appropriately between health and social care agencies.

SAP is increasingly being used as a framework for delivering services to other adults requiring care. In practice, one of the main impacts SAP practice proves is that in local areas assessments are shared between professionals. This means that service users do not have to repeat their 'stories' each time they come into contact with a different service or a new professional.

CONTINUING CARE ASSESSMENTS

Within health and social care, assessments for continuing care can feel like a minefield for many individuals and their carers. Continuing care assessments determine whether someone's needs relate to their health or to social care. If the needs are social care needs, the services that the person requires in order for their needs to be met are then means tested.

NHS continuing health care is free and can be provided in someone's own home, a care setting or within health service settings. Assessments for continuing health care are provided by health professionals (as opposed to the local authority) and decisions should be made within 28 days.

Eligibility is determined by:

- someone's *primary* need being related to their health
- the person therefore having complex needs that require health professionals to provide highly specialised support.

It is not determined by somebody's diagnosis (eg dementia) and debates over these issues can be highly emotive and difficult.

Eligibility can of course change and people who do receive continuing health care will have this reviewed at least annually.

PERSONAL HEALTH BUDGETS

Personal health budgets are being rolled out to deliver focus on:

- choice and control
- flexibility of service provision
- person-centred approaches to meeting needs.

In order for an individual to access a personal health budget:

- their needs are assessed
- a care plan is agreed
- an amount of money is allocated to meet their needs
- they decide how they want to spend the money to ensure their needs are met.

For more information on how personal health budgets are being delivered and how the learning around this is being collated, see www.personalhealthbudgets.dh.gov.uk.

THE COMMON ASSESSMENT FRAMEWORK (CAF)

There has been a Common Assessment Framework in children's services for many years. The framework means that a similar process is used to assess the needs of children and families wherever they live and from wherever they receive services. The white paper, 'Our Health, Our Care, Our Say' (Department of Health 2006) proposed a common assessment framework for adults in need of health and social care services. The aim of adopting a common framework is to remove the artificial boundary of 'older age', and provide continuity of a person-centred approach throughout adult life, geared towards self-determination and planning for independence.

The CAF has retained the core features and properties of SAP and aims to:

- support seamless delivery of services across health and social care

- avoid duplication of information collection and procedures

- provide a proportionate assessment according to an individual's level of need

- provide a person-centred assessment of needs feeding into a personalised care plan to support people.

It is likely that the single-assessment process will form the basis of a model for a national common assessment framework. The framework will aim to deliver the benefits of a holistic needs assessment for all adults with long-term conditions.

SUPPORTING INDIVIDUALS TO LEAD THE ASSESSMENT AND PLANNING PROCESS

Person-centred assessment and planning requires individuals' participation in these processes to be:

- genuine

- maximised

- not just making a token effort

- tailored around their communication needs.

As well as participating in assessments and planning, individuals can be enabled to lead these processes in a variety of ways. The methods and tools you need to consider will be different for each person, and should be specific to the context and purpose of the assessment or plan.

People can lead assessments and planning by:

- changing standard documentation so that the paperwork used belongs to them

- using advocates to enable their viewpoint to be stressed at all times or to ensure they have the opportunity to question professional judgements or jargon

- calling for their own reassessment or review

- chairing their own care planning meeting

- being prepared properly for any meeting (ie by discussing what questions they would like answered, by considering where they should sit, by making sure the time and venue are appropriate for the individual, etc)

- being involved in discussions about risk, choice and dignity

- being involved in discussions about the potential range of resources that plans could contain.

SELF-ASSESSMENT

As part of the movement in health and social care towards self-directed support, many local areas are promoting self-assessment. Self-assessment generally involves service users and carers completing assessment documentation to assess their own needs.

ADAPTING ASSESSMENT AND PLANNING DOCUMENTATION TO MAXIMISE OWNERSHIP

Many pieces of key documentation in health and social care settings have a small box, usually towards the bottom of the document, where the service user's views are recorded. Often these boxes are left blank when assessments are sampled by inspectors or managers.

Documentation can easily be adapted to ensure that people have ownership and control over it. The reasons for doing so are powerful, including:

- Plans are more likely to work if people feel that the plan belongs to them.

- Maximising control and ownership is part of the value base for the profession (working with people, not 'doing to' them).

- Documents can always be improved.

- Person-centred practice means we should do things differently for each individual – recognising individuality in documentation avoids the 'one size fits all' approach.

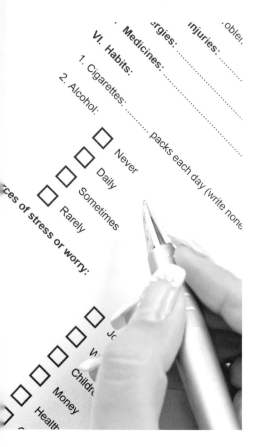

Some ideas for making these adaptations in practice include:

- ensuring that the process itself is appropriate and inclusive (eg holding meetings in the right venue at the best time for the person even if professionals have to move their diaries around for this; including people's relatives as necessary; using advocates, etc)

- moving boxes around on the form (where possible) – why not put people's viewpoint, wishes, feelings and hopes first?

- ensuring documentation meets people's communication needs (eg font size, colour of the paper, Braille, use of jargon or appropriate language, use of professional acronyms, etc)

- avoiding terms that de-personalise people, including 'patient' and 'service user' (why not write the documentation using the word 'you' instead so that this is about and for the person?)

- making sure people have their own copies of the documentation, that they are signed off by them, and that where there are differences of opinion, the person's feelings and wishes are recorded. See Chapter 4 on the duty of care for more detail about this issue and the need to be clear with people about why their wishes may not be able to be met.

PERSON-CENTRED ASSESSMENT TOOLS

A number of tools are used in person-centred planning to assist in assessment and planning. These have been developed mostly from learning disability services and are based on the work of well-known practitioners such as John O'Brien, Beth Mount and Helen Sanderson.

Many of these tools are available online and the most widely used ones are explained below. However, it is important that health and social care workers make use of the tools in their service and that they have specific knowledge on how these tools should be used with individuals.

One-page profile

This is literally a single-page profile of somebody. Nothing unique in that, you might think; however, it must not focus on needs and disabilities, as many individual user profiles do. Rather, in person-centred thinking, a one-page profile lists what other people like and admire about someone, what that person feels is important to them and what excellent support for them would involve.

Good day/bad day

This explores what makes a good day for someone – what they do, where they go, who is there, etc, and what makes a bad day. A good day would be one that the person enjoys and finds meaningful and a bad day would be one where they feel little has been achieved. Learning about what makes a good day and what makes a bad day can help inform planning so that people can have more good days than bad days.

Pyramid of success

This is a way of helping people identify the steps they need to take to work towards their goal. It also identifies who might be able to assist. Where there are difficulties or 'obstacles' to be overcome on the way to the goal, discussion can take place about how these can be addressed.

Staff-matching tools

There are many tools available to help people identify the characteristics of staff they would like to support them. These are often used when people are considering using personal budgets to employ PAs. Essentially, the idea of this is that service users have control over deciding who supports them.

Lifelines

These are a pictorial way of showing someone's life story – it helps identify where a person is at and how they got there. It can also be developed to show where they want to go to next.

4 + 1 questions

These are generally used to inform the review process and essentially involve asking four questions:

1   What have we tried?

2   What have we learned?

3   What are we pleased about?

4   What are we concerned about?

And then following this up with the +1 question, ie what do we need to do?

REFLECT

- How could assessments and planning processes be adapted in order to maximise people's involvement, ownership and control in your work setting?

- How could assessments and planning documentation be adapted in order to maximise people's involvement, ownership and control in your work setting?

FACILITATING PERSON-CENTRED ASSESSMENT

Facilitating person-centred assessment is about carrying out an assessment using all the principles of person-centred practice – key to this is taking a partnership approach to assessment.

A PARTNERSHIP APPROACH TO ASSESSMENT

Establishing a partnership approach to assessment is critical, as service users need to understand the assessment process and to experience the maximum level of control over this. Assessments generally take place at times of stress for people which can make people feel powerless and therefore asking for help is often very difficult to do. People's sense of powerlessness is often enhanced by the fact of needing services or support to have their basic needs met, or to achieve tasks that they used to do for themselves. That is why partnerships with service users need to:

- acknowledge and address issues of power imbalance by involving people fully in assessment and planning

- ensure the accessibility of information about assessments and planning

- listen to service users' perspectives, wishes and views in more than just a tokenistic way

- be transparent and open when the outcome of an assessment is not what a person hoped for, and explain why this may be and what their options are.

Partnerships with relatives and other unpaid carers are also critical because of the implications of legislation concerning carers, and also for ethical reasons because carers are often the people who:

- know the person best

- can advise on methods of communication that work

- are affected deeply by the decisions professionals make

- are rightly very frustrated when they are not fully involved in assessments.

Partnerships with other agencies are also vital in the context of holistic assessment and the reasons for this are considered in detail in Chapter 1 on the role of the health and social care worker. Other agencies may well know more about someone's unique needs or other professionals may have more specific information about a condition in their field of expertise, and it would do the person a disservice not to tap into this expertise as part of the assessment.

CO-PRODUCTION

Co-production (also referred to as co-creation and parallel production) is increasingly referred to in terms of producing assessments in partnership with service users. Co-production describes approaches to health and social care that recognise and utilise the expertise of service users in shaping their own support and encourages their involvement in service planning, delivery and improvement. It can be seen as a transformative way of thinking about partnerships, power, risks, resources and outcomes.

Recognising service users as the experts about themselves and their own needs should underpin all practice in health and social care. Service user involvement on an individual level (eg in their own assessment and planning) is essential to all good practice. Collective involvement of service users in the commissioning and development of services is also a vital ingredient for co-production to be a reality.

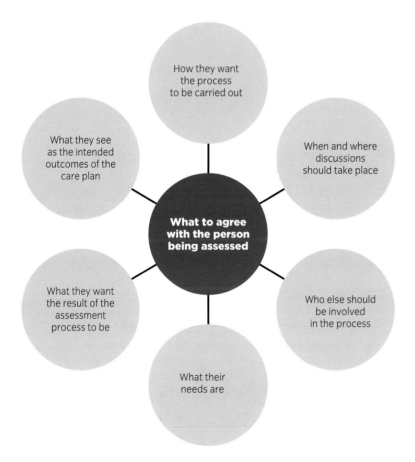

How they want the process to be carried out

When and where discussions should take place

What they see as the intended outcomes of the care plan

What to agree with the person being assessed

Who else should be involved in the process

What they want the result of the assessment process to be

What their needs are

Taking a co-production or partnership approach to person centred assessment

MESSAGES FROM RESEARCH

Service user experiences of assessment

In 2011, the Equality and Human Rights Commission published research into the experiences of older people receiving home care services. One aspect of this was considering the experiences that service users had of the assessments of their needs. This highlighted:

- Service users and carers 'praised assessments where staff had taken their time and shown skills and sensitivity in eliciting respondents' needs and preferences'.

- Many respondents said that they did not feel they were given much opportunity to say what they wanted: 'they arrange everything and just tell you what they are going to do'.

- Some people said they felt that the assessment process was never going to end – they felt the questions were intrusive and not always clear.

- Service users said that they found answering personal questions very hard work and sometimes they felt humiliated.

(Sykes and Groom 2011)

OUTCOME-FOCUSED ASSESSMENT

The concept of needs-led assessment is now being complemented by outcomes-focused assessment. This has been developed by research carried out at the University of York. According to the Social Policy Research Unit this approach is based on the social model of disability and empowerment.

Outcomes are generally seen in three dimensions:

- Outcomes involving change, eg improving self-confidence, self-care skills or changes to the accessibility of certain environments.

- Outcomes that maintain quality of life (or slow down deterioration in quality of life), sometimes referred to as maintenance outcomes.

- Outcomes that are associated with the process of receiving services, such as feeling valued, being respected, feeling listened to, etc.

Harris et al (2005) developed an outcomes framework that categorised outcomes into four areas – in many ways these four areas could be seen as needs. The three dimensions of outcomes could be applied to any of the four areas in the framework.

Key term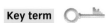

Outcomes are what people want to achieve.

Autonomy outcomes	Personal comfort outcomes
■ Access to all areas of the home	■ Personal hygiene
■ Access to locality and wider environment	■ Safety/security
■ Communicative access	■ Desired level of cleanliness of home
■ Financial security	■ Emotional well-being
	■ Physical health
Economic participation outcomes	**Social participation outcomes**
■ Access to paid employment as desired	■ Access to mainstream leisure activities
■ Access to training	■ Access to support in parenting role
■ Access to further/higher education or employment	■ Access to support for personal secure relationships
■ Access to appropriate training for new skills (eg lip-reading)	■ Access to advocacy/peer support
	■ Citizenship

(Source: Adapted from Harris et al 2005)

The outcome-focused approach is seen as a person-centred approach which involves the practitioner acting more as facilitator than assessor. Many professionals find an outcome-focused approach to be an improvement on needs-based assessment as this approach stresses that the whole point of assessment is about achieving progress and change for people.

In carrying out an assessment, professionals need to agree with people what the intended outcomes for the individual are. Service users, carers and professionals may have very different views on what the intended outcomes are, so considering this and seeking agreement early on can:

■ reduce the possibility of conflict or tensions further down the line

■ improve people's ownership and thereby their confidence

■ increase opportunities for partnership working and can mean partnerships become more effective

■ improve the likelihood of the intended outcomes being achieved.

RESEARCH

In your work setting, how do assessments and plans look at outcomes?

How are outcomes:

- identified
- mapped against the four areas above of autonomy, personal comfort, social participation and economic participation
- planned for
- recorded
- monitored?

ACCOUNTING FOR AN INDIVIDUAL'S STRENGTHS AND ASPIRATIONS AS WELL AS NEEDS

Historically, assessments have focused on listing people's deficits (what they can't do rather than what they can do), their vulnerabilities and negative past experiences. Good practice means focusing on people's strengths, abilities and resilience.

There is a specific model referred to as the strengths perspective, which highlights the way that assessments have traditionally led to what is called 'professional pathologising' (focusing on negative issues). This is poor practice and good practice focuses on strengths. The following comparison developed by Saleebey (1996) shows this clearly:

Poor practice – focusing on 'pathology'	Best practice – focusing on 'strengths'
Person is defined as a 'case'; symptoms add up to a diagnosis	Person is defined as unique; traits, talents, resources add up to strengths
Service user accounts are filtered by a professional to aid the generation of a diagnosis	Personal accounts are the essential route to knowing and appreciating the person
Professional devises treatment or care plan	Focus is aspirations of individual, family or community
Professional is the expert on the service user's life	Individual, family or community are the experts

Poor practice – focusing on 'pathology'	Best practice – focusing on 'strengths'
Possibilities for choice, control, commitment and personal development are limited by labels, diagnoses or conditions	Possibilities for choice, control, commitment and personal development are open
Professionals' knowledge, skills and connections are principal resources for service user	The strength, capacities and adaptive skills of the individual, family or community are the principal resources
Support is centred on reducing the effects of symptoms and the negative effects of emotions or relationships	Support is focused on getting on with one's life, affirming and developing values and commitments, and making or finding membership in a community

The strengths perspective promotes the idea that personal qualities and strengths can come out of and be formed by difficult life experiences. Resilience, independence, loyalty to one or more people can arise due to a painful or traumatic personal experience. People can develop great insight into their own situation, how they reached where they are currently and how they can find ways through their current issues.

An important source of strength can be cultural, community or personal stories or narratives.

The strengths perspective recognises that individuals and families have already been subjected to a range of demanding life events. Additionally, if people have had contact with health and social care services for some time they could have internalised the ideas of deficiency and needs. It is in addressing this that the professional's skills are called upon to work creatively (eg in using narrative approaches, life-story work, etc) with the service user and this can require specific training and be very demanding.

RESILIENCE PERSPECTIVE

The **resilience** perspective is closely related to the strengths perspective. Often resilience is seen as one aspect of the strengths perspective.

Resilience refers to supporting people in developing their own reservoir of skills, abilities and knowledge. This personal reservoir includes someone's social support network. Ideally, their sense of the resources they have should be developed in depth (eg strengthening existing family relationships or friendships) and across a broad range

Key term

Resilience is best defined as a person's ability to 'bounce back'. Resilience perspectives in health and social care take account of a person's strengths and the resources around them that protect them from presenting risks. The aim then is for these protective factors to be enhanced further as part of planning for that individual.

(the person is supported to try new experiences both so that they acquire new skills but also so that they meet new people).

The resilience perspective recognises that individuals can have difficulties in one area of their life. One of the ways a person overcomes a difficulty is by drawing on other aspects of their life either directly to problem solve, or indirectly so that the person has a sense that in other areas of their life they are doing well.

The strengths and resilience perspectives present both a challenge and an opportunity. To apply the strengths perspective fully, workers must move away from bureaucratic, deficit-led assessments. Workers need to engage with the service user or family in the language of hope, aspirations and outcomes. Health and social care workers can support service users by reframing statements about problems into being ones about learning from difficulties.

Crucially, the opportunity is that in a time of increasingly restricted services, if workers can engage with an individual or family and support them to identify the strengths and abilities they have in themselves and their support network, they will leave the service user or family with something to build on.

CASE STUDY

Isabella is a senior care assistant in a respite care service that provides short-term stays for younger people with learning and physical disabilities.

Isabella is supporting the parents of Tim, a young adult who uses the service to access a reassessment of their needs as carers of their son. Tim's parents are committed to him, are keen to enable him to stay with them, live as full a life as possible and engage in the community. However, Tim's father has been unwell recently and this has had an impact on the whole family, especially as Tim's mother cannot always meet Tim's personal care needs on her own.

Isabella attends an initial meeting as part of this assessment with Tim's social worker and his parents. Isabella knows that they would ideally like to have some short-term support at home and some increased respite via Isabella's service. However, during this assessment, she is concerned that the needs and issues Tim's parents are facing are being discussed, but none of the positives about how much they love their son and want things to improve and return to how they were are mentioned. Isabella knows that it has taken a lot of courage for them to ask for this assessment and for increased support, as they feel guilty about needing this and worried about whether they will qualify for any or not.

She feels that unless the strengths and positives within the family are acknowledged, that this will put Tim's parents off from continuing with their assessment.

- What could Isabella do in this situation, both at the meeting and afterwards?
- How might the strengths perspective inform this assessment and improve the quality of decision making and planning?

WORKING WITH INDIVIDUALS AND OTHERS TO IDENTIFY SUPPORT REQUIREMENTS AND PREFERENCES

By taking all of the above into account, a detailed holistic assessment should get a rounded picture of a person's:

- strengths
- protective factors (see also Chapter 5 on safeguarding)
- presenting needs
- culture
- wishes, feelings, hopes and aspirations
- carers and their viewpoints and needs
- current access to resources
- choices in terms of what other resources they might be eligible to access.

In considering all of the these, it should be possible to identify the person's specific, individual and unique support requirements, and what they are likely to prefer to access out of the range of potential resources they could choose from.

REFLECT

- How is your work informed by the strengths perspective and your understanding of resilience?
- What experience do you have of using these perspectives in assessments and plans?
- Are there any examples you can think of from your work where you could have improved outcomes by using this knowledge?

CONTRIBUTING TO THE PLANNING OF CARE OR SUPPORT

When an assessment has been completed a plan needs to be developed. In health and social care different terms are used for the plans that are developed following assessments. Plans might be referred to as care plans, daily plans, weekly plans or support plans.

It is important that a clear plan is in place for a range of reasons:

- Service users will be clear about what they can expect in terms of support.

- Family members and other informal carers will understand how a service user's needs are to be addressed.

- Direct care and support staff will understand their role in the service user's life.

- The input of all professionals will be clearer, therefore improving partnership working.

- Inspectors can be clear that a service is working towards agreed and measurable goals.

Plans should include:

- a summary of identified/eligible needs indicating the intensity, instability, predictability and complexity of needs, the associated risks to independence and the potential for rehabilitation or reablement

- a note about whether or not the service user has agreed to the plan and a reason given where this was not possible

- a note on whether or not the user has consented for information about the plan to be shared among relevant agencies and a reason where this was not possible

- the objectives of providing help and anticipated outcomes for service users

- a summary of how services will affect identified, eligible needs and associated risks

- the part the service user will play in addressing needs, including the strengths and abilities they will bring to this

- details of managing risk as appropriate – where it has been agreed that service users will accept a certain degree of risk, this must be written into the plan

- details of what carers are willing to do and related needs and support

- a description of the level and frequency of the help that is to be provided, stating which agency is responsible for what service

- details of any contributions to care costs that service users are asked to make

- the name of the person coordinating the plan and the contact number

- a contact number or office in case of emergencies and a contingency plan if things go wrong

- details about how the plan will be monitored and a date for review.

In carrying out the planning process it is useful to work through the following questions.

WHAT IS THE NEED/PROBLEM/ISSUE?

Outlining the need or the presenting issue, as identified in the assessment process, is important so that the service user and everybody involved in their care knows why the plan is being put into place. It is important to keep the focus on an agreed number of issues so that the service user is not overwhelmed. It is also important to prioritise which needs should be addressed in the first instance (in line with the theories of need explored earlier). Plans do not need to be lengthy to show they are thorough. Sometimes brevity can show more care in being appropriate to the person's needs.

WHAT ARE THE AIMS AND OBJECTIVES?

Translating identified needs into **aims** and **objectives** is perhaps where the skills and expertise of a health and social care worker are most necessary.

Turning needs into outcomes or aims needs to take account of the strengths and limitations of the service user and the situation. Sometimes it is harder for the person receiving support to see what their strengths are. Here the health and social care worker can offer their knowledge and skills to help the service user.

The easiest way to think about this is that the aim is what the service user ultimately wants to achieve. The objectives are the steps that will be taken to reach the aim (the ultimate goal).

The major new emphasis in care planning is on specifying the expected results of the care – known as the outcomes. Being clear about the criteria for measuring outcomes is also important in care planning. That is, achievable aims should be outlined – the outcomes of which can be measured.

Key terms

Aim in this context is about finding a direction or purpose.

Objective refers to the point to which operations are directed; the point to be reached; the goal.

WHAT IS THE PLANNED OUTCOME?

This question is about identifying which changes are achievable with each person and supporting the person and everyone involved in their care to recognise that change is possible. Change could entail very small steps, and planning these outcomes in stages can be a helpful way of ensuring possible solutions are broken down into specific outcomes for that individual. For one person an outcome could be independent shopping and for another it might be relearning self-care skills. The idea is that the plan is person centred and relevant to that individual at that specific time. In an age where many services are often subject to funding reviews and contracting processes and the growth of the personalisation agenda, people have the need to see that services deliver specific outcomes.

A planning tool that demonstrates this process in action can be a helpful way of services demonstrating precisely what progress they aim to make with each person. This is because talking in vague terms of 'support' may not be enough to convince some funders and individuals in charge of contracting their own care. Being more specific is also more supportive and will enable service users and their networks to have 'ownership' of the plan.

HOW WILL WE MEASURE THIS OUTCOME (INDICATORS)?

If any outcome is specific, then the plan needs to be able to show how everyone will know that change has been achieved. What are the indicators of very small changes for people? If the outcome is the person being able to access activity provision in their community, then how many activities per week is a reasonable measure of success for this person? If the outcome is improving the person's self-care skills, then how will everyone know that progress has been made? Is this about the person brushing their teeth without support or about them making a cup of tea safely and independently?

WHAT WILL THE SERVICE DO TO ACHIEVE THIS OUTCOME?

This is about clarifying what the service's role is and also what it is not. How many hours of care support are being put in? Who will be providing specific work on each identified area? What other resources could be available within the service for the service user and their carers to choose from? Also, what other agencies and services are involved in working with the person's care team (eg an occupational therapist, social worker, GP, etc)?

WHAT IS EXPECTED OF THE PERSON?

Care plans that focus only on service provision can have the air of 'doing to' people, rather than enabling and empowering users of services in line with the principles of active support, as explored in Chapter 11. Person-centred care planning should always identify what the service user will need to do in order for them to achieve the outcomes, as this enables changes to be owned by the person rather than the service. This could involve looking at the person committing to change by attending appointments in the community, being open about the barriers they may face along the way or committing to working with the care team on the agreed areas.

WHEN WILL WE REVIEW WHETHER THE OUTCOME HAS BEEN ACHIEVED?

All plans need a review timescale to be built in, so that changes are recorded and further actions identified. This can be particularly important where changes have not been as expected as this can sometimes mean that a different type of support is needed to enable the person to make the progress they hope for in that area. Setting milestones where review will occur enables the whole care team, including the person's carers, to maintain focus when things might be challenging, and ensures that reviews do not drift when a busy workload for the service can occur. Milestones will be different according to the nature of each presenting need or issue, and according to the support that is put into place.

Care plans should always be discussed and agreed openly with the whole care team, including the service user and their carers. It can be useful sometimes to have a draft of a plan ready prior to a discussion taking place but, in this instance, it is vital that people are enabled to challenge the content of their plan. After all, it is their plan and again must link with the principles of person-centred care and active support.

> **KEY POINT**
>
> **Keeping the process person centred**
> It is vital to remember that planning should always be person centred. The way in which a care plan is presented should reflect this – perhaps it needs to be presented in a pictorial way, for example. Health and social care staff need to remember that plans are about and for service users and not services.

MESSAGES FROM RESEARCH

Person-centred planning

> Successful personalised care planning needs to be developed with individuals, not done to them. It requires you to adopt a different role to the traditional 'diagnose and treater.' The healthcare professional's role is to support individuals to acknowledge, understand and adapt to living with their condition.
>
> (Department of Health 2011)

The Joseph Rowntree Foundation conducted a review in 2006 of the extent and effectiveness of person-centred planning in adult services, as well as looking at the barriers to ensuring that this approach is embedded in service contexts.

This research found that:

- Staff training and organisational culture have a profound impact on the ability of services to respond to individual needs in a person-centred and holistic way.

- Support for staff needs to be embedded in services, and managers should take a person-centred approach to how they support and supervise staff in order for this then to be modelled with service users.

- Person-centred planning requires resourcing in order to adhere properly to the value base and to be effective with individuals.

- Good relationships with family members and fully inclusive practices enable person-centred planning to work.

- An analysis and realignment of power imbalances between services, staff members, service users and carers needs to occur in order for person-centred planning to occur effectively.

(Dowling, Manthorpe and Cowley 2006)

FACTORS THAT MAY INFLUENCE THE TYPE AND LEVEL OF CARE OR SUPPORT TO BE PROVIDED

A range of factors might impact on the planning of care. These could include:

- whether an individual's objectives are achievable

- the beliefs and values an individual has

- cultural factors and preferences for individuals

- the person's own wishes and choices about what support they want at the moment (eg people do not always want the type or level of support that professionals think is best for them – see also Chapter 4 on the duty of care for more detail around ethical dilemmas)

- any risks that might be linked to achieving the care plan

- the availability of relatives, friends and others within the person's own informal networks to support the plan

- the current view on eligibility thresholds within a service or local authority area (linked to the availability of resources, the current governmental policies and constraints, etc)

- the views and wishes of the person's informal carers and any assessments of the carers' needs, along with the carers' rights as defined in carers' legislation

- the accessibility and availability of suitable local resources

- the needs, rights and wishes of other service users within group services or shared living arrangements.

AGREEING HOW COMPONENT PARTS OF A PLAN WILL BE DELIVERED AND BY WHOM

In order to be effective, actions within plans need to be SMART:

- **S**pecific

- **M**easurable

- **A**chievable

- **R**ealistic

- **T**ime-bound.

Plans should set people up to succeed, as well as stretching people's experiences in a healthy and appropriate way. Effective plans achieve all of this by:

- stating who is doing what, when, where and why

- identifying the expectations of the service user themselves, so that their active involvement in plans is paramount

- accountability, so that if someone does not do what they have agreed to, then this can be examined and addressed

- identifying timescales so that everyone knows that there is enough time for actions to be undertaken, and that the plan will be monitored and reviewed

- recording.

RECORDING PLANS IN A SUITABLE FORMAT

Most services have a format for the recording of care or support plans. It is important that you make use of the format used by your employer.

Some plans might have an extra column for recording what is discussed at the review point and any changes to the plan at that stage. Other plans might include a row for everyone signing off the plan to show agreement.

An example of a care plan might be something like the following.

What is the issue?	What is the planned outcome?	How will we measure this outcome?	What will the service do to achieve this outcome?	What is expected of the person?	When will we review if the outcome has been achieved?
Fred feels isolated and wants support to access some activities in the area where he can meet new people.	Reduce Fred's isolation.	Fred will access at least one activity per week.	We will provide support for six weeks to try out different local activities of Fred's choice, such as the chess club and gardening project.	Fred needs to decide what he would like to do each week, and whether he wants to go back to any of the activities after the first visit. Fred needs to be ready on time as agreed.	After six weeks.
Fred needs some support around self-care and hygiene.	Improve Fred's self-care and independence.	Fred will have a routine that works for him to follow to get clean and ready each day independently.	We will provide support for Fred in implementing this routine for four weeks (8am call).	Fred needs to work with us to try out routines so that he can find one that works for him. Fred's family have agreed to support him with this by reminding him of the routine and helping Fred to follow it for himself.	At the end of the six weeks (two weeks with the support in place, and four weeks of following routines independently).

ADVANCE CARE PLANNING

Advance care planning is about people making plans in advance of specific needs. For example, a person might develop an advance care plan about what they would like to happen to them if their health deteriorates.

The concept of advance care planning can feel scary for many individuals. However, advance care planning can be helpful as:

- it is entirely voluntary

- it gives people the opportunity to express their wishes and preferences at a point where this may feel useful, but before a crisis point

- it provides an opportunity for people to explore their options more fully than they may feel able to do in an emergency or when they are at their most unwell

- exploring all of the options in this way enables the person's holistic needs to be considered and addressed (eg in terms of how they wish to be cared for, their home and living circumstances, care of pets in an emergency, etc)

- the service user can still change their mind at any time in the future

- it gives people the chance to refuse treatment in advance, as well as to access treatments and care that meets their wishes and preferences

- it involves professionals, carers and family members so that everyone knows the person's wishes

- it ensures people have choices about who has legal powers of attorney and can act on their behalf.

REFLECT

Think of some of the care plans with which you have been involved. The plans do not have to be ones that you have written and led yourself, but they can be plans that you have supported.

- How do these plans meet the principles identified above for what a high-quality plan contains?

- How could plans be improved, and can you identify any opportunities to do so, either in terms of the plan format in your work setting, or for individual plans which you currently work to?

CASE STUDY

Jon is a senior support worker with a reablement team. He is working with Marvin as part of his outreach work. Marvin accesses a weekly drop-in centre at a local drug service where he engages well with his worker on a harm minimisation programme in relation to his use of amphetamines and cannabis. The current plan for Marvin focuses on reducing his drug use and harm minimisation for both him and his children who are currently on a child-in-need plan with children's social care services.

Marvin makes it known that he wants to be able to prove he can reduce his use in order to be able to show that he can keep his children safe. Until now, the plan has been for him to keep a diary and to make sure he uses drugs only when the children are staying with their mother.

- How might a plan for Marvin be developed to help him to move forwards?

- What issues of risk may need to be considered further, and who else should be involved in this assessment and plan?

- How could SMART objectives be identified and Marvin's progress measured?

SUPPORTING THE IMPLEMENTATION OF CARE PLANS

CARRYING OUT ASSIGNED ASPECTS OF A CARE PLAN

When you are part of a care plan for an individual, the following key principles apply:

- Do what you have agreed to do.

- Do this to the best of your ability.

- Be clear before you start 'doing' the delivery of the plan what your roles and responsibilities are – you cannot do something well without being very clear on your specific role.

- Be on time, professional and person centred in your approach.

- Work within the values and principles of social care.

- Treat the people you work with in the way you want to be treated yourself.

Basically, this is about working in a way that brings the values of health and social care practice to life. Nothing is more frustrating for service users and their carers when professionals do not do the above.

SUPPORTING OTHERS TO CARRY OUT ASPECTS OF A CARE PLAN FOR WHICH THEY ARE RESPONSIBLE

Part of your role may be to support others to deliver the aspects of individuals' care plans. As above, you need to demonstrate how you put the principles and values of the profession into practice when you work with and support other people as part of a care plan.

Working in partnership with others can be challenging, and some of the tensions and possible solutions in this area are covered in more detail in Chapter 1.

It is important for people who are the subject of any type of care plan to be able to see that those supporting them are:

- working together
- communicating with each other effectively
- doing their best to provide the most effective support possible
- complementing each other in terms of their approach, skills and expertise.

ADJUSTING PLANS IN RESPONSE TO CHANGING NEEDS OR CIRCUMSTANCES

As plans are implemented, it may become apparent quite quickly that the plan needs to be altered. Monitoring a care plan is covered in more detail below.

However, if you become aware that an aspect of someone's plan that you are delivering needs to change, you would be doing the person a disservice if you did not address this immediately and make the required changes. This is especially true if you are of the opinion that the current plan is causing the person distress in any way.

People's needs and circumstances can change, evolve and develop for a variety of reasons, including:

- change in the person's health needs or prognosis
- side effects of medication
- change in their relationships and networks
- change of situation for the person's carers
- moving house

- part of the plan works so well that it is no longer needed
- change in professionals working with the person as part of the plan.

REFLECT

- Think about a care plan for a person with whom you work. How do you deliver your parts of this plan to the best of your ability?
- What are some of the challenges and pressures on you in doing so?
- How do or could you work to reduce these in order to deliver your parts of the plan more effectively?

RESEARCH

- If you work as part of a team to deliver and implement a particular care plan, how are different roles and responsibilities allocated within this plan?
- Talk to the other people who are part of this plan and find out how they feel about delivering their assigned aspects of the plan.
- Where and how could specific roles and responsibilities be clarified?

CASE STUDY

Chen is a senior care assistant in a residential service for older people. He is working with Jim as part of Jim's care plan for reablement. Jim has had a stroke and has lost his confidence in doing daily tasks in the community, such as shopping and going to see his children.

The care plan had tasked Chen to look at supporting Jim to get the bus to the other side of town to see his son. Jim is really looking forward to going over there, but has not been on a bus for a long time as he always used to drive everywhere before his stroke.

The bus is 10 minutes late on the day they go to get it and is packed to standing room only. Chen and Jim board and pay the fare, but Jim becomes dizzy, overwhelmed and upset quite quickly.

- What should Chen do in this situation?
- How can Jim's care plan be reviewed immediately to ensure his needs are met?

MONITORING A CARE PLAN

Monitoring is important in any health and social care setting. In terms of care planning, it is important to look at the extent to which a care plan is working in terms of:

- meeting a person's individual needs
- responding to change (as discussed above)
- coordinating delivery of the various aspects of the care plan.

Monitoring is about:

- observing and talking to people to check how satisfied they feel with their plan and that it is meeting their needs and desired outcomes
- gathering feedback from other sources, including carers, friends, relatives and other professionals
- planning and collating evidence to inform reviews of the care plan
- using a variety of methods including observation, communication, formal feedback and reviews
- being clear as to the purpose for which information is being gathered around the impact of the care plan
- maximising the impact and effectiveness of all plans in meeting individual needs
- acknowledging that the needs of people change over time and are never static
- using agreed ways of recording this information.

Key term

Monitoring means keeping an eye on how the plan is working. Monitoring can either be done formally (on documentation such as that you prepare for a review meeting) or informally (via conversation and observation).

RECORDING CHANGES THAT AFFECT THE DELIVERY OF THE CARE PLAN

Changes can be recorded on the care plan itself (provided there is space to do so), on the person's file, or on other documentation that is specific to a service setting where monitoring information should be kept.

As discussed in Chapter 7, it is important to record and store information appropriately and according to your service or agency's policies and procedures. Recording of monitoring information should be done in partnership with the person whose care plan is being looked at in order to maximise their ownership of this, and their control of any alterations to their plan.

If the changes are significant and mean that the whole care team should be involved in looking at a more effective means of delivery to meet an individual's needs, it can be helpful to move reviews forwards so that everyone is involved in doing this together.

- How do you monitor the effectiveness of care plans in your work role?

- What are the tools and methods most in use in your work setting for monitoring of plans?

- How do you ensure that service users are involved and in control of monitoring activities?

CASE STUDY

Dee is a senior care assistant in a day service for older people. The people who attend the day service generally live at home with much of their support being provided by family members – a few service users also receive domiciliary care services.

Dee has been working with John for a long time. Recently she has observed that John looks tired when he arrives at the service, is sometimes in the same clothes and seems to be less well cared for than previously. She has also noticed that he is more withdrawn than he used to be, and he has started to sit on his own and to avoid group activities.

Dee asks John if he is alright and whether anything has changed for him. John is reluctant to talk to Dee at first, although they have always had a good working relationship. However, after a few days, he asks to speak to her and confides that his daughter has been taken into hospital. He says he is having to do a lot more for himself at home as his neighbour and his son cannot come round as often as his daughter would do normally. John is really worried that by telling Dee this, she will have to share this with his social worker and that he may lose his ability to live independently. Dee reassures him that the social worker should talk to him and to his family about how long his daughter may be unable to provide the usual level of care, and put in additional support at home for this period. John is doubtful that the social worker will listen as he feels that she never does.

- How could Dee feed back the information about how John's needs have changed?

- How could she support John if there is a review of his care plan needed at this time?

- How could Dee support John so that his voice is heard throughout this process, especially if his daughter may be unable to resume caring for him for some time?

FACILITATING A REVIEW

Reviews are an essential part of the social care process. If the review stage is missed, then support offered to an individual is likely to 'drift', plans are likely to go out of date and outcomes are less likely to be achieved. The purpose of a review is to:

- establish how far the support has achieved the outcomes set out in the care plan

- reassess the needs and issues of individuals

- help determine a service user's continued eligibility for support

- confirm or amend the current care plan or lead to closure

- comment on how individuals are managing direct payments where relevant.

REVIEW MEETINGS

Often reviews take the form of a meeting where everyone involved in providing support to the service user is represented. Usually, the care plan forms the basis of the discussion and it is amended as a result of the discussion.

A record should be made of the review and the care plan should be updated. If a 'case' is closed following a review, then the reasons for the closure should be recorded.

A review record should include:

- a review of the achievements of the care plan's objectives by assessing the realism of the original plan and its continuing relevance, checking it against the perceptions of the user and carer and those of the service providers

- reasons for success or failure of the plan

- an analysis of whether current services have been both cost effective and of the right quality

- reassessment of the current needs of the service user and carer

- a consideration of whether the eligibility level remains the same (workers should extend, reduce or withdraw services as appropriate and provide a full explanation for the service user and/ or their representative)

- re-evaluation and revision as appropriate of the original care plan objectives (setting new short-term objectives for each service provider, bearing in mind the wishes of the user and carer)

- re-definition and re-negotiation of the service contracts as necessary

- re-calculation of the cost and revision of the budget, subject to management approval, for the period leading to the next review

- identification of areas where service quality is deficient

- agreed date for the next review.

The review record should be shared with the service user and, subject to confidentiality constraints, with other contributors to the review.

WHAT REVISIONS MIGHT BE MADE AT A REVIEW?

- How do you involve service users and their carers in:
  - providing input into a review
  - leading the facilitation of a review
  - providing feedback into a review?
- How could practices in your work setting be adapted to enable this to occur more effectively?

Jane is a senior support worker in a day service for people with learning disabilities. At the day service where she works, a review meeting is being held for Trevor, a young adult who attends the service. At Trevor's meeting, he comes in at the start with his partner. The social worker, occupational therapist and the service manager start to speak about some concerns they have about Trevor's refusal to access some of the activities that are available to him.

At this point, Trevor becomes upset and frustrated. Jane, his key worker, notices this and takes him out of the meeting to find out what his views are. Trevor tells her it is his meeting and they have not asked him what he thinks. He is annoyed that everyone is talking about him and not to him, and he refuses to go back into the meeting as there is no point anyway.

- Is there anything that Jane could have done before the meeting to prevent this situation?
- What could or should Jane do now?
- How could Trevor's involvement and ownership of this plan be improved?

CASE STUDY

Chen is a senior care assistant in a residential service for older people. Gosia moved into the home six weeks ago. Chen has been working as key worker to Gosia.

A review is held after the six weeks to see how Gosia has settled in and to ensure that the care plan is right for her needs. Her review meeting involves a community psychiatric nurse (CPN), who was involved in the assessment of Gosia's needs, Gosia's social worker, who has known her for some time, and the home manager, as well as Gosia's husband, Pav. At the review, there is a debate around the care plan for Gosia and the manager from the home expresses concern that she feels Gosia's needs seem very different from the assessment and the care plan that was developed before Gosia moved in. The home manager says she feels that Gosia's condition is deteriorating rapidly.

Pav is unhappy as he says that he had been told by Gosia's key worker previously that she is settling in well. The manager calls Chen into the meeting and asks him to feedback.

- Were the right people present at the review meeting?

- How might Pav feel about the information being given to him at the review meeting?

- How might the care team look at resolving these issues at this point?

- What would Chen need to have ready in order to contribute effectively to this discussion?

Code of Conduct for Healthcare Support Workers and Adult Social Care Workers

The Code of Conduct for Healthcare Support Workers and Adult Social Care Workers states that you must be alert to any changes that could affect a person's needs or progress and report your observations in line with your employer's agreed ways of working.

CHAPTER 10
Promoting person-centred approaches

Current health and social care practice is built on the foundations of person-centred practice. The move towards person-centred practice has led to major changes in the way that health and social care services are delivered. We are moving from traditional service-led delivery of care and support towards care and support that is focused on the uniqueness of each individual.

Links to other chapters

Health and social care workers need to be person-centred in all of their practice and therefore this chapter will be useful to everyone in the field. In particular this chapter has links with chapters 2, 3, 4, 9 and 11.

THE APPLICATION OF PERSON-CENTRED APPROACHES IN HEALTH AND SOCIAL CARE

Person-centred approaches are based on a number of core values and principles which many people see as developing from the values of health and social care practice.

These values include:

- a commitment to promoting human rights
- upholding personal dignity
- seeing people as unique individuals
- promoting choice and self-determination
- respecting individuals
- listening and empowering
- working in partnership with people
- recognising and addressing potential conflict
- safeguarding needs and the capacity of individuals
- being sensitive to diversity and putting people in control.

The values of person-centred care can be described as:

- individuality
- choice
- privacy
- independence
- dignity
- respect
- partnership.

Ultimately, these all relate to individual rights. After all, the people you work with have a basic right to be treated as unique individuals with respect and dignity and to be able to make choices, etc.

THE VIPS MODEL

Dawn Brooker has developed an equation to illustrate what she sees as the four elements of person-centred care:

$$PCC \text{ (person-centred care)} = V + I + P + S$$

V: the value base that asserts the absolute **v**alue of all human lives regardless of age or cognitive ability.

I: **i**ndividualised approach, recognising uniqueness.

P: understanding the world from the **p**erspective of the service users.

S: providing a **s**ocial environment that supports psychological needs.

(Brooker 2007)

WHY IS PERSON-CENTRED CARE SO IMPORTANT IN HEALTH AND SOCIAL CARE?

Person-centred approaches must influence every aspect of health and social care practice. The approach should not simply be about the icing on the cake – person-centred approaches are the cake.

Person-centred approaches are important to all aspects of health and social care practice because:

- Every service user is a unique individual with differing circumstances and needs. As such, their needs can only be met by support that focuses on them as a unique individual.

- Everyone has a unique history and 'life story'. This will affect their needs, their life choices and their behaviour. Support and care will only be effective if it takes the unique life history into account.

- Traditional models of service delivery create climates where power is easily abused and where service users are disempowered. This increases both dependence and vulnerability.

- Person-centred care and personalised approaches have very positive outcomes for service users, eg people report improvements in general health and well-being.

- Working in a person-centred way means that you can adapt your approach when situations and/or needs change.

- Everyone wants to have control over their own life and has the right to make choices – only person-centred approaches to care promote choice and control.

- The population of the UK is becoming increasingly diverse. Personalisation leads to services that are more culturally sensitive and person-centred care promotes culturally competent practice in care staff.

- People have a legal right to make choices and to access care services which promote dignity and respect. Quite rightly, people are making more demands on services to provide more person-centred care.

- The number of unpaid carers (mostly family and friends of service users) in the UK is growing rapidly. Carers report increased satisfaction with person-centred care and they are more likely to accept support services that work on a personalised basis.

As such, all organisational policies, procedures and practices should reflect person-centred approaches to care.

RESEARCH

Look at some of the basic policies in your organisation – particularly those relating to the planning of care. To what extent do these reflect person-centred values and person-centred approaches?

USING CARE PLANS TO PROMOTE PERSON-CENTRED PRACTICE

In the past, health and social care services were generally delivered around task-centred care practice, eg a care worker would have a list of tasks to complete during a shift.

In modern health and social care practice, the delivery of care and support is focused around individualised care plans. Every individual receiving care will have their own care plan which will detail their day-to-day needs and requirements, with reference to the outcomes that are expected (see Chapter 9). In some services, care plans may be known as support plans or individual plans, but the content will always relate to how the care worker can meet the person's individual needs.

WHY SHOULD CARE PLANS BE PERSON CENTRED?

The Department of Health (2010c) states that person-centred care planning can lead to a range of benefits for individuals, commissioners, providers of services and the health and social care workforce. These centre around:

- ensuring that care and services focus on individual needs

- promoting health through information and self-care, people staying healthier for longer, ie 'adding life to years'

- promoting independence and achievement of other goals such as returning to work

- reducing health inequalities, ie raising the standard of care across the country

- promoting integration and partnership working

- stimulating genuine choices, ie those choices influencing service design and delivery

- promoting a more planned, proactive approach to health and social care services

- efficiency savings, eg reductions in hospital admissions, outpatient appointments and GP consultations.

ENSURING THAT CARE PLANS ARE PERSON CENTRED

Sometimes practice in care planning is poor and many service users receiving care from the same service have very similar care plans. Clearly, since everyone is a unique individual every care plan should be different and unique to that individual. You can evaluate whether a care plan is truly personalised by looking in turn at each of the values of person-centred practice:

- *Individuality*. In what way does the care plan reflect this person's individuality and how does it support the worker to look at how they can uphold the person's individuality?

- *Choice*. Does the care plan make the person's preferences and choices clear?

- *Privacy*. Does the care plan make clear how the person's privacy will be respected? Is the care plan kept privately?

- *Independence*. Does the care plan reflect the principles of active participation – showing how the person should participate in their own care to maximise their independence?

- *Dignity and respect*. Are issues of dignity and respect addressed in the care plan?

- *Partnership*. Is it clear that the care plan was drawn up in partnership between professionals and the service user?

Generally, are the outcomes detailed on the care plan related to person-centred values?

A number of organisations use the values of person-centred practice as the basic structure for a care plan – even so sometimes they can be very general and lack specific detail reflecting the service user's uniqueness.

CASE STUDY

Dee is a senior care assistant in a day service for older people. She is supporting a new colleague, Shaz, in her induction at the service, and Shaz has completed her first care plan for a new service user, Simon. Simon is very nervous about attending the service as he would rather be cared for by his family at home, but his son has asked for respite as part of his carers' assessment.

As part of the induction, Dee and Shaz have discussed the VIPS model and Dee has asked Shaz to look at this in her care planning. Shaz reports to Dee that she has struggled with this, as she understands person-centred values from her training, but she does not know how to reflect this model in her care plan for Simon because he is quite reserved. She is worried that he does not want to be there or to participate in the activities that are on offer.

- How could Dee support Shaz to work through the VIPS model with Simon?

- How could Shaz seek to understand Simon's world, perspective and ideas, so that he is able to influence the range of activities available at the service?

WORKING IN A PERSON-CENTRED WAY

The Department of Health (2010c) explains that to work in a person-centred way health and social care professionals and their managers need to:

- listen to people

- respect their dignity and privacy

- recognise individual differences and specific needs including cultural and religious differences

- enable people to make informed choices, involving them in all decisions about their needs and care

- provide coordinated and integrated service responses

- involve and support carers wherever necessary.

Working in a person-centred way essentially involves putting person-centred values into practice. Key to working in a person-centred way is to understand each service user as a unique person. One effective method for understanding individuals and for treating people in a person-centred way is to adopt what is known as the biographical approach.

BIOGRAPHICAL APPROACH

The biographical approach to health and social care is essentially about taking the person's life story into account when working with them. As a theory it is fundamentally simple – think about how often we read the autobiography of a celebrity to understand 'where they are coming from' or how interested people seem to be in the lives of celebrities (through magazines and papers, etc). When we meet someone new we often ask them about their lives; it shows interest and respect and gives something on which to base conversations. The biographical approach recognises this – it reflects the influence of a person's life story on them and is a key part of person-centred care.

Many health and social care workers use a biographical approach – often without recognising it.

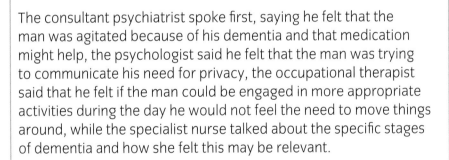

CASE STUDY

Geoff is an older man with dementia. He has recently been admitted to a hospital ward where his behaviour has become increasingly difficult for the service to manage. He has been moving furniture around the service – initially blocking the door to his room with this, then posing health and safety risks by moving furniture and equipment around in shared environments. A multidisciplinary review meeting was called to plan an appropriate response to the situation.

The consultant psychiatrist spoke first, saying he felt that the man was agitated because of his dementia and that medication might help, the psychologist said he felt that the man was trying to communicate his need for privacy, the occupational therapist said that he felt if the man could be engaged in more appropriate activities during the day he would not feel the need to move things around, while the specialist nurse talked about the specific stages of dementia and how she felt this may be relevant.

The social care worker (very quietly and lacking in confidence) said that she had spoken to Geoff and his family about his life and she discovered that the family ran a business, initially set up by him. It was a removals firm. She wondered if this might be having an effect on his behaviour.

In discussing Geoff, others had focused on their professional perspectives – while the social care worker had placed herself in the shoes of the service user and recognised the fact that every time he had been somewhere new in his life, he was there to move the furniture.

This case study illustrates the importance of taking a biographical approach to working with service users and the fact that it is essential to know about a person's life history to work with them.

Health and social care workers need to find out about a person's life story and sometimes this involves detective work. How you do this will differ, depending on what the person can tell you about themselves. The various methods that health and social care workers use in finding out about a service user's life story include:

- talking to the service user

- actively listening to everything the service user says (not just what they say verbally)

- asking family members about the person's life

- looking through photographs with the person

- reading past records and reports

- using a 'life-story book' (sometimes prepared by family members or by staff who know the person well)

- using reminiscence group work (see page 359)

- playing music, films, etc that would have been popular when the person was younger – and watching the individual for responses.

Look closer, see me

This poem shows, in a very powerful way, how it is vital to understand a person's unique life in order to work with them in a person-centred way.

What do you see, people, what do you see?
What are you thinking, when you look at me
A crabby old woman, not very wise.
Uncertain of habit, with far-away eyes,
Who dribbles her food and makes no reply.
When you say in a loud voice "I do wish you'd try!"

Who seems not to notice the things that you do.
And forever is losing a stocking or shoe.
Who, unresisting or not, lets you do as you will.
With bathing and feeding, the long day to fill.
Is that what you're thinking, is that what you see?
Then open your eyes, you're not looking at me.

I'll tell you who I am as I sit here so still!
As I rise at your bidding, as I eat at your will.
I'm a small child of 10 with a father and mother,
Brothers and sisters, who loved one another.
A young girl of 16 with wings on her feet,
Dreaming that soon now a lover she'll meet.
A bride soon at 20 – my heart gives a leap,
Remembering the vows that I promised to keep.

At 25 now I have young of my own
Who need me to build a secure happy home.
A woman of 30, my young now grow fast,
Bound to each other with ties that should last.
At 40, my young sons have grown and are gone,
But my man's beside me to see I don't mourn.
At 50 once more babies play around my knee,
Again we know children, my loved one and me.

Dark days are upon me, my husband is dead,
I look at the future, I shudder with dread.
For my young are all rearing young of their own.
And I think of the years and the love that I've known.
I'm an old woman now and nature is cruel,
'Tis her jest to make old age look like a fool.
The body is crumbled, grace and vigor depart,
There is now a stone where I once had a heart.

But inside this old carcass, a young girl still dwells,
And now and again my battered heart swells.
I remember the joy, I remember the pain,
And I'm loving and living life over again.
I think of the years all too few – gone too fast,
And accept the stark fact that nothing can last.
So open your eyes, people, open and see,
Not a crabby old woman, LOOK CLOSER, SEE ME.

(Source: McCormack, 1966)

MESSAGES FROM RESEARCH

Life-story work and reminiscence approaches

Research summarised by the Institute for Research in Innovation in Social Services (2011) into the use of life stories and reminiscence work with adults who have dementia shows that the work:

- leads to improvements in both people's mood and cognition

- generates benefits for carers and relatives of individuals, including a reduction in stress levels

- aids communication, and provides stimulation and fun

- is especially valuable when people are involved in significant changes or moves

- is most effective with people who have mild to moderate symptoms, as opposed to those with severe dementia

- has no harmful effects upon individuals.

WORKING IN COMPLEX AND SENSITIVE SITUATIONS

Health and social care workers regularly work in situations that are complex or sensitive. Such situations might include:

- those that are distressing or traumatic
- where there are threats or a person is frightened
- where there are likely to be serious consequences
- a person who has complex communication needs
- where there are issues about whether a person has capacity
- where there are conflicts between people involved in the situation.

Where a situation is complex or sensitive, a health and social care worker may be at risk of losing their focus on person-centred practice. However, it is at times such as these that the values of person-centred practice become even more important.

In order to be person centred in complex and sensitive situations, health and social care workers need to remain focused on the specific principles of person-centred practice. If the situation is particularly challenging for you then you should seek support and advice from others, including your manager.

REFLECT

Consider an individual service user you have worked with where their needs or issues have been complex and sensitive.

- How did you work with this individual to find out their unique history, preferences, wishes and needs?
- What worked well in enabling you to achieve this and what would you do differently in the future?

CASE STUDY

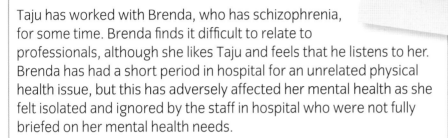

Taju is a senior support worker with a mental health charity. In his role he is used to working with people who have complex, sensitive and changing needs. He strives to ensure that he gets to know people, to understand their uniqueness, and to learn about their wishes before developing their support plan.

Taju has worked with Brenda, who has schizophrenia, for some time. Brenda finds it difficult to relate to professionals, although she likes Taju and feels that he listens to her. Brenda has had a short period in hospital for an unrelated physical health issue, but this has adversely affected her mental health as she felt isolated and ignored by the staff in hospital who were not fully briefed on her mental health needs.

When she went into hospital Brenda said she did not want anyone to know about her mental health needs as she was not going in for these issues. However, after her discharge, Brenda feels increasingly annoyed about the care she received, as well as the aftercare appointments she has to attend. Brenda says she is left waiting for hours before anyone sees her and, when she is seen, she says that no one seems to care how she is feeling. She asks Taju for support and advice around improving her experience of health services.

- What can Taju do to support Brenda in this situation?

- How could he enable Brenda to get others to adapt their actions in response to her changing needs?

- How can Taju use his experience and knowledge to support others in responding to Brenda's needs?

ADAPTING TO CHANGING NEEDS AND PREFERENCES

Over time we all change, develop, grow and want different things. People who have specific needs for care or support are no different from anyone else, and their needs and wishes will also evolve over time.

Change can come in a variety of forms:

- a change in someone's condition (either an improvement or a deterioration)

- a change in the circumstances or needs of an informal carer

- loss or grief

- a change in financial circumstances

- a new (possibly unrelated) health issue
- a change in living arrangements
- a change in the person's opinions
- change in professional involvement, eg staff turnover.

With any of these changes, or a number of them potentially occurring at once or in quick succession, this is likely to mean that:

- workers need to be aware that change has an impact on people
- individuals need the opportunity to express their wishes and feelings, and, in particular, any changes to these (don't assume that people's views are static)
- formal and informal opportunities for finding out what people think, want and prefer need to be created
- extra effort needs to be made where individuals have limited verbal communication in order to ascertain and record what they feel, enjoy and prefer
- care plans need to be updated, monitored and/or reviewed.

Remaining person centred involves being aware of the changes in people's lives, continuing to find out what people's preferences and wishes actually are at any time, and adapting the work we do in order to take account of these wishes. These adaptations can be relatively minor (eg a change in someone's diet or key worker). However, sometimes we need to be able to make radical changes to people's care plans in order to work in a truly person-centred way and to not be afraid to do so.

ESTABLISHING CONSENT WHEN PROVIDING CARE AND SUPPORT

Establishing that a person consents to an activity or to the care you are to provide is very important in all health and social care activity. As part of this it is important to understand what is meant by consent. Consent is not simply about allowing something to happen. A person consents to something when they are making an informed decision or giving informed permission.

There are particular complexities around consent in health and social care as there may be questions about whether an individual has the **capacity** to **consent**. Concerns in this area generally relate to whether someone has the mental capacity to consent. Since this is such a significant issue in health and social care there is legislation that covers this area of work.

Key terms ⊙━┉

Capacity: is about whether someone is physically or mentally able to do something.

Consent: a person consents to something when they are making an informed decision or giving informed permission.

THE MENTAL CAPACITY ACT 2005

This Act represented a fundamental change for adult health and social care services and is particularly relevant to this chapter.

Where the Mental Capacity Act breaks new ground is that it departs from the idea that an assessment of capacity is made on a once-and-for-all basis and affects all other decisions that the person makes. It recognises that the ability to be able to make rational decisions may vary for a variety of reasons and according to the complexity of what is being asked of the person.

The Mental Capacity Act has five core principles:

1　A person must be assumed to have capacity unless it is established that they lack capacity.

2　A person must not be treated as unable to make a decision unless all practicable steps to help them to make the decision have been taken.

3　A person must not be treated as unable to make a decision just because they make an unwise decision.

4　Any decision made or act carried out on behalf of a person must be in their best interests.

5　Before a decision is made or an act is carried out, consideration must be given about how this can be achieved in a way which is least restrictive of the person's rights and freedoms.

It is vital to recognise that a person's capacity to consent and to make decisions can change over time (even over a short period of time) and the Mental Capacity Act and the associated guidance makes this clear. For example, some people take medication with quite powerful side effects which are often at their worst in the morning. The ability of people affected in this way to be able to make decisions and to give consent may be poor in the morning, but this may well improve as the day goes on.

ESTABLISHING CONSENT

Just because someone needs care or support in some areas of their life, it does not mean that they consent to receive this support once and once only.

Consent should be:

- established formally in writing for some activities (eg consent to receive a service, and consent to keep a record according to the Data Protection Act 1998)

- established informally for each activity during the person's daily life where support is provided (eg asking people what they would like to eat, asking them if they want something to be done for or with them, or if they can do it for themselves, etc)

- established each time a personal care activity is commenced (eg 'Would you like me to …?', or 'Are you ready to …?')

- recorded (especially where someone does not consent to something, this should be recorded appropriately)

- informed (people need to understand what they are consenting to, and often they also need to understand the potential consequences or risks if they do *not* consent to an activity or treatment).

Consent is important:

- morally and ethically (treating people as we would want to be treated ourselves – with dignity and respect)

- legally (eg according to the Mental Capacity Act, the Data Protection Act, etc)

- in terms of the value base of the profession and the need to practise in a person-centred way.

RESEARCH

- What procedures are there in your organisation for establishing consent?

- Talk with colleagues about how they achieve this, especially when a person's capacity to consent may be restricted.

- What strategies work for others and can you adapt your own practices to test out another person's ideas?

REFLECT

- How do you establish and review consent with individuals in your work setting?

- What approaches work for you in enabling people to express their consent or to state when they do not consent?

CASE STUDY

Jane is a senior support worker in a day service for people with learning disabilities. She and the team she works with are planning the next set of activities for the service, and meet to discuss the ideas they have gathered from service users. The team normally use these ideas to generate a draft plan, which is then discussed again with the users of the service before being finalised.

One of the team, Shaun, says that some of the service users are getting bored with some of the activities in the centre, and want a greater range of activities, including more that take place in the community, such as swimming and using the local gym. Others in the team express concern that they feel that some of the quieter individuals who use the service do not get heard as much as more vocal individuals.

There is a feeling that some people cannot consent or opt out of activities as effectively as others because of their limited verbal communication, but that some service users appear to be distressed when they are taken out of the centre to new places, and that they need routine in order to thrive.

- How might Jane and the team balance the needs of individuals in this scenario?

- How could issues of consent and communication be addressed by the team?

- What could the team do to ensure that people are not forced to 'opt in' and do something they are not comfortable doing because the group setting requires this?

IMPLEMENTING ACTIVE PARTICIPATION

Active participation is closely linked to active support – you will therefore find reading Chapter 11 useful in understanding active participation fully.

Promoting active participation in health and social care work is part of the duty of care, as this links with the key concepts of empowerment and enabling people to do all that they can for themselves.

Key term

Active participation is about people being involved in their own care, as opposed to being a 'recipient' of that care (ie it is about something being done *with* someone rather than something being done *to* someone). Active participation also means that people take part in the activities of daily and independent life as much as possible.

ACTIVE SUPPORT

Active support is a person-centred model of how to interact with individuals combined with a daily planning system that promotes participation and enhances people's quality of life.

Active support is about providing the right amount of support to individuals which recognises their rights while providing opportunities for growth and skill development.

ACTIVE PARTICIPATION IN HEALTH AND SOCIAL CARE

Regardless of whether a service adopts an active support model or not, all workers in health and social care will need to demonstrate their knowledge of and commitment to active participation. This is because:

- People are not objects to be 'treated' or 'cared for', but are unique individuals who have rights, wishes and choices.

- The fact of needing care or support can mean that people feel unable to do things for themselves – professionals intervening in their lives therefore need to optimise the individual's feelings of control and competence.

- Whatever people's needs are, there are still things that they can do and want to do for themselves.

- Without the opportunity to do things for themselves, people feel more helpless and achieve poorer outcomes.

- Workers can sometimes think it is easier (or quicker) to do a task on behalf of a person or they can feel it is their role to do things. Considering how people can be more involved in their own care is about challenging these sorts of preconceptions.

- As well as being involved in their care, people have the right to be involved in tasks around their homes and activities outside their homes. The lives of people in some care settings can be isolating, dull and lonely. Working in a person-centred way is about striving for the best and most active lives for people.

Chapter 11 on active support explores these issues in more depth.

HOW TO PROMOTE ACTIVE PARTICIPATION

Active participation in social care can be promoted in a number of ways.

1 *Care tasks*. With any task that a worker could do for a person, ask the service user if they would like support to do this, or to do it for themselves *before* taking action. For example, it is important not to help someone get dressed, brush their teeth, get more comfortable, etc without first asking the key question, 'Would you like ...?' Doing so enables people to say 'no' as well as to say 'yes' when they do want help.

2 *Daily living*. Consider ways in which people can become more involved in the things we all do on a day-to-day basis. We all need to keep our homes clean, wash clothes, shop for and cook food, etc. However, people in social care settings often have a lot of these things done for them by others. The consequence can be that people's actual days can be quite empty and dull. It is useful to consider what people can do, as opposed to doing every task around the home for them because there are certain activities that they cannot do.

3 *Social inclusion*. Wanting the best for people whom we work with is about enabling them to participate in society as well as in daily living and their own care. We all benefit from contact with other people who have similar interests, beliefs or who simply acknowledge us as we go about our lives. Needing care can be isolating in itself, and working in a person-centred way is about enabling individuals to be part of society, to enjoy activities, to meet other people, and to feel valued and important.

Active participation is also promoted by:

- praise, encouragement and recognition of people's achievements

- the involvement of carers and relatives – sometimes people's carers have the best of intentions but can overprotect individuals. Active participation can sometimes need to be about ensuring that others recognise what the person *can* do for themselves

- involving people in discussions and assessments about choices and risk (see Chapter 4 on the duty of care for more detail around the dignity of risk taking)

- being sensitive to people's individual needs and going at their pace – being asked to do too much too quickly can be as off-putting as being asked to do too little

- working as a team with your colleagues so that the care and level of support that people receive are both consistent with their needs and consistent across a team

- focusing on people's strengths and talents.

REFLECT

- How does your work setting enable active participation to be at the centre of work with individuals?

- Can you suggest ideas, tools and methods to aid a greater level of active participation, either with a specific individual or on a service basis?

RESEARCH

Even if you are not undertaking the unit on active support for your diploma, it will be a good idea to read Chapter 11 and consider how the principles of active support and active participation overlap.

MESSAGES FROM RESEARCH

Active participation

The Social Care Institute for Excellence's (SCIE) website (www.scie.org.uk) has some excellent resources and research into active participation, and the benefits of this. SCIE has reviewed a range of research into active participation which strongly indicates that:

- Active participation leads to better quality of life for older adults, people with disabilities and those with mental health difficulties.

- Where people participate actively in their own care plan, they are likely to experience increased self-esteem and acquire new skills as a result of this. This can mean that they are more likely to enter employment in the future, which brings in turn material benefits for the person, as well as a resulting further increase in their self-worth.

- Service user participation brings a wide range of benefits to individuals and to society in general beyond their benefits to the person's individual care. These include benefits around policy development, service development, citizenship and improved understanding in research practices and social care theory.

(Social Care Institute for Excellence 2012)

CASE STUDY

Isabella is a senior care assistant in a respite care service which provides short-term stays for adults with learning and physical disabilities. She is working with Delilah, a service user. Delilah has autism and has been accessing the respite service once a month for a year. Part of Delilah's care plan includes her participation in tasks around the house, such as washing up, making her bed and tidying the living room. Her mother reports that this is going well at home, but Delilah has not yet consented to participate in this aspect of her plan while on respite. When people have tried to get her to help out, she has ignored them, and if they persist in encouraging her, she has become aggressive or she has covered her ears and screamed. Many staff have now given up on involving Delilah in the tasks included in her care plan – they say it is easier to just do the things themselves.

Isabella considers some of the knowledge she has of Delilah and of active participation, and talks to her colleagues about the fact that Delilah has proved at home she can do these tasks, so she should be able to take part in them at the service too. Isabella suggests a plan to ensure that Delilah sees these tasks as enjoyable and rewarding by making sure that as soon as she does a task, even for a very short time, she is rewarded by a choice of something she likes.

- How might active participation be introduced to Delilah in this way?

- What are the next steps in ensuring that Delilah sees these tasks as positive in themselves, as opposed to something that she has to endure in order to get the reward?

SUPPORTING PEOPLE'S RIGHT TO MAKE CHOICES

Making choices is about being in control of your own life, and achieving your own goals and dreams. Enabling people to make choices is therefore key to good person-centred care practice.

The choices that people make can either be simple and day to day (which drink to have, what to wear, or where to go out), or they can be extremely significant (where to live, whom to have a relationship with, what job to do, etc).

Choices in health and social care are especially important in terms of:

- the level of support people need and want to have provided

- medical treatment

- social activities and opportunities
- risk assessment (see below)
- support planning
- finance
- accommodation
- relationships with others.

The development of self-directed support has led to a far greater level of choice and control around care for many individuals than has been possible in the past.

Even with the significant focus on self-directed support and the recognition that choice and control are vital for good-quality care services, too many individuals who have care or support needs can feel that:

- decisions are made by others on their behalf
- professionals 'know best'
- other people are in control of their lives
- no one listens anyway.

Part of your role as a health and social care worker is about supporting people to make choices. Doing so is not about making decisions for people, but it can involve:

- getting the information on all of the options that are available to the person
- going through all of these, weighing up pros and cons, and considering the consequences of certain decisions
- trust, good communication and listening skills, and taking the time to do this properly with people as individuals
- checking that the person's decision is their own and that you have understood the choice they have made correctly before implementing something on their behalf
- ensuring that people's individual communication needs are addressed, so that where verbal communication is limited, people are still enabled to make all of the choices that they can make for themselves
- representing and advocating for individuals where others are not in agreement with the choices they want to make for themselves
- a good understanding of the issues around capacity as this relates equally to choice as to consent

- recording this appropriately as part of your duty of care to show that you have looked at every aspect with the person in depth

- demonstrating good practice around risk assessment and risk management in terms of choice.

REFLECT

Think about what choices you have made today and then reflect on whether the people you provide support to have been able to make as many choices as you.

- What limits the choices you can make?

- What limits the choices that the service users you work with can make?

CHALLENGES AND COMPLAINTS

The importance of complaints procedures is considered in Chapters 4 and 5 on duty of care and safeguarding. It is important to note though that working in a person-centred way has to involve:

- informing people of their rights to complain

- listening to people's concerns and acting on these

- enabling people to make choices about whether to complain formally or make an informal challenge or request to a service

- promoting people's rights to be listened to, respected and treated fairly at all times

- advocating on people's behalf where requested to do so, necessary and/or appropriate.

Sometimes, people are not able to make the choices they would like to make. This could be because of:

- changes in eligibility for a service

- cuts or closures to services

- the person's needs, circumstances or changes to these

- a decision made by others around their capacity

- safeguarding issues or concerns about risk where the risk outweighs the person's rights to make certain choices.

Even where any of these factors occur, people still need to feel listened to, to be informed of their rights to challenge or complain, and to access the support they need to have their view heard. You may be in a good position to support someone in this, or you may need to access an advocacy service on behalf of a person where the boundaries of your own role prevent you from doing so.

REFLECT

- How have you enabled an individual to make informed decisions in your work role?

- Can you think of an instance when you have had to champion this as somebody's right or to challenge others about their decision making?

- If so, how did you manage risk in a way that enabled that person to make their own decision?

MESSAGES FROM RESEARCH

Choice and control

Research indicates that choice and control are not just about ethical practice in health and social care. Choice and control are also key issues in terms of promoting people's health and well-being. The Social Care Institute for Excellence indicates that:

- choice, control, respect and dignity are interlinked as concepts in a critical way (ie you cannot promote people's dignity without enabling their choices, and without choice and control, people are not likely to feel respected)

- having choices and control enables people's skills to be maintained as much as possible, especially during periods when their health is at its lowest or when they are in hospital

- people are unlikely to participate in meaningful activities without choice and control

- staff shortages, lack of time, work pressures and an overemphasis on targets can limit workers' ability to promote dignity, choice and control.

(Social Care Institute for Excellence 2012)

CASE STUDY

Jon is a senior support worker with a reablement team. Within his role, he regularly works with people who have complex and changing needs. Jon has been supporting Tim for six weeks following Tim's discharge from hospital after a stroke. Tim is in his eighties and has felt very embarrassed about needing help with his personal care, but he has accepted Jon's support gradually and is now settling back into his own home.

A multi-agency meeting is planned to put Tim's care plan in place and, following this, Jon will be seeking to withdraw. Tim becomes upset and angry about this as he feels that he is not ready for this and he does not think that he has any choice around who will be providing the personal care for him. Tim states that he does not want women involved in his care, and he also expresses a preference for white British carers. Jon is challenged by this as he is keen to promote anti-racist and anti-sexist attitudes, and he asks to talk to Tim's social worker before the meeting.

- How can Jon and the social worker challenge some of Tim's attitudes while also promoting his right to choices?

- What solutions and ideas could help in this scenario?

- How might risk to Tim and others be managed effectively?

PROMOTING WELL-BEING

It is vital that all health and social care workers recognise the importance of well-being. You will often hear the phrase 'health and well-being'. While health refers to someone's physical and mental health, the word well-being refers more to other aspects of a person's happiness, such as:

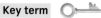

Key term

A **holistic approach** considers someone as an individual, and all of the factors that make up their life, instead of focusing only on their support needs.

Addressing well-being is really about seeing someone as a whole person and taking a **holistic approach**. This is perhaps where health and social care workers have a specialist aspect to their practice. For example, while a nurse or doctor might at prioritise someone's physical health, a health and social care worker will recognise that there are lots of other aspects to someone's well-being.

IDENTITY

Understanding identity issues is an important step in promoting well-being. Identity is partly an expression of two functions – **self-image** and **self-esteem**.

Key terms

Self-image is essentially about how we see or describe ourselves.

Self-esteem is about how we feel about or value ourselves.

In respect of adults who have contact with social care services there are various threats to their positive sense of identity, self-image and self-esteem – many of which you will covering elsewhere in the diploma. Below are some examples.

- *Societal prejudice and discrimination.* In the section on inclusion (see Chapter 3), we discussed how there can be oppression at a societal level. Many adults in society are aware of the way they are discriminated against and this can have an effect on self-confidence and generate a range of responses (including defensiveness and anger, or exacerbating mental health issues).

- *Institutional stigma.* Being in contact with health and social care services can still carry a stigma. This is partly because in the past the quality of care services for adults was poor. Even today there are examples where service provision can be very poor (see Chapter 5, pages 161–162, for examples from Mid Staffordshire Hospital and Winterbourne View. Even disregarding these high-profile cases, there are still too many residential care homes where even a short visit tells you 'I wouldn't like to live here!'

- *Individual attitudes.* The attitudes and behaviour of staff can be a key element of supporting adult service users to maintain (or develop) their identity and self-esteem. Negative attitudes and a lack of commitment to person-centred values will negatively impact on a person's self-image and self-esteem.

- *Labelling and stereotyping.* Labelling is the process by which a negative blanket term is applied to a person. The effect on other people, when they view that person, is to have a prejudiced and negative view which can lead to the person being stereotyped. The effect on the person, both of the label and of other people's actions towards them, results in the person feeling judged and this undermines their self-esteem and confidence. The person who is labelled may then act in ways that are a distortion of their true identity. Issues of labelling and stereotyping are covered in more detail in Chapter 3.

REFLECT

Look at the links described in this section between identity, self-esteem and self-image.

- How is your own identity formed by the labels that surround you as an individual?

- What factors in your own life have promoted your own sense of self-worth?

Consider this then in relation to an individual whom you have worked with in the past or whom you currently support.

- How do you and the service you work in enable that person to develop their self-worth by valuing their unique identity?

- How do the labels and societal values placed upon that person influence this, and what strategies do or could you put in place to minimise the potential negative impact of these labels and values?

PROMOTING IDENTITY, SELF-IMAGE AND SELF-ESTEEM

Health and social care workers can adopt a range of methods to promote service users' identity, self-image and self-esteem, and many services have made progress in recognising and respecting the identity of service users.

Many of the methods that can be used to promote a service user's identity, self-image and self-esteem are covered in this unit of the diploma. Below are some examples.

Meaningful activities

Many services that work with adults of working age are seeking to give more relevant options. These options include further education, training for employment and support to get a job. Day-time occupation is a key aspect of identity. Often if you meet someone new the first question is 'What is your name?', followed by 'What do you do?'

A meaningful day occupation is also a key aspect of self-esteem. Where a service user is unlikely to get a job then many services still support the service user to contribute, in some way, to their community. Many services assist service users to raise money for a charity or campaign for a local cause; this can have a direct effect on positive feelings of self-esteem.

Positive approaches to risk

Services are also developing a more positive approach to risk assessment and risk management. Often the key decisions about risk management are made in multidisciplinary meetings, but the view of the service user is now taken far more seriously as it is acknowledged that there is dignity within risk taking which people must not be denied. If services respect the service user's wishes, then often the service user can still live their life as they want to even if there is risk involved.

Addressing personal relationship needs

Personal relationships are a significant aspect of identity. This is partly because our sexuality is a key part of who we are. Some services have developed a more positive attitude to this but there are still other services where managers either overlook or ignore the needs of service users in this area.

Life-story work

In life-story work, the aim is to generate a personal record of that person's life. This record could be a book, a photo book, a memory box, a CD or DVD, and the record becomes the individual's property. Where a person has experienced many changes, life-story work can result in them understanding more about their life.

Activities around life-story work can include visiting former places where the person has lived, talking to people who have known the person over time, and keeping items in one place which remind the person of certain times in their life. All of this generates further discussion which can be recorded alongside photographs or items. Any life-story work should be unique like the individual it is chronicling.

Reminiscence work

Reminiscence work is usually associated with older people and is often done in groups. There are often props or prompts which can consist of photographs or videos from the past, clothing or household articles (also from the past). The intention is to support the person to talk about their past, both in terms of employment and personal life (right back to childhood).

Reminiscence work helps confirm a person's identity and reinforces their individuality. It has been seen as a practical application of understanding human development, giving the person the opportunity to review their life, address unresolved questions, etc.

In reminiscence work, there is usually no individual book kept (which is one difference from life-story work). However, workers could support a service user to generate one if the service user wanted one.

Other aspects of person-centred practice that promote people's identity and self-esteem include:

- enabling people to make informed choices
- reviewing consent
- establishing and reviewing the individual person's wishes, feelings and preferences
- involving a person's family, carers and friends in an appropriate way in their care planning
- responding to a person's unique communication needs and preferences
- using good listening skills
- avoiding assumptions about people's wishes and lives on the basis of a diagnosis or condition
- promoting active participation in daily living
- supporting the person with the tasks they need support with, and avoiding over-supporting them
- spending time with people
- promoting people's unique talents
- praising, giving encouragement and recognition of achievements

- involving people in society and their community – being acknowledged by others as a worthwhile and included member of society

- sharing time with other people who enjoy doing similar things.

MESSAGES FROM RESEARCH

Person-centred approaches and well-being

Research indicates high satisfaction levels and positive well-being for service users who receive good person-centred support. For example, Edwards and Waters (2008) report that in their research:

- 55% of people stated that they spent more time with people they wanted to be with

- 77% reported improvements in quality of life

- 63% reported that they took a greater part in their local communities

- 47% reported improvements in general health and well-being

- 72% reported that they had more choice and control in their lives

- 59% reported that they had more personal dignity.

CASE STUDY

Chen is a senior care assistant in a residential service for older people. He has recently developed his understanding of biographical perspectives. He is enthusiastic and keen to implement the ideas and tools he has learnt.

Chen works with Elsie, who has moderate dementia, and as part of their work together they create a photo book with support and input from Elsie's adult children. Elsie is extremely pleased with her book and shows it to the other residents. Some of them are annoyed that Elsie was 'chosen' to do this first, and some of Chen's colleagues indicate that they want to be able to do the sort of work he gets to do, but they are not given the time to do so.

- How might Chen support his colleagues in their learning around the ideas he has brought into the service?

- What might the service need to do in order to ensure that all of the residents who want to have the opportunities that Elsie has had?

RISK AND PERSON-CENTRED APPROACHES

Issues of risk and the way that risk is managed have a high profile in health and social care, which is why the issue of risk is addressed in a number of units within the diploma. It is therefore worth reading Chapters 4, 5 and 6 on duty of care, safeguarding, and health and safety. In health and social care, risk is a key issue because:

- people have the fundamental right to be safe

- workers have legal and moral duties of care to keep people safe and ensure their needs are met

- the concept itself holds dignity; people should not be more disempowered than they already may be

- the fact of needing care or support means that services and other people may be averse to the person taking risks that other people take every day

- the person may already feel that others have a greater level of control over their life than they would want them to have – people do have the right to take risks

- everyday life involves risk, eg crossing a road, driving a car, plugging something into the mains, eating things we know are not good for us, etc

- overprotecting people from risk creates learned helplessness and reduces the quality of people's lives which is not what good care practice aims to achieve

- risk assessments are part of your work role and every work setting

- people should be involved in the consideration of risk, so that informed decisions can be taken by the individual and their care team in partnership.

A POSITIVE RISK-AWARE CULTURE

If a service operates within the model of active support, it should be well on the way to promoting a positive culture in relation to risk.

Taking some risks is a daily occurrence for everyone and must be necessary if people are to take a full and active part in their communities. Government guidance makes this clear:

The possibility of risk is an inevitable consequence of empowered people taking decisions about their own lives.

(Department of Health 2007b: 8)

Most people are able to balance risk against possible benefits and will take any necessary precautions to help minimise risk. It may not be quite so easy for the vulnerable people care services support to achieve this balance for themselves. This is where support will be required. It is where the key dilemmas will occur and where getting the balance right is perhaps the most difficult. Sometimes when providing support, we can be anxious to eliminate any identified risk of harm, which can mean that a decision is made that a particular choice cannot be supported. This should only occur in extreme circumstances and where risk assessments clearly indicate the reasons the person's choice cannot be supported.

Risk assessments are designed to ensure that those making decisions are aware of all the risk factors and have considered any precautionary measures that might help to reduce identified risks. Their purpose is not to inhibit choice and prevent people making choices that carry a degree of risk, but to raise awareness so that decisions can be made with the full knowledge of possible consequences and with some anticipation of the measures that might be taken to reduce risks.

The impact of a risk assessment can sometimes be to prevent people undertaking activities that would be expected to bring pleasure and satisfaction in the lives of people being supported. The aim should be the opposite – to take preventative measures to actively reduce the possibility of the person being at risk. Key reasons why some organisations may be 'risk averse' and overly reluctant to provide positive active support to people in taking risks might include:

- *A wish to protect the individual from harm*. This is natural when working with vulnerable people and is the subject of safeguarding vulnerable adults policies, but services are now designed around the individual to an increasing extent with the aim of supporting them to be as independent as possible. An important aspect to person-centred care is recognising the 'dignity of risk'.

- *Fear of putting the organisation at risk of litigation*. Once again this is understandable in that the media regularly carry stories of legal action being taken against allegedly negligent organisations, and there are more and more advertisements by organisations promising to help individuals to claim compensation.

- *Fear of being blamed if things go wrong*. This arises if the employee has little management support when dealing with issues of risk and often where there is a perception that managers will rush to take disciplinary action against staff members should an error occur.

These feelings may be argued away as simply being unproven assumptions, but from the perspective of a lone worker or someone working as part of a small team, perhaps in people's own homes and away from a base, they may seem justified. The key to feeling secure in supporting people to take reasonable risks lies in the culture within the organisation which in turn rests upon the efforts of managers to demonstrate that they value their staff and are prepared to support them when necessary. Staff will not feel able to contribute to a positive culture around risk unless they themselves feel that they are listened to and that their views are respected by their managers. This kind of supportive culture brings benefits to all elements of managing the service, not just the management of risk.

A positive risk culture needs to be owned by senior managers within an organisation. Employees will need to feel confident that the philosophy of the organisation encourages a positive attitude towards supporting people to take reasonable risks and are more likely to develop this outlook if:

- employees are provided with sufficient training to understand the issues, including where the law stands and what is considered to be good practice

- the culture is one where there are opportunities to discuss sensitive and tricky issues concerning choice and risk, and where staff feel that they can turn to their manager or to other staff for support. Team meetings where care and support issues are routinely discussed and one-to-one supervision meetings with managers can provide opportunities for both kinds of supportive discussions. Each person's perspective should be valued and treated with respect by others including their manager. Arising from this kind of culture, there is genuine shared ownership of decisions so that no individual is left feeling that they had to take the decision alone

- a learning approach is encouraged on occasions where a problem or dilemma occurs. The team should be encouraged to review what might have gone wrong and to be involved in the process of deciding if any preventative or precautionary action needs to be taken by contributing their views, suggestions and feedback

- team members feel confident that managers will make effective use of disciplinary procedures. While it would be wrong to suggest that negligence and other failures should go unnoticed and un-actioned, if people are to learn from situations that have not gone well they must have some scope to be able to explore this and the leeway to learn new approaches for the future. This, of course, depends upon the nature of what has gone wrong and the degree of responsibility the employee had for what has happened, but there should be a sense of proportionality and fairness about any actions taken by the employer.

ENSURING RISK ASSESSMENTS AND RISK MANAGEMENT PLANS ARE PERSON CENTRED

There are some key issues to consider in order to be able to demonstrate that risk assessment and risk-management practice within a service setting is person centred.

- How involved are individuals in the initial discussion about risk?

- How are people enabled to talk through the consequences of taking an action, not taking an action, accessing a service or intervention, etc?

- How involved are carers and others who know the person well in these discussions?

- How are these discussions recorded? Are users of services involved in the recording of risk assessments (or the design of the paperwork)?

- How do assessments develop into risk-management plans?

- In what ways are these plans made unique for individuals' needs, wishes and choices?

- How is the impact of decision making reviewed with the individual concerned?

- How are risk assessments and plans updated to take account of changing needs, circumstances, wishes and learning?

- How does the service review its practices and develop its work on the basis of collective learning and training around these issues?

Working in a person-centred way is about wanting those whom we support to live as full a life as possible, whatever the nature of their needs. Living a full life is about making choices and feeling in control. All of us do things that sometimes are not what others would see as 'best' for us, but the important thing is often that we make the choice ourselves. Being person centred means that we involve people in the same way in making informed decisions about their own lives. However, because you are a professional (ie paid money to provide the best support that people need and deserve), you have to be able to demonstrate the way in which risk has been considered as part of your duty of care in your work role.

REFLECT

- How does risk assessment in your work setting enable the dignity of risk?

- Consider some of the documentation you use or a specific risk assessment that you have completed or been involved in. Can you adapt, improve or suggest ways to others in which this paperwork could be enhanced to look at the positive aspects of risk in other ways?

MESSAGES FROM RESEARCH

Risk assessment and management

The Joseph Rowntree Foundation reviewed approaches to the assessment and management of risk in adult social care services in February 2012. Some key findings include:

- There is insufficient research into how cultural, gender and socioeconomic factors influence the assessment and management of risk, and there is a specific gap in evidence around the experience of black communities in social care services.

- Carers tend to be more risk averse than users of services, especially carers of older adults.

- Practitioners report the difficulties in promoting positive risk taking while balancing safeguarding responsibilities as a key ethical dilemma across the profession.

- There is also a lack of evidence around the impact of personalisation in social care upon risk management, and around how these issues should best be addressed with people whose conditions and needs fluctuate (eg those with certain mental health conditions).

(Mitchell, Baxter and Glendinning 2012)

CASE STUDY

Zakiyah is a senior domiciliary care worker. She supports Yasmin, who is in her seventies and living in her own home, with three visits a day. Yasmin has some signs of dementia and has osteoporosis. During a visit, Yasmin's daughter asks Zakiyah to come into the kitchen to talk privately. The daughter expresses concern that her mother needs more support as she has been found wandering the streets at 10pm looking for the post box.

Zakiyah is aware that Yasmin's social worker has done a risk assessment about Yasmin's ability to live independently. Yasmin has also talked to Zakiyah about not wanting to go into a home or to be a 'burden' on her children by going to live with them. She is proud of her independence and wants to maintain this for as long as possible. Zakiyah explains to Yasmin's daughter that she will talk to the social worker about the information she has shared and that the risk assessment will be updated.

- What are some of the ethical dilemmas in this situation?

- How can Yasmin's rights and safety needs continue to be met?

- When might the line be drawn around things being unsafe for Yasmin, and how can Zakiyah support her if this is the case?

Code of Conduct for Healthcare Support Workers and Adult Social Care Workers

Issues around consent are recognised in the Code of Conduct for Healthcare Support Workers and Adult Social Care Workers, which states that you must:

- always explain and discuss the care, support or procedure you intend to carry out with the person and only continue if they give valid consent

- promote people's independence and ability to self-care, assisting those who use health and care services to exercise their own rights and make informed choices

- always gain valid consent before providing health care, care and support. You must also respect a person's right to refuse to receive health care, care and support if they are capable of doing so.

CHAPTER 11
Promoting active support

It can be difficult to get the balance right between upholding people's rights and ensuring they are protected from abuse and harm. Services trying to get this balance right can sometimes 'over-support' people to the point that they stifle them – ultimately preventing their rights.

Active support is a person-centred model that supports health and social care workers to get this balance right. Active support is about providing the right amount of support to individuals which recognises their rights and provides opportunities for growth and skill development.

While active support is used in working with people with learning disabilities, this chapter will be useful to everyone working in health and social care since aspects of active support can be useful in working with people from a wide range of backgrounds.

Links to other chapters

Even if you are not completing this unit you will find this chapter useful in your practice. Active support is a principle which is influencing all aspects of health and social care. You can particularly consider this chapter in relation to chapters 1 and 13.

WHAT IS ACTIVE SUPPORT?

Active support was first established as a model of care for people in learning disability services. It was designed as a model of support to challenge what has become known as the gift model of care provision.

- The gift model is where care is provided *for* or *to* people, eg tasks are done for or to people.

- The active support model involves working *with* people to enable them to take part in all the activities of daily life.

Active support is now the preferred model for all health and social care services.

Historically, care services were delivered on the gift model basis. Care was seen as something to be 'given'. Often the care was provided in an institutional way – as in the 'hotel model'.

THE HOTEL MODEL

The phrase 'hotel model' refers to institutional style settings organised mainly around staffing needs. They are not person centred and can offer a poor quality of life to individuals. For example, this is apparent where carers undertake all the domestic tasks and do not provide opportunities for individuals to participate in constructive activities. The ideas of the hotel and gift models overlap, but the concept of people being in a hotel is more closely related to residential care provision.

Active support has developed from the research evidence that many adults with social care needs, especially those with complex learning and/or physical disabilities, do not have the same quality of life as people who do not have these needs. The lives of individuals, particularly those in institutional care, can be dull, and their days can be unstructured, with lots of time where they do not have anything meaningful to do.

Adopting an active support philosophy and model within a service involves training, commitment, reflection, consistent application, patience, time and proactively seeking out and utilising opportunities for individuals to participate in meaningful activities.

Young people and vulnerable adults may need support to ensure that they are protected from abuse and harm, but this support must actively promote their right to make their own decisions and choices, and to be fully involved in their own care.

Services need to ensure that people are enabled and supported to take risks that are as safe as possible in order to promote their learning, life skills and competence in effective decision making.

MESSAGES FROM RESEARCH

Active support

Research demonstrates that active support is essential for the well-being of service users of all ages. Key messages from research show that:

- Active support has four key components:

  - Service users are offered opportunities to take part in everyday activities and all care tasks. 'Little and often' is the key.

  - 'Graded assistance' is about putting in the right level of support for the individual.

  - Staff focus on helping service users take part in activities 'minute by minute'. Reference is made to the concept that 'every moment has potential'. Staff find parts of even very complex tasks that all people can do and undertake other parts of the tasks themselves.

  - Staff pay particular attention to working as a team and coordinating their approaches. Staff monitor carefully the degree to which service users are taking part in everyday activities using simple record-keeping procedures. Regular staff meetings allow for plans to be modified in the light of experience and learning. 'Choice and control' for service users are essential to effectiveness.

- Service users' activities and independence both increase significantly where staff adopt active support approaches.

- The self-esteem of service users is significantly improved where active support is implemented.

- Staff job satisfaction is significantly enhanced where a service's main model of care is active support.

- Although active support has been demonstrated to be a powerful model, it has not yet had a significant impact in the delivery of most services. Typical staff performance in community services is still characterised by low levels of staff and client interaction, and little direct facilitation of service user participation.

(Mansell et al 2002; Stancliff, Jones and Mansell 2008)

> **KEY POINT**
>
> There are links between active support and:
> - positive behaviour support
> - person-centred planning
> - communication planning.

ACTIVE SUPPORT AND PERSON-CENTRED PRACTICE

Increasingly, active support is referred to as 'person-centred active support'. This is in recognition of the fact that active support must be delivered in a person-centred way and shows that this approach involves more than just providing opportunities and direct assistance for activities. The ultimate aim is to support people to live the lives they want to live, doing the things they want to do, following their agenda and respecting their decisions.

PROMOTING AN INDIVIDUAL'S INDEPENDENCE, SUPPORT-INFORMED CHOICES AND IMPROVING THEIR QUALITY OF LIFE

A range of practical changes can be made within any setting to promote active support. Even services that are not adopting the full model can utilise the key principles within this.

- *Focus on rights*. All people, whether they have social care needs or not, have the right to as full and varied a life as anyone else. This is the starting point for active support. Ensuring people's rights to things like meaningful relationships, choice and control, and access to activities is critical in order for people to enjoy the same quality of life as others.

- *Service culture and staff training*. There needs to be a commitment to the philosophy of active support within a service. Managers need to enable workers to reflect on their practice and how this promotes people's independence. Workers need ongoing training and opportunities to develop for the model to be implemented and sustained.

- *Using everyday opportunities*. Active support is not about putting on new or specific activities. Instead, it is about using the opportunities that day-to-day life provides. Meaningful activity for most of us is not about the hobbies we have, but about how we conduct our lives, eg every morning most of us follow a set routine – get up and wash, get dressed, have breakfast, brush our teeth, etc. For some people with disabilities, all or most of these things could be done for them. Active support recognises that these sorts of daily living tasks provide opportunities to build people's skills and thereby their confidence in their own abilities by providing them with the opportunity to take part in these tasks.

- *Matching the level of support to individual need*. Active support asks workers to step back from doing these things for people, and to identify the minimum level of support in order for the service user to do that activity independently. This principle can be applied in any service setting, and it can be valuable for all workers to reflect on the actual level of input that an individual needs to perform a task, as it is much more rewarding for people to experience the outcome of achieving something than to feel that others do everything for them.

> **REFLECT**
>
> Even if your service does not adopt the full model of active support, how do you promote the key principles described above in your work with individuals?

USING DIFFERENT LEVELS OF SUPPORT TO INCREASE INDEPENDENCE

The literature around active support suggests the following as an incremental way to increase people's participation in tasks:

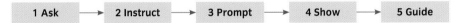

1 Ask → 2 Instruct → 3 Prompt → 4 Show → 5 Guide

- *Ask*. The idea is that people should be given the opportunity to do something without any support if they want to and can.

- *Instruct*. The next level would be to describe to them (using appropriate communication) what steps to take to achieve the task, so they can then do this themselves – again, if they want to and can.

- *Prompt*. People would then receive a prompt or reminder if they were getting stuck. The principle of 'minimal sufficiency' is critical to this. So, if an individual is managing without a prompt, do not prompt them as this reduces their ownership of their activity.

- *Show*. If someone needs a demonstration of how to do something, show them, but do not then walk away, eg if they need to be shown how to wash a plate, that is fine, but then let them wash the next one.

- *Guide*. This is about providing the minimal level of support for someone to do a task. For example, if someone needs help putting their socks on, the worker can guide them in this, but the key principles are to not do this for them, but to provide enough support so they can achieve it themselves, and then, next time, to let them do it with slightly less support and input, and so on.

> **REFLECT**
>
> Consider the ASK – INSTRUCT – PROMPT – SHOW – GUIDE model.
>
> - Can you identify occasions when you may have over-supported individuals, and how could you apply this model with someone you are currently working with?

CASE STUDY

Isabella is a senior care assistant in a respite care service that provides short-term stays for adults with learning and physical disabilities. Her service has recently decided to look at using active support as a model for improving people's experience at the service and the outcomes they achieve. Isabella goes on a training course and she is asked to share her experience and learning with her colleagues.

Most of the team seem keen to try out some of the ideas, but Jackie, who has worked in the service for many years, is reluctant. Jackie says, 'We do all of that already' and at one point states 'most of the young people won't be able to take part in that – they're here because they can't do lots of things for themselves'.

- How could Isabella challenge Jackie in a way that promotes Jackie's learning?

- What techniques could Isabella use with individuals, and how could she demonstrate the impact of these to all of her colleagues?

PROMOTING POSITIVE PARTICIPATION

ASSESSING THE LEVELS OF HELP AN INDIVIDUAL NEEDS TO PARTICIPATE IN A RANGE OF NEW ACTIVITIES

Many health and social care workers are used to working with individuals who require high levels of support in order to ensure their basic care needs are met. Undertaking work within an active support philosophy requires a shift in thinking towards *how* people can be enabled to do everything they can do, as opposed to focusing on what they *cannot* do without support.

The first stage in this shift has to be a reassessment of the following:

- *What does the individual's day look like?* This involves considering, hour by hour, what someone is actually doing, what they are involved in, and what others are doing around them and to support them.

- *Where are the opportunities for the individual to become involved in those activities?* This is likely to involve a task analysis of what the activities involve, and where other activities and tasks could be built into the person's day.

- *What is it specifically that the person needs help with?* Does their need concern understanding what is being asked of them, communication, gross or fine motor skills, behaviour that is challenging, etc?

The term 'levels of help' refers to graduated levels of assistance, from simple verbal reminders providing the lowest level of support to actual physical guidance providing the highest level. Assistance should be given flexibly according to the individual's need for help and should be focused on encouraging as much independence as possible.

The concept of matching the level of help to someone's need is very much about a reassessment and reconsideration of what that individual needs in order to take part, and avoiding assumptions about what they need to have done for them. The idea of minimal sufficiency, as described above, in terms of the support provided is important to this matching of input to individual need. The key to this is:

- do not do the things for a person that they can do for themselves

- be very certain of their abilities before you assume they cannot do something and then jump in and do it for them.

For example, look at your own morning routine as follows:

- get out of bed
- use the toilet
- shower
- get dressed
- eat breakfast
- clean teeth
- turn on the phone
- plan for the day, etc.

While most of us probably follow a set routine for the day, we still make a plan each morning of what we will do and in what order. This will include what to eat (cereal or toast), how long to shower for, whether to reply to any messages we have, etc. Some of the routine we perform on autopilot as it is instinctive, but the activities are still our own and we are not passive recipients of a routine.

For many of the people with whom we work, all of the above are activities that they cannot (perhaps yet) do fully on autopilot, or that they need some level of support or input from others to achieve. However, by matching different levels of support to different tasks, active support can be promoted. For example, consider an individual with limited mobility and complex physical care needs:

- *Get out of bed*. Can the person be supported to move certain parts of their body themselves, as well as receiving support to move other parts, so that this is done *with* and not *to* them?

- *Use the toilet*. What tools and support are available to the person to get on and off the toilet, and how are they involved in the moving and changing position?

- *Shower/bathe*. Can the person hold the sponge and soap themselves, or can you provide them with a guide to their own hands to wash themselves, instead of your washing and their sitting there still?

- *Get dressed*. To what extent can the person dress themselves (would some aids help with this?)?

- *Eat breakfast*. As above, do you hold the cutlery and move it to their mouth, or can they do this with you?

- *Clean teeth*. As above.

In order for all of this to work, the individual needs to:

- receive the right amount of support (not too much so that the task is done for them, and not too little so that they fail and feel disempowered by the approach)

- receive praise, encouragement and reinforcement

- feel that it is something that is enjoyable, that you do together, and that is valuable

- not become overwhelmed. In active support, it is better that someone undertakes a task actively for 10 seconds to start with, and that this success is then built up, rather than the task becoming a battle of wills, which would render the above three points meaningless.

Active support involves applying these principles and ideas to the whole range of activities and tasks in people's daily lives. It is not just about involvement in formal 'activities', but is about the day-to-day things that keep most of us busy, take up our time, prevent us from sitting around bored all day, and that engage us with others in our environment.

Active support is about wanting all of this for the people with whom we work, and promoting people's involvement in day-to-day living, such as:

- preparing meals

- laying the table

- cleaning up

- washing up

- caring for a pet

- walking the dog

- dusting
- doing the food shop
- packing and unpacking the shopping
- loading and unloading the washing machine
- watering plants and tending the garden
- using electronic equipment and choosing entertainment
- the list goes on for all of us.

With each of these, the level of help should be matched as described above, and the opportunities each day presents should be planned for and optimised in order to promote people's active involvement in their own lives. One way to ensure that this matching takes place effectively is to analyse in detail the precise nature, stages and skills involved in certain tasks.

USING TASK ANALYSIS

Task analysis refers to breaking down tasks into small, manageable steps as in recipes or DIY guides. The size of each step or number of steps for a specific task should vary according to the individual's ability or need for support.

In planning for active support with individuals, every task needs to be considered in detail. This means:

- looking at what the task involves (not taking for granted how you may do the task yourself)
- breaking this task into a number of small steps
- looking at the way in which the individual could access those steps
- matching the level of help the person needs to do so
- planning how to introduce the task to the person
- planning for reinforcement and encouragement.

Consider a daily task in your own life, such as loading the washing machine. The steps involved could be:

1 emptying the laundry basket onto the floor by the machine

2 sorting out whites from colours

3 putting the clothes you want to wash into the machine

4 getting the right detergent out of the cupboard

5 measuring the right amount of detergent into the cup

6 putting this detergent into the drawer in the machine

7 pouring the right amount of fabric softener into the right compartment

8 selecting the programme you want and the right temperature

9 switching the machine on.

Now consider these steps in terms of an individual who previously may not have had any involvement in the washing of their clothes, but may have had all of this done for them for all of their lives.

Using the model of:

- ask

- instruct

- prompt

- show

- guide.

You would then need to consider the right amount of support and input the individual would need, as well as the level of reinforcement, encouragement and praise for that person. Someone with complex physical needs and little verbal communication may need more guidance, for example, and may need the worker's hand to guide their own hand in doing some of these activities themselves. Another person may need more instruction and some prompting.

An individual with autism and behaviours that are challenging may need to take part in one of the steps (eg starting by emptying the basket), and to see this as enjoyable and rewarding before they will consent to moving forwards with you in the rest of the steps. As discussed below, it is better that this individual sees the task as satisfying, rewarding and their own achievement than that the involvement of them in future tasks becomes compromised by them getting 'switched off' by the procedure.

By doing this with daily tasks, and by building up people's involvement gradually and in an appropriate way to their needs and learning, this can be applied in other settings and activities in the person's life. As well as motivating people, ensuring they feel valued, and promoting independence, the other benefit of this model can be that people identify, and others notice, unique talents which would otherwise not have been uncovered.

REFLECT

Consider the task analysis above for using a washing machine.

- Can you do a similar task analysis for a daily activity in your work setting, and then apply the steps and the level of support needed to an individual with whom you work?

DIFFERENT WAYS OF POSITIVELY REINFORCING AN INDIVIDUAL'S PARTICIPATION IN A RANGE OF NEW ACTIVITIES

In order to understand how people's participation can be increased, it is useful to have an insight into adult learning and into behavioural theories around reinforcement.

ADULT LEARNING

There are a number of basic 'rules' or 'principles' of adult learning, some of which are detailed below.

The law of exercise

People learn best by actually doing something. Remember, practice makes perfect. Practising something away from the real environment will not help someone to learn. While we believe that we are helping people when we give them lots of opportunity to practise a skill, if this is not performed in the real environment with the real equipment, we may well actually be hindering an adult's learning.

So in relation to active support, it is important that a person gets regular opportunities to engage in learning new activities and that these opportunities take place in a natural environment at a natural time. For example, it would not be useful if someone were to learn to make a breakfast when they are in the kitchen of a day service in the afternoon. It would be much more appropriate for the person to learn this skill in the mornings in their own home.

The law of association

Like building anything new, knowledge needs to be built upon. New facts, skills or approaches are best learnt if they relate to something we already know, or have experienced.

Need-to-know motivation

It is clear that adults learn best when they feel that they need to know what they are called upon to learn. If an adult doesn't feel they need to know how to do something, they are unlikely to learn ('What's the point?' is a common question).

In terms of active support, it is important for the person to understand why learning a new skill will be useful to them.

Learning and empowerment

Adults learn best from a position of confidence, it is important therefore to recognise people's experience and facilitate some degree of self-confidence. If the supportive relationship is viewed as one where the learner is the 'empty vessel' and the supporter the 'full vessel' who is prepared to fill the other with knowledge, then the person learning will not learn effectively.

It is therefore helpful when promoting active support to provide lots of praise and encouragement and to put the principles of empowerment into practice.

Plateau learning

We all learn at different rates and we may experience some good days and some bad days. It is not realistic to expect steady increases in learning patterns. Plateaux will occur in our learning, though learners do not always recognise or expect this and may need some reassurance at such times.

In terms of active support, it is useful to recognise that people need time to become confident in newly acquired skills, before moving on to learning something else.

Learning continuum

Learning is a continuous experience. People continue to learn throughout their lives.

Ignore sayings such as 'You can't teach an old dog new tricks!' – people can always learn something new.

Whole or partial learning

Individual parts of a task, or knowledge, can only be assimilated when the whole is understood.

In terms of active support, task analysis is very useful, but if a person begins by engaging in only one of the small steps they need to be present when the other parts of the task are carried out so that they can see where what they have done fits into the bigger picture.

POSITIVE REINFORCEMENT AND BEHAVIOURAL THEORIES

We learn best when we receive positive reinforcement. Recognition of learning is a big incentive for future learning. Specific and realistic feedback can aid reinforcement for learning.

Positive reinforcement refers to what an individual gains from undertaking a specific task. These can include naturally occurring rewards (eg drinking a cup of tea the individual has just made) or other things that the individual particularly likes (eg praise and attention or a preferred activity) as an encouragement or reward for participating in a specified activity.

Our knowledge about reinforcement and the importance of this comes largely from the work of twentieth-century psychologists. The concept of 'conditioning' is most well known through Pavlov's experiment where dogs were given food at the same time as a bell was rung. After a short while, the dogs would salivate when the bell was rung even though no food was presented, as they had been conditioned to expect food when they heard the bell.

The application of classical conditioning to health and social care is relatively limited, though there are instances where staff could come into contact with this approach. One example is where a child who persistently wets the bed may have a sensor under the sheet of the bed. When the sensor detects urine, a buzzer or alarm sounds. This wakes the child and, after a short while, the child should wake when their bladder is full without the need to urinate in bed.

Skinner's (1971) work into operant conditioning recognises that the environment (both human generated and natural) has an effect on our behaviour. One of the insights of operant conditioning is that it highlighted that many behaviours occur randomly (we just do something or say something from out of the blue). Whether we do it or say it again will be strongly influenced by the response that we get. If we get little or no response, we may not do it again.

Operant conditioning also highlights that most behaviours are a response to a stimulus. To try to capture the processes involved in how behaviour is influenced or shaped the ABC continuum was developed. 'A' stands for 'antecedent' – an event happens and as a result the person engages in a behaviour, (B), which is a response to 'A'. Immediately, or soon after the behaviour, the consequences (C) occur.

ABC charts have commonly been used in health and social care services. Many services have developed ABC charts so that they try to understand the broader environment in which a person lives.

It is through operant conditioning that knowledge about behaviour being shaped by rewards has been developed. Rewards (or reinforcers) should be identified that the person actually likes and values. The reward should be:

- applied consistently

- given as immediately as possible after the desired behaviour occurs.

If part of the reward is intrinsic to the person (internal sense of pride, achievement, etc) then this is helpful. Many rewards are external to the person and can include the full range of rewards we all like, such as:

- enjoyable activities

- money or gifts

- social companionship or praise.

Some activities themselves lead to rewards automatically, eg preparing food or drink where the reward is the enjoyment of the food or drink.

Potentially, social praise and companionship are a significant reward and this should not be underestimated. Where a desired behaviour is complex or demanding, breaking it down and having rewards that are provided for each stage should result in the behaviour being achieved.

HOW THIS LINKS TO ACTIVE SUPPORT

Workers in health and social care need a good understanding of the above principles and theories whether active support is the service model or not. However, in active support, understanding how an individual learns, and matching the type, level and frequency of reinforcement are critical to the success of the work.

If a person responds well to verbal praise, active support requires lots of praise and encouragement to be:

- planned for

- given consistently

- given frequently.

Similarly, if a person enjoys a certain activity, this can act as a powerful reward and reinforcer when active support is used. For example, an adult with autism may not be keen on taking part in the morning routines described above initially, but planned and consistent use of symbols charts can show that by doing certain tasks, these then lead to the chosen activity as a result or reward.

The idea is that by applying all of the above in a planned way, the somebody gains an intrinsic sense of achievement and pride through doing, learns independence skills, has less time being inactive and bored, and builds up gradually into learning new tasks and activities.

HOW POSITIVE INTERACTION PROMOTES SUCCESSFUL PARTICIPATION IN A RANGE OF NEW ACTIVITIES

Positive interaction refers to supportive interaction using the levels of assistance, task analysis and positive reinforcement that help an individual to participate in constructive activity.

The concept of engagement is critical in active support. Some service providers supply not-for-profit services to adults with complex and challenging needs and promote active support. They talk about how engagement with others is part of what contributes to life being meaningful for most adults, and one of the elements that gives choice and control in life. Engagement promotes our identity, makes us feel valued and important, develops our independence, and keeps us physically and mentally well.

They describe different forms that engagement can take, such as:

- talking and listening to other people (eg being acknowledged by others and being noticed as a worthwhile individual)

- taking part in tasks as described above in terms of routines

- being part of groups and sharing experiences with others who enjoy similar interests.

Positive interaction throughout all of the tasks that are planned for is about:

- promoting this level of engagement

- wanting the people we work with to have active full days and lives

- planning how people will be involved in tasks and matching the level of help to the level of their unique need and ability

- planned reinforcement as discussed above.

Some individuals need more praise and encouragement than others, which can depend on their communication needs, their preferences and their learning styles. Some people simply do not like verbal praise at all.

If someone refuses to take part in the activity, or if they get stuck, there are some techniques to consider:

- Have they got the right level of support?

- Are the level and type of reinforcement appropriate?

- Do they understand what is being asked of them and why?

- Is this a good time to involve them in this particular activity? (Do they see the point of it right now, and do they have choice and control over the nature and timing of activities?)

- Are they having difficulty concentrating? If so, can you break it down more, allow them more space to do something at their own pace, etc? The research evidence stresses you should avoid nagging as this is demotivating.

- Are they bored? Behaviours that are challenging can be one way in which people show that they are bored and, in this case, less can be more in terms of not overwhelming people with expectations. Take a break and come back to the plan later at a more appropriate or calmer time. If the behaviour persists, the key is to:

  - ignore – do not be drawn away from the purpose of what you are trying to achieve

- redirect – ie give more support, prompt the person again, etc

- reward – praise the person as soon as they re-engage.

REFLECT

- What techniques do you use in order to reinforce people's participation?

- How do you communicate praise and encouragement, and how do individuals respond to this?

CASE STUDY

Chen is a senior care assistant in a residential service for older people. Many of the residents of the home have dementia.

Chen has been using active support principles in his work with individuals, and this has shown a marked impact in terms of increasing people's communication, and in terms of a reduction in certain behaviours that challenge the service.

Chen has worked with people around getting them more involved in daily routines, around tasks in the home and around their personal care. However, Chen is uncertain how to enable people to become more actively involved during visits out in the community.

There is a trip to the seaside coming up in a few weeks' time, and Chen would like to involve the residents in terms of getting increased participation in planning for the day, making refreshments and so on. Last year when this trip occurred, Chen felt that the residents could have been more actively involved, but sat back and had the trip 'done to them'. However, he is concerned that there needs to be an incremental plan which looks at some of the events that are likely to happen on the day before the trip itself. This is because Chen thinks that doing the whole trip differently could confuse people.

- How can Chen break down some of the tasks that the trip will involve into manageable chunks before the day?

- How can Chen plan for these tasks, encourage and reinforce individuals' participation, and build up skills before the trip?

DEVELOPING AND IMPLEMENTING PERSON-CENTRED DAILY PLANS TO PROMOTE PARTICIPATION

AVOIDING DISENGAGEMENT

Disengagement means doing no constructive or meaningful activity, and can include aimlessly wandering about, pacing, staring, sitting, lying down, purposelessly fiddling with items and so on, with no social contact.

MESSAGES FROM RESEARCH

Disengagement

Research summarised by the Association for Real Change (2012) indicates that people with learning disabilities in care homes usually receive less than six minutes per hour of input from workers to engage in meaningful activities.

Research indicates that many adults who use health and social care services spend far more of their daily lives in periods of disengagement, without stimulation from other people, and without taking part in the activities that we all undertake as part of our daily lives. Most of us cannot go out to work until we have gone through the morning routines discussed above, without shopping for the food for our breakfast, or without having clean clothes ready to wear for work. For many individuals in health and social care settings, all of these tasks can be done for them by other people, which gives the individual less to do and more time to be disengaged.

(Association for Real Change 2012)

DEVELOPING PLANS

In order to ensure that people do not spend lengthy periods of time in disengagement it is important to develop daily plans with people. Involving the individual, their carers and your colleagues in developing the daily plan for the person is critical in terms of:

- the plan being person centred
- the plan allowing the person's uniqueness and communication and cultural needs to be addressed
- the individual having an investment in their plan
- consistency in how the plan is applied in practice
- being able to measure the effectiveness of the plan.

Daily plans should look at:

- mapping out a full week day-by-day to give variety
- the person's self-care needs
- the domestic tasks that need to be undertaken where the person can become more involved
- the person's social, leisure and cultural time.

It can be useful to have both a weekly and a daily plan, as follows:

Weekly plan example

Day	Self-care activities	Domestic/household activities	Social/leisure time
Monday	Does own personal care – needs prompts about remembering deodorant and needs significant support in brushing teeth	Vacuums lounge and cleans own room	Pottery class at college
Tuesday	As above	Personal laundry	
Wednesday	As above – and takes a shower after Zumba class		Zumba class at local community centre – early evening
Thursday	As above		
Friday	As above	Food shopping	
Saturday	Likes to take a long bath in the afternoon	Bakes cakes to take to church service tea	Watches X Factor on television
Sunday	As above		Attends church service – stays afterwards to socialise and help with the teas

REFLECT

- How does this compare with a weekly plan for individuals in your service setting?
- How does this weekly plan compare with how you plan for and manage your own day-to-day living tasks, social and leisure time, and work and other commitments?
- What opportunities does this plan give for the person to engage with others?
- What would you do to develop this plan further?

Daily plans

While weekly plans can be useful to provide an overview, more detailed daily plans are important in active support because setting the timings and lengths of time an activity should take is important. You can then monitor the extent to which someone's participation changes over time.

For example, we will take Monday from the above weekly plan, and consider how this could be broken down into a more detailed daily plan.

MONDAY	Self-care	Household	Leisure
7am	Get up Toilet Shower Wash hair Shave Teeth Get dressed		
8am	Take medication with breakfast	Prepare breakfast together Wash up Put bins out	Radio
9am			Relax – free time
10am		Vacuum lounge Clean room Make tea	
11am			Cards Exercise
12 noon		Prepare and eat lunch together Wash up	
1pm			Pottery class
2pm			As above
3pm			As above
4pm			As above
5pm		Prepare and eat meal together Wash up	

MONDAY	Self-care	Household	Leisure
6pm			Relax – free time
7pm		Local shop – bread and milk	Walk
8pm		Put shopping away Wipe surfaces down	
9pm			Free time
10pm	Bedtime routine to include: Wash Brush teeth Gett undressed and into nightwear		
11pm	Sleep		

REVIEWING AND REVISING DAILY PLANS

All plans need to be kept under review to ensure that they are working. Plans should be amended regularly to reflect changing needs and circumstances. It is vital to ensure that daily plans are kept under review – perhaps a person is ready to become further engaged in activities and the plan can be adapted to reflect this.

REFLECT

Consider the daily lives of individuals in your service setting.

- What proportion of time do people spend being active and inactive?

- Can you suggest ways in which this balance can be improved?

- How can you incorporate this into individual daily plans, and into service development?

MESSAGES FROM RESEARCH

The impact of active support on valued lives

Ashman and Beadle-Brown (2006) showed that where active support was implemented:

- 50% of people showed an increase in engagement in activities

- 75% of people with severe disabilities showed an increase in their independence and skills

- the most significant contributory factor towards the outcomes achieved was staff commitment to active support and to changing the way they worked with people, as well as workers being given the time to implement strategies.

(Ashman and Beadle-Brown 2006)

CASE STUDY

Zakiyah is a senior domiciliary care worker. She provides care services to people in their own homes. The domiciliary care service provides support to all adults in need of support, although most of the service users she works with are older people.

Zakiyah has been working intensively with Marlon in his home. Marlon has a learning disability. Marlon requires intensive support around his mobility and personal care needs. Zakiyah is implementing a daily planner with the rest of Marlon's care team to enhance his quality of life using the principles of active support. Marlon's mother, who is his main carer, is also involved in implementing this approach.

Marlon becomes very distressed the first time that Zakiyah and her colleague try to involve him in a more active support approach. They have decided to do this via his morning routine initially, so that in the morning, they look at involving him more in getting out of bed, bathing, getting dressed and having breakfast.

Zakiyah tries to prompt and instruct Marlon around washing, and not just to wash him without his involvement as has been the norm. Marlon shouts 'Shut up!' and tries to hit Zakiyah when she continues trying to prompt him. Her colleague suggests it would just be easier to continue washing him as he is used to this and she feels he is getting distressed by the change being too sudden.

- What can Zakiyah do then and there?

- Should the plan for Marlon be adjusted? If so, how?

USING PERSON-CENTRED RECORDS

Since active support is a person-centred approach, records that evaluate an individual's participation in activities must also be person-centred.

DEVELOPING A PERSON-CENTRED RECORD TO MONITOR AN INDIVIDUAL'S PARTICIPATION IN ACTIVITIES

Using the activity support plans that are developed for individuals, workers need to:

- record and monitor the person's participation against these plans

- communicate any issues as part of handovers and recording so that changes to plans can be seen and necessary alterations made

- ensure there is consistency in terms of the application of the plan across the team

- ensure that there is an appropriate level of input, support and activity for all of the different individuals who access the service or setting.

An example of a person-centred daily record

Self-care

	Mon	Tue	Wed	Thu	Fri	Sat	Sun	Amount of participation
Teeth	✓	✓	✓	✓	✓	✓	✓	7 days
Showering self	✓	✓	✓	✓	✓	✓	✓	7 days
Drying self	✓	✓	✓		✓	✓	✓	6 days
Dressing	✓		✓		✓		✓	4 days
Styling hair		✓		✓				2 days

From this it is clear that the person does not engage often in styling their hair – they may need extra prompts and support in this area.

Making meals

	Mon	Tue	Wed	Thu	Fri	Sat	Sun	Amount of participation
Breakfast	✓	✓	✓	✓	✓	✓	✓	7 days
Lunch	✓		✓		✓	✓		4 days
Dinner		✓		✓				2 days
Supper	✓	✓	✓	✓	✓	✓	✓	7 days

From this it is clear that the person does not engage as much in making dinner as in making other meals – they may need extra prompts and support in this area.

Records such as these could be kept in every area of support to help in reviewing someone's participation in activities over a period of time.

REVIEWING AN INDIVIDUAL'S PARTICIPATION IN ACTIVITIES TO ASSESS CHANGES OVER TIME

As individuals gain in skills and confidence with tasks, the level of support they need is likely to change. Active support is about changing people's lives and enabling them to have a more fulfilled lifestyle, so this naturally involves an ongoing assessment of the progress they make.

These changes should be monitored in a planned, proactive and measurable way using person-centred records. As the evidence grows of the individual's ability and preferences, the:

- level of input should be gradually reduced accordingly
- type and nature of tasks should become more advanced
- time the person spends inactive should be monitored and reduced.

For example, consider the scenario earlier in this chapter where active support is used to enable someone to load the washing machine. Imagine the following:

- At first, the person is involved in emptying the laundry basket, but is reluctant to take part in the rest of the activity.
- They receive praise and reinforcement in a planned way for the achievements they make.

- They gradually increase their level of participation in other stages of the task, and receive further praise and encouragement.

- The plan then alters and grows accordingly to involve the person in unloading the machine.

- The person then gradually becomes interested in putting the washing out to dry, or folding it and putting it away, etc – eventually gaining pride in their appearance and an increasing interest in fashion.

EVALUATING AN INDIVIDUAL'S PARTICIPATION OVER TIME AS REPRESENTATIVE OF A VALUED LIFESTYLE

Person-centred active support is all about wanting the people whom we work with to have as active and fulfilled lives as possible. This includes people being involved in the day-to-day living tasks that we all need to participate in if we want to get through life, as well as engaging with others and enjoying activities which stimulate and entertain us.

In order for active support to be effective, we need to evaluate the balance of activity in people's days. Looking at the idea that people with learning disabilities usually receive six minutes of worker input associated with activities per hour, active support aims to redress this imbalance between activity and inactivity.

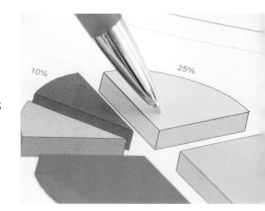

One way to do this is via planned observations. Considering individuals in the work setting, you could set up a chart that shows, hour by hour, a person's waking day and how much activity they are involved in, and then compare this with the research evidence. The chart could take the form of a graph, a table, pie charts, etc, depending on the tools available in your service and your technical skills.

In order to reflect the balance of activities of other people with valued lifestyles, the following questions need to be considered:

- How much of the activity that people are involved in is achieved independently and how much with support or input?

- We all need 'down time', but what do you consider to be an effective and relevant amount of this for yourself and for those with whom you work?

- How much activity takes place within one room and how can increased engagement in activity outside of the work setting be promoted?

- How much activity is undertaken by the person alone and how much concerns engagement with other people?

Jenny's participation record

Week of	Self-care activities	Meals	Household activities	Shopping	Leisure activities	Engaging with family and friends	Total
Jan 4	26	28	20	11	18	3	106
Jan 11	27	30	20	11	20	3	111
Jan 18	22	22	20	8	21	2	95
Jan 25	30	25	19	8	11	1	94
Feb 1	32	26	17	11	24	3	113

The numbers relate to the amount of times Jenny has participated in the planned activities outlined in a daily plan as shown above. The idea would be for the totals in the right-hand column to be shown to increase over time, and for any changes or gaps to be monitored so that the plans can be adapted and developed for Jenny.

IMPROVING THE QUALITY OF AN INDIVIDUAL'S PARTICIPATION TO PROMOTE INDEPENDENCE, INFORMED CHOICE AND A VALUED LIFE

With an analysis of the person's daily activity and engagement in place, your role is then to address any imbalance. For example, if there is a greater amount of independent activity by an individual than that involving others, can the plan be altered to increase the level of group activity in the setting? Can more work be undertaken outside of the one room (we all get a little low when we feel confined to one place all day)? How can activities in the community be promoted in order to provide more stimulation and opportunities for the person to engage with others, including other people who can be involved in including individuals in community life? How are the person's cultural, faith and communication needs addressed by other people who engage with them who may not yet know them as well as your care team?

Considering all of the above will lead to staged, planned and achievable changes being made to the person-centred active support plan. Plans should not be static and should allow for:

- reviews to be undertaken, both formally and informally

- information to be gathered from colleagues, the individual and their carers in order to inform reassessment and future planning

- the person's needs, wishes and preferences changing over time and as they gain in skills and confidence

- your own reflection and personal development in terms of informing new ideas and strategies.

REFLECT

Consider an individual with whom you work where you are working towards active support.

- How do you evaluate the individual's participation over time?

- What criteria do you (and the individuals with whom you work) use to judge whether their participation represents the balance of activity that you associate with an active and **valued lifestyle**?

Key term

Valued lifestyle refers to the balance of activities that contribute to a good quality of life for individuals, incorporating vocational, domestic, personal, leisure, educational and social activities.

Code of Conduct for Healthcare Support Workers and Adult Social Care Workers

The Code of Conduct for Healthcare Support Workers and Adult Social Care Workers states that you must:

- promote people's independence and ability to self-care, assisting those who use health and care services to exercise their own rights and make informed choices

- put the needs, goals and aspirations of people who use health and care services first, helping them to be in control and choose the health care, care and support they receive.

CASE STUDY

Dee is a senior care assistant in a day service for older people. The people who attend the day service generally live at home with much of their support being provided by family members – a few service users also receive domiciliary care services.

Dee has been using active support in the day centre in order to promote the ways in which individuals can participate in the life of the service, as well as in activities that the service arranges for people. Dee has looked at daily plans with a range of individuals who have been keen to get more involved.

These plans have included individuals helping out with serving food and drinks, using people's talents and experience in looking after the gardens and enabling people to work closely with staff in their duties around the building.

Dee has been evaluating these plans, and has noted that the people she has worked with have shown increases in their levels of well-being and happiness, and have reported that they feel more involved in the service. However, she is concerned about Alan's wife's response when she talked to her about his progress.

Alan has dementia and he used to be a caretaker in his working life, so Dee has involved Alan in some of the day-to-day work around the centre. He has seemed to enjoy this, and has spent less time sitting in his chair, watching television and looking isolated from others. Alan's wife however has asked to see Dee as she feels that Alan is tired out when he gets home now, and that he is being 'used' to do tasks that workers should be doing.

- How can Dee work with Alan's wife to communicate the plan she has been trying to implement and to involve Alan's wife in reviewing this plan?

- How can the plan be altered and amended to maintain Alan's involvement and to address his wife's concerns?

CHAPTER 12
Supporting individuals to access and use services and facilities

All workers in health and social care will need to support individuals by providing information about the range of services they can access, and enabling them to use the services they choose to access. Services and facilities might be in the community or they can be provided in people's own homes.

Links to other chapters

The way you go about supporting people who need to access and use services is vital. You will therefore find chapters 9, 10 and 11 particularly useful in relation to this aspect of practice.

UNDERSTANDING THE FACTORS THAT INFLUENCE INDIVIDUALS' ACCESS TO SERVICES AND FACILITIES

WHAT DO WE MEAN BY SERVICES AND FACILITIES?

Mainstream services and facilities

All of us access services and facilities in our day-to-day lives. These include:

- *health services*: the GP, walk-in centres, hospitals, A&E, etc

- *public facilities*: parks, libraries, swimming pools, leisure centres, children's centres, etc

- *community services*: the police, community centres, etc

- *providers of facilities to our homes*: internet providers, mobile phone providers, home shopping, the post service, refuse services, etc

- *business premises*: shopping centres, travel agents, supermarkets, pubs, clubs, private gyms, etc

- *socials and faith groups*: social clubs, activity groups, sports clubs, special interest groups, etc.

For the people with whom we work, their access to these day-to-day services and facilities can either be limited, non-existent, or wholly organised and managed by others.

Specialist service provision

Most individuals who use health and social care services will also be required, need or want to access other specialist provision, most of which is accessed on a referral basis and only available to people with specific needs. This range of services includes:

- housing services, and services that support the maintenance of housing provision

- services that assist with access to and management of finances

- specialist health services

- therapeutic services

- specialist care services and facilities

- advocacy services

- drug and alcohol services

- educational or activity-based facilities.

A range of factors will influence:

- whether people choose to access services
- what services they choose to access
- how people make use of services.

In supporting people to access and use services and facilities it is important that you understand these factors.

SOCIAL INCLUSION

Chapter 3 considers issues of social inclusion and social exclusion. One of the most straightforward ways to promote social inclusion for an individual is to enable them to access and use a wide range of services.

Being part of society and included within a community means having contact with people, and being valued and recognised by the people with whom you come into contact. Each person can be visualised using an ecomap (see below) as having a few layers of connectivity around them:

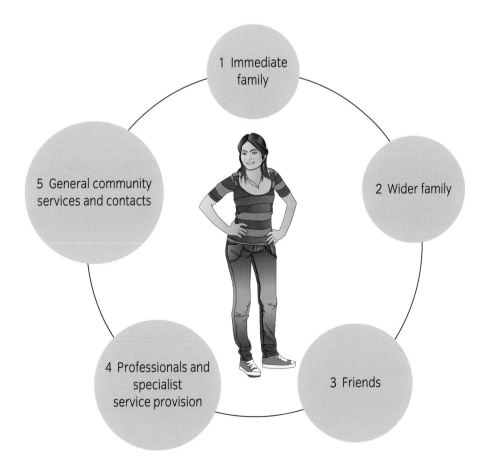

If individuals are not enabled to access the outer layer, then it is easy to see how they may feel cut off from their community, and therefore isolated and devalued. People need to be able to access the mainstream services and facilities in their areas, as well as the specialist provision to which they are entitled. If their access to either of these types of services is limited because of the barriers explored below, there is likely to be a resulting impact on:

- the individual's sense of belonging

- their feelings of self-worth and self-esteem

- their level of isolation and stress

- the level of stress experienced by those who care for them.

Having a range of services and facilities which you access, both in terms of mainstream and specialist provision, is about:

- social inclusion – people being a part of their communities and being valued, whatever needs they have

- having a varied and interesting life

- getting to know other people from different backgrounds

- feeling valued

- learning new skills, discovering talents, and achieving things that you (or others) may have thought you could not achieve before

- fulfilling your unique potential.

RECOGNISING THE BARRIERS THAT PEOPLE CAN FACE IN ACCESSING SERVICES AND FACILITIES

The types of barriers that people encounter in accessing services are the same whether these services are universal or specialist. The barriers may be:

- physical

- psychological

- financial

- linked to communication and information.

PHYSICAL BARRIERS

These can include:

- access to buildings where services are provided (eg doorway width, lifts, ramps etc)
- people being able to get to where a service is provided (transport issues, especially for people in rural areas, and the financial implications of transport can be huge for people)
- access to toilets, hearing loops and other specific facilities the individual requires.

PSYCHOLOGICAL BARRIERS

These can be extremely powerful for people and prevent people from moving forwards in their lives. For example, people may be embarrassed about the very fact that they have a certain condition or need a certain service, and actually going to talk to someone about this may be difficult for them to think about. People may also be fearful of others finding out about their needs, or they may fear the worst if they do find out more about a medical diagnosis and their own prognosis.

As well as fear and embarrassment, psychological barriers also include:

- issues linked to mental ill health or depression
- cultural barriers (people feeling that a service is not going to be inclusive of their needs and culture – see also below about how information is communicated)
- issues concerning confidence and self-esteem, eg in leaving the house, using public transport to get somewhere, walking into somewhere new on their own, etc
- concerns about being labelled or stigmatised.

FINANCIAL BARRIERS

As discussed above, if you have to go somewhere to access a service or a facility (as opposed to the service coming to you), there is likely to be a cost implication in terms of getting there. For many individuals, this can be prohibitive, and this can be a particular issue for people in isolated rural communities and areas without good transportation links.

Access to some services and facilities also are either means tested or you have to pay to access them, such as:

- leisure centres or gyms
- activity provision
- clubs and outings.

Without the means to do so, access is impossible. Some specialist care services also require people to make a financial contribution to the cost of care. Often service users are reluctant to pay these costs for a range of reasons, including a lack of money.

COMMUNICATION AND INFORMATION BARRIERS

As is explored in Chapter 2, if an individual's communication needs are unmet, they will not be able to participate in or understand what services are available to them, how services may benefit them, or how to access provision.

As well as the means and methods for communication, it is also important to consider what is communicated about services by you and by the services themselves. Services need to be appealing and inclusive in order for anyone to feel it is worthwhile accessing them.

Information can, however, sometimes be communicated by services or by others in a way that is:

- misleading
- inaccurate
- discriminatory
- inaccessible
- seen as excluding individuals.

Inclusivity is about language, but it is also about imagery on leaflets, how buildings look, staff presentation and attitude, and the facilities provided. In terms of language, though, when you describe a service, or when a service describes itself in its literature, the following should be considered in order to confront information barriers:

- Ensure that there is a range of formats available, including large print versions of leaflets and versions in languages other than English.
- Focus on how people benefit from the service and the outcomes it can have for people generally or for the individual concerned.
- Show where the service is located and public transport routes to get there.

OVERCOMING BARRIERS TO ACCESSING SERVICES AND FACILITIES

There are four key steps to overcoming barriers:

1 Find out what the barrier is for the individual.

This sounds obvious, but:

- Don't assume you know. Someone may actually be really confident about going into new situations and environments, but may be embarrassed to tell you that they cannot afford to join a group. The person knows themselves better than you will ever know them, so do not assume you understand what their barrier is. Different barriers affect different people in different ways.

- Listen and take the time to find out the individual's perceptions, worries, hopes and fears.

- Ask the right questions, eg open and not closed questions ('How would you feel about …?', 'Have you ever thought about …?', 'What might be your worries about …?').

- Consider all four types of barriers that people face (the individual you are working with could face any one of these or any combination of them all).

2 Explore with the person how they feel barriers can be overcome.

Again, this is about avoiding assumptions. If you approach someone in an insensitive way, even with the best of intentions, you can make the person more reluctant to participate in activities or access services, so take the time to find out what the person's views are on how their own goals can be achieved.

If you assume that a lack of confidence means they need you to go with them for the first time, whereas the person actually wants a peer or friend to go with them (and not you as a 'worker'), you can actually do more damage than good. If you assume that the barrier concerns access and transport and offer the person a lift, they may actually miss out on what they see as part of the experience in using a bus again for the first time in years, and so on.

Health and social care work is about being person centred, and listening to the individual's own hopes, fears and goals. The focus must be on how the person involved feels the barriers can be overcome. As a professional you can of course give some ideas, but make sure the person and their family, if involved, are the people who decide how the barrier can best be overcome.

3 Make a plan together to put ideas into practice.

Doing this together is important for the reasons outlined above. Making a plan is useful because it enables some of the potential pitfalls to be identified in advance and strategies considered, shared and agreed to prevent the experience from being a negative one.

A plan dealing with someone's confidence and their anxiety about going to a new service will be very different from a plan dealing with someone's physical access to public transport and a facility. Planning for both types of scenario involves thinking through these barriers in advance, and contacting providers to ensure that they have the necessary access requirements in place.

Making a plan also involves people in risk assessment in an inclusive and empowering way. The key question can be, 'What is the worst that could happen?' Thinking this through together, making contingency plans, and weighing up the advantages and disadvantages of trying out a new activity is important in enabling someone to manage and take appropriate risks in their own lives.

> **KEY POINT**
>
> Be risk aware rather than risk averse when supporting people to make use of services and facilities.

4 Test out the plan and review it together.

There is no harm in doing a 'dry run' together if that is what will promote an individual's independence and confidence. Any plan needs to be tried and reviewed, so that the individual's needs are met, and so that you enable them to learn about how they tackled their barriers, and how they could do so again in the future.

Once the plan has been put into action, review what happened and see whether any changes need to be made. If plan A didn't work – start again and make a plan B.

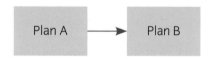

SUPPORTING INDIVIDUALS TO CHALLENGE INFORMATION ABOUT SERVICES THAT MAY PRESENT A BARRIER TO PARTICIPATION

As stated above, sometimes people can talk about services or facilities in a way that does not show off their benefits to their best advantage. Likewise, services sometimes do not do themselves justice in their literature, on their website, or in other ways in which they present themselves to the public. In these ways, information can be a barrier, because it can be:

- misleading
- inaccurate

- discriminatory
- inaccessible
- excluding individuals.

One of the roles of the health and social care worker is to challenge discrimination and poor practice, and also to enable and support users of services to do this for themselves.

There are several scenarios where people may wish to (or need to) challenge provision that presents them with barriers to participation, including:

- a lack of access for people with disabilities
- a lack of leaflets in large print, other languages, Braille, etc
- unreasonable pricing
- a lack of space or dignity in changing facilities
- staffing ratios that exclude people who need extra support, or mean they have to wait for a long time to see someone who can help them
- out-of-date information, eg on opening times, contact numbers, etc
- unapproachable or unwelcoming frontline staff in a service.

It is important to spend time with the individual and consider the following questions:

- Do they want to challenge the issue themselves? If so, how and when?
- Do they want you to do this with or for them?
- Do you have any moral duty to challenge, or any personal duty as a citizen to challenge, even if the person does not want this challenge to be about them and their experience of a service or facility?

REFLECT

Consider the four types of barriers that people may experience in accessing services.

- Which of these barriers have you or do you experience yourself?
- Which of these barriers are most powerful and difficult to overcome for the users of your service?
- How do you or how does your service strive to address these barriers and be as inclusive as possible?

MESSAGES FROM RESEARCH

Barriers for people from minority groups in accessing dementia services

Research from the Social Care Institute of Excellence (2011) shows that the increasing diversity of the UK's population and an ageing population represent some key issues in terms of dementia services:

- Black people and those from other ethnic minority groups are currently under-represented in dementia services.

- There are lower levels of awareness about dementia and relevant services in black and minority ethnic communities, and there is increased stigma around dementia in some communities.

- Some people prefer services to be 'culturally specific', and others prefer mixed services.

- There needs to be specific effort to target adults and carers of adults with dementia in black communities and minority groups, and training for staff on culturally competent care practices.

(Moriarty, Sharif and Robinson 2011)

CASE STUDY

Isabella is a senior care assistant in a respite care service that provides short-term stays for younger people with learning and physical disabilities.

Tom has been having respite at Isabella's service for over two years. One day, when he is being collected by his parents, Tom's parents tell Isabella that they have not had a review of Tom's care plan for over a year, and they are starting to struggle a little more in managing things at home as they are getting older and as Tom's dad lost his job earlier in the year.

Isabella suggests that they could contact Tom's social worker to ask for a review and for an update of their carer's assessments. They are reluctant to do this, though, even when she offers to do this on their behalf, as they say, 'There are plenty of people out there worse off than us' and 'We don't want them to think we can't cope with Tom'.

- What barriers are Tom's parents facing to accessing services?

- What sorts of services and facilities could have an impact on their lives?

- How could Isabella help to address or reduce these barriers?

SUPPORTING PEOPLE TO SELECT SERVICES AND FACILITIES

When you are identifying services and facilities that could meet an individual's needs, the following key issues and questions need to be considered.

- Are you looking at universal services in the community, or the person's access to specialist provision?

- How are you promoting the person's inclusion into society via universal facilities? Do we always look at the people whom we work with as 'users' of services, as opposed to leaders, volunteers and contributors to services? It can be really helpful to look at local volunteering opportunities as these can be widely ranging (from conservation to supporting others, and from transport to animal care). Volunteering can offer people a real sense of importance in 'giving something back' to society and others. This concept is often something that can be denied to those who themselves have needs.

- If you are looking at specialist services, can the person refer themselves, or do they have to be referred by you or other professionals?

- How do you know you are presenting the full range of options to somebody? We all know what we know – but there is often a lot more out there than we know about. So, how do you research (with the individual) the full range of possible service provision?

- If you are gathering information to present to an individual, how do you apply the concept of 'minimal sufficiency'? That is, can you present a brief summary of your research, and then let them look into ideas in depth themselves?

- Are there any issues around bias in what you present to people? Do you have better relationships with some people in some services? Have you had specific positive or negative experiences of certain provision in the past? Do you take a view that some services are more effective than others, and, if so, what is this based on? Do you need to update your knowledge of some services? Should you visit some in person yourself to check out your knowledge, build relationships and challenge your own prejudice?

- Are the ideas you are looking at based on what you think is best for the person, or what they think is right, best and appropriate for themselves? How are you applying your professional power and ensuring you do not misuse this power? (See Chapters 3 and 4 on equality and duty of care.)

- How are the person's cultural needs being considered in the range of ideas you gather and present?

> **KEY POINT**
>
> Knowledge is power. One of the key aspects of empowering people is to ensure that they have access to information. People don't know what they don't know – so you really need to think through how you can provide information about a wide range of services and facilities to service users.

- How will your presentation of all of this meet the person's communication needs? How will you ensure you do not overwhelm them with information or, on the other hand, make them feel they have very little in the way of options?

- How does the information you have gathered relate to the person's assessment, their needs and the outcomes they hope to achieve? The actions you agree to take with an individual regarding access to services should be linked back to these, so that progress and achievements can be noted and celebrated, allowing further goals and growth to be considered.

GATHERING INFORMATION

There are a range of sources for researching the provision in a local area, including:

- the local newspaper

- free papers

- talking to the service user, their carers and friends about what they know already

- local libraries often provide information about a range of local services

- leaflets in local community centres and cafes, etc

- the Citizens Advice Bureau (CAB)

- local CAB volunteer coordination organisations

- the local council (many have access centres which have information available and advisers who can help)

- go to leisure centres, faith venues, etc and find out what is on

- talk to other colleagues and professionals

- the internet – working with service users to access information on the internet together can be a useful way of getting to know their prior experiences, discussing any barriers and working out how they feel about the options generated immediately.

AGREEING WITH AN INDIVIDUAL THEIR PREFERRED OPTIONS FOR ACCESSING SERVICES AND FACILITIES

When you have worked through the whole range of options by researching what services are available, the next stages are as follows:

1 Narrow down the options with the person.

2 Look at the practicalities – the when, where and how.

3 Consider any barriers to accessing services in detail.

4 Find out if there is any further information which the person would like before committing to a plan. If you do not know something, be upfront about this, and agree that you will find out and come back to them with this information in a timely way.

5 Look at the outcomes the person hopes to achieve for themselves by accessing these services. (See also Chapter 10 person-centred practice as there are clear links with how services should enable outcomes to be achieved.) These could be outcomes concerned with making changes in a person's life (eg via specialist support services), or with reducing isolation, making new friends, learning new skills, and social inclusion (eg via access to universal facilities). As discussed above, focusing on the outcomes that a service has shown with others can be a powerful way of 'selling' the benefits of accessing it.

6 Consider together the level of support that the person wants in order to access each service, so that the person's independence is maximised.

7 Make a provisional plan for trying out the services and agree a timescale to review this together.

REFLECT

When you support people to select services and facilities, you have an influence over what they choose to access based on what you decide to present, and the way in which you 'sell' different ideas to them.

- How do the factors described above influence what you present to people and how you present it?

- Are there examples you can think of when you could have expanded the range of options, so that the individual had a wider range of choices available to them?

KEY POINT

The key aspect for health and social care workers is to promote choice. See pages 351–353 in Chapter 10 for more information on supporting people to make informed choices.

MESSAGES FROM RESEARCH

Access to services for people with learning disabilities

The Mental Health Network NHS Confederation's (2012) research identified that:

- there are specific barriers and training needs for staff in identifying when someone with a learning disability has a mental health need

- information about medication is often completely inaccessible for people with learning disabilities

- services do not take account of how difficult new or unfamiliar environments can be when adults with learning disabilities need to access in-patient care

- GPs need to conduct regular health checks for people that take account of their mental health as well as their physical well-being.

In terms of physical health, there is also extensive research to show that adults with learning disabilities experience far poorer physical health outcomes than others.

Emerson and Baines (2010) examined the whole range of physical health conditions and the inequalities faced by people with learning disabilities in each area of their physical health. They highlight that these outcomes are poorer because of the barriers that people face in 'accessing timely, appropriate and effective health care' – ie if people's needs were identified earlier, and if they received a more appropriate, personalised and effective response, the outcomes would be better.

(Emerson and Baines 2010; Mental Health Network NHS Confederation's 2012)

CASE STUDY

Jane is a senior support worker in a day service for people with learning disabilities. Many of the service users she works with have profound learning disabilities along with physical disabilities. Jane is responsible for organising day service activities and she supervises a small group of day service assistants.

Jane and her team are making plans for the next few months' activities, and, as part of this, they are considering how their service users can access services and facilities in the community as well as at the centre. Some individuals want to go shopping and go for a coffee afterwards, some want to do a signing course at the local college, and some want a 'pamper day' at a spa. Some of Jane's staff are concerned about the ratio of workers required to enable this to happen and about the cost of some of these activities. Suggestions are made about the staff having some training in beauty therapy and signing so that the activities can take place at the centre instead of needing to be off-site.

- What are some of the tensions in this discussion?

- How might Jane manage some of these tensions and promote inclusion?

- How might the issues raised by the staff members be addressed?

SUPPORTING PEOPLE TO ACCESS AND USE SERVICES AND FACILITIES

With the provisional plan in place, the next stage is to outline the resources, and the exact level of support that the person will need (and want) in order to access the services that they have chosen in their plan. This may involve:

- filling out application forms (enabling the person to do this for themselves as much as possible)

- working out finances together

- considering transport, and maybe a 'dry run' if there is a need for public transport to get to a service

- actioning the ideas that the person has chosen to address any barriers they have, eg they may want to meet a worker from a service or visit a building before going there for a club for the first time. People often want to meet another person who has used or who does use a service, or someone who is part of a group, so that they know a familiar face when they first attend

- working out what your role, and that of other support staff, will be. Planning this in detail is useful as this avoids 'over-supporting' individuals, and ensures that they are involved in the discussions around the level of assistance they may need in order to access a facility. Some individuals may need someone to go with them on the bus to get somewhere, but then may need very little in the way of assistance during an activity, such as a class at a local college. Others may have more complex needs and may require far more input in order for them to participate, enjoy and achieve their outcomes at the same activity.

CARRYING OUT AGREED RESPONSIBILITIES TO ENABLE THE INDIVIDUAL TO ACCESS AND USE SERVICES AND FACILITIES

The following are the key principles to consider.

- Do what you say you were going to do (no more and no less).

- Monitor the plan on an ongoing basis. Even if a review is planned in due course, there is no harm in changing a plan sooner if an individual needs this to happen.

- Work towards a gradual, planned and appropriate reduction or withdrawal of support in accessing services. You should hope and expect that people become more confident over time, particularly in the context of clubs, groups and classes, and that they forge links and relationships there if this is the planned goal. In this instance, your role should reduce over time in a planned and proactive way, so that the individual's independence and control over their own continuing access to the facility are maximised.

ENSURING INDIVIDUALS' RIGHTS AND PREFERENCES ARE PROMOTED WHEN ACCESSING AND USING SERVICES AND FACILITIES

Promoting people's rights and preferences is about:

- recognising that challenges may be needed, eg if a service or facility is excluding someone from using the service

- enabling people to challenge issues for themselves where possible

- recognising that people's preferences (and tastes) change over time. They may start a painting class, enjoy this, and then want to do a pottery class, or they may want to then try something completely different. Doing more of the same is not always what most of us want – we often enjoy a continuity of some activities and the challenge of something new

- in this context, workers need to strive to challenge their own assumptions about what is best for an individual, to use their observation and communication skills to consider the person's preferences, and to change the plan when needed

- these changes can occur at certain planned review points or they can take place sooner. This is especially the case if issues around people's safety or rights are identified which mean that the person is unhappy to continue attending somewhere, or if professionals identify and report formal concerns with or on behalf of an individual around a service's practices.

REFLECT

Consider an occasion when you supported an individual to try something new.

- Did the person have any anxieties about this?

- How did you carry out your responsibilities and support the person appropriately?

- How did you avoid 'over-supporting' the person in this situation?

MESSAGES FROM RESEARCH

Older people from black and minority communities

In 2010, Age Concern (now Age UK) published 'Later matters: tackling race inequalities for BME older people'. This research looked at some key issues in the Yorkshire and Humber areas, which are relevant elsewhere:

- Older people are more likely not to know about the range of services they can access, and not to know who can tell them what they are entitled to access.

- Services need to improve in terms of cultural competence (the examples of culturally appropriate catering and the provision of prayer facilities were cited).

- Leaflets and printed materials need to be visibly made available in other languages and formats (ie not having the non-English versions in a drawer so that people have to, first, know that these exist and, second, have to ask for one).

- Black older adults and older people from minority communities are more likely to have had poor prior experiences of services, so they are therefore more likely to be reluctant to access services in the future.

- Alongside this, professionals too often assume care is provided within the family in black and minority communities. There are issues for people in identifying themselves as carers around pride and stigma, which means that carers often too do not get the help they need.

(Age UK 2010)

Taju is a senior support worker with a mental health charity. He works some of his time in a drop-in centre for people with mental health problems and the remainder of his working week is spent in outreach services providing ongoing practical and emotional support for service users.

As part of his role, Taju is often involved in supporting individuals to access services to help in times of financial crisis, and when housing issues are a major concern for them. Taju recognises that people's mental health can be deeply affected by instability and uncertainty around their practical, financial and housing needs.

Taju has worked with Simone for some time, who has bipolar disorder. Simone is extremely concerned that the local housing association has written to her saying that her tenancy is at risk because of her teenage children's antisocial behaviour in the community. Simone's children have a social worker and she has started a parenting course, but she feels that everyone is getting at her and that the children do not stick to the boundaries she tries to put in place.

Taju offers to arrange a meeting with housing and Simone so that she can discuss how hard she is trying to keep the situation under control. He wants her to explain the impact on her well-being and on her parenting, if she remains under constant threat of eviction.

- What support might Taju need to provide Simone before, at and after this meeting?
- What other services may Simone benefit from accessing?

SUPPORTING INDIVIDUALS TO REVIEW THEIR ACCESS TO AND USE OF SERVICES AND FACILITIES

EVALUATING WHETHER SERVICES OR FACILITIES HAVE MET AN INDIVIDUAL'S ASSESSED NEEDS AND PREFERENCES

As with any plan, monitoring and reviewing its effectiveness is critical. Again, there are links here with Chapter 9 on assessment, planning and reviewing.

Evaluating people's access to services is something that you and the person will be doing from day one. It is important to know how they have found the experience of accessing a service or a facility, because if that first experience is a bad one, they are unlikely to go back a second time anyway.

Doing a more formal evaluation of the impact of a service upon a person's life may be something that you do with them prior to a planned review meeting, and this evaluation should look at:

- the outcomes that the person hoped to achieve

- the way in which the service has promoted these outcomes

- any gaps or areas the service could improve

- any changes the person wants to make to the plan now

- the next steps, ie do more of the same for a further period of time, make a partial change to the plan or to make a complete change of plan.

Services themselves should also be seeking feedback from users in order to ensure they are meeting people's needs and to aid service development and improvement.

SUPPORTING AN INDIVIDUAL TO PROVIDE FEEDBACK ON THEIR EXPERIENCE OF ACCESSING AND USING SERVICES OR FACILITIES

It is important to try to ensure that feedback is always constructive. What makes feedback constructive is not whether a person is saying a service is good or bad. The *way* feedback is given is what makes it constructive (or not).

Service users need to be able to provide feedback on their experience of accessing services and facilities in order for:

- their experience to be heard and valued

- changes to be made to their plan where necessary

- services to develop and improve

- issues around poor practice, safeguarding or discrimination within services to be addressed.

It can be difficult for any service, or any individual, to hear negative feedback, even where the intention of the person giving this is for things to improve. Where people make complaints, their aim is usually for others to have a better experience than they did. It is useful though to consider ways of supporting people to give feedback in a manner that comes across as constructive. You may also be involved in giving feedback to a service provider on behalf of an individual and then you need to ensure that the feedback is constructively given.

GUIDELINES FOR CONSTRUCTIVE FEEDBACK

- *Positive*. Good feedback should always start and finish with a positive. This is often referred to as the positive sandwich.

- *Specific*. Feedback should deal clearly with specific issues, particular instances and behaviours rather than making vague or sweeping statements.

- *Descriptive*. Feedback should use descriptive rather than evaluative terms, eg 'my perception was that when you repeated the same question several times the person became confused', rather than 'your questioning technique was confusing'.

- *Actionable*. Feedback should be directed towards behaviour that the other person can do something about, eg 'if you slowed down your delivery, it would probably be easier for the person to follow what you were saying', rather than 'your accent is hard to understand'.

- *Prioritised*. Feedback should concentrate on the two or three key areas for improvement.

- *Well-timed*. The most useful feedback is given in a timely way, so feedback about services should be given as soon as possible after the person has used the service.

- *Clear*. Feedback should avoid jargon wherever possible and the person communicating feedback should ensure that their communication is clear.

Your role may be to gather or present feedback to others, or to representatives from services, on behalf of individuals. The aim of this feedback is about change, improvement and increased satisfaction, so it is important that feedback is shared with this in mind.

It is also important that if you do give feedback on behalf of someone, that it is their feedback you share, and not your own opinion, unless you are asked to give this specifically.

DIFFERENT PEOPLE, DIFFERENT APPROACHES

Different people will want to give feedback about their experiences of using services in different ways. You should work with the individual you are supporting to think about how they would like to give feedback and work with them to support them in providing feedback in the way they choose.

The most important thing you can do is to stress how important it is that the person gives feedback – so that services can be responsive to peoples' needs and continually improve what they do. Some people do not like to give feedback, particularly if it is negative, as they may fear that it will affect their entitlement to receive services or they may feel that people or services may perceive them to be a troublemaker.

EVALUATING THE SUPPORT PROVIDED FOR AN INDIVIDUAL IN ACCESSING AND USING SERVICES OR FACILITIES

It is important to seek feedback from service users on how they feel about the support that you have provided. This is a key aspect of working in partnership with service users.

As discussed above, the principle behind evaluating the type and level of support that workers provide to an individual in order to enable them to access services is about a planned reduction or withdrawal of this support. People should hopefully feel enabled by the support that is provided to do whatever they want to do for and by themselves where possible. Therefore, if the level of support can be reduced, minimised or withdrawn, then this can be a powerful step towards promoting the person's independence, self-esteem and social inclusion.

IDENTIFYING AND AGREEING ANY CHANGES NEEDED TO IMPROVE THE EXPERIENCE AND OUTCOMES OF ACCESSING AND USING SERVICES OR FACILITIES

Having looked at monitoring and evaluating an individual's access to services, feedback and reviewing the level of support, the next and final stage is to agree any changes to the current plan. These changes could be in terms of:

- a change of plan (eg looking at different services, changing preferences or new experiences the person would like to try)

- a change in the level of support provided for the person's continued access to a service

- a change in some aspect of a service's offer to a person (eg concerning access, what is provided there, opportunities, etc)

- a change in the outcomes and goals a person is seeking to achieve (eg they may have wanted to try out a drama group, and, having done so, they may now want to volunteer in running it; or they may want to learn backstage skills instead of acting or performing).

Any changes should of course be planned for, agreed with the individual, and again monitored on an ongoing basis to ensure that individual needs continue to be met, and that people are supported and empowered to live full, engaging and valued lives.

REFLECT

- How do you evaluate and record whether a person's access to services and facilities has been beneficial to them?

- How do you ensure that people in your service setting are able to access universal as well as specialist provision?

- Can you suggest areas where your service or practice could improve in terms of looking at people's social inclusion needs in more depth?

CASE STUDY

Jon is a senior support worker with a reablement team. He works with service users on a short-term basis to try to maximise their independence. His input is intensive but limited to six weeks' duration. Many of the people he works with have recently been discharged from hospital. Jon works closely with the occupational therapists, physiotherapists and social workers on the team to develop individual reablement plans for service users.

Jon is looking at an exit plan with Ben who, following a heart attack, is now doing well at home. Ben says he is getting all the help he needs and he feels pleased with all the support he has had, but Jon is worried that when he withdraws, Ben will become increasingly isolated as he has not wanted any support in accessing community-based services and universal facilities.

When Jon asks Ben about this, Ben says that the only 'community service' he used to access was the pub, and it was years of drinking and smoking that led to his heart attack. He says he does miss his friends whom he used to see there, but he knows he cannot go back to his old way of life.

- How can Jon explore ways of Ben staying in touch with his old friends, and taking up new or healthy activities with some of them?

- How can Jon enable Ben to do this for himself, and support him with the areas of moving forwards where he needs support?

KEEPING IT PERSON CENTRED

We have discussed the importance of keeping practice person centred in health and social care. It is vital that you maintain a person-centred approach when supporting individuals to use services and facilities.

Apply the principles of person-centred practice to all of your work in this area.

- *Individuality*. Recognise the service user as a unique individual. Just because one person has found a service useful doesn't mean that another person will.

- *Choice*. Ensure that the individual has a range of options and that you enable them to make an informed decision by providing them with a range of information.

- *Privacy*. Always respect a person's privacy. If a service requests information about an individual, check with the individual that they are happy for you to share the information, or, better still, enable them to provide the information themselves.

- *Independence*. Ensure that you do not 'over-support' an individual and that you promote their independence at all times.

- *Dignity*. Work in a way that promotes the person's dignity.

- *Respect*. Respect the person's wishes and preferences.

- *Partnership*. Work in partnership with the service user at all times.

These principles can also be used to support a service user to evaluate the whole range of other services that they have used. For each service or facility the person has accessed, they could consider how well these principles were addressed, and you could support them to ensure their views are heard and ideas actioned by other providers, so that these services change, adapt and improve in their approaches based on feedback from individuals.

CHAPTER 13
Providing support to maintain and develop skills for everyday life

All health and social care workers will be supporting individuals with their skills for everyday life in some way. Many of the people we work with need support to undertake tasks that are part of day-to-day living, and to ensure that their own needs are met. Providing support with these tasks in ways that enable and empower people is a critical part of a skilled worker's role.

There are close links between the content of this chapter and those on person-centred practice and active support, so it is worth reading Chapters 10 and 11 in tandem with this one to ensure your knowledge has the maximum depth.

Links to other chapters

It is particularly relevant to consider this chapter in relation to its links with chapters 4, 11 and 12.

WHAT DO WE MEAN BY SKILLS FOR EVERYDAY LIFE?

Many users of health and social care services require support with their skills for everyday life. These might include:

- skills for personal care needs (eg washing, bathing, cleaning teeth, dressing, eating, etc)
- mobility skills
- communication skills
- relationship skills
- memory skills
- skills to manage living independently (eg shopping, cleaning, budgeting, etc)
- skills to get where they want to go (eg using money, using public transport, driving, etc)
- job skills (eg gaining employment, doing the job they want to do, developing a career, etc)
- technical skills (eg using computers, DIY skills, etc).

Part of your work role is likely to involve consideration of some of these skills with each person you support. Identifying the skills that people need and want to develop, maintain or regain is part of good assessment practice, and you will be involved in developing and implementing plans for individuals in these areas.

The specific skills that individuals need and want to develop will depend on a variety of factors, including:

- the individual's skills, abilities and strengths
- their individual needs and circumstances (eg for some people, the plan may need to focus more on their basic care skills or mobility because of the nature of their needs, and for others you may be working more on independent living)
- the reason for the person accessing a service (eg if an individual has had a traumatic event, or a hospital admission, they may have lost some of their basic skills and may access a rehabilitation or reablement service specifically to redevelop these skills)
- their hopes, goals and the outcomes they want to achieve (see Chapter 9 on facilitating person-centred assessment for more detail on outcome-focused assessment)
- where they live and the availability of support, adaptations in their homes and other people in their network
- their carers' views, wishes and needs.

METHODS FOR DEVELOPING AND MAINTAINING SKILLS FOR EVERYDAY LIFE

There are a variety of different methods which can be useful in helping people to develop and maintain skills. Which methods you use will differ according to the individual, their needs, the skill you are working on and the boundaries of your work role. The key principle is always that of promoting the individual's independence in line with the value base of the profession. This means that people should be enabled to do everything for themselves as far as they are able and to learn the skills they need for life so that they do not need ongoing support from others in all areas of their life.

The methods might involve:

- active participation (see Chapter 10 on promoting person-centred approaches)

- active support (see Chapter 11)

- praise, encouragement and reinforcement (in ways that are appropriate to the individual)

- using technological aids (eg communication aids)

- adaptations to the person's home or your service's environment (eg mobility aids, aids to bathing, alerting others to difficulties, cooking, etc)

- using a specific teaching or training approach (eg the 'ask – instruct – prompt – show – guide' as described in Chapter 11), which is sometimes called 'train and fade'. The idea is that the input provided should reduce as the person learns and becomes more comfortable with the specific skill, so that their independence is promoted

- group work to promote learning of a skill among several individuals

- forward or backward chaining approaches.

FORWARD OR BACKWARD CHAINING APPROACHES

Chaining approaches are based on task analysis (ie breaking down tasks into small, manageable steps as in recipes or DIY guides). The size of each step or number of steps for a specific task should vary according to the individual's ability or need for support (see Chapter 11 on active support for more information on task analysis).

Chaining then involves the individual undertaking one of the small steps with the worker undertaking other steps. As the individual becomes more confident with the specific step, they then go on to carry out more steps with the worker carrying out less, until eventually the individual can carry out the whole task themselves.

> **KEY POINT**
>
> Forward chaining involves the individual starting with the first step and then building from there, while backward chaining involves the person starting with the final step and then working backwards.

BE CREATIVE

A wide range of techniques can be used to enable people to learn new skills. For example, one innovative technique that has been successfully used with adults with learning disabilities is 'feed-forward'. This involves people being encouraged to carry out small parts of a task and being filmed doing this. The film clips are edited to show a sequence of the person completing the whole task. This method has been shown to be effective in enabling people to develop skills more quickly. This will not work for everyone, but it demonstrates how creativity in enabling people to learn can be very effective.

Some services work specifically around reablement, either within the community, following hospital discharge or on a residential basis. The focus of these services is always on enabling individuals to maintain, regain or develop skills, so that they do not become dependent on the service, and can return to living as independent and full a life as possible. Reablement professionals use a range of the techniques described to support individuals in maintaining, regaining and developing skills.

WHY MIGHT INDIVIDUALS NEED SUPPORT TO MAINTAIN, REGAIN OR DEVELOP SKILLS?

The reasons why individuals may need support with their everyday living skills are as diverse as the users of health and social care services. The reasons will be unique to the person themselves and their specific needs and circumstances.

Someone may need to ...	Because of ....
Maintain skills	dementia (eg maintaining independence and memory skills)
	mental health needs (eg maintaining the household and access to networks at times of crisis)
	a physical health condition or learning disability, where the tendency of carers and service providers could be to 'over-support' the individual in a way that de-skills them

Someone may need to ...	Because of ....
Regain skills	a traumatic life event
	a sudden illness
	hospitalisation (research shows that people can become de-skilled after losing their independence suddenly)
	a loss in their confidence in their own abilities
	a change in their existing condition or needs, or the development of an additional health need which leads to a need for certain skills to be relearned
Develop skills	a disability that has meant that others have done things for them possibly all of their lives until this point (ie they have not had the opportunity to develop skills before)
	access to new technology and aids that were not previously available

HOW CAN MAINTAINING, REGAINING OR DEVELOPING SKILLS BENEFIT INDIVIDUALS?

We all benefit from being able to do things for ourselves in terms of:

- confidence in our own abilities
- pride in our own skills
- feeling we have achieved something
- feeling we are learning new things and progressing towards our goals
- access to encouragement and praise
- increasing our self-esteem and feelings of worth
- our contribution to society.

All of these feelings are developed from childhood where we learn from doing, trying new experiences, and from the way in which significant others in our lives provide experiences and encouragement to us. If people are cushioned from new experiences, or if they do not have the same access to opportunities (because of their needs or because others do not promote their right to inclusion), they are likely to feel that:

- they cannot do things for themselves (this is often referred to as 'learned helplessness')

- they do not know where to start in learning a new skill

- their lives will always be the same and never change.

Promoting people's opportunity to maintain, regain or develop skills is about promoting their right to inclusion, and also to living as full a life as possible where their needs may be static or deteriorating. Your role in enabling individuals to live independently, learn new skills, access opportunities and develop (or re-develop) their confidence can be critical in challenging the above feelings and in promoting the person's well-being.

REFLECT

Put yourself in the position of a person with whom you have worked or with whom you are working now.

- Consider the level of support that this person needs with day-to-day living, and how you might feel about needing this type and level of support yourself.

- If you were in this position what could others do to enable you to maintain independence?

- What would work best for you, and are there any interventions you would feel uncomfortable with?

MESSAGES FROM RESEARCH

Young adults' views on their skill development

Morris's 2001 research for Scope has many themes which are just as current today. This research was based on the experiences of 44 young adults with high levels of support needs, and Morris found the following:

- Professionals can be extremely averse to risk (eg instead of safe lifting, 'no lifting' policies can be instigated) and this can lead to practices that exclude service users.

- Young adults face specific barriers to the transition to adulthood and moving to independence. Too many assessments are focused on whether people are eligible for a service, as opposed to what their actual needs are, and this can lead many people into feeling that institutional care is the only means of ensuring that their day-to-day living needs are met.

- The young adults in the study reported isolation, loss of relationships and feeling 'shut away' from their local communities. There are no governmental policies that talk about 'friendship' as a means of social inclusion and active participation, and yet friendship (with peers who have disabilities or who do not) is the most important concept for young adults themselves.

SUPPORTING INDIVIDUALS TO PLAN FOR MAINTAINING AND DEVELOPING SKILLS FOR EVERYDAY LIFE

Supporting individuals to maintain, regain or develop daily living skills involves following the basic social care process (see Chapter 9) in that it involves:

Assessing the person's needs. Working with the individual to identify skills for everyday life.

Planning support. Planning the methods that will best support the individual to develop, maintain or regain the identified skills.

Implementing the plan. Supporting individuals to retain, regain or develop skills for everyday life in line with the plan.

Review. Reviewing the progress the individual has made and whether the methods being used are working. The plan will probably need changing following the review.

WORKING WITH AN INDIVIDUAL AND OTHERS TO IDENTIFY SKILLS FOR EVERYDAY LIFE

Identifying the specific skills that a person wants to maintain, regain or develop is the first part of good assessment practice. The principles of this are covered in the chapter on person-centred assessment and the key principles to consider are:

- Avoid making assumptions (eg that someone cannot perform a skill because they have a certain condition or label).

- Involve the individual fully, and start from their wishes, hopes and goals.

- Use self-assessment tools appropriately (and do not rely solely on these).

- Consider the outcomes the person wants to achieve.

- Be specific about which skills are important in terms of the individual's safety, personal care and basic care in the first instance.

- Work up from these to consider other skills that the person may require to achieve their goals and aspirations. You could draw on Maslow's hierarchy of needs (see pages 297–299) to help you work up from the basics.

A variety of other people will be involved in these discussions and assessments, such as the individual's family, carers and friends, your colleagues, any advocates or supporters the person has, and other professionals.

CASE STUDY

Chen is a senior care assistant in a residential service for older people. Many of the residents of the home have dementia.

Martin has recently moved to live at the home, and Chen has been working with Martin to retain his independence and day-to-day living skills. Martin has dementia and needs support with getting dressed, eating and personal care. Chen has been working to put in an ask–instruct–prompt–show–guide model using some of his knowledge about active support, so that Martin is enabled to do everything for himself that he can.

Chen is concerned that although Martin has responded well to his work with him, his health needs are continuing to increase and other colleagues are beginning to do things for Martin which Chen knows he can still do for himself with minimal help.

- How can Chen challenge some of his colleagues' thinking in terms of these issues, so that the approach of the whole care team is more consistent?

- How can Martin be enabled to live as full and independent a life as possible?

KEEPING THINGS 'AGE APPROPRIATE'

Sometimes the skills that people need to regain or develop are skills that traditionally people learn in childhood. This means that often people cannot think of different ways to learn a skill – which means that they might support an individual to learn a skill in a childlike way. Adults will find a childlike approach patronising and it will diminish their motivation and ability to learn. It is therefore vital to think about an age-appropriate way for a person to learn a skill – and to ensure that the support you offer (eg the feedback you give) is age appropriate.

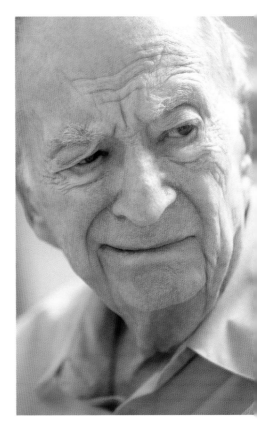

ASSESSMENTS OF DAILY LIVING SKILLS

There are several tools that specifically look at assessing people's skills in relation to daily living. Many of these are used by professionals, such as occupational therapists, who specialise in assessing daily living skills.

Some of these assessment tools include the Katz ADL scale, the Lawton IADL scale and the Bristol Activities of Daily Living Scale (BADLS). These assessment tools generally separate the skills needed for everyday life into different areas and then evaluate how independently a person can carry out these tasks, often using scales that rate the person's level of independence. The tools generally consider either basic activities or instrumental activities – or a combination of the two.

Basic activities for daily living

Often referred to as BADLS (the Bristol Activities for Daily Living Scale), these are generally seen as consisting of self-care tasks, including:

- bathing and showering (washing the body)
- bowel and bladder management
- dressing
- eating (including chewing and swallowing)
- functional mobility (moving from one place to another while performing activities).

Instrumental activities of daily living

Often referred to as IADLs (instrumental activities of daily living), these are seen as more than basic skills, but are those that enable an individual to live independently. These include:

- housework
- taking medications as prescribed
- managing money
- shopping

- use of telephone or other form of communication
- using technology (as applicable)
- transportation within the community.

Many scales for instrumental activities use the reminder SHAFT (shopping, housekeeping, accounting, food preparation, telephone/ transportation).

SKILLS AND TASKS: UNDERSTANDING THE DIFFERENCE

In supporting people with daily living skills it is important to recognise the difference between skills and tasks.

- Tasks are something that needs to be done.
- Skills are what you need in order to achieve a task.

If people have been used to achieving a task in one particular way for a number of years they often confuse the task with the skills. Perhaps the clearest example of this is shopping. If someone has always gone to the shops to buy their food they may confuse the shopping task with the way that they do this (ie the skills that they use such as handling money, lifting items into and out of the trolley, communicating with workers in shops, etc). If someone loses the skills to go to the shops, they may feel that they can no longer shop. However, shopping online is increasingly popular and although the person may have lost some of the skills they need to go to their local shop and buy food, they can still shop (perhaps by learning new skills to use the computer).

A further example is where somebody has always cooked their food using a gas cooker. If they develop dementia they might begin to leave the gas on and this can create significant risks. Family members might feel strongly that the person can no longer 'cook' for themselves, but perhaps they could use a microwave for cooking instead.

Essentially, it is important to separate the skills from the task, so that in helping people to either maintain or regain skills they can learn a different way of achieving the task. After all, it's not particularly important *how* we do something – just that we do it. There are always lots of different ways to do anything.

AGREEING A PLAN WITH AN INDIVIDUAL FOR DEVELOPING OR MAINTAINING THE SKILLS IDENTIFIED

Once you have identified the skills that someone needs and wants to work on, the next stage is to agree a plan with them to state how these skills will be developed or maintained. The plan may include:

- their hopes and their goals (short, medium and long term)

- the type and level of support needed to achieve these goals

- roles and responsibilities, including those of others such as the person's family, carers and friends

- any risks associated with learning the skill and specified ways to address these

- any aids, adaptations or technology that could support the plan and the person's independence

- timescales

- ways to monitor the plan.

Some activities and skills may need to be broken down into manageable 'chunks', and this may be especially relevant in involving some individuals in planning. For example, someone with a complex learning disability may want to learn cooking skills, and this may need to be broken down quite specifically. You would consider the types of meals the person would like to cook, and then you might look at the skills and level of support needed for each as follows:

Skill	Support
Shopping for ingredients	Family to do shopping list
	Worker to support the person to use the bus to go to the shop
	Person to communicate with the shop assistant and pay for the ingredients
	Worker to support with carrying the shopping
Chopping and preparing vegetables	Worker to model safe use of knives
	Support the individual to do the chopping using some guiding

Skill	Support
Frying the meat	Talk through the need for meat to be cooked properly Worker to let the individual do this and monitor safety closely
Using the oven	Worker to demonstrate and model this, and then let the person do this for themselves
Washing up and food hygiene	Talk this through together Worker to remind the individual of the importance of food hygiene Minimal support/reminders when washing up as the individual is used to doing this
Serving the meal	None needed

CONFLICTS THAT MAY ARISE WHEN PLANNING AND WAYS TO RESOLVE THEM

When you are making plans of any sort with individuals, conflicts can arise and your role may include seeking agreements and compromises when this does occur. Conflict could develop between:

- you and the individual
- you and the person's carers and family members
- the individual and other professionals
- you and your colleagues.

The most common area of conflict can be between individuals who want to develop skills and their family members or carers. This is not because carers do not want what is best for the person, but they may have several anxieties around the plan, including:

- fear that the person may hurt themselves
- wanting to protect them from not succeeding at a task or achieving a goal
- believing that they are not capable of something
- possibly, worries that greater independence may mean their relationship with the person changes.

Sensitivity around these issues and worries is of course important, but the key thing to bear in mind is that the plan belongs to the individual, and the hopes, goals and outcomes they are striving towards are their own. You may be involved in advocating for someone and expressing their wishes, or you may need to access an independent advocacy service for them, so that their voice can be heard in planning meetings.

It may be useful or necessary to bear in mind the issues around risk assessment when addressing any of these conflicts and this is covered in detail in Chapter 10. The idea of a positive culture around risk and the need for dignity in promoting people's right to make choices are critical considerations.

The person may also have some conflict internally around wanting to develop new skills and the potential fear associated with this. Where people have been de-skilled, or where they have not had the opportunity to develop certain skills in the first place, the impact of learned helplessness can be powerful. Your sensitivity in working through this will have an impact in terms of the outcome for the person, and in the resulting effect on their self-esteem. Change can be difficult for many of us, even where the change is likely to be positive, and change can be especially difficult for some individuals with autism.

Your own skills in managing conflict are important, and are likely to include:

- naming the issue and enabling each person to explain their position and work through their feelings
- looking at all of the possible options before making decisions
- seeking solutions and compromises
- maintaining your professionalism
- ensuring the individual's voice is heard and that their dignity is maintained
- recording agreements when they are reached.

SUPPORTING THE INDIVIDUAL TO UNDERSTAND THE PLAN

If a plan is to be effective it is vital that the individual understands the plan and any processes, procedures or equipment needed to implement or monitor it.

Plans only have their maximum impact when the individual concerned has:

- involvement
- understanding

- commitment
- the right level and type of support.

Your role will include ensuring that people have all of this in place, and that they are motivated and supported to achieve their own goals. Your own skills around engagement, communication and providing the right level of support will be critical in the success of the plan.

Attribution theory, drawn from psychology (see Weiner 2005), shows that:

- if people succeed in doing something, their self-esteem and confidence grow
- if they feel they have failed at something, then the reverse happens
- if they attribute their success to their own skill development and effort, then they are more likely to feel positive about approaching future tasks
- if they attribute success to some other factor (eg a worker's input or 'luck'), then there is less of a resulting positive impact.

How you praise, encourage and reinforce individuals in their achievements can therefore be important in what they take from an experience. Chapter 2 on communication outlines that some people prefer less praise than others, and 'over-encouraging' people can sometimes seem false. When a person attempts a new skill, focus on their efforts (even where they find something difficult or where they do not initially succeed at something), and their development of the skill itself.

People may need access to equipment, technology, aids or adaptations in order to learn a new skill, and a wide range of new tools is now available to support people's independence and communication. Where someone accesses a new piece of equipment (especially a technical aid), remember that:

- they are likely to need training in all aspects of how to use it
- the equipment may need safety checks and insurance
- they need to know what to do if the equipment breaks
- they may need ongoing training or support with its use (it is especially important to keep technological tools up to date and working).

REFLECT

- What is your experience of involving people in plans to maintain or develop their skills for everyday life?

- What has worked well for you around ensuring that people are involved in their own plans?

- How have these plans promoted people's independence?

- Is there anything that you have learned works less well or anything that you would not do again when involving people in this way?

CASE STUDY

Jon is a senior support worker with a reablement team. He works with service users on a short-term basis to try to maximise their independence. His input is intensive but limited to six weeks' duration. Many of the people he works with have recently been discharged from hospital. Jon works closely with the occupational therapists, physiotherapists and social workers on the team to develop individual reablement plans for service users.

Jon has been agreeing a plan with Sophie following her discharge from hospital. Sophie is in her early twenties and was involved in a serious car accident. She is keen to do all that she can for herself, to live as independently as she did before the accident, and is planning a return to work in the medium term.

However, Sophie's home needs adaptations in order to ensure she can access the property, the bath and the kitchen cupboards. Sophie is extremely frustrated that the funding for these adaptations has to go through a panel to be agreed and that there is no timescale in place for the changes to be made when she is discharged.

- How can Jon support Sophie's independence while she is waiting for the funding to be agreed and the adaptations to be made?

- Who else needs to be involved in discussions about Sophie's independence and day-to-day living in the meantime?

IMPLEMENTING THE PLAN TO SUPPORT INDIVIDUALS TO RETAIN, REGAIN OR DEVELOP SKILLS FOR EVERYDAY LIFE

In implementing the plan to support the individual, there are a number of areas to consider. We will go through the key areas, and then look at the first two, active participation and feedback, in more detail.

- *Active participation*. This refers to the extent to which an individual is involved in the plan for their own skills.

- *Feedback*. A person's need for the right amount of feedback and encouragement, and their preferences for how they receive feedback.

- *Empowerment*. Ensuring that an individual is not 'over-supported' and that they are enabled to develop their own skills for themselves.

- *The level of challenge*. Getting the balance right between the task being so difficult that someone may not achieve the outcome, and it being so easy that they can perform the task already without support.

- *Involving others*. Consistency of approach across a person's care team is crucial, as is the involvement in implementing the plan from significant others in the individual's life.

- *Recording*. While implementing the plan, it is important to consider how evidence of its impact will be monitored and recorded.

Promoting active participation

Active participation and its importance is covered in Chapter 11. Your work role will involve promoting this by:

- giving an individual the right amount of support to meet their needs (as identified in their plan)

- not doing things for someone that they can do themselves

- assisting the person to develop, maintain or regain the skills that they need and want to have

- ensuring consistency across the person's care team and network in how a skill is supported

- giving the person the right level and type of encouragement in their achievements (as outlined above)

- reducing the amount of support you and others provide as the individual learns a skill, feels confident in repeating this activity and gains independence.

Where you are supporting someone to maintain a skill, it is equally important not to 'over-support' them. Some people's needs may mean that they need your input on certain days, but not all of the time. Being vigilant and sensitive to this is part of maintaining people's independence and their self-esteem.

GIVING POSITIVE AND CONSTRUCTIVE FEEDBACK

Giving feedback to people is one of the most effective ways of enabling them to maintain and develop skills. Chapter 8 on personal development covers receiving feedback and the principles involved in giving feedback are similar. People's learning is only likely where feedback is given in a constructive way.

When giving feedback to individuals, it is useful to consider the following:

- *Be positive*. Focus on what the person has achieved and remember that most people only take feedback on board if they have heard positives first. Feedback is often thought of as a sandwich:

    - Say something positive.

    - Give constructive feedback.

    - End with a positive.

- *Consider your timing*. Sometimes you need to give feedback immediately in order for the other person to understand your meaning, and take ideas on board. However, sometimes, the right timing is critical and people need to be in the right frame of mind in order to hear any feedback (whether this is good or bad).

- *Employ your active communication skills*. Look at the person you are feeding back to, maintain an open body language and listen to their communication.

- *Focus on the individual*. Receiving feedback is not easy, especially if you feel that you are not achieving something as quickly or as well as you want to. The person is likely to be disappointed if this is the case, and to have put a lot of effort into the task, so sensitivity is critical.

- *Recognise the person's learning and development*. Remember that people are working to learn, maintain or regain skills, and that this takes time. Encouragement is vital if people are to keep motivated.

- *Be specific*. If you are giving the person constructive feedback, this needs to be specific, with ideas on how they can develop their skill further. For example, it is less useful to say to someone washing up 'You missed a bit', when you could say 'When you washed that plate, there was a bit of food on the back from the plate that was underneath it. It will help to make sure you do both sides each time you wash one'.

- *Check the person's understanding and reactions*. As always, it is useful to check that the person agrees and understands your ideas for their continued skill development. It is also important to make sure that your feedback is not upsetting to them, and that they are happy with the way you feed information back to them, as this both builds your relationship with the person and aids your own development. It is also helpful to check that they found what you said helpful and constructive, and not critical.

- *Write down the feedback*. Many people find a written record of feedback useful to reflect on afterwards.

In receiving feedback, people take either a negative (closed) style or a positive (open) style. The following table summarises this.

Negative/closed	Positive/open
Defensive: defends actions, objects to feedback	Open: listens without frequent interruption or objection
Attacking: turns the table on the person providing feedback	Responsive: willing to truly 'hear' what is being said
Denies: refutes the accuracy or fairness of the feedback	Accepting: accepts the feedback without denial
Disrespectful: devalues the person giving the feedback	Respectful: recognises the value of the feedback
Closed: ignores the feedback	Engaged: interacts appropriately seeking clarification where needed
Inactive listening: makes no attempt to understand the meaning of the feedback	Active listening: listens attentively and tries to understand the meaning of the feedback
Rationalising: finds explanations for the feedback that dissolve personal responsibility	Thoughtful: tries to understand the personal behaviour that has led to the feedback
Superficial: listens and agrees but does not act on the feedback	Sincere: genuinely wants to make changes and learn

WHAT IF AN INDIVIDUAL BECOMES DISTRESSED OR UNABLE TO CONTINUE?

If someone becomes distressed at any time, they will show this in their behaviour, their communication or their body language. As always, you need to remain sensitive to the person's needs and wishes, and this is especially important when the person is practising a new skill or trying a new experience.

If the individual is distressed or unable to continue, it is important to stop what you are doing (as the task could be hurting them or upsetting to them). It is often helpful to go into a different environment in order for people to feel calmer and for an immediate stressor to be removed, so that they can explore with you the right course of action to take.

Next, there are some key questions to consider:

- Can they tell you how they are or were feeling about the task?

- Is this the right time to be doing this task?

- Are they in pain?

- Is this the right task to have on the person's plan?

- Have they got the right level of support (eg lifting something could be extremely difficult, and you need to get the level of support right so the person feels safe in doing this task)?

- Do they need aids or adaptations in order for this task to be possible?

- Do they just need a break or are they finding the activity boring?

- If they need a break, when would be the right time to return to the activity and try again?

- Is the task too big for them and does it need breaking down further?

- Do you need to take advice from others before deciding what to do next?

Remember that finding something difficult is not about failure, but sometimes people may see struggling as a failure. Reassuring the person, agreeing a plan for what to do next, adjusting the support, or changing the goal are all useful to consider, so that the person's self-esteem is not affected by the experience and so that their goals can still be achieved.

REFLECT

- How do you ensure that the feedback you give to individuals is constructive?

- Have you ever had an experience where someone has reacted badly to feedback you have given, or where they became distressed and unable to continue with a day-to-day living task?

- What did you do in this situation?

- What worked well and what would you do differently in the future?

OPTIMUM CHALLENGING

In learning something new or regaining a skill we previously had, it is important to consider how challenging this is for a person. If the person is faced with something that is too easy for them, they may feel patronised and become demotivated. However, if they are faced with something that is beyond their current ability, then they may become frustrated and demotivated.

In order to maintain people's motivation to learn, they should be given something that stretches their ability but is achievable. As they achieve the challenge, then a further step can be introduced to maintain their motivation. This is referred to as optimum challenging. It can be difficult to maintain the balance between something that is too easy and something that is beyond their current ability – which is why a good-quality assessment and ongoing monitoring are vital.

MESSAGES FROM RESEARCH

The outcomes of supporting people to regain skills

Various research studies indicate that reablement that focuses on supporting people to regain skills has very positive outcomes:

- People using reablement welcome the emphasis on helping them gain independence and better functioning.

- Reablement approaches improve outcomes, particularly in terms of restoring people's ability to perform usual activities and improving their perceived quality of life. From a social care perspective, there is a high probability that reablement is cost-effective.

- Reablement achieves cost savings through reducing or removing the need for ongoing support via traditional home care. There is some limited evidence that it also reduces health care costs.

- Managers and care workers are generally positive about reablement, valuing its flexibility and the more responsive way of working with people.

- Complaints about reablement mainly relate to handover (to a traditional home care provider) and a lack of help with domestic tasks.

- Requirements for training, closer supervision of care workers and longer, more responsive and flexible visits all contribute to the greater costs of reablement compared with conventional home care. However, the higher price of reablement is likely to be offset by longer-term savings from reduced social care-related needs.

(Francis, Fisher and Rutter 2011; Glendinning et al 2011)

CASE STUDY

Isabella is a senior care assistant in a respite care service that provides short-term stays for younger people with learning and physical disabilities.

Isabella is working with Shanice, who is a new member of staff in the service. Isabella has observed Shanice's work with Simon, who has attended the service for several years. Part of Simon's care plan is for him to be supported with his day-to-day living skills, such as shopping, washing his clothes and tidying his room.

On a couple of occasions Isabella observes that when Shanice is trying to keep Simon on task, she can get quite tense when he does not follow the plan. This in turn has a negative effect on Simon, who then refuses to continue participating. Shanice asks Isabella for ideas and support as she says she is finding Simon's behaviours quite challenging to manage.

■ How can Isabella support Shanice to give Simon constructive and engaging feedback which keeps him motivated to participate in the tasks?

THE LADDER OF LEARNING

This is a theory drawn from psychology and used widely in understanding people's motivation to learn (Cameron and Green 2012). The idea is that we all go through four phases when we try to develop a skill.

1 Unconscious incompetence

When asked to undertake a new skill, we don't know what we don't know. It could be said that we're incompetent but that we are unconscious of this. In a way, this is quite a comfortable stage – it could be seen as 'blissful ignorance'. We don't know that we can't do something. However, as we attempt to undertake the new task, we quickly realise that there is a lot more involved than we think and we move on to:

2 Conscious incompetence

Now we become aware of what we can't do, we realise that we can't perform the skill. This is a very uncomfortable and potentially painful stage. Many people are socialised to believe 'there's no such word as can't' and becoming conscious of our 'incompetence' is distressing.

At this phase, some people decide to concede defeat – to give up on the task. People can develop quite sophisticated defence mechanisms to ensure that people around them aren't aware of their

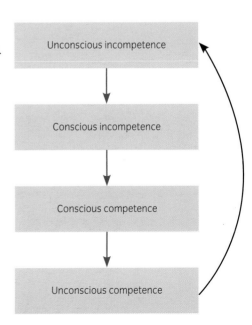

'incompetence'. Think of the highly developed systems that some adults with literacy difficulties have developed.

Others seek out support and new and useful experiences in order to get through this stage, learn the task and move on to the next stage.

3 Conscious competence

When we have recently learned a new skill we are very aware, or conscious, about it. Think about a new driver who is saying 'mirror, signal, manoeuvre' every time they go out in a car. While we may be anxious to ensure that we get things right, this is probably the most comfortable and safe stage in which to be. We are aware of what we are doing, so we are likely to continue to question ourselves and are probably getting it right! The danger is that we will probably, at some point, move on to the next stage.

4 Unconscious competence

This is where we have become so familiar with the task and confident about our abilities that we almost go into an autopilot mode. The potentially dangerous aspect of this is that when we are unconscious about something, how do we know that we are still doing it right? Think how many of us (if we are honest) wouldn't pass our driving test today if we had an examiner sitting in the car on one of our usual journeys. When we are unconscious about something, we slip into bad habits, we take shortcuts – maybe we have actually slipped back to the first phase (unconscious incompetence). If we are unconscious, how do we know? Obtaining feedback from others and continually reviewing how we do things can help us move from unconscious competence back to conscious competence (that is we stay alert to what we are doing).

Understanding the ladder of learning is really useful in supporting service users to maintain skills they have, to regain skills they used to have and to develop new skills.

MAINTAINING SKILLS

To help people to maintain the skills they have, it is important to recognise that they will maintain their skills most effectively if they can be maintained in the stage of conscious competent. This means that they need to have the opportunity to keep using the skills and to maintain their awareness of the different aspects of their skills.

REGAINING SKILLS

If someone used to have a skill and they have lost it for some reason, they will be very conscious of their 'incompetence'. At the conscious incompetence phase, people can easily slip into allowing others to do the task for them because they feel so 'useless'. They may also become angry because they are frustrated at their inability. They may not recognise that they can do the task again by using different skills, ie they can achieve the same outcome in a different way. People will need specifically tailored support to see them through the phase of 'conscious incompetence.'

DEVELOPING NEW SKILLS

Where people are learning a skill for the first time, they will start at the first stage – unconscious incompetence – which means that they are unaware of what skills they might need in order to achieve a task. They may therefore be overwhelmed when they are beginning to learn the task and may feel that they are never going to be able to do it. Regular praise and encouragement will help people move to the next stage, as will techniques such as breaking down a task into smaller parts and enabling the person to learn one task at a time.

REFLECT

Think of a time when you couldn't do something (it doesn't matter what the 'thing' is).

- How did you feel?

- Did you continue to try to learn the task or did you give up?

- How might you be able to relate your experiences to the ladder of learning?

REVIEWING AND EVALUATING SUPPORT FOR DEVELOPING OR MAINTAINING SKILLS FOR EVERYDAY LIFE

You will find the information on pages 324–331 particularly useful when considering how you review plans and evaluate the effectiveness of the support provided for maintaining and developing skills.

AGREEING CRITERIA AND PROCESSES FOR EVALUATING SUPPORT

In the context of people learning new skills, or working to maintain or regain skills, it is useful to consider the following:

- How is the individual kept at the centre of all evaluation? It is their plan and their skills being worked on, so start from their experience and viewpoint, and use others to enable you to understand and appreciate this if they cannot tell you verbally how they felt about the support provided.

- Who else needs to be involved in the evaluation of support?

- What creative and motivational methods can you use or develop to get a helpful and detailed evaluation? Are there tools available in your service setting, or can you obtain evaluations in a more creative way than via a tick-box feedback form?

- How do you enable the person to give feedback on the plan in their own words?

- What formal mechanisms need to be considered, planned for and utilised in order for support to be properly evaluated, and for changes to plans to be agreed?

In terms of the criteria for evaluating if support has been effective in helping somebody to redevelop or maintain their skills, consider:

- Are there observable changes in their skill level?

- How are changes and improvements recorded?

- How involved does the person feel in the plan, and in their involvement and participation in the development of their skills?

- Has the person learned something that has helped them work towards achieving a goal or outcome they hoped for?

- Has an outcome been achieved by a skill being learned?

REVISING THE PLAN

Evaluating if a plan is effective is only useful if this information is then used to make changes and revisions to that plan. Most plans work to an extent, but monitoring, evaluating and reviewing plans usually leads to evidence showing that:

- some aspects are working or have worked (if the person has achieved a certain outcome, then it is useful to consider what their next goal is, and what skills they would like to develop next to achieve this)

- some aspects are working less well and the plan needs to be adjusted to improve its impact (eg providing more support with a certain skill)

- some aspects are not working at all and either the level or type of support or the plan itself needs to change.

Revisions to a plan should be done in partnership with the individual, and any others who are involved in implementing the plan, as discussed above.

People's needs, circumstances and wishes are subject to continual change and evolution, so we should expect plans to change in light of these. Also, good plans have an impact, so this means that the plan itself should evolve as the person ideally achieves their goals and outcomes. If a plan does not 'work' first time though, that just means that other ideas need to be trialled – it does not mean that the person's goals are not achievable.

Revisions should also be recorded in line with agreed paperwork and procedures, so that everyone is clear about what's involved in the person's current plan.

REFLECT

What criteria and processes do you use in your own work role to evaluate the support that both you and your service provide to individuals around their skills for everyday life?

MESSAGES FROM RESEARCH

What skills do staff need?

Research around supporting people to regain and develop skills indicates that staff require particular skills, as follows:

- Active assessment is vital to supporting people to learn or relearn the skills necessary for daily living, so health and social care staff need skills in assessment which fully involve the individual.

- The delivery of reablement depends on suitably trained care workers. Care workers require specific training in reablement. Ongoing refresher training or shadowing of experienced workers is vital to sustain this approach.

- Occupational therapy skills are central to reablement. These can be accessed by training reablement staff rather than having an occupational therapist as a team member.

(Francis, Fisher and Rutter 2011; Glendinning et al 2011)

CASE STUDY

Jane is a senior support worker in a day service for people with learning disabilities. Many of the service users she works with have profound learning disabilities along with physical disabilities. Jane is responsible for organising day service activities and she supervises a small group of day service assistants.

Jane has been evaluating the level of support with personal care that staff in the service provide for service users. Jane's impression is that staff can sometimes 'over-support' people and do things for them that many individuals could do for themselves, or where less support could be more enabling.

Jane conducts some planned observations around mealtimes and how people are supported in clothing themselves for outdoor activities. Jane is surprised that she identifies that across the team there are some quite different working practices, and some of the more experienced workers are the ones who she feels are 'over-supporting' individuals. Jane considers various options for working on this, including picking this up in individual staff supervisions, putting the issue on the agenda for a team meeting and booking a team day around active participation.

- Which of these options would you favour and why?

- How would you rather be challenged by Jane if you were one of the experienced members of staff who Jane feels is 'over-supporting' individuals in the service?

CHAPTER 14
Supporting individuals with specific communication needs

Communication is a vital part of a health and social care worker's role. If you are working on this unit as part of your qualification, you will be working with people who have specific and perhaps complex communication needs. If you haven't recently read Chapter 2 on communication, then take another look at it to remind yourself about the basics of communication. This chapter goes into more detail about interacting with individuals who have specific communication needs. The process of getting to know the specific needs, and suitable aids and adaptations for individuals is covered, as is enabling individuals to communicate with people other than yourself.

Links to other chapters

This chapter builds on the content of chapter 2. It also has links with chapters 8 and 10.

Environmental issue	Consider
Atmosphere	Sometimes environments can feel very formal, which can inhibit informal relaxed communication
	Everyone will recognise that sometimes there is an atmosphere in a room that can affect communication (think about the saying 'you could cut the atmosphere with a knife in here!')
	Uncomfortable atmospheres can make people reluctant or even fearful to communicate

USING COMMUNICATION THAT IS NOT BASED ON A FORMAL LANGUAGE SYSTEM

Most people will have experiences of using communication that isn't based on formal language, eg have you ever been on holiday to a country where people spoke a language other than your own? You probably used gestures and facial expressions much more than you do at home. Many people have had an experience of being in a crowded bar or club where you can hardly hear each other – and again you probably found yourself using gestures to communicate.

Where people do not have a formal language system they might use many different forms of communication – just as you might do on holiday or in a crowded bar. Individuals may have communication preferences and abilities in:

- gesture
- facial expression
- behaviour
- vocalising sounds
- pointing (eg with hands or eyes)
- typing words
- music.

People may communicate in these ways because of:

- a learning disability
- a sensory loss
- physical disability (eg their body affecting their ability to use speech or gestures)
- mental health needs (eg communication needs which are caused by specific types of mental health disorder)

- dementia
- any combination of the above.

People's communication needs and specific requirements may also be influenced by whether they have had specific communication needs since birth, or whether a condition has developed during their adult life.

The area of health and social care in which you work will also determine your prior knowledge about why individuals in your own work setting have specific communication needs.

REFLECT

Have you ever been unable to communicate through speech, eg maybe you were on holiday in a country where you couldn't speak the language or perhaps you lost your voice?

- How did this make you feel?
- How did you communicate?

COMMUNICATION METHODS AND AIDS

There are a variety of methods and aids that can support individuals to communicate. Your assessment and understanding of the individual is considered later in this chapter, and is critical to ensuring that the right methods and aids are put in place for the person. You will not be doing this in isolation as a worker, but are likely to work with colleagues and other professionals, including social workers and speech and language therapists, to ensure that the whole range of available tools are considered. Methods could include:

- planned and focused use of regular words to develop specific language skills via routines

- any form of **augmentative and alternative communication** (AAC), eg visual cues such as photographs, symbols, charts and signs

- specific models for AAC, eg Picture Exchange Communication Systems (PECS), Treatment and Education of Autistic and related Communication-Handicapped Children (TEACCH), Widgit, Symbol World, Talking Mats (the most up-to-date information on these and others can be found online)

- touch

- Braille

- use of the deafblind manual alphabet

- sign language.

Key term

Augmentative and alternative communication (AAC) is used to describe a range of techniques that health and social care workers and other professionals use in order to aid communication and support people to understand. AAC can be pictorial (eg using photographs and symbols to mark out what will be happening and in what order), or it can be where sign and gesture are used in order to communicate certain words or ideas.

Aids could include:

- technological solutions

- hearing assistance aids

- human aids (eg translators or advocates)

- written aids (eg pen and paper, laptop, etc)

- music.

THE POTENTIAL EFFECTS ON AN INDIVIDUAL OF HAVING UNMET COMMUNICATION NEEDS

Think about your own experience and a time where you have felt unable to communicate, or when you felt that the other person was not listening or taking your point of view on board. Consider how this felt, and apply these feelings to the people with whom you work. Individuals needing support are no different from anyone else and experience all of the same emotions.

However, people are also likely to experience additional feelings and difficulties if they are unable to express those emotions verbally, such as:

- increased frustration

- feelings of powerlessness

- helplessness

- anger

- disappointment.

These feelings can be demonstrated via:

- behaviours that show this frustration (eg pacing, shouting, aggression)

- disengagement from services

- loss of trust in specific workers or in staff members generally

- becoming more withdrawn or other changes in behaviour

- depression.

Also, if people's communication needs are and remain unmet, it is far more likely that their care or support plan will not be centred around their specific needs and wishes. This then means that the plan is less likely to meet those needs, and it is less likely for the person to achieve the outcomes that they and others hope for. It is also important to note that if we do not ensure people can communicate their needs, we are potentially colluding in abuse of that person as we are denying them one of their fundamental human rights.

REFLECT

Consider an individual whom you have worked with where you observed that their communication needs were unmet (either by other services, colleagues or by yourself).

- How did this person display their feelings about being unable to communicate?

- How did you or others address the communication issue, change practices and promote the individual's rights?

CASE STUDY

Jane is a senior support worker in a day service for people with learning disabilities. Many of the service users she works with have profound learning disabilities along with physical disabilities. Jane is responsible for organising day service activities and she supervises a small group of day service assistants.

Over recent weeks, Jane has observed that Bartek, who accesses the service, has been increasingly withdrawn. Bartek started attending two months ago, and he presented initially as bright, happy and engaging, but he has become a lot quieter and has been spending long periods of time sitting on his own.

Jane asks for a meeting with Sue, Bartek's key worker. Sue says that she has been worried about Bartek too, and she has been monitoring the situation for his review meeting. Sue feels that Bartek is unhappy because he has more specific communication needs than the service had been made aware of before he started attending. She feels that too much verbal communication confuses Bartek and he does not respond to the PECS system which is part of the service.

- What can Sue and Jane do to promote Bartek's rights?

- How can they take these issues forwards?

- Who else will need to be involved in the discussion and review of Bartek's communication needs?

UNDERSTANDING BEHAVIOUR AS A METHOD OF COMMUNICATION

The most straightforward way of understanding any behaviour is, as has been said many times, to recognise the behaviour as a form of communication. While the question, 'What is this person communicating?' sounds very straightforward, it is very often missed. One of the major problems when a person has reached the stage of exhibiting behaviours that are challenging to services is how to find out what is being communicated. Sometimes finding the answer to the very straightforward question is extremely complicated and staff might almost feel like a detective with few clues to go on.

Whenever a health and social care worker encounters a behaviour that is challenging, they need to ask themselves (and colleagues) questions that will help 'detect' what the person is communicating. The following questions, though by no means exhaustive, may be a good starting point.

WHAT IS THE PERSON COMMUNICATING?

Health-related reasons

- Is s/he in pain, eg dental pain?
- Has the person suffered an injury that hasn't yet been noticed, eg a sprained ankle?
- Is the person suffering from stomach problems?
- Does she have premenstrual syndrome (PMS)?
- Is the person tired due to disturbed sleep?
- Is s/he constipated?
- Does the person have sensory impairments, eg a hearing impairment, tinnitus, a visual impairment?

Situational reasons

- Is the person being asked to do something they don't like?
- Is s/he being overloaded with information/demands?
- Is s/he bored?
- Is the person uncomfortable in some way, eg are they hot or cold? Is their clothing uncomfortable?
- Have there been changes that the person had little control over and/or little notice about?

- Has the person had to stop doing something they liked doing?

- Does the person engage in the behaviour with certain staff or when certain service users are around?

- Are there any triggers, eg when staff arrive to start work, loud noises, etc?

- Do staff attend to the person as a result of the behaviour?

- Do staff leave the person alone as a result of the behaviour?

- Is the person given confusing and conflicting information by staff and/or carers?

- Are they angry? If so, why are they angry?

General reasons

- Does the person need something?

- Is the person feeling insecure?

- Are there new staff around? How can the person be sure they can trust staff?

- Can the person communicate their needs in other ways?

- Could the person have been abused in the past?

- Is the person with others who display behaviours that challenge services and so:

  - models their behaviour

  - feels that to be noticed s/he needs to do something significant, etc?

- Has the behaviour been established over many years? Any positive changes may be gradual. Can staff perceive these improvements and acknowledge them to the person themselves?

- Does the person have a sense of control over their life only when they engage in the behaviour, in that it prevents staff action/plans?

The extent of this list of questions demonstrates how difficult it can be to detect what a person is trying to communicate through their behaviour. However, the main starting point is to recognise the behaviour as a method of communication and then start to try to identify exactly what the behaviour is communicating. Poor practice involves simply labelling the behaviour as 'challenging behaviour' and not attempting to determine what the behaviour is communicating.

APPLICATION OF SKILLS

Person-centred communication charts

One of the person-centred thinking tools that is used most widely across all areas of social care is communication charts. These recognise the fact that communication is a form of behaviour, recording communication in the following (or a similar) way:

What is happening? Where? When?	When Rose does this …	We think it means …	And we should …
Anytime	Scratches at her legs	Rose wants to use the toilet	Ask Rose discreetly if she wants to use the toilet, then assist her to the bathroom
In the mornings and less often at other times	Hits at her face	Rose is thirsty	Offer Rose a drink

ESTABLISHING THE NATURE OF SPECIFIC COMMUNICATION NEEDS AND WAYS TO MEET THEM

Chapter 9 on facilitating person-centred assessment covers the basic social care process that involves assessing needs, planning ways to meet the identified needs, implementing the plan and then reviewing whether the plan has worked. Addressing people's communication needs is no different – you must start with an assessment and ensure that the individual's communication needs are met in all aspects of their care.

IDENTIFYING THE INDIVIDUAL'S SPECIFIC COMMUNICATION NEEDS

This is basically about carrying out an assessment of the person's communication needs. As in all assessments, you must work to keep things person centred and work in partnership with the service user and others who are important.

Working with the individual

This can be achieved by:

■ *Observation*. Consider observing the person on different days, at different times of the day, in different environments and activities, and with different people (including family members, colleagues, friends and other professionals). Observation should be done in partnership with the individual, and they should know when and why you are observing them. Observations should be recorded in order for evidence-based conclusions to be drawn.

■ *Spending time with the person*. This sounds obvious, but you cannot draw any conclusions about a person's needs unless you know them well yourself. You can only get to know someone, and build a relationship and trust with them, through spending time with them, doing things together, and learning yourself about their communication and other preferences.

■ *Reading assessments and reports* from other professionals which the person shares with you.

Working with others

Others could include:

■ colleagues

■ other professionals who know the person (eg social workers, speech therapists, a GP, etc)

■ advocates

■ family members

■ friends.

All of these people will know about the person and how they communicate. They may have different perspectives, experiences of the person and opinions. Relatives and carers may sometimes be very protective of the person and may argue passionately for a particular viewpoint. It can be difficult to counter this sometimes if your own professional opinion (based on your own observations, experience and knowledge of the person) differs from theirs.

KEY POINT

It is important to take people's viewpoints into account, but to base your own judgement on your own knowledge of the person, your observations and your professional expertise.

Using the 'assessment triangle'

When you are assessing any particular needs it is important to use the triangle approach. This means getting information from:

■ what you see (your own observations)

■ other people (feedback from others)

■ reports and records about the person.

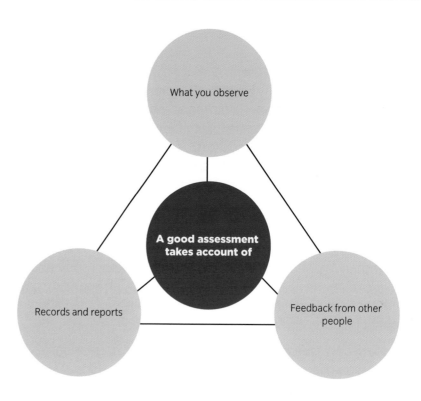

What you observe

A good assessment takes account of

Records and reports

Feedback from other people

UNDERSTANDING SOME SPECIFIC COMMUNICATION NEEDS

APHASIA (ALSO KNOWN AS DYSPHASIA)

In the UK, a stroke, or cerebrovascular accident (CVA), is the most common cause of **aphasia**. A significant number of people with learning disabilities also have some level of aphasia.

A distinction is made between receptive aphasia, which indicates the inability to understand the language of others, and expressive aphasia, which indicates a difficulty in saying what you wish to say. In expressive aphasia someone may have no speech or may mix words up, make errors and confuse words, eg saying 'yes' when they mean 'no', although they can usually understand others. People with aphasia often lose the ability (if they had it) to read and write.

How aphasia affects someone needs individual assessment. Expert assessment and advice from a speech and language therapist should always be sought. Depending on the cause, treatment may be possible.

The impact of aphasia on individuals is significant and can lead to extreme frustration for the person and their carers. The speech and language therapist will be able to advise on ways to manage and minimise the impact of communication difficulties and help reduce the understandable frustrations even if treatment itself is not possible or appropriate.

ECHOLALIA

Echolalia is commonly associated with people who have autism and it is thought that up to 75% of people with autism have echolalia (Prizant 1983). For many years it was regarded as a distinct feature of autism. Many professionals and writers now point out that echolalia is a normal way for people to learn language – in children who do not have autism it peaks at around 30 months of age.

There are two types of echolalia: *immediate*, which refers to the repetition of language just spoken by others, and *delayed*. An example of immediate echolalia is when a person with autism answers a question by repeating the question. An example of delayed echolalia is the repetition of a TV advert over and over again.

There is some debate around the function and treatment of echolalia in people with autism. There are arguments that it indicates the ability to learn language and the person with autism has become 'stuck' at a normal phase of learning. Others have used echolalia to teach people with autism the names of objects. However, for many people with autism it can get in the way of social interaction and lead to frustration for them and their carers. It is certainly recognised that people with autism are more likely to exhibit echolalia when they feel unsure or uncertain about what to say. Therefore most professionals focus on teaching ways to manage it. Professional advice from a speech and language therapist is needed to assess a person's echolalia and to advise on its management.

> **Key term** 🔑
>
> **Echolalia** refers to repetitive speech, specifically the 'echoing' of another person's speech.

PERSONAL COMMUNICATION PASSPORTS

Developed in the 1990s by Sally Millar, a specialist speech and language therapist at the Communication Aids for Language and Learning (CALL) Centre, personal communication passports are a person-centred and practical way of supporting people who cannot easily speak for themselves. Passports aim to:

- present someone positively as an individual, not as a set of 'problems' or disabilities
- provide a place for their own views and preferences to be recorded and drawn to the attention of others
- describe their most effective means of communication
- draw together information from past and present, and from different contexts, to help staff and conversation partners understand them and have successful interactions
- reflect a 'flavour' of their unique character.

Some organisations have developed and adapted this approach and refer to the system as individual communication profiles or something similar.

IDENTIFYING THE COMMUNICATION METHODS OR AIDS THAT WILL BEST SUIT THE INDIVIDUAL

When an assessment has taken place, the next step is planning ways to meet the needs. Therefore, when a person's communication needs are clear, the next step is to identify what methods can be used to support them to communicate.

Health and social care workers will contribute to multidisciplinary discussions and decisions about what communication methods or aids are most suitable. The key things to consider when contributing to these discussions are:

- basing decisions on observation, knowledge and a range of perspectives looking at someone's needs in their entirety

- basing decisions on the wishes and feelings of the person as far as you and others have been able to ascertain these

- recording what has been considered and why a certain course of action is chosen

- ensuring that somebody has the right level of training and support from you and from others in using whatever method or aid is chosen (this is especially important at first, but can be necessary on an ongoing basis too)

- monitoring and reviewing their access to whatever method or aid is chosen and putting in more support as is needed or changing the plan if it is not working.

AAC: GETTING INTO THE DETAIL

An awareness of augmentative and alternative communication (AAC) is very important. AAC supplements or replaces speech using both unaided and aided methods of communication. Unaided methods involve the service users' own body, eg signing, body movements, vocalisations, eye pointing, etc. Aided communicaton uses additional resources and equipment, eg symbols, objects, voice output communication aids (VOCAs) and other gadgets. AAC can be further divided into four sections:

- *Communication medium*: how the meaning is transmitted, either aided or unaided as described above.

- *Means of access to the communication medium*: eg body movements, joystick, keyboard, switches, etc.

- *A system for representing meanings*: sign languages and use of symbols. These are many and various and some are specifically developed for people with learning disabilities.

- *Strategies for interacting*: initiating conversation, maintaining it by taking turns, using questions, etc – many of the things we maybe take for granted.

The Royal College of Speech and Language Therapists states that augmentative and alternative communication is typically used by some people with cerebral palsy, autism, learning disabilities and developmental apraxia of speech. AAC is very specialised and there is much to learn about it, so always seek specialist advice if a service user uses a communication system with which you are unfamiliar.

BRAILLE

Braille is a system widely used by blind people to read and write. It was devised in 1821 by Louis Braille. Each Braille character is made up of six dot positions arranged in a triangle. A dot can be raised at any of the six positions.

BRITISH SIGN LANGUAGE

British Sign Language (BSL) is the most common form of sign language in the UK. It has its own structure and is a unique language – it is not particularly related to spoken English. BSL is the preferred language of between 50,000 and 70,000 people in the UK.

There is significant regional variation in British Sign Language – similar in a way to the difference in regional accents in spoken language. BSL was recognised by the British government as an official minority language in 2003.

MAKATON

Makaton was devised by Margaret Walker, a speech and language therapist, in the 1970s. It is a language system based on British Sign Language where key words are signed in word order alongside speech. This means that information is given in a very visual way. Makaton has been shown to be not only an effective form of signed communication, but also an effective method in encouraging the development of speech. Makaton is predominantly used with people with learning disabilities.

ACCESSING INFORMATION AND SUPPORT ABOUT SPECIFIC COMMUNICATION NEEDS

There is a range of information and support available for both identifying and addressing people's specific communication needs.

Knowing how to access the support you need is usually more important than trying to know everything yourself all the time. People also find it annoying when professionals pretend they are an expert on something they do not fully understand, and it is fine to say to people that you do not know something, but that you will find out and come back to them with the right information.

It is vital that you know the limitations of your own expertise and that you feel confident in asking for the input you need when you need it. Accessing support when you need it is a strength and not a failure, and it shows both your commitment to your own professional development and creates a role model for those you work with who may find it difficult to ask for help. All the people we work with have different needs and we should also expect those we support to challenge us and teach us new things – this is one of the most important and rewarding aspects of the work we do.

Support can be available from:

- colleagues

- other professionals, eg speech therapists, occupational therapists, psychologists

- people's records (assuming you have informed consent to be able to access these)

- carers, relatives and friends

- the internet

- books, journals and magazines

- specific organisations (eg Scope or Mencap. You may find Mencap's learning disability helpline invaluable for some issues).

SPEECH AND LANGUAGE THERAPISTS

Speech and language therapists, previously referred to as communication therapists, work with people who have problems with communication or with chewing and swallowing. Speech and language therapists can work with people on a one-to-one basis or in group sessions.

OCCUPATIONAL THERAPISTS (OT)

The role of the OT focuses on supporting people to maintain, develop and regain their fine motor skills. Some assistive technology requires people to have good fine motor skills (eg computers, laptops and tablets).

PSYCHOLOGISTS

A psychologist could be involved in assessing and treating a person's mental health needs (eg depression or anxiety). Psychologists use specific models, such as cognitive behavioural therapy (CBT), and working on people's thinking, understanding and behaviour in these ways can support them to communicate their needs more effectively.

PSYCHIATRISTS

A psychiatrist is a doctor specialising in mental health, who could be involved in assessing and treating a specific health need, such as dementia, depression or schizophrenia.

BEHAVIOUR SUPPORT STAFF

All behaviour is about communication – this applies whether someone's behaviour is positive (in communicating their wishes in a socially acceptable way) or negative. Behaviour support teams may be involved in assisting understanding of what someone is trying to communicate through their behaviour or in supporting individuals to develop other means to express themselves.

REFLECT

Consider an occasion where someone you worked with challenged your assumptions or beliefs about their communication needs and wishes.

- How did this challenge take place?

- How did you adapt your work or enable their plan to change from this?

- How did what you learned from this person inform future actions in your work with them and others?

MESSAGES FROM RESEARCH

Communication equipment

Scope conducted some research into people's access to and experience of AAC. This research is part of a campaign, 'No Voice, No Choice', to ensure that anyone who needs AAC has access to what they need. Scope's findings were as follows:

- 1.5 million people in the UK have specific communication needs.

- 600,000 people might benefit from access to AAC.

- Only 60% of communication aids come with any form of guarantee or warranty, and 43% of these guarantees are only valid for one year.

- Most respondents reported issues around the size, design or access to their communication equipment.

- 73% of people had an aid that had broken, and most of them had difficulties or delays in getting this aid replaced.

- Only 19% of respondents had any training in how to use their communication aid, and 44% of the people's carers had not had any training or support.

(Scope 2009)

CASE STUDY

Chen is a senior care assistant in a residential service for older people. Many of the residents of the home have dementia.

Chen has been doing some research into communication and he believes that many of the residents in the service would benefit if the staff team were trained in AAC techniques. There is some resistance in the staff team towards using signs, touch and symbols to support communication as they feel that this could be perceived as patronising by service users and their family members. One worker says that although they would like the training, they feel that, 'People have communicated verbally all their lives, so why would we need to start signing at them instead now?'

- How could Chen challenge some of the workers' perceptions and develop their understanding around AAC?

- How could Chen demonstrate that using appropriate levels and types of AAC could improve outcomes for residents?

INTERACTING WITH INDIVIDUALS USING THEIR PREFERRED COMMUNICATION

Good practice in communicating with people with specific needs involves:

- preparing the environment to ensure that it promotes effective communication
- using methods of communication that the individual prefers
- monitoring people's responses
- adapting and improving your practice.

PREPARING THE ENVIRONMENT TO FACILITATE COMMUNICATION

Preparing the environment in order to facilitate communication is essential. If the environment is not right, people may struggle to engage, to hear or to understand the messages you are trying to give them. Equally importantly, you may misunderstand or not be able to hear what they try to communicate to you.

The environment in which you work should be prepared to feel welcoming and to enable communication to take account of individual needs.

PLANNING AND MANAGING THE ENVIRONMENT IN ORDER TO FACILITATE COMMUNICATION

Issue	Think about
Access and equality	Can the person access the room and does the room feel comfortable for them?
	Are there any obvious obstacles or barriers to physical access that you need to address before any communication can take place?
	Does the room or building comply with the Disability Discrimination Act (DDA) guidelines?
Temperature	Is the room is too hot or too cold? We all find it hard to concentrate if we feel either extreme, and being too warm can make some people feel tired and/or irritable.

Issue	Think about
Seating	Seating can have a huge impact on communication, eg if two people are talking and one person is sitting on a chair which is much higher than the other this will give the impression of one person looking down on another. If there are lots of seats they can be positioned in a way that encourages communication between people. The comfort and suitability of chairs are also essential to consider for some individuals with specific physical needs in order for an environment to be accessible for them in the first place.
Interruptions	Ensure that you won't be interrupted if at all possible. This might just be about closing the door or indicating that the room is in use. Mobile phones can be especially irritating and insensitive in some situations.
Power imbalance	Some environments enable people to communicate more freely than others. This can be in relation to a range of issues, such as the layout of the room. Could this be changed to enable better communication?
Imagery	What do people see when they walk into the room? What images are on the walls? Is there a window and, if so, what is the view out of it? The presence or absence of positive images can also be a factor in how people communicate and interact.
Noise	If the room is very noisy, can this be changed? Sometimes it is about something as simple as closing a window if there is a lot of noise outside. Some people also find a room that is too quiet difficult as they enjoy background noise and find music or listening to a radio station can help them to concentrate and engage. For other people, even low levels of background noise can be highly distracting.
Safety	Does the other person feel safe and secure in this environment? This could relate to a range of issues, such as what is the room usually used for, how the person accesses the room and how they feel about being in that place.

Issue	Think about
Lighting	Think about the lighting in the environment. This might involve considering issues such as whether the room is sufficiently lit so that people can see you. This can be especially important when someone uses and needs a greater level of non-verbal communication.

On the other hand, if you want to communicate with someone about something that is personal and perhaps distressing, maybe you don't want the room to be too strongly lit (eg with bright strip lighting), as this can feel 'clinical'.

As with everything, the lighting that will be appropriate for the circumstance and the individual will vary, but the main thing is that you put thought into this. |
| Level of formality | How relaxed and enabling does the environment feel? This could be linked to what the room is usually used for, the imagery, temperature, lighting, etc. This could also be necessary to consider in terms of:

- the layout of the room

- the presence or absence of a desk or table

- the type of seating

- your own positioning in relation to the person with whom you are communicating. |

USING AGREED METHODS OF COMMUNICATION TO INTERACT WITH THE INDIVIDUAL

Once a communication plan has been agreed and an agreed method or aid put into place, it is important that this is introduced to the individual in the right way and used consistently by everyone who needs to support them with this.

There is no point going through all of the processes outlined in this chapter unless the agreed methods are used consistently and appropriately. You should be prepared to do this, to monitor the person's responses, to seek further training if you need it, and to input into formal reviews of the plan.

MONITORING THE INDIVIDUAL'S RESPONSES DURING AND AFTER THE INTERACTION TO CHECK THE EFFECTIVENESS OF COMMUNICATION

Monitoring people's responses to any plan is important, but especially so when communication methods or aids are being introduced and utilised. It is therefore vital that you monitor the individual's responses during and after any interaction to check the effectiveness of the communication.

Initially, people may need time to get used to a means of communication or an aid, and it is important not to give up straight away if understanding is not reached. However, it is equally important not to be afraid to change and develop the plan if it is clear that improvements need to be made in order for better communication to be achieved.

People may respond to a new type of communication in many different ways:

- positively (eg smiling, laughing, showing they understand the message given, giving you feedback, etc)

- with frustration or annoyance

- with confusion (watch for non-verbal signals that they do not understand)

- by finding something difficult at first and needing more support (eg in using the functions or switches on a technological device)

- by withdrawing from an activity altogether or disengaging (this can mean more support is needed or it could be the wrong time to try this method with the individual).

ADAPTING YOUR OWN PRACTICE TO IMPROVE COMMUNICATION WITH INDIVIDUALS

By monitoring people's responses to our own communication, and our application of agreed methods and aids, we can see and implement ideas for development of our own communication practice. This is an ongoing activity in terms of professional development, especially as learning takes place with every individual you work with, and because people's needs and communication change and develop constantly.

You may adapt and develop your own practice by:

- changing your verbal communication (eg reducing the number of words you use; changing your accent, tone and speed of your speech; choosing simpler or more appropriate vocabulary to use with a person; reducing your use of acronyms or jargon, etc)

- developing your knowledge around acceptable and unacceptable non-verbal communication in order to meet someone's cultural needs better

- developing your skills, knowledge and experience in AAC

- acting on feedback from the person, colleagues or your assessor

- making changes in terms of how you plan for and manage the environment in your work setting

- making changes to your service's written information, leaflets, documentation or website.

KEY POINT

Remember, it is not the responsibility of those you work with to communicate with you. It is your responsibility to find the best ways of communicating with them, and communication is about both what you say and how you listen.

REFLECT

Reflect on a time when a new method or aid for communication was introduced to an individual you have worked with.

- How, when and why was this method or aid introduced?

- How were the person's responses monitored?

- What worked in enabling the person to access and understand this method or aid, what worked less well, and why?

MESSAGES FROM RESEARCH

Written communication

Written information can be overwhelming for many people, regardless of whether they have a learning disability or not.

Based on research about what works in practice Mencap (2013) produced a guide for services about producing written information, which is useful for reviewing service documentation and leaflets. Some key points are:

- Use the right words (eg avoid jargon, use bullet points, use active verbs).

- Consider where words are on the page (eg avoid using columns, keep a point on a single line where possible).

- Use pictures and use them to show the meaning of the words in a helpful and clear way (eg an image of a clock to show the time for something).

- Choose the font, colours and paper carefully.

- Make a leaflet easy to hold (eg an A5 booklet) and make information available in other formats (eg online, on a CD, etc).

(Mencap 2013)

Dee is a senior care assistant in a day service for older people. The people who attend the day service generally live at home with much of their support being provided by family members – a few service users also receive domiciliary care services.

Dee is reviewing some of the leaflets the service provides about other agencies, as well as their own policies on safeguarding and data protection. Dee feels that many of the leaflets, documents and posters that are visible and available in the service are not particularly accessible. Many are wordy, use jargon and are not available in other formats or languages.

Dee decides to get a small group of users together to look at the service's own leaflet and policy statements to see how these can be improved. The group is very keen that these materials are improved and agree with Dee about her concerns. The group makes lots of suggestions for changes, and would like Dee to approach some of the other agencies about their written materials, especially the local social work teams, as they feel that some of the booklets that social workers use are hard to follow.

Dee takes this information to her managers and they agree to change some of the policy statements, but they advise that the cost of reprinting lots of leaflets is prohibitive at the moment. They also advise Dee against approaching social work teams with her feedback as they feel this may damage relationships and reduce referrals to the service.

- What can Dee do now?
- How might she and the service users feel?
- What other options may be available?

PROMOTING COMMUNICATION BETWEEN INDIVIDUALS AND OTHERS

Relationships and communication are very closely linked, as outlined in Chapter 2. Supporting people to establish and maintain a range of relationships is a key aspect of promoting well-being, and therefore it is important for health and social care workers to promote effective communication between service users and a range of other people.

SUPPORTING INDIVIDUALS TO DEVELOP COMMUNICATION METHODS

Communication methods are unique to all of us, and every living creature communicates. Part of our responsibility in health and social care is to develop our understanding of the ways in which the people we work with communicate. Workers also need to support individuals to develop their communication skills so that:

- they can understand others

- others can understand them

- the individual can build meaningful relationships via interaction with others.

Developing individuals' communication methods and skills is a complex task that takes time, skill and commitment. Supporting people to communicate requires mutual effort and trust. Some key ways of enabling this trust to be built include:

- spending time with people and treating them as individuals

- spending time doing things they enjoy

- making sure your own communication is appropriate (eg your choice of words, your use of gesture and eye contact, your use of AAC, etc)

- acknowledging when someone does communicate with you (being attentive and noticing the small efforts as well as the bigger achievements)

- checking you have understood what they have communicated (eg repeating something back to check)

- giving praise and encouragement

- planning for opportunities that will promote communication (eg discussing a television programme, talking about daily tasks such as shopping, activities in the community, etc)

- utilising the opportunities as they present during someone's daily life.

Modelling this with others will enable their skills to develop and will demonstrate, in a practical and concrete way, that the individual can communicate, that they have preferred methods of doing so, and that others can understand the person's communication if they attend to it in the same way.

PROVIDING OPPORTUNITIES FOR THE INDIVIDUAL TO COMMUNICATE WITH OTHERS

Individuals need to communicate with others, as well as with you and other workers. Part of your role includes planning for opportunities for people to do so. Others might include:

- other users of a service

- family members and friends

- professionals from other agencies

- people in the community.

These opportunities should be planned for, with the person ideally, so that the individual feels in control of this process and not overwhelmed by it. This can be especially important where you are developing someone's use of a communication method or aid, and enabling their close family and friends to utilise this effectively; or where you are supporting someone who may be anxious about interacting with professionals or people they do not know.

Opportunities could include:

- discussion groups (talking about a topic, issue, event or anything else)

- everyday activities (using a bus, buying something in a shop, going to a cafe, etc)

- meetings or reviews

- social and leisure activities

- cultural and faith activities

- any task someone is doing (eg where an active support approach is being modelled with an individual – see also Chapter 11).

SUPPORTING OTHERS TO UNDERSTAND AND INTERPRET THE INDIVIDUAL'S COMMUNICATION

When you are trying to make yourself understood by others, it is very frustrating if you cannot do so. Think about times when this has happened to you or when you have struggled to understand others (eg when you have been abroad, when people have spoken too fast or in a strong accent which you have struggled to follow).

This is something that some people we work with experience all of the time. Part of your role in supporting individuals will involve ensuring that they are understood by others. However, it is vital that you achieve this in a sensitive way that does not make the person feel excluded or further disempowered by their communication difficulties.

Within service settings (yours or those of other agencies), this can be something that is achieved via:

- planning meetings (involving the individual)

- training courses and staff development

- supervision.

In public, this is something that you need to consider with the individual – how they would prefer you to ensure others understand them. Involving people in planning for this is important, because if you step in too soon and 'interpret' what they say, they are likely to feel annoyed or upset. Likewise, this would be the case if the person wanted your support and you did not provide this.

If someone you work with is communicating something to a member of the public (eg in a shop, library, cafe, church, activity centre, etc), and the other person is struggling to understand them, some top tips include:

- Avoid saying 'he said' or 'she said' as this excludes the person.

- Apply any agreement you have made about how much support you will provide to the individual and when you will provide this.

- Try repeating what the person has said and checking with them that this is what they wanted to say.

- Ensure the other person communicates directly back to the individual (and not with you in a way which excludes them).

SUPPORTING OTHERS TO BE UNDERSTOOD BY THE INDIVIDUAL BY USE OF AGREED COMMUNICATION METHODS

As above, it may be important in your role for you to enable others to use agreed communication methods so that they can engage with an individual. The same avenues for developing this are available within service settings, and, again, this can be harder to achieve with members of the public, but is no less important. Your skill in involving individuals in planning for these events, involving them at the time and in any discussion, and in modelling good practice in communication with members of the public is critical. This is especially important as within your role you may be also challenging assumptions that some people may have about users of services and their level of ability.

REFLECT

- What opportunities do you provide for individuals whom you support to communicate with others?

- How do you enable others to understand the individual's preferred means of communication, and to use methods and aids that the person uses effectively?

- How could you develop and improve your own practice, and that of others, around this?

CASE STUDY

Taju is a senior support worker with a mental health charity. He works some of his time in a drop-in centre for people with mental health problems and the remainder of his working week is spent in outreach services providing ongoing practical and emotional support for service users.

Taju is working with Betty. She has depression which she experienced following a stroke. This stroke has also meant that Betty has some difficulties with communication, and that she feels frustrated when people cannot understand her or when they do not give her time to express what she wants to say.

Betty asks Taju if he can accompany her to see her GP as she is having her medication reviewed, and she feels that her GP does not always listen to her. During this visit, Taju observes that the GP has some difficulties understanding Betty, and while she is describing some of the side effects of her current medication the GP interrupts her.

Taju understands that the GP's time is under pressure, but is concerned that he has not given Betty time to communicate fully her experience of the current medication and her wishes. Taju knows Betty is anxious about changing her medication because the last time she did so she was unwell for several weeks while she got used to the tablets she now takes. However, the GP seems to want to try Betty on something new and Taju is concerned that Betty does not feel she has had her views heard.

- What can Taju do in this situation?

- How can he challenge the GP and ensure Betty is able to communicate with him effectively?

SUPPORTING THE USE OF COMMUNICATION TECHNOLOGY AND AIDS

To support the use of communication technology and specific aids, health and social care workers should use the basic health and social care process of assessment, planning, intervention and review. This means:

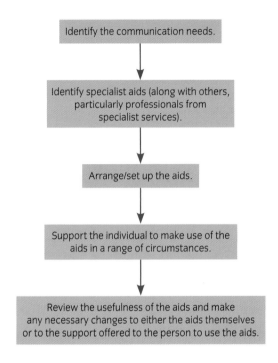

Identify the communication needs.

↓

Identify specialist aids (along with others, particularly professionals from specialist services).

↓

Arrange/set up the aids.

↓

Support the individual to make use of the aids in a range of circumstances.

↓

Review the usefulness of the aids and make any necessary changes to either the aids themselves or to the support offered to the person to use the aids.

IDENTIFYING SPECIALIST SERVICES RELATING TO COMMUNICATION TECHNOLOGY AND AIDS

The pace of change in terms of technology continues to accelerate, and this is especially useful when considering how technological aids can enable people to communicate. Twenty years ago, some of the technology we now take for granted was either inconceivable or in a relatively primitive format. Now there is a huge range of resources available, such as:

- voice-assisted software

- tablets and smartphone devices

- devices where people can point with their eyes to letters or words to be understood

- talking houseware items to enable day-to-day living tasks to be undertaken.

Identifying specialist services is therefore a complex matter as experts in the field struggle to stay fully up to date with the wide range of tools, aids and technological solutions. The website www. communicationmatters.org.uk is extremely useful as it contains:

- information on conferences
- details of local roadshows
- research
- links to other sites
- discussion forums
- newsletters.

Support in identifying services and aids will also be available from your managers, colleagues and other professionals (eg social workers, speech and language and occupational therapists). Other professionals may also need to be involved in meeting the cost of these aids and in considering the range of options for individuals to access.

SUPPORT TO USE COMMUNICATION TECHNOLOGY AND AIDS

Different people will need different amounts and types of support when they begin to use new communication aids or pieces of technology. Being introduced to something new can be overwhelming for many people, and the aid is far less likely to be effective in achieving the planned outcomes if the individual feels they have been unsupported around its use.

Research (Scope 2012) shows that if people are not supported and trained, then devices are not effective, and that solutions need to be considered for:

- ongoing training and support (especially for developing technologies and for people whose conditions may deteriorate)
- guarantees and insurance of devices
- training for colleagues, family members and friends so that consistency of approach is maintained.

The type of support needs to be matched to the individual, and appropriate to their needs. Consider the first time that you saw a new device and learned how to use it (eg a DVD player, the internet, a smartphone, etc). It probably felt beyond you at first, and you needed either time, support, a manual, or to explore the device and its use. People's learning styles and preferences in how they approach something technical for the first time also need to be considered. Some people prefer to read the manual and then feel confident, while others prefer to 'play around' with a device to explore its functionality.

Training in an aid or technology could either be something that you do informally, or that is planned for across a service in a more formal way.

Colleagues may need just as much support, or even more support, as users of services for new devices. This support could include:

- how to set up a device or aid

- how to switch it on (where the switches are)

- what the different functions are and what they do

- troubleshooting tips

- looking at any necessary risk assessment of a device or aid

- working through concerns individuals have about a device

- supporting individuals who see a communication aid as a sign that their verbal communication has gone for good.

ENSURING THAT COMMUNICATION EQUIPMENT IS CORRECTLY SET UP AND WORKING PROPERLY

It is absolutely vital to ensure that any communication technology or device is properly set up and maintained. Some devices may need to be installed by a qualified professional, and others may be more portable and easy to set up within a service or someone's home. Risk assessment around this is likely to be necessary, especially where an electronic device has trailing wires. Anything electronic also requires PAT (portable appliance testing).

If a device or aid is not set up properly, then the individual using it is likely to find this frustrating and they may be more likely to give up using it before they see the benefits. Some devices may also need regular checks and updates (eg of specific software) and ongoing maintenance. If they do not receive this maintenance, they may be likely to fail while the person is using the aid. Again, this is frustrating and disempowering for people, especially for those who have become reliant on an aid in order to ensure they are understood.

REFLECT

- What has been your own experience of accessing communication aids, learning how to use them and getting help with aids when there are issues with how they are working?

- Where can you access additional support and guidance with this in your own work setting or service?

MESSAGES FROM RESEARCH

Communication and technology

The National Institute on Deafness and other Communication Disorders (NIDCD) reports that research is currently taking place on a range of areas relating to communication and technology, as follows:

- *Improved devices for people with hearing loss.* Researchers are developing devices that help people with varying degrees of hearing loss communicate with others. One team has developed a portable device in which two or more users type messages to each other that can be displayed simultaneously in real time.

- *Improved devices for non-speaking people.* Researchers are developing a personalised text-to-speech synthesis system that synthesises speech that is more intelligible and natural sounding to be incorporated in speech-generating devices. Individuals who are at risk of losing their ability to speak can prerecord their own speech, which is then converted into their personal synthetic voice.

- *Brain–computer interface research.* A relatively new and exciting area of study is called brain–computer interface research. Scientists are studying how neural signals in a person's brain can be translated by a computer to help someone communicate.

(National Institute of Deafness and Other Communication Disorders)

CASE STUDY

Isabella is a senior care assistant in a respite care service that provides short-term stays for younger people with learning and physical disabilities.

Isabella has had some training in using Widgit on a tablet as this is something that Mark, who has used the service for several years, has recently started to access. Isabella has found this difficult to learn, as she is not used to tablets and she has put a lot of time and effort into this. Previously, Mark has found communication difficult. He tends to show his frustration via challenging behaviours when he feels people are not listening and when he cannot express what he wants to. However, his social worker has reported to Isabella that the Widgit app is really helping Mark as he feels that this technology belongs to him.

When Mark arrives for his weekend stay, Isabella asks his parents about the tablet and how this is going. They say that they have left it at home as last night Mark threw it across the room so they feel it can't be working for him if he is still getting angry like this.

- What can Isabella do in this situation?

- How can she ensure Mark can communicate in his preferred way and challenge his parents without being disrespectful?

REVIEWING COMMUNICATION NEEDS AND SUPPORT

In order to contribute effectively to a review, health and social care staff need to have followed the plan in place and monitored its effectiveness (as is detailed in Chapter 9). A key part of monitoring is to collate information, so that the review can be evidence based (which means that decisions are based on evidence of what is and what isn't working).

Information about individuals' communication could come from:

- your own observations
- feedback from the person themselves (eg about how a device, method or aid is working for them)
- their relatives, carers and friends
- your colleagues and managers
- other professionals.

It may be part of your own work role to collate all of this information (eg in preparing for a review meeting), and gathering this in a meaningful way will be useful for your own records, personal development and practice in meeting the somebody's needs.

Your service may have proformas for recording this information, or it could be part of your work with an individual to develop a personal record in order to track their progress and preferences. A range of person-centred assessment tools can assist with collating and recording the information.

EVALUATING THE EFFECTIVENESS OF AGREED METHODS OF COMMUNICATION AND SUPPORT PROVIDED

Evaluating the effectiveness of any plan is important, so that progress can be evidenced and so that the support provided can be altered if it needs to be. People's communication is not static, and is likely to change and develop, especially if a new device or aid is introduced, or if they have a health condition that affects their communication and either improves or worsens.

When you evaluate any plan, it is important to have the facility to compare your observations and assessments against an initial baseline assessment. This is a process that has to involve the individual and others who know and work with them in order for it to be effective. An example follows.

Jim's communication of ...	Initial observations	Changes with the tablet device in place
Hungry	Shouts and clicks his tongue	Able to point at symbol on the tablet for meal
Annoyed	Shouts; can hit out	Shows emoticons and is beginning to respond to discussions around reasons for frustration
Excited	Claps his hands and smiles	As before; also uses emoticons sometimes, depending on the reason for feeling excited
Boredom	Yawning or closing his eyes and refusing to participate	As before; sometimes will use the tablet, but can switch this off if he feels he wants a change of activity immediately
Sadness	Crying; shouting; sometimes hitting out	Depends on the reason – working on this using the tablet

Continuing to develop communication skills and using new methods is important for all of us. This is especially true in the digital age as new means of communication become available to us all of the time. In our verbal communication, we all continue to develop our vocabulary, and language itself changes and evolves over time too. The continued development of communication has to be equally important for individuals whom we support because:

- this maintains people's confidence and builds self-esteem as they develop skills

- people have an equal right to communicate and to have access to available resources

- technology changes and dates quickly, so may need to be regularly updated
- it is our role to enable and empower people, which involves supporting their growth and ongoing development of all of their skills.

Working with others will involve keeping up to date with new information as part of your own personal and professional development, and sharing resources and best practice across teams and agencies. Supporting individuals to keep developing communication could be about:

- teaching new vocabulary in a planned way
- using and developing opportunities for communication as part of active support and social inclusion
- reviewing and adapting a communication plan or passport
- accessing new aids, tools and training.

REFLECT

Can you identify an occasion where you have supported the continued development of communication practices with an individual in your work? This could have involved changes to practices or communication aids following a formal review of the support provided, or it could be a more informal adaptation you made to your work following observation or feedback.

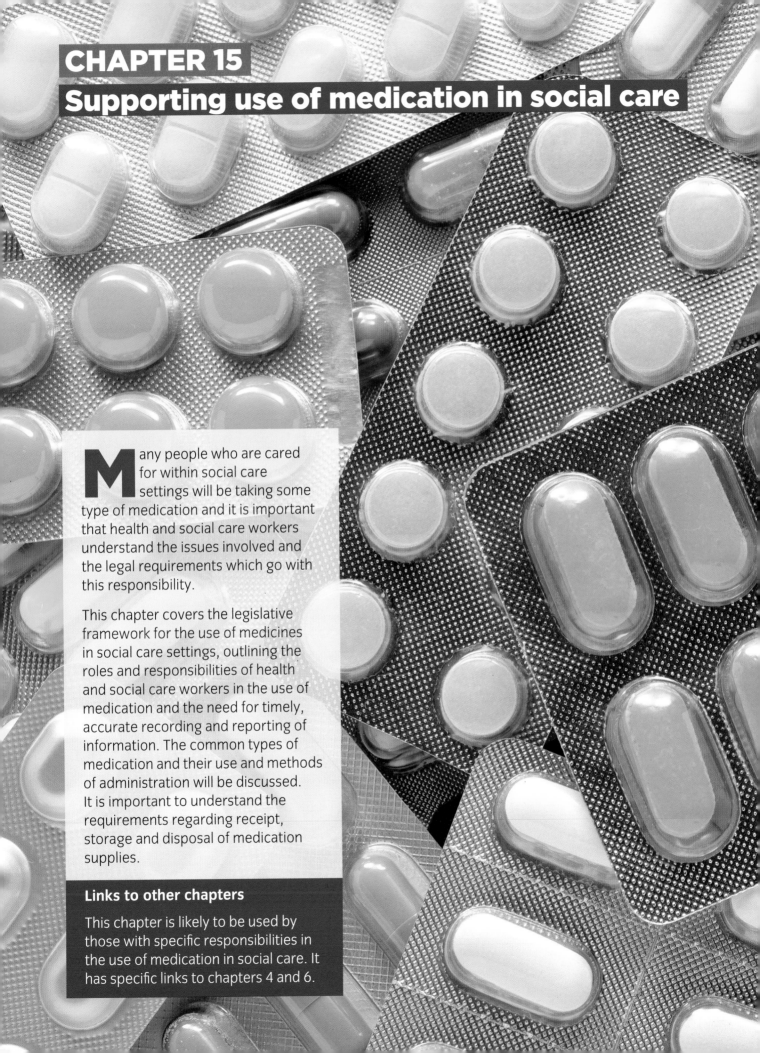

CHAPTER 15
Supporting use of medication in social care

Many people who are cared for within social care settings will be taking some type of medication and it is important that health and social care workers understand the issues involved and the legal requirements which go with this responsibility.

This chapter covers the legislative framework for the use of medicines in social care settings, outlining the roles and responsibilities of health and social care workers in the use of medication and the need for timely, accurate recording and reporting of information. The common types of medication and their use and methods of administration will be discussed. It is important to understand the requirements regarding receipt, storage and disposal of medication supplies.

Links to other chapters

This chapter is likely to be used by those with specific responsibilities in the use of medication in social care. It has specific links to chapters 4 and 6.

UNDERSTANDING THE LEGISLATIVE FRAMEWORK FOR THE USE OF MEDICATION IN SOCIAL CARE SETTINGS

It is very important that health and social care workers understand the legislation surrounding the various issues related to the use of medication. The purpose of this legislative framework is that it protects both the person being cared for and the professionals caring for them. The various Acts and regulations cover all aspects of medication use, from the actual medicines to the workplace and social care, mental health and patient confidentiality issues.

LEGISLATION GOVERNING THE USE OF MEDICATION IN SOCIAL CARE SETTINGS

The following pieces of legislation are relevant to all workers in health and social care and dictate ways of working and procedures to be followed.

LEGISLATION COVERING MEDICINES

- Medicines Act 1968
- Human Medicines Regulations 2012
- Misuse of Drugs Act 1971
- Misuse of Drugs Regulations 2001
- Misuse of Drugs (Safe Custody) Regulations 1973
- Health Act 2006
- Controlled Drugs (Supervision of Management and Use) Regulations 2006
- Control of Substances Hazardous to Health (COSHH) Regulations 1999
- Hazardous Waste Regulations 2005

Medicines Act 1968

This Act governs the control of medicines, both for human and veterinary use, covering the manufacture, prescribing, dispensing, administration, storage and disposal of medicines.

Human Medicines Regulations 2012

These regulations replace nearly all of the earlier UK medicines regulations (ie most of the Medicines Act 1968 and over 200 statutory instruments). They describe the processes involved in the authorisation of medicinal products for human use (covering the manufacture, import, distribution, sale and supply of those products), the labelling and advertising of products, and the monitoring and investigating of any adverse effects of medicines of all types reported by health professionals or the public (including herbal and traditional medicines).

Misuse of Drugs Act 1971

This Act was introduced to control dangerous or otherwise harmful drugs and it controls their possession, supply, manufacture, import and export. Drugs controlled under the Act are called controlled drugs (CDs) and are divided into three classes: A, B and C. The maximum penalties that can be imposed for breaking this law are dictated by the class of drug involved.

Misuse of Drugs Regulations 2001

The use of controlled drugs in medicine is permitted by the Misuse of Drugs Regulations (MDRs). The MDRs were created under the 1971 Act and deal with licensing issues around production, possession and supply of substances classified under the Act.

Misuse of Drugs (Safe Custody) Regulations 1973

These regulations outline the storage and safe custody requirements for controlled drugs and are enforced by the Home Office via the police. The degree of control depends on the premises within which the drugs are being stored. Particularly stringent requirements apply to retail premises and certain care homes.

Health Act 2006

Under this Act the concept of a 'controlled drug (CD) accountable officer' was introduced. All designated bodies such as health care organisations and independent hospitals are required to appoint an accountable officer and any issues regarding controlled drugs are dealt with by this person and their team.

The Act imposes a duty of collaboration on all bodies to share intelligence on controlled drug issues and gives the police and other nominated people power of entry to inspect stocks and records of them.

Controlled Drugs (Supervision of Management and Use) Regulations 2006

These regulations came into effect in England on 1 January 2007 and set out the changes covered by the Health Act 2006.

Control of Substances Hazardous to Health (COSHH) Regulations 1999

These regulations require the employer to protect all employees from any potential hazards posed by substances and materials they may come into contact with while performing their job. Some medicines are more hazardous to a care worker's health than others. Cytotoxic drugs are used to treat various conditions, including cancer, rheumatoid arthritis and Crohn's disease, eg methotrexate.

Hazardous Waste Regulations 2005

Waste medicines from a patient's home and from a residential care home can be returned to a pharmacy for destruction. Waste medicines from nursing and dual-registered (residential and nursing) homes are classed as industrial waste and must be disposed of by consignment or transfer to a suitably authorised person/facility. If medicines from a nursing home are returned to a pharmacy, both the home and pharmacy are in breach of the law. Pharmacies are not able to accept any sharps for disposal even in sharps boxes.

KEY POINT

It is important not to touch medication while assisting individuals with their medicine. It is important to take extra precautions, such as wearing gloves, when handling cytotoxic drugs, especially women of reproductive age, as these can damage an unborn baby.

LEGISLATION COVERING MENTAL HEALTH

- Mental Health Acts 1983 and 2007
- Mental Capacity Act 2005
- New Mental Capacity Act Guidance 2011

Mental Health Acts 1983 and 2007

The Mental Health Act 1983 aimed to ensure that people with serious mental disorders could receive treatment irrespective of their consent if it was necessary to prevent them harming themselves or others. The Act put safeguards in place to protect the patient, strengthening their rights to seek independent reviews of their treatment.

The 2007 Act is largely focused on public protection and risk management. The amended legislation extends the powers of compulsion and introduces compulsory community treatment orders, making patients' compliance with treatment a statutory requirement.

Mental Capacity Act 2005

This Act provides a clear legal framework for people who lack capacity and those caring for them by setting out key principles, procedures and safeguards.

New Mental Capacity Act Guidance 2011

The Care Quality Commission (CQC) provides guidance on various issues around the care and needs of people with mental health issues who are receiving social care.

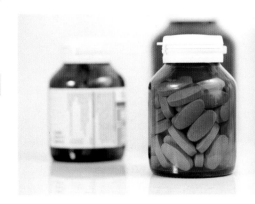

THE LEGAL CLASSIFICATION SYSTEM FOR MEDICINES

The Medicines and Healthcare products Regulatory Agency (MHRA), an agency of the Department of Health, is responsible for ensuring that medicines and medical devices are effective and are acceptably safe.

The MHRA assesses data provided by manufacturers regarding the safety, quality and effectiveness of a medicine and, if satisfied, grants marketing authorisation (this used to be called a product licence). This system of licensing means that both prescribers and patients can have confidence that the medicine has been fully scrutinised before its release.

Medicinal products for human use fall into three legal classes, as defined by the Medicines Act 1968:

- GSL (general sales list)
- P (pharmacy)
- POM (prescription-only medicines).

GSL medicines

General sales list (GSL) medicines are medicines that can be sold from registered pharmacies but also from other retail premises. These other retail premises must be able to 'close so as to exclude the public', eg a corner shop but not a market stall.

An extra condition applies to the sale of GSL medicines from a pharmacy – they can only be sold from a pharmacy when the 'responsible pharmacist' is on duty.

Key terms

A **drug** is any substance that when taken into the body affects the way that the body functions.

Brand name is the name given to a new medicine by a manufacturer. It is protected by copyright and will be used in advertising campaigns. Examples include Panadol® which is a brand of paracetamol and Anadin® which is a brand of aspirin. See also *generic name*.

Generic name is the official name given to the active ingredient when a medicine is developed; examples include paracetamol and aspirin.

A **medicine** is a drug that is used to diagnose, prevent or treat an illness.

REFLECT

- Can you think of any examples of GSL medicines, eg medicines you have seen on sale at a petrol station shop?

P medicines

Pharmacy (P) medicines are medicinal products that may only be purchased from a registered pharmacy, from a registered pharmacist or a person acting under the supervision of a pharmacist. P medicines have the P symbol printed on the box.

P

OTC medicines

Together GSL and P medicines are known as 'over the counter' (OTC) medicines or non-prescription medicines. Some OTC medicines are associated with additional legal and professional considerations, eg paracetamol and pseudoephedrine have limits set on the quantity that may be sold and certain cough medicines are restricted to over six-year-olds.

Prescription-only medicines (POM)

A prescription-only medicine or POM is a medicine that can generally be sold or supplied only on presentation of a legally written prescription from an appropriate prescriber. Although the bulk of prescriptions are written by doctors, other health care professionals, including dentists, some nurses and pharmacists, may also legally prescribe POMs. POMs have the POM symbol printed on the box.

POM

Controlled drugs (CD POM)

Certain POM medicines are further categorised as controlled drugs (CDs) under the Misuse of Drugs Act 1971 and the Misuse of Drugs Regulations 2001. Under the regulations there are five classes of CD, each with a different requirement for ordering, storage, supply and record keeping, eg preparations containing morphine. The packaging carries the symbols POM and CD.

POM | CD

Some medicines are classified under more than one category depending on their formulation, strength, quantity or what they are to be used for.

> **REFLECT**
>
> Can you think of a medicine that falls into more than one legal category?

Paracetamol is a GSL medicine when sold in a pack of 16, but is classified as a pharmacy (P) medicine when sold in a pack of 32 and is a prescription-only medicine (POM) when supplied as a pack of 100.

Morphine also falls into three legal categories, kaolin and morphine suspension is sold as a pharmacy (P) medicine for the treatment of diarrhoea; it is a prescription-only medicine (POM) in Oramorph® solution 10mg/5ml used for pain relief, and is a controlled drug (POM CD) in the stronger Oramorph® concentrated solution 100mg/5ml and in products such as MST® tablet and Zomorph® capsules.

LEGAL REQUIREMENTS FOR PRESCRIPTIONS

A prescription may be written only by an appropriate practitioner and the information that must be written on the form is determined by the law. In England there are four colours of prescription form in use and different types of prescribers use different coloured forms.

- Prescriptions written on green forms by GPs or nurse and pharmacist prescribers, hospital doctors, supplementary prescribers or out-of-hours centres are known as FP10 forms.

- Dentists who are prescribing on the NHS use a yellow FP10D form and prescribe from an approved list of medicines that are included in the dental formulary.

- Some nurses with limited prescribing rights will use lilac forms which are printed with information about the prescriber. They should only prescribe products that they are personally authorised to prescribe.

- The fourth type of form is the blue FP10MDA form used for instalment prescribing of controlled drugs to addicts, such as methadone for daily collection.

Prescriptions must be written in indelible ink; a faxed copy of a prescription is not a legal prescription.

REFLECT

Using prescriptions you have been given or have seen as an example, what information do you think is legally required on a prescription?

INFORMATION REQUIRED ON A PRESCRIPTION

- Name and address of patient.

- Date of birth for children under 12 years of age. It is worth noting that electronically generated prescriptions have DOB for every patient but this is not a legal requirement.

- Medicine name, form and strength. Medicines can be prescribed by brand or generic name but the NHS encourages generic medicines as these are of equal quality to the brand but are generally of much lower cost.

- Quantity to supply.

- Dose to be taken.

- Prescriber's signature – this must be in indelible ink.

- Date – a prescription is valid for six months from the date it is written, apart from a prescription for a controlled drug which is only valid for 28 days.

- Name and address of the prescriber and their NHS identifier. This can be pre-printed on a pad for handwritten prescriptions or computer printed when generated using the practice's computer.

ELECTRONIC PRESCRIPTION SERVICE (EPS)

The NHS is currently introducing an electronic prescription service (EPS) and there are several areas of the country where this is live already. The big change with EPS is that the legal prescription is the electronic version. In some cases the prescriber may issue a paper token but this is not a prescription – if the patient presents it at a pharmacy the pharmacy must retrieve the electronic version from the NHS server in order to be able to dispense the medication. Essentially all of the prescription requirements for information included remain – the information is simply produced, stored and transferred electronically.

REPEAT (BATCH) DISPENSING

Repeat dispensing makes it easier for patients with chronic conditions to obtain repeat prescriptions, speeding up services and relieving pressure on GP surgeries. Repeat or batch dispensing is an essential NHS service and is offered by every pharmacy. It makes better use of pharmacists' skills, helps patients get the most out of their medicines and reduces wastage. Each time a patient collects their medicines the pharmacist checks for problems and ensures that they only supply the items the patient needs that month.

Not every patient is suitable to have their medicines by repeat dispensing; it works for patients on a stable medicine regime whose condition is well controlled. They are issued with a batch of prescriptions that cover a period of up to a year and which the patient lodges with the pharmacy of their choice, and if the patient's condition changes the batch can be cancelled.

The repeat dispensing service should not be confused with 'repeat items' – this term simply refers to medicines that the GP authorises for the patient to tick and order a prescription when they need a further supply. Each month a new order has to be given to the surgery and a new prescription printed and signed by the prescriber.

PRESCRIPTION CHARGES

In England the NHS levies a charge for each item on a prescription; the amount is set by the government and generally changes on 1 April every year. Under current regulations, all patients under 16 and over 60 years of age are automatically exempt from paying prescription charges. Other categories of exemption are awarded for various reasons, eg low income, medical grounds (such as diabetes, thyroid problems), those under 19 years of age in full-time education.

The back of the prescription must be completed, the type of exemption must be ticked and a declaration signed. To reduce fraudulent exemption claims, the NHS requires the pharmacy to check for proof of exemption when the prescription is collected (eg a pre-payment card, a medical exemption card, an HC2 certificate, a students' union card). The fine for making a false declaration is £1,000 and the person signing the declaration is fined rather than the patient.

Prescription charges differ in England, Wales and Scotland.

PRIVATE PRESCRIPTIONS

Private prescriptions are written by medical practitioners but are not part of the NHS. The legal requirements for information to be included on these prescriptions are the same as for the NHS (see above). Because the supply is not part of the NHS the patient pays for the medication with the price dependent on the cost of the medicine.

If a patient does not consult a medical practitioner through the NHS the practitioner is not able to write an NHS prescription, so that even if a patient would qualify for free NHS prescriptions, there are no exemptions from private prescription payments. For instance, many dentists now see patients privately.

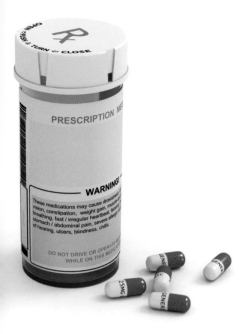

LABELLING REQUIREMENTS

Under the law certain information must be included on the label that the pharmacy adds to the medicine when it is dispensed, including:

- the name of patient

- the name of the medicine, its form and strength (the medicine name on the label must be the name the prescriber used on the prescription)

- the quantity supplied

- the dose to be taken

- the date dispensed

- a 'keep out of reach of children' warning

- any other warning labels required, such as 'with or after food', and any special storage information, such as 'store in a fridge'. These warnings may also include handling precautions

- the name, address and telephone number of the supplying pharmacy.

CASE STUDY

Zakiyah is a senior domiciliary care worker. She is visiting Sarah at her home and notices that Sarah is often very drowsy. When she talks to Sarah, Zakiyah finds out that she got some new tablets from the doctor recently because she had been very itchy. She has been taking them in the morning and the itch seems better but she says she is finding it hard to stay awake. Sarah shows Zakiyah the bottle; the label says: 'Hydroxyzine tablets 25mg. Take ONE daily'.

- Who could Zakiyah ask for medicines advice on Sarah's behalf?

- The pharmacist explains that the medication has a side effect of drowsiness and that Sarah would be better taking them at night.

- If Sarah were to take one tablet at night, is this still following the GP's directions?

- Do you think the GP meant Sarah to take the drug in the morning?

- Would there have been a clearer way to word the directions so that this problem could have been avoided?

EMERGENCY SUPPLIES

Many GP surgeries require 24 or 48 hours' notice to produce a prescription. If a prescription has not been ordered early enough and a patient has run out of their medication it may be possible to purchase a small supply if it is a GSL or P medicine. However, if it is a prescription-only medicine (POM) the prescriber may be able to produce an emergency prescription to allow the medication to be dispensed. The pharmacist is also legally allowed to make an emergency supply of a POM under certain conditions (at their professional discretion).

Emergency supplies may be made at the request of the prescriber and if the supply is agreed the prescriber must supply the pharmacy with the prescription within 72 hours of the request. In some circumstances a copy of a newly produced prescription is faxed to the pharmacy to aid accuracy of supply, but the fax is not a legal prescription and the actual prescription must still be presented to the pharmacy with the 72-hour deadline. With the exception of phenobarbital for epilepsy, no controlled drug may ever be supplied as an emergency supply.

Emergency supplies may also be made at the request of a patient, provided the pharmacist interviews the patient (not the carer), preferably face to face, and is satisfied that there is an immediate need for the POM and that it is not practical for the patient to obtain a prescription without undue delay. This type of emergency supply is not covered by an NHS prescription and the pharmacist is entitled to levy a charge for the medication. If the pharmacist does not feel it is appropriate to make an emergency supply, they should give the patient advice on where to get a prescription, eg at an NHS walk-in centre, a minor injuries unit or at an A&E department.

POLICIES, PROCEDURES, AGREED WAYS OF WORKING – WHY THEY MUST REFLECT AND INCORPORATE LEGISLATIVE REQUIREMENTS

When working in social care settings it is important that all health and social care professionals work in a standardised way ensuring that all individuals receiving care and support receive the same level of service. Working within the framework of the law safeguards both the giver and receiver of care.

Each care provider, whether local council, private company or voluntary organisation, must have a set of policies and procedures covering the many aspects of the day-to-day provision of care in social settings. These are developed with consideration to all of the various forms of legislation that apply to care provision and also to any guidance documents produced.

When used properly, medicines help to control disease, give relief from symptoms and prolong life. They are powerful compounds that have the capacity to cause side effects as well as giving relief and so it is especially important that medicines are administered under the guidance of specific policies and procedures.

An extremely useful guidance document, 'The handling of medicines in social care', is produced by the Royal Pharmaceutical Society of Great Britain. It should be available at your place of work or alternatively you can also download it from www.rpharms.com/support-pdfs/handling-medicines-socialcare-guidance.pdf.

The Care Quality Commission (CQC) issues guidance for care providers to help them understand the issues involved when developing their policies. When the care provider is a local council any local regulations must also be reflected in the policies it uses.

Care providers need written policies that cover various aspects of handling and administering medicines, considering both the medicines and the rights of the individual. When a care provider produces an agreed way of working this must incorporate all of the appropriate policies and procedures and must comply with the law. In other words, a provider cannot have its own policy that bypasses the law.

A medicines policy

This must cover the ordering, receipt, storage, administration and disposal of medicines (both prescribed and non-prescribed) as well as record keeping, and also incorporate individuals' rights with respect to confidentiality, dignity and level of care. The policy should be written so that anyone who is new to the care home can read the policy and would be able to carry out the procedures covered in the policy as they relate to that home.

COMMON TYPES OF MEDICATION AND THEIR USE

You are not expected to be an expert in medication: remember you do have access to medical professionals to help you and who will be happy to answer questions. However, as time goes on you will start to recognise the names of the medications, especially the most common ones. Having an understanding of how these medications affect people is also useful in providing care.

LAXATIVES

These are taken to treat or to help prevent constipation and many people take them. Constipation may be a side effect of another medication, so the patient is treated with a medicine to counteract an

unwanted effect of another medicine. Common laxatives are lactulose, compound macrogol powders (eg Movicol®) which work by increasing the amount of water in the bowel, and fibre products such as ispaghula husk (eg Fybogel® and Isogel®) which work by bulking up the stool. Senna works by stimulating the bowel but has the disadvantages that it can cause abdominal cramp and, if used regularly, requires an increasing dose to have the same effect. Occasionally an individual may need a suppository or enema but these would be administered by a nurse.

PAIN RELIEF (ANALGESICS)

Pain relief may be prescribed for a variety of conditions for either short- or long-term use. Generally, the stronger the painkiller the more likely it is to cause side effects and so it is best for individuals to be stabilised on the mildest analgesic that gives relief.

For mild to moderate pain the most commonly prescribed drug is paracetamol which is safe at the recommended dose, is well tolerated and non-habit forming. It can be used for a variety of conditions such as dental pain, period pain, sprains and broken bones, or it can be used longer term for pain associated with conditions such as osteoarthritis. Although aspirin can also be used it has the disadvantages of causing gastric irritation, it is unsuitable for those aged under 16 years of age and cannot be taken by patients who are taking warfarin.

Compound analgesics contain a simple analgesic (such as paracetamol or aspirin) with an opioid component such as codeine. Commonly prescribed compound analgesics are co-codamol (paracetamol and codeine) and co-dydramol (paracetamol and dihydrocodeine). They are available with varying strengths of opioid; however, evidence for any greater benefit is lacking, while the incidence of side effects is much greater, and so most reference sources recommend simple analgesics.

Opioid analgesics are usually used for moderate to severe pain and are subject to the controlled drug regulations. They are very useful but do have many side effects and are habit-forming. Examples include codeine, tramadol, morphine, buprenorphine and fentanyl. The analgesic ladder uses a three-step approach for treating pain and was developed by the World Health Organization (WHO). The concept is that there are three levels of pain and the best way to treat it is to use a stepwise approach.

Step 3: Severe pain
Use opioid analgesic (morphine is the gold standard opioid). Use either alone or in combination with paracetamol.

Step 2: Moderate pain
As pain levels increase, consider a mild opioid (eg codeine) either alone or with paracetamol.

Step 1: Mild pain
At this level use the mildest analgesia (paracetamol is the gold standard).

Depending on the condition being treated other drugs to treat, for example, anxiety or agitation may need to be added at some stage (this can be on any rung of the ladder).

NON-STEROIDAL ANTI-INFLAMMATORY DRUGS (NSAIDS)

This group of drugs are used for short-term relief in conditions such as pain from a fracture or sprain, dental pain, period pain and migraine. When a single dose is given they produce similar pain relief to paracetamol, but when used regularly, at a full dosage, they have pain relieving and anti-inflammatory properties. They have been found to be useful in rheumatoid arthritis and in advanced osteoarthritis, but recent safety data has shown that use of NSAIDs can increase the risk of cardiovascular events (eg heart attack and stroke) and so the lowest dose for the shortest length of time should be used. Current prescribing advice relating to NSAIDs advises the use of ibuprofen or naproxen and a move away from the prescribing of diclofenac which carries a higher risk of cardiovascular side effects. All NSAIDs can cause gastric irritation and so should not be taken on an empty stomach. Some asthmatics are allergic to NSAIDs and so they should be used with caution in asthmatic patients and the patient warned to stop taking them if their asthma control worsens.

ANTIHISTAMINES

These drugs are used to treat allergies, such as hay fever and skin reactions to chemicals, soap powders, etc, and are usually given as tablets and liquids, eg loratidine, cetirizine, chlorphenamine.

ANTIBIOTICS

Antibiotics are used to treat bacterial infections but have no effect on viral infections. Due to the problem of antibiotic resistant bacteria (such as MRSA) prescribers are now encouraged to prescribe antibiotics only when absolutely necessary and, where possible, after sensitivity test results are received identifying the most effective antibiotic for the identified infection. It is also very important that the patient takes as prescribed and finishes the course.

Amoxicillin is a broad-spectrum antibiotic often used for chest infections and dental infections. Cefalexin is another broad-spectrum antibiotic used for urinary tract infections that do not respond to other antibiotics, as well as to treat chest, ear, sinus and skin infections. Erythromycin is an effective antibiotic but it has the disadvantage of causing nausea and vomiting in some patients. Metronidazole is very useful to treat dental infections if the patient cannot take amoxicillin and is also used to treat surgical infections and can be used in *Clostridium difficile* infections.

INHALERS FOR ASTHMA AND CHRONIC OBSTRUCTIVE PULMONARY DISEASE (COPD)

Inhalers can contain a reliever drug or a preventer drug.

Relievers can be short acting, such as salbutamol (Ventolin®), terbutaline (Bricanyl®) and ipratropium bromide (Atrovent®), or long acting, such as formoterol (Oxis®) and salmeterol (Seretide®). They relax the airways in the lungs and give immediate relief to asthmatics who are struggling to breathe (these inhalers are often colour-coded blue or green).

If an asthmatic regularly needs to use a reliever inhaler the prescriber may add in a preventer which gives better control of the symptoms. Preventer inhalers contain steroids such as beclometasone (Clenil® and Qvar®) and fluticasone (Flixotide®) which work by reducing inflammation in the lungs and so reduce the swelling and mucous in the airways – this makes it less likely that the patient will need the reliever drug. These inhalers tend to be colour-coded brown or purple/pink.

Another type of chest condition treated with inhalers is chronic obstructive pulmonary disease (COPD). Unlike asthma this condition is irreversible. As COPD progresses, the drugs prescribed will change. Salbutamol can be used at all stages, but ipratropium bromide will be discontinued and may be replaced with a longer-acting reliever such as tiotropium (Spiriva®) used once a day, giving some relief from symptoms. They may also be prescribed a combination device containing a steroid with a long-acting reliever. Seretide 500 Accuhaler® is licensed for use in COPD.

Inhalers are available in a variety of dispensers including metered dose (gas expelled) or powder-based inhalers. In order to receive the maximum benefit from inhaled medication it is very important that the inhaler device is used correctly. Your local pharmacist can help with advice on how to use the various devices.

HIGH BLOOD PRESSURE (HYPERTENSION)

Blood pressure (BP) is regularly checked as a measure of an individual's heath. There is a target range for blood pressure rather than one 'correct' BP and as we age our BP tends to rise. However, if the BP becomes too high it puts an individual at increased risk of cardiovascular events, such as strokes or heart attack. Losing weight, increasing the level of exercise and stopping smoking can all improve the BP but when these measures are not enough medication will be prescribed and will be a long-term therapy as it is not a cure.

Common drugs used to treat blood pressure include diuretics (water tablets), such as bendroflumethiazide, furosemide and amiloride. There are various other classes of drugs which are used to lower BP including ACE inhibitors (enalapril, lisinopril, perindopril), beta blockers (atenolol, bisoprolol), alpha blockers (doxazosin), angiotensin receptor blockers (ARBs) (candesartan, irbesartan, losartan), centrally acting drugs (methyldopa, moxonidine) and calcium channel blockers (amlodipine, diltiazem, felodipine, lercanidipine).

CHRONIC HEART FAILURE

Chronic heart failure is a progressive condition. The heart gradually deteriorates and the aim of treatment is to relieve symptoms and prolong life. Many drugs used to treat it are also the same drugs that are used to control blood pressure. ACE inhibitors such as enalapril are used in all stages, usually combined with a beta blocker such as bisoprolol and carvedilol. In addition, diuretics such as spironolactone can be used in heart failure and digoxin may be used to improve symptoms.

ANTIDIABETIC DRUGS

Diabetes mellitus occurs because of a lack of insulin or resistance to its action.

Type 1 diabetes is the form of the disease where the patient is unable to produce insulin in their pancreas and so they are treated with insulin injections. Historically, the insulin used was from animal origin but now human insulin is available, produced using biotechnology. Insulins vary in how quickly they act and how long the effect lasts, and patients will be treated with insulin in a dosage regimen tailored to their disease and lifestyle, with insulin doses varied dependent upon blood glucose monitoring.

Type 2 diabetes is due to either a reduced insulin production, a resistance to the effects of insulin, or a combination of the two.

Treatment of type 2 diabetes is with a variety of medications such as metformin, gliclazide, glibenclamide, acarbose, exenatide, sitagliptin.

ANTI-EPILEPTICS

These drugs are used to treat epilepsy and must be given regularly to either reduce the number of fits or to keep the patient free of fits. Common drugs used to treat epilepsy are carbamazepine (Tegretol®), lamotrigine (Lamictal®), phenytoin (Epanutin®), sodium valproate (Epilim®) and topiramate (Topamax®). A much older drug which is still prescribed for some patients with epilepsy is phenobarbital.

ANTIDEPRESSANTS

Drugs used to treat depression fall into four groups – two older groups and two with more modern drugs in them.

The tricyclic antidepressants can also be used to treat panic and other anxiety disorders and include drugs such as amitrptyline, dosulepin and lofepramine.

Monoamine oxidase inhibitors (MAOIs) are not used so often because of a danger of dietary and drug interactions but phenelzine (Nardil®) is still prescribed for some patients.

The newer generation of antidepressants include selective serotonin reuptake inhibitors (SSRIs) such as citalopram, paroxetine, and sertraline.

The final group is a collection of 'others' and includes commonly seen drugs such as duloxetine, mirtazepine and venlafaxine.

ANTIPSYCHOTICS

Antipsychotics are also known as neuroleptic drugs and in the past they were termed 'major tranquilisers'.

They can be used as a short-term treatment to calm disturbed patients regardless of the underlying problem (eg schizophrenia, brain damage, mania, toxic delirium or agitated depression) and can also be used to alleviate severe anxiety. These drugs are used to treat psychotic symptoms in schizophrenic patients, many of whom will require long-term treatment.

The older neuroleptics such as chlorpromazine generally cause worse side effects than the newer drugs such as amisulpride, olanzapine (Zyprexa®), quetiapine (Seroquel®), risperidone and aripiprazole (Abilify®).

Antipsychotics drugs pose particular risks of serious side effects for the elderly, especially those with dementia. A great deal of work is being done to reduce their usage in these patients.

ANTIPARKINSON

Parkinson's disease is a progressive, degenerative disease of the nerve cells which cannot be cured, but symptoms can be relieved by treatment with drugs such as cabergoline, pramipexole, ropinirole, co-beneldopa (Madopar®) and co-careldopa (Sinemet®), selegeline, procyclidine.

ANTICOAGULANTS

Warfarin is the most commonly used anticoagulant. It is used to treat blood clots such as deep vein thrombosis (DVT), pulmonary embolism and to prevent clots forming on artificial heart valves. It is also used to treat atrial fibrillation (AF).

The dose must be carefully tailored to the needs of the patient and blood tests are required every 1–2 days during the initial treatment phase. Then, as the patient is stabilised, testing will be less frequent, possibly at 12-week intervals. The test measures the clotting time of the blood and is reported as the international normalised ratio (INR) and depending on the result the warfarin dose may be adjusted. Warfarin is available in 0.5mg, 1mg, 3mg and 5mg tablets, and each strength is a different colour to reduce the chance of errors. (In some areas of the country only 1mg tablets are prescribed as a safety precaution.)

Warfarin should be taken at 6pm in the evening. This is because the blood sample for the INR testing is taken in the morning and the result comes back the same day. This means that if a dose change is needed, the new dose can be started on the day of the test.

It is also important to be aware that if a dose of warfarin is missed the next doses should not be doubled or increased in any way in an attempt to compensate for the missed dose. A note of any missed doses should be made on the yellow card so that when the next INR test is performed the clinic is aware and can factor this in to any decision about possible dose changes.

Many drugs interact with warfarin and it is important that patients on warfarin inform all health care professionals who treat them and should ask for advice when purchasing medicines from a pharmacy.

Aspirin is also often used to lower the risk of clots that cause heart attack or DVTs. Low molecular weight heparins are also used in injection format for shorter terms in the treatment on pulmonary embolism or DVT. Newer antiocoagulants, such as dabigatran and rivaroxaban, may be prescribed as these have the advantage of providing a stable level of anticoagulation on a regular dose which doesn't require the constant monitoring and adjustment as needed with warfarin. The disadvantage of these newer drugs is that, unlike warfarin, their effects are irreversible – in the event of a dosing error there is no antidote. This problem means that in practice most patients needing anticoagulant therapy for DVTs and AF are still receiving warfarin.

OTHER CONDITIONS THAT MAY REQUIRE REGULAR MEDICATIONS

Dementia

Dementia is a condition of permanent mental deterioration and treatment should only be started and supervised by a specialist in the field. The drugs are used in the mild to moderate phase of the disease and work by enhancing the patients' cognitive skills (the skills involved with problem solving, concentration and memory, in short, the skills needed to carry out everyday tasks).

Attention deficit hyperactivity disorder (ADHD)

Drugs prescribed for ADHD should be prescribed by a specialist following diagnosis and ideally after psychological therapies have been tried. The most commonly prescribed drug for ADHD is methylphenidate (Ritalin®, Equasym®). An alternative in the over-18 is atomoxetine (Strattera®).

CHANGES TO AN INDIVIDUAL'S PHYSICAL OR MENTAL WELL-BEING

Changes to a service user's physical or mental well-being may indicate an adverse reaction to a medication. In your role you will probably get to know the individuals in your care very well over time and so you are ideally placed to notice changes in the individual. You are the expert in this situation as, with your first-hand knowledge of the patient, you will probably notice when they are 'not themselves' before the GP does.

All medicines have side effects, but that does not mean that every person taking the medicine will suffer from every possible side effect, nor that the side effect will mean that the medication has to be discontinued. Sometimes the side effects are mild and outweighed by the benefit derived from the medication. Common side effects to medicine include rashes, nausea, diarrhoea, drowsiness and confusion. Sometimes the side effect is used to enhance the benefit derived from the medication, eg cold remedies that cause drowsiness help the patient to sleep despite their symptoms.

When an individual starts on a new medication it is a good idea to read the patient information leaflet (PIL) that is supplied with the medicine. It will give information on how it works but also about known side effects, meaning you will know what to look out for.

An adverse drug reaction (ADR) is when an individual suffers harm from medication used in the normal way and at a normal dose, and can develop after a single dose or after prolonged treatment. This type of problem could include a severe allergy to the medication and is an unexpected consequence of taking the medication.

The important thing is to be vigilant and if you suspect that an individual is suffering from a side effect or ADR you must report it at once. Tell your manager, contact the pharmacy for advice and contact the prescriber. Never be tempted to wait to see if the individual 'gets used to the medicine'. Ask for advice and let the prescriber make the clinical decision.

If the reaction is severe, take emergency action by calling 999 for an ambulance if necessary. A severe allergic reaction, known as anaphylaxis, although rare, can be fatal if not treated promptly. Signs and symptoms of anaphylaxis may include:

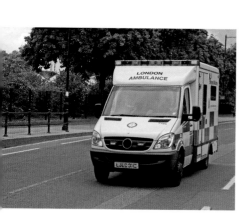

- raised itchy red rash

- swelling of eyes and lips

- breathing difficulties and wheezing

- swelling of the throat

- faint and dizzy feelings

- nausea

- vomiting

- sore, red, itchy eyes.

Emergency action must be sought by ringing 999 if symptoms are affecting:

- airways (eg swelling of the tongue)

- breathing (eg shortness of breath or wheezing)

- circulation (eg dizziness or fainting).

ROLES AND RESPONSIBILITIES IN THE USE OF MEDICATION IN SOCIAL CARE SETTINGS

The various roles and responsibilities in the use of medication can be seen in relation to the three stages of:

- prescribing medication
- dispensing medication
- supporting the use of medication.

PRESCRIBING MEDICATION

The first step in the chain of care is diagnosis of someone's medical condition. This may be done by a GP or the individual may be referred to hospital for a second opinion or further tests. Once the diagnosis is made, the clinician must decide on an appropriate treatment and if this involves medication then it is their responsibility to write a prescription. The prescription must be written according to the legal requirements set out in the various Acts discussed earlier.

Hospital prescriptions

When a patient is seen as a hospital outpatient they may be given a prescription. There are two types of prescriptions issued by hospitals:

1 internal, which can only be dispensed at the hospital

2 external (FP10HP) which can be taken to any community pharmacy for dispensing.

If you accompany an individual to hospital check which prescription type has been issued as the internal prescriptions are only legally allowed to be dispensed by the hospital pharmacy (even if it is run by one of the national pharmacy chains, ie it cannot be taken to one of their branches outside the hospital).

DISPENSING MEDICATION

A prescription will usually be presented for dispensing at a pharmacy. The pharmacy team is made up of various professionals led by the pharmacist. The final responsibility for all dispensing of medicines rests with the pharmacist and it is their job to ensure that the prescription is written legally and they also perform a clinical check, assessing the appropriateness and safety of the prescription. They will look for possible dosage errors and will also check their patient medication records (PMR) to check for any potential interactions with medication that the individual is already taking.

The medicines are assembled by either a dispensary assistant, registered pharmacy technician or pharmacist, a label is produced which must comply with the pharmacy legislation, and before the medicine is handed to the patient or their representative a final accuracy check will be carried out.

Legally, the pharmacist is able to dispense a prescription, self-check their work, then hand the item out; however, in most pharmacies it is considered best practice for two people to check each other. In practice, this means that if the item is dispensed by the pharmacist it will be checked for accuracy by a registered pharmacy technician.

In some pharmacies there are accuracy checking technicians (ACTs) who are registered pharmacy technicians who have gone on to do an extra qualification which allows them to accuracy check prescriptions after they are dispensed. Where an ACT carries out the final accuracy check the pharmacist will have carried out the clinical check and still retains legal responsibility for the accuracy of the dispensing.

In some rural locations, some GPs operate as dispensing practices. In these practices the dispensing process is carried out by dispensers and registered pharmacy technicians under the GP's authority, but there is no pharmacist involvement in the dispensing process. This means there is one less safety check on the medication as there is no pharmacist clinical check performed.

SUPPORTING THE USE OF MEDICINE

Individuals of all ages often rely on others to help them with their medication and the level of help required varies between individuals. For example, someone may rely on a family member or friend to collect their prescription or to help them to remember when to take it.

In a social care setting, where an individual needs help from a health and social care professional, the help can be given with consideration to the preferences of the individual, but also must be done with regard to all of the policies and procedures governing the service.

If somebody needs a prescription to be collected on their behalf, they may have a preferred pharmacy and wherever possible this should be respected. The health and social care worker may support the individual to take their medicine by simply reminding them it is time to take it, or they may need to be more involved, ie removing it from the packaging, offering it to the individual and recording whether it has been taken. They need to watch out for deterioration in health or for possible side effects and to call in health care professionals as appropriate. They also need to report concerns to family members as appropriate but to bear in mind the individual's right to privacy.

RESPONSIBILITIES IN RELATION TO USE OF OVER-THE-COUNTER (OTC) REMEDIES AND SUPPLEMENTS

Individuals may decide to take non-prescription or OTC medication such as multivitamins, cough and cold relief products and herbal remedies, and outside of the care environment this choice is down to the individual. However, as a health and social care professional it is important to understand the legal position. There are two distinct areas to consider.

OTC MEDICINES PURCHASED BY THE INDIVIDUAL OR FAMILY MEMBER

When purchasing an OTC medicine for themselves an individual would normally seek advice on its appropriateness. It is the same when you are assisting someone in social care; they and their family should always be discouraged from purchasing medication without telling the care provider or care home. As a professional, you want to 'allow' the free choice of the individual but you will need to check with the pharmacy and/or prescriber as to the suitability of the medicine. If it is agreed that it is suitable, the medicine needs to be stored safely and the OTC medicine would be recorded on the individuals' medication administration record (MAR) sheet.

OTC MEDICINES PURCHASED BY THE CARE HOME

It is possible for care homes to decide to 'hold' a selection of OTC medicines in stock 'just in case' they are required. To do this they must have a homely remedy policy which states which products will be purchased, which conditions they will be used for and for how long. Generally products will be short acting, such as paracetamols, cough medicine, indigestion medicine, simple laxatives. The home may seek advice from their supplying pharmacy as to the choice of medicines and advice on how to write the policy. Once drafted, the policy needs to be sent to the relevant GPs with information on which of their patients it would apply to. The GP(s) will then inform the home as to whether they approve the policy or prefer to be called out to see the individual in each instance.

Homely remedies must be purchased by the care home and stored securely, but must be kept separate from prescription medicines so that there is no confusion as to which are the homely remedies. The administration of the homely remedy must be recorded in the home's homely remedy record and on the individual's MAR sheet – the dose, time and the reason for using the homely remedy should be recorded.

Many care homes choose not to keep homely remedies under a homely remedy policy.

CASE STUDY

Dee is a senior care assistant in a day service for older people. Today, Geoff attends for the first time; his wife normally cares for him but he is visiting the centre to give his wife a little respite time.

He has a brown envelope in his pocket and at lunchtime he says that he has medication to take. He hands over the envelope which has 'lunchtime' written on it and Dee discovers it has two different tablets inside.

- Should Dee support Geoff to take these tablets?

- How should the medication be packaged?

- What information would Dee need in order to be able to be to support Geoff with his medication?

- What does she need to say to Geoff's wife about the medication and what will be needed in order for Dee and her colleagues to be able to support Geoff?

- What records should Dee keep if she assists with Geoff's medication?

TECHNIQUES FOR ADMINISTERING MEDICATION

When a medicine is developed by a pharmaceutical company, it spends considerable time and a large amount of resources on testing the drug for effectiveness and safety. Another major part of development is deciding on the formulation (form) to use; the company is looking for a way to deliver the drug to the part of the body where the effect is needed while causing the minimum number of side effects. It also needs to think about how stable the drug is (eg is it affected by sunlight, moisture, temperature?).

If a medication is to be taken internally it has to consider things like whether the drug would be affected by the acid in the stomach, would it be absorbed at all and how quickly it would be broken down by the body.

The final decision on formulation is the product of a combination of all of these factors and so it is important to understand how to correctly administer the different formulations to ensure that the individuals in your care get the maximum benefit from their medication.

INTERNAL/SYSTEMIC MEDICINES

For a medicine to have an effect it must get to the part of the body that is being treated (the site of action). **Internal medicines** are delivered into the body by a variety of routes including oral, sublingual, parenteral and transdermal.

Oral

Oral medicines are swallowed and will not have any effect on the body until they have been absorbed from the gut and the drug delivered to the site of action.

- *Tablets and capsules* are swallowed whole, with water, and must dissolve in the gut before they begin to be absorbed. For standard tablets and capsules this generally takes about 20 minutes. If a drug has an unpleasant taste a sugar coating can be added to mask the taste and make it easier to take.

- *Effervescent or soluble tablets* can be prescribed for a more rapid **onset of action**. These are dissolved in water before they are swallowed and so begin to be absorbed as soon as they are taken. They can also be useful for individuals who have difficulty swallowing tablets or capsules.

- *Syrups, suspensions and solutions* are another form of medicine that begin to be absorbed as soon as they are swallowed. When administering a liquid dose form, it is important to shake the bottle before using it so that the drug is evenly spread through the medicine. The dose should be carefully measured using a 5ml spoon or an oral syringe in order to ensure that the correct amount of drug is taken.

- *Slow-release preparations.* Some tablets and capsules are specially formulated to slow down the rate at which they dissolve and the drug is absorbed. This can prolong the time the dose lasts and reduce the number of doses needed over the course of a day. The rate at which slow-release forms dissolve and are absorbed will be affected by antacids so should not be taken within an hour of each other. Slow-release dosage forms should be swallowed whole and never chewed or broken. If an individual cannot swallow them whole then contact the prescriber and ask for an alternative form.

Sublingual route

The mucosal membrane of the mouth has an excellent blood supply and drugs are rapidly absorbed into the bloodstream when they are either sprayed or allowed to dissolve under the tongue or between the gum and upper lip. This route gives a rapid onset of action and is used for glyceryl trinitrate in either tablet or spray form to treat angina. If an individual is vomiting, an anti-nausea medication such as prochloperazine (Buccastem®) can be given by this route. Midazolam is given sublingually to treat status epilepticus.

Key terms

An **internal** or **systemic medicine** is a medicine that is taken into the body and is then carried all around the body by the circulatory system (blood), so that it reaches the part of the body needing treatment.

Onset of action refers to when the medicine begins to have an effect on the body. Depending on the form of medicine used the onset of action will vary.

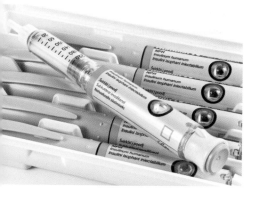

Parenteral route (injections)

Injections can be useful if a patient needs medication but is unconscious or if the speed of the onset of action is important.

- Subcutaneous (SC) injections are given just below the surface of the skin. Insulin is administered this way.

- Intravenous (IV) injections are given directly into the blood via a vein and so the drug very rapidly spreads around the body. They have a rapid onset of action as there is no absorption time – they are delivered directly into the circulatory system. Some antibiotics are given by this route, especially in severe infections.

- Intramuscular (IM) injections are given deep into a muscle. The drug does not get into the system as quickly as an IV injection; it is gradually absorbed from the muscle. Drugs for nausea such as prochloperazine are given IM which may be a great benefit if the patient is vomiting.

- Intra-articular injections are given directly into a joint, such as steroids for arthritis or tendonitis (Adcortyl®, Betnesol® or Depo-Medrone®).

- Depot injections are slow-release injections. They are given deep into the muscle and the drug is generally formulated in an oily base and is slowly released into the body to give a long duration of action. The contraceptive injection Depo-Provera® and some antipsychotic drugs are given this way.

Transdermal

Drugs can be applied to the skin and they are slowly absorbed into the system. This route is used for strong pain relief (buprenorphine and fentanyl patches), nicotine replacement therapy patches and hormone replacement therapy which can be in the form of patches or a gel.

It is important to read the instructions with the patches as different drugs need to be applied to different parts of the body. Always choose a hair-free area. When applying and removing patches, care should be taken not to touch the underside to avoid coming into contact with the drug. After removal, the patch will still have some drug left in it and should be disposed of with medicines waste.

Other routes

Some drug forms are used to deliver topical drugs to the site of action; however these same routes can be used to deliver systemic medication. Nasal sprays and pessaries can be used to deliver hormones systemically, suppositories can be used to deliver pain relief, eg paracetamol or diclofenac, and rectal diazepam solutions can be used to treat status epilepticus.

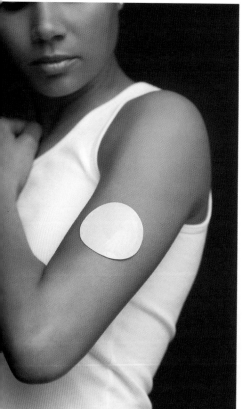

TOPICAL MEDICINES

Ointments and creams

Often an active ingredient is formulated as both an ointment and a cream, and the prescriber can choose which is more appropriate for the patient. Ointments are greasy and are most often used on dry skin. They are more difficult to remove from the skin than creams. Creams have an aqueous (water) base which makes them more easily removed with water.

Sometimes items such as creams are not seen as important as tablets, but if an individual suffers from a skin condition such as eczema the relief from moisturising emollient creams and anti-inflammatory steroid creams should not be underestimated. Gloves must always be worn when handling creams or ointments.

When using steroid creams and ointments, it should be remembered that these contain a powerful medication and, unlike moisturising creams, they should not be applied in a thick layer, but applied sparingly.

When you open a tube or pot, mark it with the date. In a care home setting, a general rule would be to discard large tubs one month after opening and tubes three months from opening. This is to reduce the risk of the product becoming contaminated – the tube has a smaller opening and so can be used for longer as it is less likely to be affected by airborne contamination.

Lotions

Like ointments and creams, lotions are applied to the skin. They are much more fluid than ointments and creams, and can be in an aqueous or an alcoholic base. Care should be taken with alcoholic lotions as they are flammable (avoid naked flames). Again, gloves should always be worn.

Inhalers

There are many types of inhaler devices available – pressurised metered dose (MDI), breath-actuated, or dry powder, and they are designed to deliver drugs to the surfaces of the lungs to treat conditions such as asthma and COPD. It is important that the device is used correctly and pharmacists, nurses and doctors will be happy to help individuals with inhaler technique.

If using an MDI it should be shaken before use, the individual should breathe out and, as they breathe in, press the aerosol to release the dose. A breath-actuated device will release a dose triggered by the in-breath. As the drug is breathed in, the individual should hold their breath for a count of 10 (if comfortable doing so) in order for the drug to stay in contact with the lung tissue and exert its effect. If a second puff is needed, the individual should wait a minute before taking it and shake the device between each puff.

Key term

Topical medicines are applied directly to the part of the body that needs treating.

If the drug is a steroid, rinsing the mouth with water after taking the dose will reduce the chances of the individual developing oral thrush which is a common side effect of using steroid inhalers.

When using both a reliever and a preventer inhaler, the individual should use the reliever first; this will help to relax the airways, and, after about 10 minutes, if they then use the steroid inhaler the drug will penetrate deeper and they will get greater benefit from it. It is not necessary to use the reliever before every dose of steroid; only if the individual is suffering symptoms at the time the steroid dose is due.

For patients who are very short of breath and struggle to use their inhaler, spacer devices such as the Volumatic® and Aerochamber® can be used. The inhaler fits into the space and the patient can then breathe gently from the device and the medication reaches the airways.

Eye drops and ointments

Medication for eye conditions is applied directly to the eye in the form of drops or ointment. These are sterile until opened and most must be discarded four weeks after opening (there are some exceptions to this and the PIL should give this information; alternatively check with the pharmacy). When opening eye preparations note the date of opening, both on the MAR sheet and on the product packaging, to ensure it is not used beyond its opened shelf life.

Eye preparations should be used with care and the tip of the applicator should not touch the eye as this will lead to contamination of the product. If using two drops of the same preparation, wait 30 seconds between administrations and if two different products are to be used, a space of 15 minutes between them should be allowed to avoid one preparation rinsing away the other.

Nasal and ear drops

Follow the manufacturer's instructions and, as with eye preparations, the tip of the applicator should not touch the part of the body being treated.

Nasal sprays

Nasal sprays can be used to deliver medication to the nasal membranes, eg steroid sprays to reduce inflammation in rhinitis and decongestant sprays for colds. They should be used in accordance with the manufacturer's directions – with the head slightly forwards (not tipped back).

Paints

These are applied to areas needing treatment such as nails with a fungal infection. Check the manufacturer's instructions as to how often they should be applied and be aware that many of these products are flammable.

Rectal medicines – suppositories, enemas, foams

When used to deliver topical medication these products deliver the active ingredient into the rectum where it exerts its effect. This may be as a laxative (suppositories and enemas) or as a local anti-inflammatory to treat haemorrhoids or inflammation due to conditions such as Crohn's disease. It is likely that the rectal medication will be administered by a nurse; however the care worker should think about the need for privacy and dignity while helping the individual prepare to have their medication administered.

Vaginal preparations – creams and pessaries

These are used to treat local problems such as vaginal thrush or dryness. Creams for vaginal use generally come with an applicator; pessaries may or may not. As with suppositories, a nurse will administer the product, but privacy should be provided for the individual.

MATERIALS AND EQUIPMENT THAT CAN ASSIST IN ADMINISTERING MEDICATION

It is important to be organised and have everything ready before you begin the medication round, so collect items such as gloves, a jug of fresh water and glasses. Keeping the working area clean and tidy is more hygienic and also makes it less likely that things will go wrong, so work in a logical manner. It is important that any distractions are avoided. Often in care homes staff are given a tabard to wear with words similar to 'Please do not disturb me, I am giving medication' – this is an attempt to reduce interruptions which in turn can reduce mistakes.

You will need to get the medicine ready; if this is locked away you will need the keys to the treatment room, drug cupboard and medicines trolley. Some individuals may have devices to help with medication taking, eg spacer devices for inhalers, and you will need to ensure these are clean and ready too.

You need the MAR sheets so that you can record whether medication was taken, refused or spat out, etc.

In the file with the MAR sheets you may find useful notes detailing an individual's specific needs and peculiarities around taking medication, eg care homes have details such as 'Margaret is capable of taking her own medication'; 'Dorothy needs reassurance while taking her medication'; 'Brian likes to take his white tablet first'; 'Peter has a habit of hiding his tablets, please watch carefully', and so on. Be aware that extra information may be included on the care plan and know where these are stored so that you can access the information if you need to.

RECEIVING, STORING AND DISPOSING OF MEDICATION SUPPLIES SAFELY

RECEIVING MEDICATION SAFELY

It is important that you have the correct medicines available for all of the individuals in your care and a well organised system for managing the medication will help to ensure that this happens.

Order only the medication that is needed each month and keep a record of what was ordered, check the prescriptions when collected from the surgery against your order list and then send the prescription to the pharmacy for dispensing.

Record keeping is very important as you need a written audit trail so that you can follow the 'journey' of medication from entry into the home until it is either taken by the individual or destroyed.

So when the medicines are delivered, you need to check them off against your order list and check and sign for the quantities delivered. This can be done on the MAR sheet.

STORING MEDICATION SAFELY

Medicines must be stored in a suitable place at the correct temperature and humidity, usually in a cool, dry place and away from light. The temperature of the storage area should not be above 25°C.

> **REFLECT**
>
> Think about where you store your medicines at home, and then after reading this section think about whether this is the most appropriate place.
>
> Medicines should be stored securely; if you are assisting an individual in their own home, encourage them to consider where they keep them and bear in mind any visitors with children. Consider storing them in a high cupboard or one with a childproof lock.

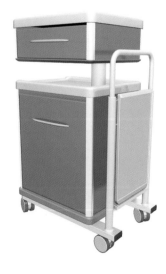

Care homes

In a care home, medicines are stored in a locked trolley, cupboard or room, and the keys kept by the person in charge. Medicine key security is very important. These keys should be kept on a separate fob so that they are always available for the designated person to have them and be able to use them to access the medicines. When it is not in use, the medicines trolley must be secured to a wall and if the worker is called away during the drug round they must always secure the trolley before leaving it.

Internal and external medicines should be stored separately in locked cupboards where space permits; otherwise they can be stored clearly separated and labelled in the same cupboard.

If individuals self-medicate, they must have lockable storage facilities in their room.

Some medicines require refrigeration, eg insulin, certain antibiotic syrups and eye drops. The fridge should be kept locked and the temperature maintained between 2 and 8°C. There should be a max/min thermometer which should be reset every 24 hours, ie after each temperature reading. A daily log of the maximum and minimum fridge temperature should be kept. In smaller homes, if no medicine fridge is available, the medication may be kept in a lockable box, clearly marked as medicines, and stored within the kitchen fridge. Again, temperature logs must be kept.

Oxygen equipment presents special considerations because it supports combustion and so increases fire risk. Cylinders must be stored in a dry, clean, well-ventilated area, away from heat, and any suspected problems with leaks, etc should be reported to the manager who will contact the supplier. If any spare cylinders are kept in the treatment room they should be secured to prevent them falling over, either in a trolley or chained to the wall. The home needs to display a notice to say that compressed gas is being stored on the premises and warning notices prohibiting smoking and naked lights must be displayed anywhere oxygen is stored or being used. This includes residents using oxygen concentrators as well as cylinders. Notices can be obtained from the oxygen supplier.

SAFE DISPOSAL OF UNUSED OR UNWANTED MEDICATION

There are various reasons why medication may no longer be required – the individual may have decided they do not want to take the medication or the GP may have changed their medication, the medication may only be required infrequently and has gone out of date, or perhaps the individual has died.

If a medication is no longer required it must be securely stored, clearly separated from other medicines, until it is removed from the home.

Following a death, the individual's medicines should be retained for seven days before disposal in case there is a coroner's inquest.

Unwanted medicines must be disposed of safely, in a way that poses no threat to other individuals or the environment. They should never be disposed of in the refuse bin or thrown down the sink, toilet or sluice.

There are certain regulations that must be considered in social care settings when returning unwanted medicines.

Pharmacies will accept unwanted medicines from individuals and residential homes – they store them securely until they are collected by a waste contractor for safe incineration.

Nursing homes

By law, pharmacies are unable to accept medicines for disposal from nursing homes which must have their own contract with a waste company.

Controlled drugs (CDs)

Even when no longer required, controlled drugs (CDs) are still subject to conditions set out in the Misuse of Drugs Regulations and must be kept in the CD cupboard until they are returned for disposal. In care homes, all CDs are logged in the CD register and must be signed out when sent for destruction. If they are returned to a pharmacy they are then entered into the pharmacy CD destruction register; the date, quantity, type and who has returned the controlled drug will be recorded.

Pharmacies have special kits for CD disposal (DOOM® kits) which have a resin in them which solidifies when mixed with liquid, and this means that the controlled drug cannot be removed from the pot. These DOOM® kits are then stored safely and incinerated with the other medicines waste.

Nursing homes dispose of their unwanted CDs as described above, except that they cannot return them to a pharmacy and so have a supply of DOOM® kits for their own use.

Transdermal CD patches, such as fentanyl, will still have some drug in them when they are removed from the skin and must be handled with care. Do not touch the side of the patch which was in contact with the skin. Fold the patch on itself, sticky sides together, and dispose of the used patch as for other CDs.

Sharps

Sharps (needles, lancets, etc) cannot be returned with normal waste – they must be placed in a sharps bin at the point of treatment to reduce the risk of needlestick injuries. Arrangements for disposal of full sharps bins vary around the country. In some areas pharmacies are unable to accept sharps bins as they do not have access to the sharps collection service. Some health centres will take back sharps bins or there may be certain hubs that act as collection points. You will need to find out what the arrangements are in the area where you practise.

Record keeping

Members of the public do not get a receipt from the pharmacy for returned medicines; however in a social care setting you must follow the procedures set down by your employer.

If you assist an individual in their own home and use MAR sheets you may ask the pharmacy to sign the MAR sheet to say what was returned. Care homes will have a record book for returns where the home lists all of the medicines being returned, and the pharmacy will sign the record when they accept them. The pharmacy may keep a copy of the return sheet. As discussed above, CDs are also subject to further record keeping.

PROMOTING RIGHTS WHEN MANAGING MEDICATION

There are a number of basic principles to follow when supporting the use of medication. Many of these relate to good practice in care and are covered throughout this book.

CONSENT

Anyone whose work involves treating or caring for people must ensure they have the individual's consent to any proposed action. It is a fundamental and legal right that an individual can determine what happens to their own body and this encompasses all aspects of care including managing medication. The Department of Health's guidance for individuals and for carers and clinicians on delivering care states that:

It is a general legal and ethical principle that valid consent must be obtained before starting treatment or physical investigation, or providing personal care, for a person. This principle reflects the right of patients to determine what happens to their own bodies, and is a fundamental part of good practice. A healthcare professional (or other healthcare staff) who does not respect this principle may be liable both to legal action by the patient and to action by their professional body. Employing bodies may also be liable for the actions of their staff.

(Department of Health 2009: 5)

Consent can only be given by the individual and it is important that they understand the information and the implications of the choice they are being asked to make in order for it to be 'informed'. If it is felt that the individual does not have the capacity to give consent a spouse or family member cannot simply step in and give consent.

If an individual makes a choice that you do not consider reasonable this is not an indication that they are incapable of making a choice – the test is whether they understand the implications of their choices.

An assessment of the individual must be carried out and this must not be influenced by organisational pressures or your personal opinions. It may be decided that an individual has the capacity to make some choices but not others, eg in the early stages of dementia.

Where it is decided that an individual is not capable of giving or refusing consent, you can still lawfully provide treatment as long as it is in the person's 'best interests'. While the spouse and close family cannot give consent on behalf of the individual, they should be included in the decision making where possible.

Legally, the health professional responsible for the person's care is responsible for deciding whether or not a particular treatment is in that person's best interests. Ideally decisions will reflect an agreement between clinicians, professional carers and those close to the service user.

Key term

Active participation is about people being involved in their care, as opposed to being a 'recipient' of that care (ie it is about something being done with someone rather than something being done to someone). Active participation also means that people take part in the activities of daily and independent life as much as possible.

SELF-MEDICATION OR 'ACTIVE PARTICIPATION'

Some individuals want to retain responsibility for their own medication and it is important that this is recognised and that the individual is supported in this decision.

DIGNITY AND PRIVACY

The rights of the individual to be treated with respect at all times are fundamental when delivering care. Consider issues of privacy when having a conversation about medication; do not talk about sensitive issues where conversations can be overheard and think about talking loudly to an individual who is hard of hearing – they may hear you, but who else can hear too? It is important that you do not assume that an individual will be unable to understand issues around medication, but also consider whether they need someone with them during certain conversations, eg a family member who may help them remember what was said.

CONFIDENTIALITY

The individual has the right to expect confidentiality and so information should only be shared with persons who can reasonably be expected to need that information. You must be aware of with whom it is acceptable to discuss medication issues, ie the treating clinician and other health professionals such as nurses and pharmacists involved in the care of the individual. Remember, you must never discuss the individual outside of work.

REFLECT

- What information do you think is acceptable to share with a close family member or friend of the individual?

- How would you decide?

CASE STUDY

Jon is a senior support worker with a reablement team. He is part of the team working with Frank following his recent discharge from hospital. Frank has to take regular medication for blood pressure and to control his cholesterol. He is also diabetic and needs to take his metformin three times a day. Before he went into hospital, Frank was able to manage his medication, but after being in hospital he has got used to the nurses dealing with his medication for him.

- Should Jon assume that Frank can no longer manage his medication?

- What if Frank's only problem was not being able to open childproof tops?

Following an assessment it is decided that Frank is happy to manage his medication, but Frank is concerned that he may forget an odd dose.

- What sort of simple strategies could Jon suggest for Frank?

- If it was decided that Frank needed more help, such as a 'blister pack' for his medication, whom would Jon need to contact to discuss this?

- Who would Jon need to liaise with in order to ensure that Frank had a safe and reliable system in place for ordering, obtaining and taking his medication once the six weeks had finished?

USING RISK ASSESSMENT TO PROMOTE AN INDIVIDUAL'S INDEPENDENCE IN MANAGING MEDICATION

Where an individual is receiving help with medication in social care they must have consented to this. Some individuals will want to retain responsibilities for their own medication management and these individuals will need to be risk assessed.

When carrying out a risk assessment, the care provider must consider how the individual will cope with the various aspects of self-management of their medicines, including ordering and safe storage of medication, how usage will be monitored and documented. They must assess the level of competence of the individual with consideration given to their ability to understand the need for the medicine as well as their memory and manual dexterity.

A physical disability need not be a barrier to self-medication, eg medication can be supplied with non-childproof tops for individuals with arthritic hands. It is possible that compromises may be reached; eg some individuals look after their own inhalers or creams and other medication use is supported by health and social care workers.

When deciding that an individual is not able to self-medicate, several factors will have influenced the decision. Not only does it depend on the individual but also on the type of medication or the condition being treated. When we think of poor memory we think of missed doses but what if someone takes repeated doses as they 'can't remember having their tablets today'. Some medicines result in problems if not taken correctly, eg alendronic acid is more likely to cause severe side effects if the dosage instruction is not followed. Conditions such as diabetes, epilepsy and Parkinson's are poorly controlled if medication is not taken at the correct times and dose.

It must also be remembered that the individual's level of competence may change and so it is important to reassess them regularly to see if they are still able to self-medicate. It may be that an annual review of this is sufficient but also be aware that during an acute illness, eg infection, they may require help with medication so the process of risk assessment should be dynamic and reactive.

ETHICAL CONSIDERATIONS

In implementing the principles outlined a number of ethical dilemmas might occur. You will find Chapter 4 useful in considering how to respond to ethical dilemmas generally. With specific regard to the use of medication, the ethical issues that might occur are as follows.

Confidentiality and information sharing

When an individual is happy to take their medication, the situation is fairly straightforward. Your ethical issues are more likely to concern confidentiality and sharing of information as discussed above.

Refusing medication

When the issue of consent is considered it is important that the individual is assessed as to their ability to understand the choices they make. If an individual has been assessed as competent to consent or refuse to their medication regimen, and they refuse to take it then you may have a conflict. It is important to remember that they have the right to make a decision that you do not agree with, but you may consider the follow actions:

- Try to explore the reasons behind their decision with them, eg a vegetarian may refuse to take gelatine capsules but if the medication is supplied in an alternative form it may be acceptable to them.

- Consider whether the individual is acting voluntarily (ie is not under pressure from anyone – this may be a safeguarding issue).

- Ensure that the individual has enough information to make the decision. Do they fully understand the consequence of their refusal and its detrimental effect on their health?

- Where an individual refuses to take their medication, the health and social care worker should discuss this with their manager and inform the prescriber and the supplying pharmacy. The decision about telling the family presents another ethical dilemma as the individual has the right to choose.

The only exception to the competency and consent rule is that for individuals where treatment is being provided for mental disorder under the terms of mental health legislation. If they refuse treatment for their mental disorder, specialised guidance should be obtained. The law does not give any power to treat an unrelated physical disorder in these individuals if they refuse treatment.

Covert administration

For individuals who have been assessed as unable to give consent, then, as discussed previously, the health professional responsible for the person's care is responsible for deciding whether or not a particular treatment is in that person's best interests.

Covert administration should not be considered for individuals who are capable of giving consent. For certain patients who cannot make an informed decision but refuse to take their medication, covert administration may be necessary and justified.

It should be done within the existing legal and best practice frameworks to protect the individual receiving the medication and the care workers involved in giving the medicines. When the decision is being considered, the prescribing clinician, supplying pharmacy, social services and the individual's family will have been included in the process. It must be well documented and regularly reviewed.

Key term

Covert administration is where medication is administered in a disguised format without the knowledge or consent of the individual receiving it, eg in food or in a drink.

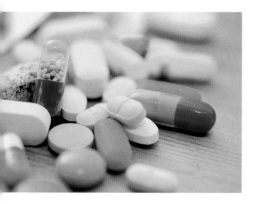

SUPPORTING THE USE OF MEDICATION

ACCESSING INFORMATION ABOUT AN INDIVIDUAL'S MEDICATION

Each individual who is receiving some sort of social care will have a care plan with details of their care needs, medical conditions and treatment plans. For a detailed record of their medication, you may check the MAR sheet which lists all medication currently prescribed and for the current month it will be marked up to show doses taken and any missed or refused doses. Older MAR sheets will be stored at the home and can be accessed if you need to check further back.

You should also have access to medical information and know whom to ask for advice.

Medication is supplied with a patient information leaflet (PIL) which is written in accessible language as it is produced for patients rather than clinicians. It will detail what the medication is used for, gives normal dosage ranges and any special instructions about how or when to take the medicine. It also lists possible side effects and any special storage information. *The British National Formulary* (*BNF*) is an excellent source of information for health care professionals and is produced every six months so that information is up to date. This can be used to check information about medication if you need more detailed information than is provided in the PIL.

> **REFLECT**
>
> - Find the *BNF* at your place of work and see when it was printed – is this new enough? Will it still be reliable?

USEFUL SOURCES

If you have internet access you can visit the *BNF* online and register as a health care professional for access to the latest version of the *BNF*. See www.bnf.org.

You can also contact your supplying pharmacy who will be happy to help with questions and give advice relating to medication.

The prescriber will also give help and advice so you may want to contact the surgery, eg to clarify when a medication should be taken.

A useful website with information for health professionals and also available in patient-friendly terms is www.patient.co.uk.

SUPPORTING AN INDIVIDUAL TO USE MEDICATION IN WAYS THAT PROMOTE HYGIENE, SAFETY, DIGNITY AND ACTIVE PARTICIPATION

Medication may be supplied in bottles or boxes from the pharmacy or may have been supplied in a compliance aid in order to help the individual remember when to take their medication and also whether they have taken a particular dose. For care homes the medication may be supplied in a monitored dosage system (MDS). There are several systems on the market, eg Nomad® and Venalink®, and the choice of system will have been agreed between the pharmacy and the care home. Most systems are only suitable for tablets and capsules, and there are some drugs that are not suitable for packing in these systems as the quality of the medicine would be affected either by humidity or light, eg Epilim® tablets and any effervescent tablets.

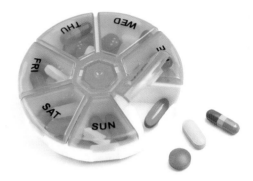

Medication must always be given from the container in which it was dispensed by the pharmacy. You must never pop it from the blister into another container in advance of the drug round. This is also true if the individual is going to be away from home at the time of the drug round. Putting tablets into an unlabelled container or envelope to take with the service user is not allowed.

As previously discussed, when supporting an individual to use medication you must promote hygiene, safety, dignity and active participation. Think about having a clean tidy area, be well organised, with everything ready before starting the process – eg medication, record chart, water and cup, etc. Wash your hands and wear gloves, if appropriate, and avoid handling medications. Remember to treat the individual with respect, explain what is happening and encourage them to be interested and to understand the process, giving reassurance where required.

You must always take the medication to the individual in the packaging supplied by the pharmacy.

ENSURING THE MEDICATION IS USED OR ADMINISTERED 'CORRECTLY'

'Correctly' in this situation means that you must ensure that:

1 the correct individual receives

2 the correct medication

3 in the correct dose

4 by the correct route

5 at the correct time

6 with agreed support

7 with respect for dignity and privacy.

It is crucially important to correctly identify the individual who you are supporting. This may be straightforward if you are visiting them in their own home; however in care homes there is more potential for confusion. If you approach an individual and ask them if they are 'George Brown' they may say 'yes' when this is not true – they could be hard of hearing or they may be confused. A better way to determine identity is to ask them their name; this is more likely to elicit an accurate response. It is also good practice to have a recent photograph of each resident in the medication folder – this is particularly helpful for new or bank staff.

Check the name on the MAR sheet to match the individual with the record sheet.

Select the medication for the individual; again check the name on the medication label to ensure you have the correct medication. For each medication you must check that it is the correct drug, that the strength and the dose are correct, and that the form is suitable for the route of administration and has not expired. For each of these variables you must check both the MAR sheet and the label on the medication. If you notice that a medicine looks different from what you were expecting, do not give the medication until you have confirmed it is correct. You could ring the pharmacy and confirm with them (it may simply be that the generic medication was prepared by a different manufacturer who uses a different colour, but you must never assume). Trust your instinct; if you think it may be wrong, check first. If it is incorrect it is better for the individual to miss a dose while the error is corrected than for them to have been given the wrong medication.

Ensure that you are looking at the correct time slot on the MAR sheet and that the medication is the correct one for the time of day. You must be sure you are giving morning medication if you are completing the morning medication round.

You must tell the individual that you have their medication ready for them to take as they have the right to refuse the medication at each administration. Check in the individual's care plan as to whether they require any particular support to take their medication. Some need a simple prompt or perhaps encouragement and reassurance while others may need more practical help.

If the medication is prescribed PRN (when required), such as analgesia, you must ask the individual if they need the medication at this time. Check the care plan and medication notes to determine maximum frequency and whether the individual can tell you when they need their PRN medication.

You must sign the MAR sheet immediately after the medication is given. It is unacceptable to sign the MAR prior to giving the medication or to fill it in later during a quiet time. This could lead to problems, such as the individual refusing the medication, your forgetting exactly what happened, or a colleague thinking you have missed giving the medication and so giving another dose.

Remember that to keep the audit trail accurate you must sign for each medication at the time it is given, and if a dose is refused you must also note that on the MAR sheet. You will see the codes along the bottom of the MAR sheet so you can record why a dose was not given. Your choices might be:

A = refused

B = nausea or vomiting

C = hospitalised

D = social leave

E = refused and destroyed

F = other ....

The final code allows you to record another reason if it is not covered by the other options.

CASE STUDY

Chen is a senior care assistant in a residential service for older people. He is supporting service users to take their medication in the residential care home where he works. One of the elderly residents, Barbara, needs to take medication to control her blood pressure as well as donepezil (Aricept®) for her dementia. Today Barbara is refusing to take her medication.

- Where might Chen get information about Barbara and the support she needs to take her medication?

- If Chen discovers that gentle reassurance is all that is usually required but today Barbara still refuses her medication, what records should Chen make?

- Who should Chen tell?

- Can Chen simply hide the medication in Barbara's food?

- Who needs to be involved in any decisions taken regarding Barbara's medication?

ADDRESSING ANY PRACTICAL DIFFICULTIES THAT MAY ARISE WHEN MEDICATION IS USED

It is important to understand what to do when difficulties arise when medication is being used.

Medication not available

If medication is unavailable this needs to be recorded on the MAR sheet. In the example above you could use 'F = other' and write 'unavailable' on the dotted line. It is not enough to simply record the medication as not available – you need to speak to your manager and alert them to the problem. Contact the pharmacy for advice on the importance of the medication and the urgency needed when addressing this problem. As discussed earlier, the pharmacist may be able to make an emergency supply; however you will need to contact the GP to request an urgent prescription.

Lost medication

If medication is lost several issues must be addressed. You need to conduct a thorough search for the medication; it is important that it is not available for anyone else to take in error. You need to let your manager know and you will also need to contact the prescriber for a new prescription. If the medication is a controlled drug (CD) you will also need to let the CD accountable officer know.

Missed medication

If a dose of medication is missed it is important to find out if the dose should be given when the omission is noticed or whether the dose should be left untaken. It would be best to contact the pharmacy for advice on what to do in this situation because it will depend on the medication as to what the recommended action should be.

Spilt medication

If a tablet is dropped on the floor you need to pick it up. It should be disposed of and another tablet taken from the pack. If you use blister packs you would take a tablet from the end of the pack; this will mean the immediate dose is not missed and will give you time to contact the surgery to request a prescription for a replacement.

If liquids are spilt, they should be mopped up with regard to all of the health and safety issues. Do not leave wet patches on the floor which someone may slip in and be aware that you should not leave the medicines trolley unattended while you go to get equipment to deal with the spillage. If there is no medication left for the patient to take then you must deal with the incident in the same way as when medicine is not available. (Remember there may be a back-up bottle in the medication cupboard so do check this before missing the dose.)

Individual decides not to take their medication

We have discussed the rights of the individual to refuse to take their medication but this needs to be documented on the MAR sheet. Also let your manager know and if they are routinely refusing medication you will need to discuss this with the pharmacy and the prescriber.

Difficulty in taking medication in the prescribed form

If the individual is struggling to take their medication, eg they cannot swallow tablets, contact the pharmacy who may be able to suggest alternatives and then the prescriber can be contacted about the possibility of changing the form prescribed.

Wrong medication used

If the wrong medication is used you must immediately let your manager know. You can contact the pharmacy for immediate advice and you must advise the individual's GP. Delay could prove fatal so this error must be dealt with urgently. Local policies should also be followed as many organisations will have an incident-reporting document or process.

Vomiting after taking medication

After taking oral medication it takes about 20 minutes for the tablet to dissolve and then it begins to be absorbed into the body. Unless the individual is sick immediately after taking the dose, it is very difficult to assess how much of the drug will have been absorbed. You should therefore seek expert advice on what to do in this situation. Do not simply give another dose and do not assume it is alright to miss this dose, eg if it is an anti-epileptic drug the individual will be at increased risk of fits if the dose is missed.

Adverse reaction

If you suspect an adverse reaction tell your manager, contact the pharmacy for advice, contact the prescriber or if you think the reaction is severe or life threatening (eg anaphylaxis) call 999.

Discrepancies in records or directions for use

If you check the MAR sheet and there are any discrepancies tell your manager so that the discrepancy can be investigated.

If the MAR sheet and the label directions do not match, again contact your manager. It may be that the prescriber has given a verbal instruction to change the directions after the medicine was dispensed, but this should be written in the care plan and should be annotated on the MAR and signed by the staff who accepted the instruction and the staff member who witnessed the verbal instruction being taken. Never just assume it is correct; double-check with the prescriber if necessary and do not give the medication until the discrepancy is resolved.

PRN medication – how often can it be taken?

If you are unsure how often a PRN medicine can be taken within a 24-hour period, you can check with the pharmacy for the safe maximum daily dose. The information will also be available in the BNF. However, even if you determine what the maximum daily dosage would be, this does not tell you what the prescriber intended the patient to take. If you are present while they are prescribing ask them to clarify this for you. If you come across this issue after the prescriber has left the home you could contact them at the surgery and ask for clarification.

ACCESSING FURTHER INFORMATION OR SUPPORT

Very often you will know the individual you are supporting to take medication and be familiar with their regular medicines. However, you should consider accessing extra information if they are prescribed a new medication, especially if it is one with which you are unfamiliar.

You should not hesitate to look up information in PILs, speak to your manager or contact the pharmacy and/or the prescriber if you run into any of the issues described above.

RECORDING AND REPORTING ON USE OF MEDICATION

As discussed earlier, it is important that all aspects of the care given to an individual should be recorded. With respect to medication, this record should include exactly what was given and when, along with observations about the individual's condition and any other relevant information.

MEDICATION ADMINISTRATION RECORD (MAR) SHEETS

MEDICATION ADMINISTRATION RECORD

MEDICATIONS	HOUR	1	2	3	4	5	6	7	8	9	10	11	12	13	14	15	16	17	18	19	20	21	22	23	24	25	26	27	28	29	30	31

NURSE'S ORDERS, MEDICATION NOTES, AND INSTRUCTION ON REVERSE SIDE

CHARTING FOR MONTH:		Page of
Primary Care Physician:		Telephone No.
Specialist(s):		Telephone No.
Allergies: Adverse Drug Reactions:	Pharmacy:	Telephone No.
Diagnosis:		
Medicaid Number	Medicare Number	Complete entries checked By: Title: Date:
Patient:		Location:

INSTRUCTIONS: a. Put initial in appropriate box when medication given.
    b. Circle initials when medication refused.
    c. State reason for refusal on nurse's notes.
    d. PRN Med: Reason given and results should be noted on Nurse's Medication Notes.

CHARTING CODES:
A-Charted in error
B-Patient refused
C-Patient out of facility

D-Drug not given Indicate reason in Nurse's Medication Notes.
E-See Nurse's Notes

F-Patient did not retain medication

DATE	1	2	3	4	5	6	7	8	9	10	11	12	13	14	15	16	17	18	19	20	21	22	23	24	25	26	27	28	29	30	31	DATE
Temperature/ Pulse																																Temperature/ Pulse
Blood Pressure																																Blood Pressures

NURSE'S MEDICATION NOTES

PATCH SITE/ INFECTION SITE CODES:
1-RIGHT DORSAL GLUTEUS
2-LEFT DORSAL GLUTEUS
3-RIGHT VENTRAL GLUETEUS

4-LEFT VENTRAL GLUTEUS
5-RIGHT LATERAL THIGH
6-LEFT LATERAL THIGH

7-RIGHT DELTOID
8-LEFT DELTOID
9-RIGHT UPPER ARM

10-LEFT UPPER ARM
11-RIGHT ANTERIOR THIG
12-LEFT ANTERIO THIGH

13-UPPER BACK LEFT
14-UPPER BACK RIGHT

15-UPPER CHEST LEFT
16-UPPER CHEST RIGHT

Date/Hour	Medication/Dosage	Reason	Results/Response	Hour/Initials

The MAR sheet is a legal document which provides an audit trail for medication within the home. It must be filled in at each drug round and signed as each medication is offered and either taken or refused. If the dose is one or two to be taken, the number taken should also be noted on the MAR sheet. For PRN medication there is often space on the back of the MAR to detail what was given and why it was appropriate at that time, ie document the reason the PRN medication was given.

MAR sheets must be retained for a minimum of six years after the last entry was made. For children they must be retained until the young person's 25th birthday (or 26th if they were 17 at the conclusion of treatment).

CARE PLANS

The care plan should be completed with information on medication taking and any notes on the individual's condition. Details of visits from GPs and nurses should be noted on the care plan along with any diagnoses, tests ordered and medication issues. Any concerns should be noted on the care plan. This is then a complete record of the ongoing condition and the care given to the individual, and it can be accessed by all relevant parties involved in that individual's care.

REPORTING CONCERNS

Any concerns about medication should be reported to your manager. Contact the pharmacy for advice and also contact the prescriber or the health care professional in charge of the care of the individual. Depending on confidentiality issues, the individual's family may also be informed if you have concerns.

Always make a written record of any action taken; a brief note can be added to the MAR sheet but also make an entry in the care plan. Depending on where the care is provided there may also be a local policy to comply with – the care provider company may have a report book or diary that must be completed. Documenting actions taken will help to prove you followed correct procedures and acted on your concerns if there is any kind of enquiry at a later date.

REPORTING USE OF MEDICATION AND ANY ASSOCIATED PROBLEMS

Routine medication use

You may need to report medication use to another health and social care worker, eg when shifts change. This could involve confirming that all was in order with a medication round or highlighting issues, such as refusal of a medicine or unavailability, etc.

If you attend a medical consultation with the individual you may be asked about their regular medication; taking a copy of the MAR sheet to the appointment would be a useful way to convey this information.

REFLECT

- How would you know if someone under your care was allergic to a particular medicine?

- The prescriber and pharmacist should have this information, but what if the individual had been seen by a locum GP and the family had collected the medication from a pharmacy not usually used by the individual?

KEY POINT

If an individual's family enquire about medication issues you may need to talk to them about this but bear in mind confidentiality issues.

Side effects

If you suspect an individual is suffering from a side effect from their medication you should report this to your manager straight away. Discuss it with the pharmacist who may be able to advise that it is a common side effect and may settle in a week or two. Alternatively, they may advise you to get in touch with the prescriber to discuss a change of medication. The vital thing is that you seek advice and do not just 'wait and see' if the problem passes.

If you suspect a serious adverse drug reaction (ADR), again act urgently and speak to your manager, the pharmacy and the prescriber. If you suspect the problem is life threatening, eg the airway, breathing or circulation is affected, call 999 without delay.

If you suspect a problem with medication always follow policies and procedures.

Medication error

As with the problems discussed above, you must report a medication error to your manager, the pharmacy and the prescriber, and for an error you will need to inform the individual and potentially their family. You must never try to cover up an error. Act promptly because any delay may worsen consequences, even resulting in death of the individual depending on the nature of the error.

Once a mistake occurs every action you take should be documented – it is important to show that you followed the correct procedures.

As soon as you have done all that you can to ensure the safety of the individual, make detailed notes about the circumstances leading up to the error. It is good to do this straight away while events are clear in your mind as you may be asked to explain what happened at some time later.

In the aviation industry every accident is investigated and lessons learned are put into practice to reduce the likelihood of a similar accident happening again. This type of approach is now used in medication error incidents, so even if you think the mistake was 'simply human error', you should expect a risk analysis to follow. The result should be an improvement of policies and procedures so that the whole organisation learns from the error. Organisations should adopt a fair blame culture and every error should be treated as a learning opportunity to improve practice.

If you have correctly followed procedures and an error occurs, it will not necessarily result in dismissal, but any attempt to cover up a mistake will result in some form of sanction.

To recap, in order that an individual can receive timely and appropriate treatment and the incident be properly investigated, it is absolutely vital that any error and possible causes are reported promptly and honestly.

MESSAGES FROM RESEARCH

Helping older people take prescribed medication

The Social Care Institute for Excellence research briefing on helping older people to take prescribed medication in their own home (2005) reports that:

- 45% of medication prescribed in the UK is for older people aged 65 and over

- 36% of people aged 75 and over take four or more prescribed drugs

- as many as 50% of older people on prescribed medication may not take their medicines as instructed

- older people living at home fail to take their medication as instructed for both unintentional and intentional reasons

- unintentional reasons include a lack of easily understandable information about how and when to take their drugs, difficulties reading labels and opening containers, and the need to take many different drugs or many doses

- alarm clocks, positioning medication in visible places and taking it at routine times, such as mealtimes, have all been found by older people to be helpful in reminding them to take their medications

- intentional reasons for not taking medicines as instructed include concerns about the value or effectiveness of medicines, their side effects and the inconvenience of taking the drugs at the prescribed times and frequency.

CHAPTER 16
Knowledge and understanding in health and social care

A great deal of work is taking place in health and social care designed to 'professionalise' the workforce and the term 'professionalisation agenda' is now in regular use in the field. This professionalisation of health and social care is particularly important in ensuring that service users are receiving the best possible support available.

This chapter covers the theoretical and legislative basis for your work and for specific interventions with people. It also covers evidence-based practice in detail. The knowledge in this chapter is needed as the field becomes increasingly professionalised – this means it is more essential than ever for you to be able to explain to others not only *what* you are doing, but *why* you are doing it.

Links to other chapters

The content in this chapter is relevant to all other chapters in this book and it will support readers to complete all units of their qualification. It is particularly linked to Chapter 8.

WHY KNOWLEDGE IS THE FOOD OF HEALTH AND SOCIAL CARE PRACTICE

Shakespeare famously said that 'music be the food of love', and, on similar lines, knowledge is the 'food' of health and social care. A very extensive knowledge base exists in the sector which reflects the diversity of health and social care practice.

The danger of not working on developing our knowledge in health and social care is that, as a practitioner, you become reduced to simply doing as you are instructed without understanding why you are doing it. This can be compared to warming up a ready-made meal. Ready-made meals are not the most nutritious or tasty, and often there is a lack of satisfaction in what you have prepared. However, if you cook using a range of ingredients which you have to hand, the food is much more satisfying and generally more tasty. As you develop your cooking skills, you will discover that you don't need to use your cookbook every step of the way. Just checking your recipe every now and again means you will develop your own ideas and produce better results. You can go to your cookbook for new ideas as well.

That is very much like knowledge in health and social care practice. You will have used this book to complete your diploma and hopefully it has helped you to develop your knowledge. You will want to look back at it every now and again as your skills develop and you need to revisit a 'recipe'.

Many health and social care workers feel that they are very much 'hands-on' workers and that knowledge isn't necessarily something for them to focus on. Without this knowledge, however good they are, there is a gap at the centre. Best (holistic) practice in health and social care involves knowledge. It is important to know why you do what you.

In health and social care, knowledge provides more than simply 'food for thought' – it provides the essential nutrients that enhance, inform and provide validity for professional practice.

DIFFERENT TYPES OF KNOWLEDGE

In 2006, Cameron and Boddy drew on a range of research studies that considered the knowledge and education required for effective health and social care practice. They noted a distinction between three forms of knowledge:

- *Tacit knowledge*. Sometimes referred to as practice wisdom, this is the knowledge derived from experience and from personal qualities.

- *Functional knowledge*. This is the knowledge that might be specifically required to perform defined tasks to an agreed standard. This is the kind of knowledge that has historically featured most heavily in competence-based qualifications.

- *Professional knowledge*. This type of knowledge is described as combining 'professional skills (including specific competences) and practical experience with a strong theoretical underpinning'.

(Boddy and Statham 2009: 13)

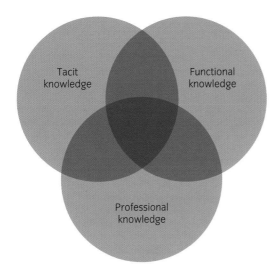

KNOWLEDGE, SKILLS AND VALUES

It is widely recognised that good practice is made up of knowledge, skills and values and these interrelate to produce effective professional practice. This means that the knowledge that you have and the values that you hold will impact on the skills you can use in your work.

The Diploma in Health and Social Care recognises the way in which knowledge affects skills and the fact that knowledge is a vital component of effective professional practice.

MAKING USE OF KNOWLEDGE

With the increased professionalisation of health and social care, the importance of knowledge is becoming more apparent in the qualification framework used in the sector. For example, within the Qualifications and Credit Framework (QCF) there are some purely knowledge-based units. However, it is not *having* knowledge that is important. The most important aspect of knowledge is what the health and social care worker *does* with that knowledge and how they use it.

Qualifications in the field recognise this and regularly refer not only to the learner 'knowing' something but 'knowing how to ...', 'understanding' and 'explaining'. This means that candidates not only need to demonstrate they know something, eg by describing a piece of knowledge, but that they know how to make use of this knowledge in their practice.

Using knowledge effectively is about three key aspects.

1 *Evidence-based practice*. This is about understanding that the work you do should be informed by the best-available research, evidence and knowledge of what is most effective practice.

2 *Law-informed practice*. Your practice has to be informed and guided by relevant legislation. This chapter covers what this actually means, and how you can ensure the fullest range of legislative knowledge is applied in your work.

3 *Theory-informed practice*. This is essential to effective health and social care. Professional practice is practice that is informed by theory. This is what makes the difference between a professional and someone who acts on instinct or 'gut feelings'.

The remainder of this chapter explores each of these three areas in turn.

EVIDENCE-BASED PRACTICE

The Canadian medical group at McMaster University, who first used the term 'evidence-based practice', defined it as a process which considers:

the conscientious, explicit and judicious use of current best evidence in making decisions about the care of individuals.

(Sackett et al 1997)

One definition of evidence-based practice used widely by a range of government bodies states that:

Although there are many complex definitions of evidence-based practice, it can be succinctly described as the systematic use of the best available evidence of what works when reaching decisions about how best to treat, care for or support patients and clients. Crucially, evidence-based practice involves the integration of the individual practitioner or clinician's expertise with the best available evidence from research, as well as with the preferences of the individual client or patient.

(Department for Children, Schools and Families 2008)

Evidence-based practice is often taken to refer to the use of research in practice. Strictly speaking, however, the term for this would be research-minded practice. Evidence-based practice is increasingly seen as using a range of evidence in practice, which is drawn not only from research, but also from knowledge of legislation, theory and practice. This is one of the main reasons that qualifications in health and social care require candidates to have an understanding of legislation, theory and research. If workers are committed to the principles of evidence-based practice, then they should be able to easily identify the specific knowledge in relation to theory, legislation and research that is influencing their daily work.

The process of evidence-based practice is outlined in the following diagram:

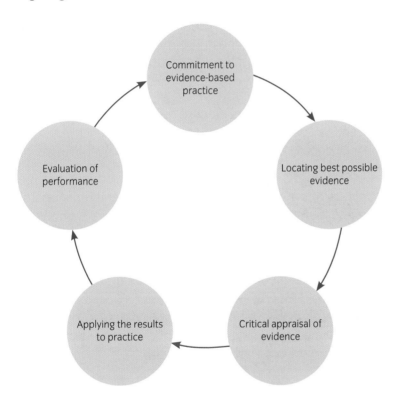

COMMITMENT TO EVIDENCE-BASED PRACTICE

Evidence-based practice is essential because it:

- can assist in developing best practice

- assists in explaining process, practice and actions, and therefore results in improved accountability for practice

- helps to ensure that resources are effectively targeted, which leads to increased efficiency and possibly more resources to use elsewhere.

For these reasons, most health and social care professionals have a commitment to evidence-based practice. Candidates for health and social care qualifications will also have the added incentive that they have to make use of evidence-based practice to meet the standards of their qualification.

LOCATING THE BEST POSSIBLE EVIDENCE

This is potentially one of the most challenging aspects of evidence-based practice. There is a great deal of research, legislation, policy and theory relating to the field – how do you find it and how do you know you have found the 'best possible information'?

Locating research

There is a substantial amount of research relating to the care sector. This can mean that there is almost 'too much' for you to sift through to find some research that might be relevant to your practice. So here are a few ideas to help:

- *Conference reports/papers*. Recent research is often presented at conferences. Even if you do not attend a conference you may still be able to get a copy of the papers presented by looking online.

- *Government publications*. The government produces a range of documents referring to research and often also publishes its own research papers. The easiest way to access these is generally through the relevant governmental department's website.

- *Research reports*. Organisations generally publish their own research reports. If you are a member of an organisation, such as Action Against Elder Abuse, the Alzheimer's Society or the British Institute of Learning Disabilities, you will find out about these and may receive summaries. Alternatively, the reports are often available from the organisation's website.

Research organisations

A number of specific research organisations exist in the field. They each have a website and most provide links or direct access to a range of research, eg:

- Social Care Institute for Excellence (SCIE) (www.scie.org.uk). SCIE also operates Social Care Online (www.scie-socialcareonline.org.uk), which is useful for research information, and a people management site (www.scie-peoplemanagement.org.uk), which is particularly relevant for managers.

- Research in Practice for Adults (www.ripfa.org.uk).

- Economic and Social Research Council (ESRC) (www.esrcsocietytoday.ac.uk).

- National Centre for Social Research (NatCen) (www.natcen.ac.uk).

E-bulletins

A number of websites offer regular updates (including news on important research) which are worth registering for, eg:

- The Social Policy and Social Work Subject Centre (www.swap.ac.uk) offers updates and has a number of research articles on its site.

- The Local Government Association (www.local.gov.uk/adult-social-care) offers updates and local and regional responses to government policy, as well as a 'knowledge hub' on its website.

- Skills for Care e-news (www.skillsforcare.org.uk).

- Local networks, eg North West Dignity Group, local care alliances, employer networks.

- Equality and Human Rights Commission (www.equalityhumanrights.com).

Journals

Examples include:

- *Journal of Social Service Research*

- *Journal of Health and Social Policy*

- *Health Service Journal*.

There are also a host of regular magazines in the field, such as Community Care online (www.communitycare.co.uk). These are now more regularly carrying summaries of recent research projects.

CRITICAL APPRAISAL OF EVIDENCE

Critical appraisal is probably the most important aspect of evidence-based practice, but one which is often missed. The danger of skipping this stage is that evidence might be flawed or out of date, and therefore knowledge might be irrelevant. It is not uncommon for services to be making use of legislation that is not relevant to the country in which they are based, for example.

Critical appraisal in itself is a vast area and there are a range of published tools which provide comprehensive details on how to critically appraise research evidence in particular. This is too vast an area to consider in detail in this publication. However, what we would say is that it is vital to question whatever evidence (knowledge) is gathered. We have put together some questions for you to consider, but these are by no means exhaustive.

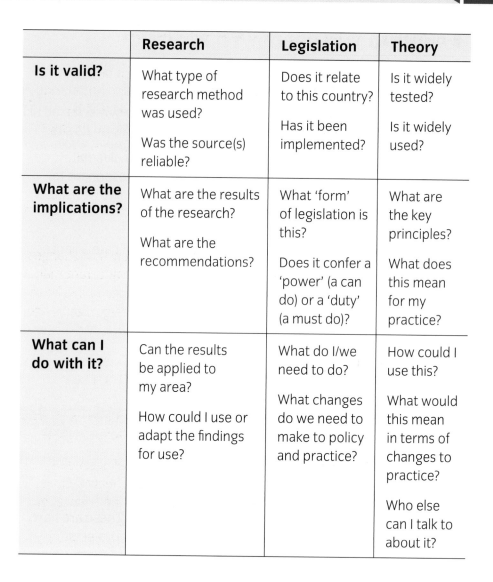

	Research	Legislation	Theory
Is it valid?	What type of research method was used? Was the source(s) reliable?	Does it relate to this country? Has it been implemented?	Is it widely tested? Is it widely used?
What are the implications?	What are the results of the research? What are the recommendations?	What 'form' of legislation is this? Does it confer a 'power' (a can do) or a 'duty' (a must do)?	What are the key principles? What does this mean for my practice?
What can I do with it?	Can the results be applied to my area? How could I use or adapt the findings for use?	What do I/we need to do? What changes do we need to make to policy and practice?	How could I use this? What would this mean in terms of changes to practice? Who else can I talk to about it?

It is important to note that these are basic questions for what is a complex process. When critically appraising research in particular, you will need to ask more detailed questions about the validity of the research, but the key to this stage of the process of evidence-based practice is to take a questioning approach.

It is important to note at this point that no research is perfect. However, through critically appraising what has been written in a paper, we can consider whether a study is good quality to use in our decision-making. Although it may be time consuming, it is essential to be able to distinguish a good piece of research from a poor one. This should prevent practice decisions being based on unreliable information, which could result in a poor decision being taken on the basis of unreliable evidence.

(RIPFA 2008)

APPLYING THE RESULT TO PRACTICE

This is another absolutely key aspect to evidence-based practice. There is no purpose to having a wealth of knowledge and not making any use of it in practice. The evidence that is generated must be shared with others and applied to practice. Evidence-based practice isn't simply about having knowledge. It is about what workers do with their knowledge – how do they use it?

EVALUATION OF PERFORMANCE

When knowledge has been applied to practice, it is likely that changes have been made to service delivery in some way. It is important that the changes are reviewed or evaluated to ensure that they have been effective. This 'evidence' then feeds back into the process of evidence-based practice.

Evidence-based practice is now a key concept in health and social care, with a great deal to offer the field. Evidence-based practice is particularly important in improving decision-making processes and supporting the continual development of staff and services. It is an area that no effective worker in health and social care can afford to ignore.

It is important that health and social care workers develop skills in evidence-based practice. In terms of working towards qualifications, this will be partly about incorporating and demonstrating knowledge with evidence of competent performance – knowledge and performance cannot be separated (ie it's not just about what you do, but why you do it).

Remember:

Knowledge + skills + values = competence

REFLECTIVE PRACTICE AND EVIDENCE-BASED PRACTICE

Evidence-based practice and reflective practice are closely linked as recognised by a number of writers. The process of evidence-based practice presented in this chapter in many ways reflects the process of reflective practice.

Chen is a senior care assistant in a residential service for older people. Many of the residents in the home have dementia.

Chen has been studying some of the evidence around reminiscence work and active support in order to improve the services offered to the residents. Chen is keen to evaluate the extent to which applying these models of practice can improve people's experiences in the service, and he shares some of the research into the impact of the models with his colleagues in a team meeting.

Chen's manager asks if he can summarise a critical appraisal of the evidence in order for this to be presented to the management team.

- How might Chen locate the best available research information?

- How could Chen present the research information in a meaningful and engaging format?

- What methods might Chen need to plan for in order to evaluate the impact of applying these approaches in the service setting?

RESEARCH AND RESOURCES

Many organisations and services have to tender for contracts in order to continue funding their work, or complete funding bids to external bodies in order to develop new work. This is especially common in the voluntary and private sectors, and many public sector services are now also involved in this in order to continue accessing funding and resources.

Knowing about research, evidence and best practice can enable organisations to access resources and monies because:

- organisations that are responsible for commissioning work need to show that they are putting the resources towards a service provider that has the best knowledge about 'what works'

- using evidence and research to show that you understand what works shows that you will deliver the best value (and outcomes) for the money you receive as a service

- it would be irresponsible to commit public money, or money donated to charity, to organisations that did not show an understanding of the need to stay up to date with the best current knowledge.

LAW-INFORMED PRACTICE

It is worth clarifying what is meant by legislation. Many people take legislation to mean Acts of Parliament. Actually, Acts of Parliament would be referred to as law and the word legislation is about much more than this.

The following diagram demonstrates how legislation is much wider than just Acts of Parliament.

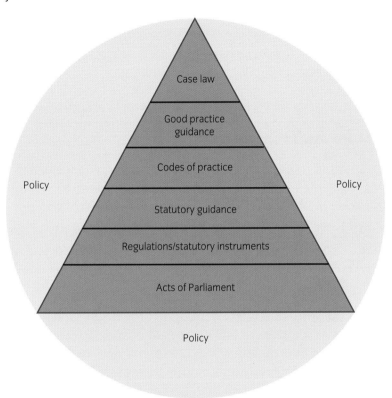

ACTS OF PARLIAMENT

There are more than 60 Acts of Parliament that might have an impact on the provision of care services. The key Acts of Parliament are covered in this book.

REGULATIONS/STATUTORY INSTRUMENTS

Acts of Parliament often include a clause that gives the senior minister involved (usually the Secretary of State) the power to introduce regulations at a later date.

These regulations detail more specific law on areas covered by the Act. This is done by means of a statutory instrument which goes before Parliament, but which is not usually debated. Regulations are used extensively for health and safety. We have covered a number of the key regulations in this book – particularly in Chapter 6 on health and safety.

STATUTORY GUIDANCE

Major Acts of Parliament may be followed at a later date by guidance. These do not have the same force of law as Acts or Regulations, but they explain and clarify the law and offer guidance on best practice.

CODES OF PRACTICE

Some Acts of Parliament have an associated code of practice, eg the Care Standards Act 2000 placed a responsibility on the regulatory bodies for social care (eg the General Social Care Council) to issue codes of practice for social care. It is vital that all staff working in care are fully conversant with the relevant codes of practice.

GOOD PRACTICE GUIDANCE

The government issues a range of good practice guidance which changes regularly. Health and social care workers need to be familiar with the good practice guidance relevant to their area of practice, and take active steps to keep up to date with developments.

CASE LAW

Case law is the term used to describe the process by which the courts decide on matters of law as a result of specific cases presented to the courts. The wording in some Acts of Parliament is ambiguous, and many individual circumstances do not neatly fit into specific situations. This means that increasingly people are taking social care, health and educational organisations to court when they feel that a particular agency has come to a decision that they disagree with and that they feel does not uphold legal requirements.

Some cases result in judgements that have implications far wider than the original case. One example of this is what has become known as the Bournewood ruling. This involved a case where a man with learning disabilities was kept in Bournewood Hospital for some months, even though he wasn't legally detained and his carers wanted him to come back home to live with them. The case went to the European courts and is formally known as *HL v UK* (2004). This case led to what became known as the Bournewood gap and the government then introduced the Deprivation of Liberty Safeguards (or DOLS) through the Mental Health Act 2007 as an amendment to the original Mental Capacity Act 2005.

POLICY

The diagram on page 541 clearly shows policy as encircling all of the other forms of legislation we have covered. This is for two reasons:

- The government publishes National Policy Guidance which essentially brings together the principles of all the forms of legislation covered and which often subsequently leads to new legislation and therefore changes in the 'triangle'.

- Organisational policies should reflect all of the legislation covered – changes in any area of the triangle should influence changes in organisational policy.

Health and social care professionals need to be able to identify what is law and what is policy. They need to keep up to date with changes in legislation and policy to ensure that their practice is legal and informed by policy and procedure.

A straightforward analogy of the relationship between law and policy is to think of a car. Laws would be represented by the engine. Once in place, laws and legislation are the main driving force. This is especially relevant where the particular law lays a duty on to service providers. The provider must move to fulfil its legal obligation. It's not unusual to find that some services have been driven to engage in various changes because of one law or another.

However, an engine on its own is not very useful – it can't go anywhere without wheels and bodywork.

Government policy is the chassis and bodywork. It dresses up the engine and mounts it on wheels. This means that the engine can move and get to where it wants to or needs to go. Government policy adds depth to the law.

To pursue the analogy – organisational policy is the cabin within which the driver and passengers sit. The car's bodywork (government policy) establishes the amount of room (the boundaries) within which an individual social care organisation can work. The government wants to cultivate diversity within service provision, therefore it does not detail exactly how social care organisations should carry out the tasks that they are required or expected to do.

In theory, it should be the service users who are in the driving seat. They are using the car to get them where they want to be. Often, however, managers of the service may need to take the driving seat to ensure that services get to where they need to be to provide the best possible outcomes for service users.

One of the main issues for health and social care workers is that just when they think they have worked out the engine (the law), it changes. It is essential that health and social care staff ensure they keep up to date with legislation and policy developments. This constitutes basic practice – after all, you wouldn't drive your car unless you regularly checked your oil, water and brakes, would you?

CASE STUDY

Isabella is a senior care assistant in a respite care service that provides short-term stays for young adults with learning and physical disabilities.

Isabella has been asked by her manager to review the service's safeguarding and health and safety policies and statements in order to check that these are up to date, accurate and in line with current legislation.

- What will Isabella need to consider in order to do this?

- Where can Isabella find the most up-to-date and accurate information?

- How could she ensure that policies are presented in a way that they can be understood and applied consistently by her colleagues?

- How could she ensure that policies are presented in a way that they can be understood by the service's users?

THEORY-INFORMED PRACTICE

Theory-informed practice is often rejected by health and social care workers who see themselves as 'practical' or as 'hands-on practitioners' who want to get on with the job. However, theory-informed practice is really important to good practice in health and social care. To recognise the importance of theory-informed practice it is important to begin with understanding what theory is.

WHAT IS A THEORY?

Theories in social care are nothing more than an attempt to explain social relationships. Theories have been developed since it became clear that there were similar patterns or repeating cycles of behaviour both in an individual's life and in the lives of lots of different people.

Since theories have been expressed by academics and social scientists, they often use an academic language. Don't let that put you off. Theories are life, dressed up! Many theories actually have a very simple message. Albert Einstein who developed what is probably the most famous theory of all – the theory of relativity – famously said:

A theory is the more impressive the greater is the simplicity of its premises, the more different are the kinds of things it relates to and the more extended the range of its applicability.

There has been some debate about what actually constitutes a theory. Generally, a theory helps to explain a situation and perhaps how it came about. In science a theory is seen as helping to:

- describe (eg what is happening)

- explain (eg why it is happening)

- predict (eg what is likely to happen next).

Sometimes theories are also seen as helping to plan intervention and bring about change (eg 'What can I do to bring about a change in this situation?'). Health and social care workers need to be able to describe the situation they are working with, explain why they think this came about, what they can do to bring about some form of change, etc. In doing so, they will be drawing on some form of theory. They may, however, not always be aware of this.

In health and social care, there are several different types of theory. An understanding of these different types or forms of theory can be helpful in recognising that all workers within health and social care do use a range of theories in any given situation.

Beckett (2006) separates theory into 'formal' theory and 'informal' theory. We have known some people use these terms inappropriately – formal theory being taken to mean theory that is presented more academically and informal theory taken to mean theory that is more accessible and understandable (and therefore not academic). However, this is a misunderstanding.

Formal theory is basically theory that can be named and traced back to a writer or an academic. Informal theory is the worker's own ideas about a situation. As this is often developed through experience, both practice experience and personal experiences, this type of 'theory' is also referred to as practice wisdom (Doel and Shardlow 1993).

WHY DO WE NEED TO APPLY THEORY TO PRACTICE?

While individual social care theories have different purposes, using all kinds of theory in our work offers health and social care professionals some important benefits:

- Theories can help make sense of a situation. Using theory, health and social care professionals can generate ideas about what is going on, why things are the way they are, etc.

- Using theory can help to justify actions and explain practice to service users, carers and society in general. The aim is that this will lead to health and social care becoming more widely accountable and ultimately more respected.

- In work with individuals, making use of the theories that relate to their specific situation will give workers more direction in their work.

- Using theory can give a reason that explains why an action resulted in a particular consequence. This can help staff to review and possibly change their practice in an attempt to make the practice more effective.

It is clear that theory is important in practice – both for work with service users and for health and social care to be more valued in society. Recognising the importance of the term 'theory' and what it can offer is part of the move towards the professionalisation of the social care workforce.

There is an old saying, often attributed to Susser but which may have originated from Leonardo da Vinci, that 'Practice without theory is to sail an uncharted sea; theory without practice is not to set sail at all'.

Imagine a boat setting out to sea in a good breeze, without a map or compass. This is like practice without theory – how will the crew know when they have arrived at their destination? If they do (by chance) arrive safely in a port they like, how would they ever be able to repeat the journey? On the other hand, a boat might bob along tied to its bollard, safely in the harbour. It might well have every direction finding device known, but isn't going anywhere. This is like theory without practice. It's pointless.

HOW DO WE APPLY THEORY TO PRACTICE?

There is no single approach to applying theory to practice. We all apply theory to practice every day, but what we may not be able to do is name the theory and use the academic language that has built up around it. But theory 'seeps in'.

Some people claim that they don't use theories, but that they use common sense. But whose sense is common? Is your sense the same as everyone else's? Just because someone cannot imagine another way to view something doesn't mean that they aren't using theory. It just means that their unconsciously held theories are what their 'sense' is composed of.

In applying theory to practice, it is helpful to remember the following points:

- No single theory can explain everything. When someone engages in an action (or inaction), the reason for their behaviour can be rooted in a range of causes or motives.

- Related to the first point, recognise that some theoretical approaches just don't work with some people.

- Take a critical approach to theory. If it doesn't 'work', why not? Can you adapt aspects so that it is helpful?

- Always apply the value base to theory. Much of the theory used in the sector is from outside of health and social care practice. Theory may have its roots in education, psychology or even industry and engineering. As such, it may not incorporate social care values and everyone in the field should take responsibility for applying these.

- Different professionals may draw on different theories given the same presenting situation. There is no right or wrong approach – just boundaries of good practice.

- Theories of different types may be used at different points in intervention in a situation.

- Some theories may complement each other, others may clash and may therefore not be appropriate to use together.

- An anti-oppressive approach is always vital. Any theory should be evaluated from an anti-oppressive standpoint, so that the impact of any approaches towards somebody considers their individuality in the context of their own lives.

CASE STUDY

Taju is a senior support worker with a mental health charity. He works some of his time in a drop-in centre for people with mental health problems and the remainder of his working week is spent in outreach services providing ongoing practical and emotional support for service users.

Taju is working with a student who is on placement in the service. He is acting as the student's work-based supervisor, so he manages and supports her workload, and an offsite assessor meets her fortnightly to assess her competence.

After supervision with her assessor, the student tells Taju that she finds these sessions extremely challenging, as her assessor keeps pushing her to identify which theories she is applying in her work. The student says she doesn't really think about theories much and she feels that her skills around engagement are being overlooked while the assessor focuses too much on academic issues.

Taju feels that the service does apply lots of relevant theories in understanding the needs of individuals who access the service, and in supporting them to move on in their lives.

- How can Taju challenge the student's thinking and support her to develop her ability to explain the theories she applies in her work?

WHICH THEORIES ARE RELEVANT IN HEALTH AND SOCIAL CARE PRACTICE?

A wide range of theory can support best practice in health and social care. Some services specifically work on particular models and approaches, and you will be familiar with those used in your service. We have covered a range of the theories that you might find useful in your work in the different chapters of this book, eg:

- concepts of need (see Chapter 9)

- the strengths perspective and the concept of resilience (see Chapter 9)

- theories about partnership working and conflict (covered in Chapter 1)

- theories around power imbalance, empowerment and understanding how this affects people's lives are covered throughout this text, and specifically in Chapter 3.

Systems theory is very relevant to all aspects of health and social care practice, though it does not 'fit neatly' into a specific chapter.

SYSTEMS THEORY

Like many theories, systems theory has, at its heart, a straightforward claim. For systems theory, one of the key starting points is that no person is an island. Everyone has contact with other people. Some of the people are family, some friends and others are people who represent an organisation. The relationships we have with all these people and organisations form a 'web' (or system) around us. The system around us should sustain us and enrich us. There should be a sense of harmony, balance or smooth working in our system. Using systems theory in social care work is often referred to as taking an ecological approach.

Systems theory recognises that a person's support network can be placed under strain because of a change in circumstances. This change may be a new event (eg acquired disability of the service user or close family member) or the change could be something progressive. The new or increased strain results in the system not working smoothly. By mapping a person's whole system, the worker should be able to work out the source of the system overload. In order to enable the system to operate smoothly, an individual or agency may need to be introduced (either short or long term) to balance the system again. In this way, systems theory is not personal. It does not seek to label the service user or family members.

The Social Care Institute for Excellence suggests that systems theory is relevant to social care work because:

- it describes and explains the recurring patterns of behaviour found in families, groups and organisations

- it concentrates on the relationship between the parts rather than parts in isolation

- unlike linear thinking, a straightforward cause and effect approach, systemic thinking offers a different perspective. It suggests there are multiple causes and effects involved and we are actively involved as a part of the problem and its solutions.

(Social Care Institute for Excellence 2004:18)

In their work on systems theory, Pincus and Minahan (1973) suggested that society and people operate within three systems:

1 *Informal systems* include family, friends, neighbours and work colleagues. These provide advice and emotional support and also contribute to our sense of worth and personal functioning.

2 *Formal systems* include clubs and societies, trade unions and other types of groups that can provide support.

3 *Public systems* include the police, council and local government services, hospitals and schools. These systems tend to have service-related functions, and duties and powers in their delivery to the community.

It can be suggested that when people are experiencing difficult or traumatic times they will turn to public systems for support and assistance to help them overcome the problems. Systems theory offers the view that when people are confronted with challenges that they are not able to resolve within their support system they experience conflict and difficulties.

This is the stage at which professional workers may intervene and support people to address their presenting needs. Through direct work and applying a problem solving and supporting approach, workers can develop a plan and design and implement services through effective partnership working with the service user.

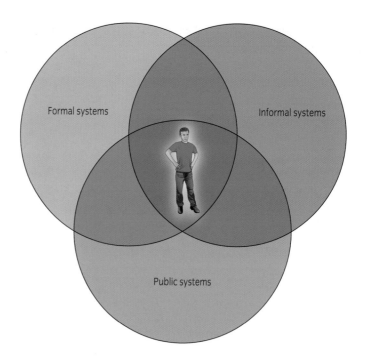

Formal systems

Informal systems

Public systems

The requirement is for the practitioner to assess the underlying problems and what has led to them being manifested. This will also include the need to consider the personal issues, structural forces and any disadvantage that the service user has experienced.

Pincus and Minahan (1973) also developed a framework for practitioners to use with helping relationships to resolve the difficulties. The model highlights the need for the worker to locate the cause of the problem and what impact the problem is having on the system. The model refers to four aspects of the system and any intervention.

- The 'change agent system'. This refers to the worker and the agency they are representing.

- The 'client system' focuses on the service user and their system.

- The 'target system' makes reference to the desired outcomes.

- The 'action system' is the work that is agreed between the service user and the worker in order to resolve the identified issues.

An alternative way to view systems theory is to focus on the aspect of balance. The worker draws up a list of difficulties the service user is facing as well as positive aspects of their life (eg supportive relationships). If the list of difficulties or problems is longer than the positive aspects, then the worker needs to introduce more positive aspects to try to re-establish a balanced system.

Systems theory is not without its critics, and commentators have suggested that it ignores the diversity of black and minority ethnic communities because it does not address the causes and effects of structural inequality.

However, systems theory is useful since it does express a basic human truth. We all rely on others to one extent or another. By looking at people's systems (support networks) we are able to recognise the strengths that people have.

Systems theory has been applied in several services, eg:

- In adult services, systems theory has been extensively used to maximise support for people. Often this focuses on immediate family (carers) and the involvement of health and social care professionals or services to either fill gaps or to sustain relationships (service user/carer relationship) that are under strain.

- In learning disability services, systems theory is at the heart of person-centred planning. Services should cultivate the opportunity for the service user to establish a range of informal and formal systems.

- Family therapy services have placed significant value on seeing the family as a whole and considering how they interact with each other within their family system.

It can be helpful when considering systems theory to see the service user at the centre of a set of systems in a visual way. Each system has its own set of terminology, and its own values, norms and expectations. It is helpful to see these various systems as interlinking circles, as the interface between the person and each system is key to their development and opportunities. Systemic thinking requires the worker to see the person in the round in order to understand the impact of social and familial structures on that individual. Only with this understanding can a plan be formed that attempts to effect change in the areas where changes and choices are possible.

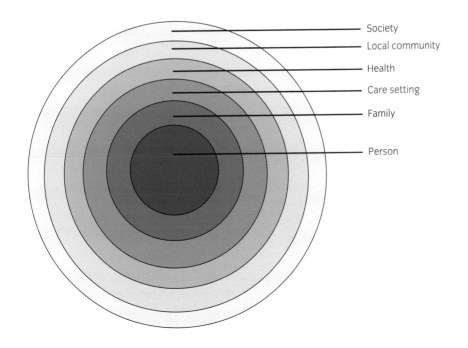

Society
Local community
Health
Care setting
Family
Person

SOCIAL PEDAGOGY

Social pedagogy has a long history within many European countries – particularly Denmark, France, Italy, Germany and the Netherlands. It has not really been practised in the UK, but is now a growing field of interest with government policy on children's services referring more and more to social pedagogy.

The historical roots of social pedagogy are about working with children and taking an individual educational approach. However, it is now widely used as an approach in working with adults in Europe and is therefore very likely to be used as an approach in adult services in the UK in the future.

ThemPra states that:

Social pedagogy is an approach covering the whole lifespan of people, and with recognition to lifelong learning as well as social pedagogues' person and care-centred value base, social pedagogy has become the preferred way of working with adults as well. Considering the need for improvement in adult services – for refugees, prisoners or older people in care, to mention but a few – England would benefit from conceiving social pedagogy in the broadest possible way and striving to implement it across all welfare services.

(ThemPra 2009)

Essentially, social pedagogy is about educating people (children and adults) in a way that recognises their role as active learners, so that they can take a full and healthy role in a diverse society. There are key issues within the concept of social pedagogy around diversity, inclusion and opportunity as the social pedagogue (professional, educator or social care worker) seeks to provide opportunities and learning for those excluded or disadvantaged within society.

Cameron states that:

The social pedagogue works with the whole person, and supports their all-round development. Pedagogues employ theories, professional knowledge, and creative and practical skills with groups and on an individual basis. They acknowledge uncertainty and constantly review situations and decisions, in dialogue with colleagues. Human rights and participation underpin social pedagogy.

(Cameron 2007)

The idea of social pedagogy then is similar to schools' provision of personal, social and health education (PSHE), which is sometimes now referred to as citizenship or SEAL (social and emotional aspects of learning). The differences between a teacher of PSHE and a social pedagogue, however, concern the focus in social pedagogy on the

> **KEY POINT**
>
> Social pedagogy is about how professionals can empower, enable and support people and their learning.

individual's needs as a learner and on the practitioner's approach to their role. The concept of social pedagogy applies equally to work with adults as well as children. This is because the role of the pedagogue:

- focuses on the individual, even when working in group settings
- seeks to promote and model positive social relationships
- applies knowledge from across the range of disciplines as described above.

APPLICATION TO SOCIAL CARE PRACTICE

In social care and social work, it is easy to see how social pedagogy applies in how 'direct work' is practised with individuals or groups of service users. Rather than there being a set 'curriculum', this work tends to focus on addressing specific issues to meet individual needs. This could include life-story work (see Chapter 10), therapeutic work or discussion about different ways of tackling a difficulty the person is facing. Approaches like active support and supporting service users to develop new skills or maintain existing skills draw on pedagogy as an approach.

The ThemPra Society describes how central the relationship between the pedagogue and the learner is. The building of relationships is seen as crucial to creating trust and ensuring that learners feel empowered and enabled to learn. Again, this is unlikely to feel new to most people working in health and social care, but the idea is that through this relationship, trust is built, which in turn enables the person to feel safe to learn and to discuss and reflect on challenges and issues as they present in their life. The relationship between the person and the professional needs to be authentic (so the person knows that the professional genuinely cares about their well-being as well as just being someone who is paid to be in their lives), but built upon professional standards and boundaries.

Alongside this process of reflection upon issues that naturally present as learning opportunities, the pedagogue seeks to provide positive learning experiences that enable the person's learning to occur. This learning can take place in any setting or environment and is not about worksheets or formal teaching, but instead is about the whole person ('holistic learning'), their needs, rights, choices and relationships with others. Positive learning experiences are crucial to social pedagogic practice because:

> **KEY POINT**
>
> Everyone working in social care is a pedagogue at some point.

The power of experiencing something positive – something that makes us happy, something we have achieved, a new skill we have learned, the caring support from someone else ... raises our self-confidence and feeling of self-worth, so it reinforces our sense of well-being, of learning, of being able to form a strong relationship, or of feeling empowered.

(ThemPra 2009)

The key concepts of social pedagogy are therefore about:

- promoting each person's well-being
- holistic learning
- positive, empowering and professional relationships between the pedagogue and the person accessing services
- empowerment.

It could be argued that everyone working in health and social care takes on the role of a social pedagogue at some point. Most of us probably don't call it that! However, as social care is subject to increasing professionalisation and as the concept of social pedagogy gains momentum in the UK (as it is already doing in parenting work, residential child care and family support), more health and social care workers are likely to encounter the term.

Social pedagogues in Europe are generally qualified with a degree in social pedagogy and it is interesting to note that degrees in social pedagogy have now begun to be offered in the UK.

While it is unlikely that health and social care workers will be qualified as social pedagogues they may find that taking a social pedagogical approach is useful in their work and that they find social pedagogy a useful way of describing their professional expertise. Health and social care workers are often involved in working with service users in an educational capacity to enable them to access opportunities and relate to others positively. Social pedagogy allows workers to examine how they use their skills to enable others to grow, develop and learn, and is likely to continue to grow in the UK as a field.

DEVELOPING YOUR CAREER

As you progress in your career as a professional health and social care worker you will find that your knowledge and the way that you use this will become ever more important in your practice. If you decide to work towards becoming a manager of health and social care services, for example, you will need to develop your knowledge and understanding in relation to organisations, leadership and management. Developing a commitment to evidence-based practice is essential for you in developing your career pathway for the future.

GLOSSARY

active listening is about really listening to what a person is saying and showing them that you are listening to them. There are several techniques that can help workers to be active listeners. While they might seem obvious, they are effective. In busy working environments they can easily be forgotten.

active participation is about people being involved in their own care, as opposed to being a 'recipient' of that care (ie it is about something being done *with* someone rather than something being done *to* someone). Active participation also means that people take part in the activities of daily and independent life as much as possible.

aim in this context is about finding a direction or purpose.

aphasia (also known as dysphasia) is a language disorder, marked by deficiency in speaking and/or understanding others, caused by damage to the brain.

augmentative and alternative communication (AAC) is used to describe a range of techniques that health and social care workers and other professionals use in order to aid communication and support people to understand. AAC can be pictorial (eg using photographs and symbols to mark out what will be happening and in what order), or it can be where sign and gesture are used in order to communicate certain words or ideas.

axon is the main body of the neuron cell.

brand name is the name given to a new medicine by a manufacturer. It is protected by copyright and will be used in advertising campaigns. Examples include Panadol® which is a brand of paracetamol and Anadin® which is a brand of aspirin. See also *generic name*.

capacity is about whether someone is physically or mentally able to do something.

commission is where something is done by somebody who understands the implications of their act. For example, hitting someone would be an act of commission.

consent is when a person agrees to something when they are making an informed decision or giving informed permission.

covert administration is where medication is administered in a disguised form without the knowledge or consent of the individual receiving it, eg in food or in a drink.

cross-infection is when an infection spreads from one person to another.

diagnosis is the identification of an illness or other problem by examination of the symptoms.

discrimination is where someone is treated less favourably than another person.

diversity refers to difference. Everyone is unique and different in some way. There is a wide range of diversity in every population.

double discrimination refers to oppression based on two characteristics.

drug is any substance which when taken into the body affects the way that the body functions.

DSM stands for the Diagnostic and Statistical Manual of Mental Disorders.

echolalia refers to repetitive speech, specifically the 'echoing' of another person's speech.

encouragers: In behavioural theory, an encourager is something that encourages and motivates a person to repeat an activity. An encourager could be praise, a smile, a treat, a break, or anything that the person finds rewarding and which recognises their achievements.

equality is about treating people in a way that ensures that they are not placed at a disadvantage to others.

ethics are about how we see right and wrong, but ethics are generally drawn from our understanding of responsibilities and so are closely linked with professional standards, codes of conduct and legislation. Ethics are closely related to the duty of care in health and social care.

exclusion describes a situation where people face discrimination on many levels and are effectively 'excluded from society' – that is where they have no voice and are not recognised in their society.

generic name is the official name given to the active ingredient when a medicine is developed; examples include paracetamol and aspirin. See also *brand name*.

hazard is a possible source of harm.

holistic approach considers someone as an individual, and all of the factors that make up their life, instead of focusing only on their support needs.

holistic approaches to assessment take account of all of the needs that people have and look at the person 'in the whole'. This means looking at people's culture, environment, resources, social networks, and all of their levels of need.

ICD stands for International Classification of Disorders.

inclusion is the word used to describe the opposite of social exclusion. It is where action is taken to address the effects of discrimination, and to strive towards preventing or ideally eliminating oppression.

infantilisation relates to the way in which people who have disabilities can be treated as though they were a child when they are actually an adult.

internal or **systemic medicine** is a medicine that is taken into the body and is then carried all around the body by the circulatory system (blood), so that it reaches the part of the body needing treatment.

intersectional multiple discrimination is where a person experiences discrimination because they belong to a number of groups which may be treated less favourably than others. The difference where discrimination is 'intersectional' as well as multiple is that where the discrimination is intersectional, this means that the person's different identities interact in such a way that it is impossible to separate them out from each other. The person's whole experience of being treated differently is not because of one aspect of their uniqueness, but it is about how their *differences* (plural) intersect with each other.

job description is a written outline of the role and responsibilities of a specific job.

leading question is a question that gives the person being asked a clear indication about the expected answer. For example, 'He hit you, didn't he?'

learned helplessness is where a person feels they have no control over their situation, and where events have made them feel that this will never change. The term comes from the field of psychology. People's health, well-being, motivation and socialisation can be severely affected when they experience the feeling of helplessness.

medicine is a drug that is used to diagnose, prevent or treat an illness.

monitoring means keeping an eye on how something is working. Monitoring can either be done formally (on documentation, such as those prepared for review meetings), or informally (via conversation and observation).

morals are about our belief in what is right and wrong, and are often associated with faith and our personal values.

multiple discrimination is discrimination against someone on the basis of two or more characteristics at the same time. People can belong to more than one or two groups who experience discrimination, and people can experience 'double disadvantage' or 'multiple disadvantage'.

neuron is a specialised, impulse-conducting cell that is the functional unit of the nervous system. Most of the cells in the human brain are neurons.

neurotransmitters are the chemicals that carry information in the brain.

objective refers to the point to which operations are directed; the point to be reached; the goal.

omission is where something is not done (accidentally or on purpose). For example, not providing an adequate standard of care for a service user would be an act of omission.

onset of action is when the medicine begins to have an effect on the body. Depending on the form of medicine used the onset of action will vary.

outcomes are what people want to achieve.

paraphrasing refers to rewording something in a way that is either easier for someone to understand or that shows the other person that you have understood what they were communicating to you. When you paraphrase, it is important to keep the original meaning so that this is not distorted.

patient-identifiable information is any personal or sensitive information that can identify a patient.

person specification is a list of criteria (skills, knowledge, experience, values and qualifications) that you need in order to do your job. These may either be 'essential' or 'desirable'.

personal values refer to values that are important to an individual. See also *professional values*.

policy in health and social care is a written statement explaining the service or agency's expected approach to an issue, area of practice, or key aspect of people's work. Policies can be local and/or national.

prejudice is where an individual makes a judgement based on either inadequate or inaccurate information that leads to the development of irrational preferences. One of the main features of prejudice is rigidity or inflexibility of ideas. This means that new information may not have an impact on prejudicial views.

procedure is an agreed and understood way or order of doing something in work

professional boundaries, in work settings, refer to the limits of what we are allowed to do, and what is appropriate in our relationships with service users and other people.

professional values refer to values that are important in a particular profession. See also *personal values*.

prognosis is the likely course or outcome of a medical condition.

reflecting on experiences is essential to good practice and professional development. Reflecting is about reviewing events and experiences, analysing information, using knowledge and supervision to consider issues and concerns, and taking a proactive stance in how you take responsibility for the development of your own learning and practices. In terms of communication within health and social care, reflecting also has another very significant meaning. Reflecting involves repeating the important things that are being said back at speaker. This can encourage the speaker to say more. However, the listener shouldn't interrupt the speaker but simply reflect things back to show that they have understood and to encourage the speaker to say more. Reflecting is important to demonstrate that you are listening to someone, and to check that you have heard correctly. When you repeat key words it tells the person speaking that you are hearing them correctly and that what they are saying is important.

resilience is best defined as a person's ability to 'bounce back'.

risk is the likelihood that a hazard will actually cause harm.

safeguarding is defined by the government as 'a range of activity aimed at upholding an adult's fundamental right to be safe. Being or feeling unsafe undermines our relationships and self-belief, our ability to participate freely in communities and contribute to society. Safeguarding is of particular importance to people who, because of their situation or circumstances, are unable to keep themselves safe' (Department of Health 2010).

self-esteem is about how we feel about or value ourselves.

self-image is about how we see or describe ourselves.

single equality duty: The Equality Act 2010 introduced a 'single equality duty' on all public bodies when they are making plans and strategic decisions. The single equality duty means that services need to be targeted at people who are disadvantaged, instead of at groups who have specific characteristics in common. This focuses the duty of those planning services on to the goal of equality itself. The single equality duty tasks public bodies to:

- eliminate discrimination
- advance equality of opportunity
- foster good relations.

synapse is a junction between two nerve cells, consisting of an extremely small gap across which impulses pass by diffusion of a neurotransmitter.

topical medicines are applied directly to the part of the body that requires treatment.

triple jeopardy refers to oppression based on three characteristics.

valued lifestyle refers to the balance of activities that contribute to a good quality of life for individuals, incorporating vocational, domestic, personal, leisure, educational and social activities.

values are what is seen as important.

USEFUL WEBSITES

Age UK
http://www.ageuk.org.uk/documents/en-gb/factsheets/
fs24_self-directed_support-direct_payments_and_
personal_budgets_fcs.pdf?dtrk=true
An age UK guide to self-directed support

Alzheimer's Society
www.alzheimers.org.uk
A membership organisation which works to improve the quality of life of people affected by dementia

Alzheimer's Research UK
www.alzheimersresearchuk.org
The UK's leading dementia research charity specialising in finding preventions, causes, treatments and a cure for dementia

Beat
www.b-eat.co.uk
Provides information for people affected by eating disorders

British National Formulary
http://www.bnf.org/bnf/index.htm
Provides UK healthcare professionals with information on the selection and clinical use of medicines

Care Quality Commission
http://www.cqc.org.uk
The independent regulator of all health and social care services in England

Change
www.changepeople.co.uk/
A leading national human rights organisation led by disabled people

Communication Matters
http://www.communicationmatters.org.uk
A UK organisation supporting people who find communication difficult

Department for Education
http://www.education.gov.uk/childrenandyoungpeople/
strategy/integratedworking/a0072915/information-
sharing
Guides for practitioners and managers around sharing information

Department of Health
https://www.gov.uk/government/uploads/system/
uploads/attachment_data/file/153462/dh_119973.pdf.
pdf
Essence of Care 2010 guide to best practice in communication

Economic and Social Research Council (ESRC)
www.esrcsocietytoday.ac.uk
The UK's largest organisation for funding research on economic and social issues

Health & Safety Executive
www.hse.gov.uk
Health and Safety publications as well as a useful Health and Safety in health and social care services section

Improving Access to Psychological Therapies (IAPT)
www.iapt.nhs.uk
National Institute for Health and Clinical Excellence (NICE) guidelines

International Stress Management Association
www.isma.org.uk
Provides information on promoting wellbeing and performance

Joseph Rowntree Foundation
http://www.jrf.org.uk/publications/transforming-social-
care-person-centred-support
Research from the Joseph Rowntree Foundation into person centred support

Local Government Association
http://www.local.gov.uk/adult-social-care
Provides updates and local and regional responses to government policy

London Deanery Faculty Development
http://www.faculty.londondeanery.ac.uk/e-learning/
feedback/giving-feedback
Provides information on the principles of giving effective feedback

Mencap
www.mencap.org.uk
Website for valuing and supporting people with learning disabilities

http://www.mencap.org.uk/sites/default/files/
documents/2008-04/make%20it%20clear%20apr09.pdf
Make It Clear guide from MENCAP

Mind
www.mind.org.uk
Provides advice and support on mental health problems
and campaigns to improve services, raise awareness
and promote understanding

Mind Tools
http://www.mindtools.com/pages/article/newLDR_81.
htm
Information on conflict resolution

National Institute for Health and Care Excellence (NICE)
http://www.nice.org.uk/nicemedia/
live/10998/30320/30320.pdf
NICE & SCIE guidelines on supporting people with
dementia and their carers in health and social care

National Centre for Social Research (NATCEN)
www.natcen.ac.uk
UK's leading independent social research institute

National Institute on Deafness and Other Communication Disorders (NIDCD)
http://www.nidcd.nih.gov/health/hearing/Pages/
Assistive-Devices.aspx#7
A guide to assistive devices for people with hearing,
voice, speech, or language disorders

Patient.co.uk
www.patient.co.uk
Information on health, lifestyle, disease and other
medical related topics

People First
http://peoplefirstltd.com
An organisation, run by, and for people with learning
difficulties

Personal Health Budgets NHS England
http://www.personalhealthbudgets.dh.gov.uk
A website providing information and news about the
Department of Health's personal health budgets policy

Plain English Campaign
www.plainenglish.co.uk
An independent campaign against misleading public
information

Research in Practice for Adults
www.ripfa.org.uk
A charity that uses evidence from research and people's
experience to help understand adult social care and
improve how it works

Royal Pharmaceutical Society of Great Britain
www.rpharms.com/support-pdfs/handling-medicines-
socialcare-guidance.pdf
A guide to handling medication in social care work

SCOPE
http://www.scope.org.uk/help-and-information/
communication/no-voice-no-choice
No Voice No Choice research from the UK disability
charity that supports disabled people and their families

Skills for Care
http://www.skillsforcare.org.uk/developing_skills/e-
learning/e-learning.aspx
Provides a range of e-learning resources from Skills for
Care

http://www.skillsforcare.org.uk/developing_skills/
leadership_and_management/providing_effective_
supervision.aspx
Guide to effective supervision in social care

Social Care Institute for Excellence (SCIE)
www.scie.org.uk
An independent charity working with adults, families
and children's social care and social work services
across the UK

http://www.scie.org.uk/adults/safeguarding
SCIE website has a range of useful information and
resources in relation to adult safegaurding

http://www.scie.org.uk/publications/elearning/
communicationskills
E-learning resources on the principles of good
communication skills and how to apply these to practice

http://www.scie.org.uk/publications/guides/guide23/
messages/mean.asp
SCIE knowledge review into partnership work

http://www.scie.org.uk/publications/reports/report36/
index.asp
SCIE research into self-directed support

www.scie-peoplemanagement.org.uk
A people management website which will be particularly
relevant for managers

www.scie-socialcareonline.org.uk
SCIE also operate social care online – a fantastic website
for research information

Social Policy and Social Work Subject Centre
www.swap.ac.uk
Provides updates and has a number of research articles
on its site

The Equality & Human Rights Commission
http://www.equalityhumanrights.com
Provides information and guidance to individuals on equality, discrimination and human rights issues

The National Archives Department of Health
http://webarchive.nationalarchives.
gov.uk/20130107105354/http://
www.dh.gov.uk/en/Publichealth/
Scientificdevelopmentgeneticsandbioethics/Consent/
index.htm
Department of Health guidance on consent

Think Local Act Personal
www.thinklocalactpersonal.org.uk
A national, cross sector leadership partnership, promoting work with personalisation, community-based social care

University of Kent
http://www.kent.ac.uk/tizard/active
Information on person-centred active support

World Health Organization
http://www.who.int/features/qa/62/en/index.html
World Health Organization guide to mental health

Write Enough
www.writeenough.org.uk
Information on effective recording in children's services

BIBLIOGRAPHY

Age UK (2010) 'Later matters: tackling race inequalities for BME older people'. Available online at www.ageconcernyorkshireandhumber.org.uk/uploads/files/FINALmapping%20and%22good%20practice%20guide%20(2).pdf (accessed 4 January 2013).

Age UK (2013) 'Self-directed support: direct payments and personal budgets'. Factsheet 24. Available online at www.ageuk.org.uk/documents/en-gb/factsheets/fs24_self-directed_support-direct_payments_and_personal_budgets_fcs.pdf?dtrk=true (accessed 19 March 2013).

All-Party Parliamentary Group on Dementia (2012) *Unlocking Diagnosis: The Key to Improving the Lives of People with Dementia.* London: HMSO.

Alzheimer's Research UK (2013) 'Dementia statistics'. Available online at www.alzheimersresearchuk.org/dementia-statistics (accessed 4 February 2013).

Alzheimer's Society (2012) 'Fighting stigma'. Available online at www.alzheimers.org.uk/site/scripts/documents_info.php?documentID=1815 (accessed 10 February 2013).

Alzheimer's Society (2013) 'How can I help my memory?' Available online at www.alzheimers.org.uk/site/scripts/documents_info.php?documentID=871 (accessed 4 February 2013).

Ashman, B. and Beadle-Brown, J. (2006) *A Valued Life: Developing Person-Centred Approaches So People Can Be More Included.* London: United Response.

Association for Real Change (2012) 'Research: active support'. Available online at http://arcuk.org.uk/activesupport/2012/04/05/research (accessed 4 January 2013).

Association of Directors of Social Services (2005) 'Safeguarding adults: a national framework of standards for good practice and outcomes in adult protection work'. York: ADSS. Available online at www.adass.org.uk/images/stories/Publications/Guidance/safeguarding.pdf (accessed 7 May 2013).

Basnett, F. and Maclean, S. (2000) *The Value Base in Practice: An NVQ Related Reference Guide for Staff working with Older People.* Rugeley: Kirwin Maclean Associates.

Beat Eating Disorders (B-eat) www.b-eat.co.uk (accessed 5 March 2013).

Beckett, C. (2006) *Essential Theory for Social Work Practice.* London: SAGE.

Boddy, J. and Statham, J. (2009) *European Perspectives on Social Work: Models of Education and Professional Roles.* London: Thomas Coram Research Unit, Institute of Education, University of London.

Borisoff, D. and Victor, D.A. (1998) *Conflict Management: A Communication Skills Approach.* Second edition. Boston: Allyn and Bacon.

Bradshaw, J. (1972) 'The concept of social need', *New Society*, 496: 640–643.

Brand, D., Green, L. and Statham, D. (2010) Facts about FACS 2010: a guide to Fair Access to Care Services. London: Social Care Institute for Excellence. Available at www.scie.org.uk/publications/guides/guide33/files/guide33.pdf (accessed 7 May 2013).

British Institute of Learning Disabilities (2002) 'Factsheet: communication'. Kidderminster: British Institute of Learning Disabilities. Available online at www.bild.ogrg.uk (accessed 3 May 2013).

Brooker, D. (2007) *Person-Centred Dementia Care – Making Services Better.* London: Jessica Kingsley.

Calderstones Partnership NHS Trust (2013) 'Learning disabilities facts and figures'. Available online at www.calderstones.nhs.uk/about-us/learningdisabilities.php (accessed 23 January 2013).

Cameron, C. (2007) 'Social pedagogy and the children's workforce'. Available online at www.communitycare.co.uk/Articles/2007/08/08/105392/social-pedagogy-and-the-childrens-workforce.htm (accessed 19 January 2010).

Cameron, C. and Boddy, J. (2006) 'Knowledge and education for care workers: what do they need to know', in J. Boddy, C. Cameron and P. Moss (eds) *Care Work: Present and Future.* London: Routledge.

Cameron, E. and Green, M. (2012) *Making Sense of Change Management: A Complete Guide to the Models, Tools and Techniques of Organizational Change.* Third edition. London: Kogan Page.

Care UK (2013) 'Fact sheet: person-centred planning'. Available online at www.careuklearningdisabilities.com/uploads/pdf/Factsheet_person_centred_planning.pdf (accessed 18 January 2013).

Carr, S. (2010) 'Enabling risk, ensuring safety: self-directed support and personal budgets', Adult Services SCIE Report 36. Available online at www.scie.org.uk/publications/reports/report36/index.asp (accessed 12 January 2013).

Carson, D. and Bain, A.J. (2008) *Professional Risk and Working with People: Decision-Making in Health, Social Care and Criminal Justice*. London: Jessica Kingsley.

Changing Lives Service Development Group (2008) 'Personalisation: a shared understanding'. Available online at www.socialworkscotland.org.uk/resources/pub/sharedunderstandingofpersonanlisationpaper.pdf (accessed 24 April 2011).

Commission for Health Improvement Investigations (CHI) (2003) Investigation into matters arising from care on Rowan ward, Manchester Mental Health andSocial Care Trust'. London: The Stationery Office. Available online at www.elderabuse.org.uk/Documents/Other%20Orgs/Abuse%20Report%20-CHI%20Rowan%20Ward.pdf (accessed 23 April 2013).

Commission for Health Improvement Investigations (CHI) (2004) 'Lessons from CHI investigations 2000–2003'. London: The Stationery Office. Available online at http://image.guardian.co.uk/sys-files/Society/documents/2004/03/25/CHI_investigationlessons.pdf (accessed 23 April 2013).

Commission for Social Care Inspection (2008) 'Raising voices: views on safeguarding adults'. London: Commission for Social Care Inspection. Available online at www.csci.org.uk and from www.warwickshire.gov.uk/Web/corporate/wccweb.nsf/Links/6EA919F805F3B54180257885002E4C6B/$file/CSCI+raising_voices_views+on+safeguarding+adults.pdf (accessed on 23 April 2013).

Communication Matters (2013) www.communicationmatters.org.uk (accessed 5 March 2013).

Department for Children, Schools and Families (2008) 'Evidence based practice'. London: DCSF. This publication has now been archived and is no longer available online.

Department for Education (2013) 'Information sharing'. Available online at www.education.gov.uk/childrenandyoungpeople/strategy/integratedworking/a0072915/information-sharing (accessed 19 March 2013).

Department of Health (2000) 'No secrets: guidance on developing and implementing multi-agency policies and procedures to protect vulnerable adults from abuse.' Available online atwww.elderabuse.org.uk/Documents/Other%20Orgs/No%20Secrets.pdf (accessed 23 April 2013).

Department of Health (2001a) 'A national service framework for older people'. London: Department of Health.

Department of Health (2001b) 'A safer place – combating violence against social care staff'. London: Department of Health.

Department of Health (2001c) 'Valuing people: a new strategy for learning disability for the 21st century'. London: Department of Health. Available online at www.dh.gov.uk/en/Publicationsandstatistics/Publications/PublicationsPolicyAndGuidance/DH_4009153 (accessed 29 January 2013).

Department of Health (2002) 'The single assessment process: guidance for local implementation'. London: Department of Health.

Department of Health (2005) 'Independence, well-being and choice: our vision for the future of social care for adults in England'. London: Department of Health. Available online at www.official-documents.gov.uk/document/cm64/6499/6499.pdf (accessed 7 May 2013).

Department of Health (2006) 'Our health, our care, our say: a new direction for community services'. London: Department of Health. Available online at www.official-documents.gov.uk/document/cm67/6737/6737.pdf (accessed 29 April 2013).

Department of Health (2007a) 'Wet, soap, wash, rinse, dry'. Available online at www.dh.gov.uk/en/Publicationsandstatistics/Publications/PublicationsPolicyAndGuidance/DH_063674 (accessed 26 October 2012).

Department of Health (2007b) 'Independence, choice and risk: a guide to best practice in supported decision making. London: Department of Health. Available online at www.worcestershire.gov.uk/cms/PDF/Independence,%20choice%20and%20risk.pdf (accessed 17 April 2013).

Department of Health (2007c) 'Putting people first: a shared vision and commitment to the transformation of adult social care'. London: Department of Health.

Department of Health (2009a) 'Safeguarding adults: a consultation on the review of the "No secrets" guidance'. London: Department of Health.

Department of Health (2009b) 'Valuing people now: a new three-year strategy for people with learning disabilities'. Available online at www.dh.gov.uk/en/Publicationsandstatistics/Publications/PublicationsPolicyAndGuidance/DH_093377 (accessed 29 January 2013).

Department of Health (2009c) 'Reference guide to consent for examination or treatment: second edition'. London: Department of Health. Available online at https://www.gov.uk/government/uploads/system/uploads/attachment_data/file/138296/dh_103653__1_.pdf (accessed 13 May 2013).

Department of Health (2010a) 'A vision for adult social care: capable communities and active citizens'. London: Department of Health.

Department of Health (2010b) 'Practical approaches to safeguarding and personalisation'. London: Department of Health. Available online at www.communitylivingbc.ca/wp-content/uploads/Practical-approaches-to-safeguarding-and-personalisation.pdf (accessed 23 April 2013).

Department of Health (2010c) 'Personalisation through person-centred planning'. London: Department of Health. Available online at www.thinklocalactpersonal.org.uk/Browse/SDSandpersonalbudgets/Supportplanning/?parent=2673&child=7588 (accessed 7 May 2013).

Department of Health (2011) 'Statement of government policy on adult safeguarding'. Published 16 May 2011, gateway reference: 160. Available online at www.gov.uk/government/publications/adult-safeguarding-statement-of-government-policy (accessed 23 April 2013).

Department of Health and NHS Commissioning Board (2012) 'Compassion in practice: nursing, midwifery and care staff. Our vision and strategy. Available online at www.commissioningboard.nhs.uk/wp-content/uploads/2012/12/compassion-in-practice.pdf (accessed 18 March 2013).

Doel, M. and Shardlow, S. (1993) *Social Work Practice*. Aldershot: Gower.

Douglas, A. (2008) *Partnership Working*. Abingdon: Routledge.

Dowling, S., Manthorpe, J. and Cowley, S. in association with King, S., Raymond, V., Perez, W. and Weinstein, P. (2006) 'Person-centred planning in social care: a scoping review. Available online at www.jrf.org.uk/system/files/9781859354803.pdf (accessed 18 January 2013).

Edwards, T. and Waters, J. (2008) *It's your Life – Take Control*. Hertford: Hertfordshire County Council.

Emerson, E. and Baines, S. (2010) *Health Inequalities and People with Learning Disabilities in the UK*. London: Learning Disabilities Observatory supported by the Department of Health.

Finnegan, P. and Clarke, S. (2005*) One Law for All: The Impact of the Human Rights Act on People with Learning Difficulties*. London: Values Into Action.

Francis, J., Fisher, M. and Rutter, D. (2011) 'Reablement: a cost-effective route to better outcomes', SCIE Research Briefing 36. London: Social Care Institute for Excellence.

Gardner, A. (2011) *Personalisation in Social Work: Transforming Social Work Practice*. Exeter: Learning Matters.

Gibbs, G. (1998) *Learning by Doing: A Guide to Teaching and Learning Methods*. Oxford: Further Education Unit Oxford Polytechnic.

Glendinning, C., Jones, K., Baxter, K., Rabiee, P., Curtis, L., Wilde, A., Arksey, H. and Forder, J. (2011) *Home Care Reablement Services: Investigating the Longer-Term Impacts*. York: Social Policy Research Unit.

Goldsmith, L. (1999) *Recording with Care: Inspection of Case Recording in Social Services Departments*. London: Social Services Inspectorate and Department of Health.

Griffiths, S (2009) *Personalisation, Choice and Empowerment: A Political and Economic Reality Check*. London: Social Market Foundation.

Harris, J., Foster, M., Jackson, K. and Morgan, H. (2005) *Outcomes for Disabled Service Users*. York: Social Policy Research Unit, University of York.

Health and Safety Executive (2006) 'Five steps to risk assessment'. Available online at www.hse.gov.uk/pubns/raindex.htm (accessed 26 October 2012).

Helen Anderson Associates (2013) 'Presence to contribution tool'. Available online at www.helensandersonassociates.co.uk/reading-room/how/person-centred-thinking/person-centred-thinking-tools.aspx (accessed on 17 January 2013).

Henwood, M. and Hudson, B. (2008) 'Checking the facts'. Available online at www.guardian.co.uk/society/2008/feb/13/long termcare.socialcare1 (accessed 1 May 2011).

Higham, P. (2005) 'What is important about social work and social care?' Available online at www.ssrg.org.uk/assembly/files/patriciahigham.pdf (accessed 26 October 2009).

Holland, K. (2011) 'Factsheet: learning disabilities'. Kidderminster: British Institute of Learning Disabilities.

Honey, P. and Mumford, A. (1982) *Manual of Learning Styles*. Berkshire: Peter Honey Publications.

In Control (2009) 'Self-directed support: social workers contribution'. Available online at www.in-control.org.uk (accessed 1 April 2011).

Institute for Research in Innovation in Social Services (2011) 'Insights 04: supporting those with dementia: reminiscence therapy and life story work'. Available online at www.iriss.org.uk/resources/supporting-those-dementia-reminiscence-therapy-and-life-story-work (accessed 17 April 2013).

International Stress Management Association (2009) 'Top-ten stress-busting tips'. Available online at www.isma.org.uk (accessed 29 December 2010).

Johnson, M. (2005) *Evidence Based Practice in the Social Services: Implications for Organisational Change*. California: School of Social Welfare, University of California.

Jorm, A.F. and Reavley, N.J. (2013) 'Depression and stigma: from attitudes to discrimination', *The Lancet*, 381 (9860): 10–11.

Just Associates (2006) *Making Change Happen: Power. Concepts for Revisioning Power for Justice, Equality and Peace*. Washington: Just Associates.

Kübler-Ross, E. (1969) *On Death and Dying*. London: Routledge.

Leadbetter, C. (2008) 'The rise of the "I can" economy: personalisation, participation and prevention'. Presentation at CBI Public Services and Personalisation Conference on 26 June 2008.

Local Government Ombudsman (2009) 'Six lives: the provision of public services to people with learning disabilities'. Available online at www.ombudsman. org.uk/improving-public-service/reports-and-consultations/reports/health/six-lives-the-provision-of-public-services-to-people-with-learning-disabilities (accessed 15 March 2013).

Luengo-Fernandez, R., Leal, J. and Gray, A. (2010) *Dementia 2010: The Economic Burden of Dementia and Associated Research Funding in the United Kingdom*. Cambridge: Alzheimer's Research Trust. Available online at www.dementia2010.org (accessed 19 January 2013).

Mansell, J., Elliot, T., Beadle-Brown, J., Ashman, B. and Macdonald, S. (2002) 'Engagement in meaningful activity and 'active support' of people with intellectual disabilities in residential care', *Research in Developmental Disabilities*, 23 (5): 342–352.

Maslow, A. (1970) *Motivation and Personality*. New York: HarperCollins.

McKinlay, J. (1994) 'A case for refocusing upstream: the political economy of illness', in P. Conrad (ed) *The Sociology of Health & Illness: Critical Perspectives*, seventh edition (pp. 551–561). New York: Worth Publishers.

McCormack, P. (0000) [To follow].

Mencap (2008) 'Advocacy'. Available online at www. mencap.org.uk/document.asp?id=2113 (accessed 21 September 2008).

Mencap (2013) 'Make it clear: a guide to making easy read information'. Available online at www.mencap. org.uk/sites/default/files/documents/2008-04/make%20it%20clear%20apr09.pdf (accessed 12 January 2013).

Mental Health Network NHS Confederation (2012) *Equally Accessible? Making Mental Health Services More Accessible for Learning Disabled or Autistic People*. London: NHS Confederation.

Mid Staffordshire NHS Foundation Trust Inquiry (2010) 'Independent inquiry into care provided by the Mid Staffordshire NHS Trust January 2005 – March 2009'. London: The Stationery Office. Available online at www.midstaffsinquiry.com/assets/docs/Inquiry_Report-Vol1.pdf (accessed 7 May 2013).

Milczarek, M., Schneider, E. and Gonzalez, E. (2009) *European Risk Observatory Report. OSH in Figures: Stress at Work – Facts and Figures*. Luxembourg: European Agency for Safety and Health at Work.

Mind (2013) 'Mental health facts and statistics'. Available online at www.mind.org.uk/mental_health_a-z/8105_mental_health_facts_and_statistics (accessed 17 April 2013).

Mitchell, W., Baxter, K. and Glendinning, C. (2012) *Risk, Trust and Relationships in an Ageing Society*. Joseph Rowntree Foundation programme paper. Updated review of research on risk and adult social care in England. York: Joseph Rowntree Foundation.

Moriarty, J., Kam, M., Coomber, C., Rutter, D. and Turner, M. (2010) 'Communication training for care home workers: outcomes for older people, staff, families and friends', SCIE Research Briefing 34. London: Social Care Institute for Excellence.

Moriarty, J., Sharif, N. and Robinson, J. (2011) 'Black and minority ethnic people with dementia and their access to support and services', SCIE Research Briefing 35. London: Social Care Institute for Excellence.

Morris, J. (2001) *'That Kind of Life': Social Exclusion and Young Disabled People with High Levels of Support Needs*. London: Scope.

National Institute on Deafness and other Communication Disorders (NIDCD) (2013) 'Assistive devices for people with hearing, voice, speech or language disorders'. Available online at www.nidcd. nih.gov/health/hearing/Pages/Assistive-Devices. aspx#7 (accessed 20 January 2013).

NICE–SCIE (2007) *Dementia: The NICE–SCIE Guideline on Supporting People with Dementia and their Carers in Health and Social Care*. Leicester and London: The British Psychological Society and the Royal College of Psychiatrists. Available online at www.nice.org.uk/nicemedia/live/10998/30320/30320.pdf (accessed 20 January 2013).

Office for Disability Issues (2010) *Public Perceptions of Disabled People: Evidence from the British Social Attitudes Survey 2009*. London: HMSO.

Osser, D. (2000) *Violence Against Social Care Staff: Qualitative Research*. London: Research Perspectives. Available online at www.scie-socialcareonline.org.uk/repository/fulltext/ukswviolence.pdf (accessed 17 April 2013).

Parker, C., Barnes, S., McKee, K., Morgan, K., Torrington, J. and Tregenza, P. (2004) 'Quality of life and building design in residential and nursing homes for older people', *Ageing and Society*, 24: 941–962.

Pincus, A. and Minahan, A. (1973) *Social Work Practice: Model and Method*. Itasca Peacock.

Prime Minister's Strategy Unit in collaboration with the Office of the Deputy Prime Minister, Department of Health, Department for Work and Pensions and Department for Education and Skills (2005) *Improving the Life Chances of Disabled People*. Available online at http://webarchive.nationalarchives.gov.uk/20130401151715/https://www.education.gov.uk/publications/standard/publicationDetail/Page1/DFES-1968-2005 (accessed 1 May 2013).

Prizant, B. (1983) 'Language acquisition and communicative behavior in autism: toward an understanding of the "whole" of it', *Journal of Speech and Hearing Disorders*, 48: 296–307.

Rethink (2011) 'Early intervention teams: services for early psychosis', Rethink Mental Illness Factsheet. London: Rethink. Available online at www.rethink.org (accessed 17 April 2013).

RIPFA (2008) 'Critical appraisal skills'. Available online at www.ripfa.org.uk/aboutus/archive/skills.asp?TOPcatID=6&TOPcatsubID=4&id=4 (accessed 12 October 2008).

Sackett, D.L., Strauss, S.E., Richardson, W.S., Rosenberg, W. and Haynes, R.B. (1997) *Evidence-Based Medicine: How to Practice and Teach EBM*. Second edition. Edinburgh: Churchill-Livingstone.

Saleebey, D. (1996) 'The strengths perspective in social work practice: extensions and cautions', *Social work*, 41: 296–305.

Scope (2013) 'No choice, no voice: a sustainable future for alternative and augmentative communication'. Available online at www.scope.org.uk/help-and-information/communication/no-voice-no-choice (accessed 6 July 2013).

Seabrooke, V. and Milne, A. (2004) 'Culture and care in dementia: a study of the Asian community in north west Kent'. Available online at www.mentalhealth.org.uk/content/assets/PDF/publications/culture_care_dementia.pdf (accessed 10 February 2013).

Skills for Care (2012) *The State of the Adult Social Care Sector and Workforce in England 2012*. From the National Minimum Dataset for Social Care (NMDS-SC). Leeds: Skills for Care.

Skinner, B.F. (1971) *Beyond Freedom and Dignity*. Indianapolis: Hackett Publishing.

Social Care Institute for Excellence (2004) 'Leading practice: a development programme for first-line managers'. Available online at www.scie.org.uk/publications/guides/guide27/ (accessed 17 April 2013).

Social Care Institute for Excellence (2005) 'Helping older people to take prescribed medication in their own home: what works?', SCIE Research Briefing 15. Available online at www.scie.org.uk/publications/briefings/briefing15/ (accessed 6 February 2013).

Social Care Institute for Excellence (2012) 'Meaning and importance of participation: outcomes of participation'. Available online at www.scie.org.uk/publications/guides/guide17/participation/outcomes.asp (accessed 21 December 2012).

Stancliff, R., Jones, E. and Mansell, J. (eds) (2008) 'Research in active support', *Journal of Intellectual and Developmental Disability*, 33 (3): 194–195.

Sykes, W. and Groom, C. (2011) *Older People's Experiences of Home Care in England*. Equality and Human Rights Commission Research Report 79. Manchester: Equality and Human Rights Commission. Available online at www.equalityhumanrights.com/uploaded_files/research/79_older_peoples_experiences.pdf (accessed 17 April 2013).

The NHS Knowledge Network Scotland (2013a) 'Genetics and learning disability: introduction'. Available online at www.knowledge.scot.nhs.uk/home/portals-and-topics/learning-disabilities-portal/topics--glossary/managing-physical-health--well-being/genetics--learning-disability---introduction.aspx (accessed 22 January 2012).

The NHS Knowledge Network Scotland (2013b) 'Communication and learning disability: an introduction'. Available online at www.knowledge.scot.nhs.uk/home/portals-and-topics/learning-disabilities-portal/topics--glossary/communication/communication--learning-disability---an-introduction.aspx (accessed 10 February 2013).

The Scottish Government Changing Lives Service Development Group (2008) *Personalisation: A Shaved Understanding; Commissioning for Personalisation; A Personalised Commissioning Approach to Support and Care Services*. Available online at www.knowledge.scot.nhs.uk/media/CLT/ResourceUploads/9087/PersonalisationPapers.pdf

ThemPra Social Pedagogy Community Interest Society (2009) 'Social pedagogy: theory meets practice'. Available online at www.socialpedagogy.co.uk/concepts.htm (accessed 19 January 2010).

Think Local, Act Personal (2011a) 'June 2011: The biggest survey yet of people's experiences of personal budgets'. Available online at www.thinklocalactpersonal.org.uk/Browse/ SDSandpersonalbudgets/Measuringresults/ (accessed 10 December 2010).

Think Local, Act Personal (2011b) 'Personal budgets: taking stock, moving forward'. Available online at www.thinklocalactpersonal.org. uk/_library/Resources/Personalisation/TLAP/ Paper5TakingStockMovingForwards.pdf (accessed 2 January 2013).

Think Local, Act Personal Partnership (2012) 'Think local, act personal'. Available online at www/ thinklocalactpersonal.org.uk/_library/Resources/ Personalisation/TLAP/THINK_LOCAL_ACT_ PERSONAL_5_4_11.pdf (accessed 10 April 2012).

Thomas, K.W. and Kilmann, R.H. (1974) *Conflict Mode Instrument*. Mountain View America: CPP Inc.

UNISON (2012) 'UNISON duty of care handbook: for members working in health and social care'. Available online at www.unison.org.uk/acrobat/19786_Duty%20 of%20care%20rev4.pdf (accessed 17 April 2013).

United Nations Department of Economic and Social Affairs (2008) 'Promoting social integration'. Expert group meeting held 8–10 July 2008, Helsinki, Finland. Convened in preparation for the 47th session of the Commission for Social Development. Available online at www.un.org/esa/socdev/social/meetings/ egm6_social_integration/documents/AIDEMEMOIRE_ REVISED.pdf (accessed 17 April 2013).

Weiner, B. (2005) 'Motivation from an attributional perspective and the social psychology of perceived competence', in A.J. Elliot and C.S. Dweck (eds), *Handbook of Competence and Motivation* (pp.73–84). New York: Guilford.

World Health Organization (2007) 'What is mental health?' Available online at www.who.int/features/ qa/62/en/index.html (accessed 8 January 2013).

World Health Organization (2013) '10 facts on dementia'. Available online at www.who.int/features/ factfiles/dementia/en/index.html (accessed 4 February 2013).

INDEX